General Science

Class 6-12 (Old+New)

General Science

Class 6-12 (Old+New)

Authors
Digvijay Singh *(Physics)*
Abhishikha Kaushik *(Chemistry)*
Juhi Bhatia *(Biology)*

ARIHANT PUBLICATIONS (INDIA) LIMITED

Administrative & Production Offices

Regd. Office
'Ramchhaya' 4577/15, Agarwal Road, Darya Ganj, New Delhi -110002
Tele: 011- 47630600, 43518550

Head Office
Kalindi, TP Nagar, Meerut (UP) - 250002
Tel: 0121-7156203, 7156204

Sales & Support Offices

Agra, Ahmedabad, Bengaluru, Bareilly, Chennai, Delhi, Guwahati, Hyderabad, Jaipur, Jhansi, Kolkata, Lucknow, Nagpur & Pune.

PRICE ₹185.00

PO No. : TXT-59-T068785-1-26

Published by Arihant Publications (India) Ltd.

For further information about the books published by Arihant, log on to www.arihantbooks.com or e-mail at info@arihantbooks.com

Follow us on   

Few Words

NCERTs are the Foundation in the Journey of IAS...

Civil Service Examinations are the most prestigious, tough and challenging examinations in India.

Being the toughest exam, it automatically consists of a vast and a detailed syllabus. Aspirants often find it difficult to cover the entire syllabus and lack a right direction for a proper and a systematic study for the exam.

The most important aspect of this preparation journey are the NCERT books. Every year approximately **35-40 questions** directly or indirectly asked from NCERT books.

NCERT books also play a key role in understanding the Basic Concepts; so that aspirants can easily form the basic foundation of the entire syllabus. But due to the demand for many NCERT books which are required for study, it becomes exhausting to cover each and every NCERT book.

NCERT MCQs series presented by Arihant Publications covers MCQs from Class 6th to 12th NCERT books (both Old & New) in a comprehensive manner.

Features of Revised Edition

- Each and Every Question is designed as per Latest Pattern of UPSC and State PCS.
- The chapter-wise questions given in the sequential form in the series along with the source of the questions.
- 100% Error free and detailed explanations will make the preparation easy and convenient.
- Additional coverage of Tamil Nadu Board and NIOS Books.
- 3 Practice Sets also provided for overall practice related to subject.

The book is adorned with questions prepared by a team of experts along with a vital role played by the Project Management team with members: Mona Yadav (Project Manager), Manshi Gupta (Project Coordinator), Seema Saini (Proof Reading TL), Pradeep Chaudhary (DTP TL), Bilal and Ankit Tyagi (Cover and Inner designer).

We hope this book will help the aspirants to achieve their goals of clearing UPSC as well as State PCS exams. Your valuable suggestions have always inspired us to strive for useful, authentic and more trustworthy publications.
So your inputs and suggestions are welcomed for subsequent editions.

We wish you all the very best for your preparation and journey!!

Authors

CONTENTS

NCERT
MCQs

Units and Measurement

Units and Measurement

Physical Quantities and Units

Physical Quantities

- The quantities which can be defined and measured e.g. Length, force, temperature etc.
- A physical quantity have a numerical magnitude and a unit.

Fundamental Quantities

- The quantities which are independent of each other. e.g. Mass, temperature, length, time, electric current, amount of substance, luminous intensity.

Derived Quantities

- The quantities which are derived from fundamental quantities. e.g., Work, force, pressure, etc.

Supplementary Quantities

- Two physical quantities which are neither fundamental nor derived. e.g., Plane angle and solid angle.

Fundamental Units

- The units which are used for the measurement of fundamental or base quantities. e.g., Kilogram, kelvin, metre, second, ampere, mole and candela.

Derived Units

- The units which are obtained from the fundamental units. e.g., Joule, newton, metre^2, etc.

Supplementary Units

- The units which are used for the measurement of supplementary quantities, e.g. Radian and steradian.

Definition of Fundamental and Supplementary Units

Metre

- The length of the path travel by light in vacuum during a time interval of 1/29, 792, 458 of a second.

Kilogram

- The mass of 5.0188×10^{25} atoms of C^{12} isotope.

Second

- The time interval in which cesium-133 atom completes 9192631770 vibrations in-an atomic clock.

Kelvin

- The fraction of 1/273.16 temperature of the triple point of water.

Ampere

- The current which produces a force of 2×10^{-7} N/m between two straight parallel conductors of infinite length placed one metre apart in vacuum.

Mole

- The amount of substance, which contains as many elementary entities of a substance as there are atoms in 0.012 kg of carbon-12.

Candela

- The luminous intensity in given direction, of a mono-chromatic source that emits radiation of frequency 540×10^{12} Hz.

Radian

- The angle subtended at the centre of a circle by an arc equal in length to the radius of the circle.

Steradian

- The solid angle subtended at the centre of a unit sphere by a unit area on its surface.

Important Practical Units

Bigger Units of Length

- **Astronomical Unit** The Average distance of the Sun from the Earth
  1 AU = 1.496×10^{11} m
- **Light Year** The distance travelled by light in vacuum in one year
  1 Ly = $3 \times 10^8 \times 365 \times 24 \times 60 \times 60$ m
  = 9.461×10^{15} m
- **Parsec** The distance at which one astronomical unit subtends an angle of one arc second in one parsec.
  1 Parsec = 3.08×10^{16} m = 3.26 Ly

Smaller Units of Length

- 1 Decimetre = 10^{-1} metre
- 1 Centimetre = 10^{-2} metre
- 1 Millimetre = 10^{-3} metre

Bigger Units of Mass

- 1 Quintal (qu) = 100 kg = 10^2 kg
- 1 Metric tonne (mt) = 1000 kg
- 1 Mega gram (Mg) = 10^3 kg
- 1 Giga gram (Gg) = 10^6 kg
- 1 Tera gram (Tg) = 10^9 kg
- 1 Solar Mass = 1.989×10^{30} kg
- 1 Chandrashekhar limit = 2.8×10^{30} kg

Bigger Units of Time

- 1 Minute (min) = 60 second
- 1 Hour (h) = 60 min = 3600 second
- 1 Day (D) = 24 h = 86400 second
- 1 Year (yr) = 365 days
  = 3.15×10^7 second

Smaller Units of Time

- 1 Millisecond (ms) = 10^{-3} second
- 1 Microsecond (μs) = 10^{-6} second
- 1 Nanosecond (ns) = 10^{-9} second
- 1 Picosecond (ps) = 10^{-12} second

SOURCE *New NCERT Class VI Chap 7 (Motion and Measurement of Distance), New NCERT Class XI Chap 1 (Units and Measurement), Tamil Nadu Board Class IX (Measurement)*

1 **If P, Q & R are physical quantities, having different dimensions, which of the following combinations can never be a meaningful quantity?**

(Chap 1, Class-XI, NCERT)

1. $\frac{(P-Q)}{R}$ 2. $\frac{PQ}{R}$

3. $PQ-R$ 4. $\frac{(R+Q)}{P}$

Codes

(a) 1 and 4 (b) 2 and 4
(c) 2 and 3 (d) 1 and 3

Ans. (a)

Exp. Principle of homogeneity of dimensions states that in a correct equation, the dimensions of each term added or subtracted must be same. Every correct equation must have same dimensions on both sides of the equation.

According to the problem, P, Q and R are having different dimensions, since sum and difference of physical dimensions, are meaningless, i.e., $(P-Q)$ and $(R+Q)$ are not meaningful.

So, in (2) and (3), PQ may have the same dimensions as those of R.

Hence, they cannot be added or subtracted, so we can say that (1) and (4) are not meaningful.

2 **Match List-I with List-II and select the correct answer from the codes given below**

(Chap 1, Class-XI, NCERT)

List-I (Physical Quantities)	List-II (Units)
A. Acceleration	1. Joule
B. Force	2. Newton metre^{-2}
C. Work done	3. Newton
D. Pressure	4. Metre/second^2

Codes

	A	B	C	D
(a)	1	2	3	4
(b)	3	4	1	2
(c)	2	3	4	1
(d)	4	3	1	2

Ans. (d)

Exp. The correct matching is A-4, B-3, C-1, D-2.

Acceleration The unit of acceleration is metre/second^2 or m/s^2. It is the change in velocity divided by time.

Force It is measured in Newton (N). A force is a pull or push upon an object resulting from the object's interaction with another object.

Work done It is measured in Joule (J). When work is done, an equal amount of energy is used up. So, its unit is same as that of energy.

Pressure The unit of pressure is pascal (Pa) or Newton metre^{-2}. It is defined as the physical force exerted on an object.

3 **Which of the following statement is correct?**

(Chap 1, Class -XI, NCERT)

(a) Mole is the fundamental unit of amount of substance.
(b) The unit of electric current is coulomb.
(c) The fundamental unit of time is hour.
(d) In SI unit, temperature is measured in celsius.

Ans. (a)

Exp. Statement (a) is correct as mole is the fundamental unit of amount of substance. One mole is defined as the amount of substance of a system which contains as many elementary entities as there are atoms in 0.012 kg of carbon-12.

Statements (b), (c) and (d) are incorrect.

The SI unit of electric current is Ampere (A), while electric charge is measured in Coulomb (C).

The fundamental unit of time is second (s). In terms of SI unit, temperature is measured in kelvin, while 1° C is equal to 273 K.

4 **Consider the following statements, choose the correct option given below.**

(Unit 1, Class-IX, Tamil Nadu Board)

Statement I The scientifically correct expression is "The mass of the bag is 10 kg".

Statement II In everyday life, we use the term weight instead of mass.

(a) Statement I is correct but Statement II is incorrect.
(b) Statement I is incorrect but Statement II is correct.
(c) Both Statements I and II are correct.
(d) Both Statements I and II are incorrect.

Ans. (c)

Exp. Both Statements I and II are correct.

Kilogram is the SI unit of mass, while the unit of weight is newton.

We use the weight for most daily purpose such as measuring our mass because the weight of an object is more useful to know.

5 **Match List-I with List-II and select the correct answer from the codes given below the lists.**

(Chap 1, Class-XI, NCERT)

List-I (Quantity)	List-II (Units)
A. Weight	1. Newton
B. Wavelength	2. Angstrom
C. Pressure	3. Pascal
D. Energy	4. Joule

Codes

	A	B	C	D
(a)	2	1	3	4
(b)	1	2	4	3
(c)	1	2	3	4
(d)	2	1	4	3

Ans. (c)

Exp. The correct matching is A-1, B-2, C-3, D-4.

Weight The weight of an object is the force with which it is attracted towards the earth. Weight is vector quantity, it acts in vertically downward direction and its SI unit is Newton (N).

Wavelength It is the distance moved by the wave in the time of one complete oscillation of a particle of the medium. Wavelength of wave can be measured in metre, Angstrom, Nanometre etc.

Pressure It is the force acting perpendicularly on a unit area of an object. It is a scalar quantity. The SI unit of pressure is N/m^2, which is also called Pascal.

Energy It is the ability to do work. It is always essential for performing any mechanical work. An object having the capability to do work is said to possess energy. The SI unit of energy is Joule.

6 Consider the following statements. *(Chap 1, Class-XI, NCERT)*

1. Energy E, velocity v, and time t are taken as the fundamental units and dimensional formula for energy per unit area will be $[Ev^{-2}T^{-2}]$.
2. The physical quantities not having same dimensions are momentum and Planck's constant.

Which of the statements given above is/are correct?

(a) Only 1 (b) Only 2
(c) Both 1 and 2 (d) Neither 1 nor 2

Ans. (c)

Exp. Both the statements (1) and (2) are correct.

We know, $\frac{[E]}{[A]} = [Ev^{-2}T^{-2}]$, thus energy will be E and velocity v.

Momentum and Planck's constants have not same dimensional formula because momentum $[MLT^{-1}]$ and Planck's constant $[ML^2T^{-1}]$.

7 Consider the following statements. *(Chap 1, Class-XI, NCERT)*

1. Megawatt is the unit of measurement of electricity, which is produced in power stations.
2. The unit of atmospheric pressure is Bar.
3. Dobson is the unit of measuring the thickness of ozone layer.

How many of the above statements are correct?

(a) Only one (b) Only two
(c) All three (d) None of these

Ans. (c)

Exp. All three statements are correct.

Statement 1 Megawatt (MW) is the unit of measurement of electricity, which is produced in the power generation station. For commercial purposes and in the house, the electric power is used in kilowatts.

Statement 2 Bar is the unit of atmospheric pressure. It is not a part of SI unit, it is the metric unit of pressure. The bar is still used in descriptions of pressure because it is about the same as atmospheric pressure.

Statement 3 Dobson is the unit of measuring the thickness of ozone layer. Dobson Unit (DU) is defined to be 0.01 mm thickness at STP (Standard temperature and Pressure). The unit is named after GMB Dobson (Gordon Miller Bourne Dobson), one of the first scientists to investigate atmospheric ozone. One Dobson unit is equivalent to 2.687×10^{20} molecules of ozone per square metre.

8 Consider the following statements about the elastic tape measurement. *(Chap 7, Class-VI, NCERT)*

1. The length of the elastic tape varies and depends upon the force by which it is stretched.
2. Measurement would vary when measured by the same person.
3. Measurement would also vary if different persons measure the same distance.

Which of the statement(s) given above is/are correct?

(a) 1 and 2 (b) 2 and 3
(c) 1 and 3 (d) All of these

Ans. (d)

Exp. All of the given statements are correct about the elastic tape measurement.

An elastic measuring tape is a common measuring tool and is a flexible ruler which is used to measure size or distance. It consists of a ribbon of cloths, plastic fiberglass or metal strip with linear measurement markings.

An elastic measuring tape gives an incorrect length because the length of the elastic tape varies with the amount of force.

Measurement with the elastic tape would also be different if the same person measures with it or different persons measure with same elastic tape.

9 Which one of the following pairs is not correctly matched? *(Chap 1, Class-XI, NCERT)*

(a) 1 cm, 0.39 inch
(b) 1 feet, 30.5×10^7 nanometre
(c) 1 micrometre, 10^{-4} centimetre
(d) 1 Picometre, 10^{-9} centimetre

Ans. (d)

Exp. Pair (d) is not correctly matched because 1 Picometre is equal to 10^{-12} metre or 10^{-10} centimetre.

Pairs (a), (b) and (c) are correctly matched.

$$1 \text{ inch} = 2.54 \text{ cm}$$

$$1 \text{ cm} = \frac{1}{2.54} \text{ inch} = 0.39 \text{ inch}$$

$$\begin{aligned} 1 \text{ feet} &= 0.3048 \text{ metre} \\ &= 0.3048 \times 10^9 \text{ nanometre} \\ &= 30.5 \times 10^7 \text{ nanometre} \end{aligned}$$

$$\begin{aligned} 1 \text{ micrometre} &= 1 \times 10^{-6} \text{ metre} \\ &= 10^{-6} \times 10^2 \text{ cm} \\ &= 10^{-4} \text{ cm} \end{aligned}$$

10 Consider the following statements.

(Unit 1, Class-IX, Tamil Nadu Board)

1. A physical balance is less sensitive than a beam balance.
2. One celsius degree is an interval of 1 K and zero degree celsius is 273.15 K.
3. A physical balance measures small difference in mass up to 1 mg.

How many of the above statements are correct?

(a) Only one (b) Only two
(c) All three (d) None of these

Ans. (b)

Exp. Only two statements (2 and 3) are correct but one statement (1) is incorrect.

Statement 1 A balance is said to be sensitive when it can register small difference in weight. A physical balance is a modified and hiqhly sensitive version of the beam balance. Thus physical balance is more sensitive than a beam balance.

Statement 2 One celsius degree is an interval of 1K, and zero degree celsius is 273.15K. An interval of one celsius degree corresponds to an interval of 1.8 fahrenheit degree on the fahrenheit temperature scale.

Statement 3 The minimum amount of mass which can be measured by the physical balance is 1 mg. Hence, a physical balance measures small difference in mass up to 1 mg.

11 Consider the following statements.

(Chap 1, Class-XI, NCERT)

1. Impulse and momentum has same dimension.
2. The dimensions of specific heat capacity and latent heat are same.
3. Electron volt is a unit of charge.

Choose the correct options considering above statements.

(a) Only 1 (b) 1 and 2
(c) 1 and 3 (d) Only 3

Ans. (a)

Exp. Statement (1) is correct as the dimension of impulse and momentum are $[M^1L^1T^{-1}]$.

Statements (2) and (3) are incorrect. The dimension of specific heat is $[M^0L^2T^{-2}K^{-1}]$ and latent heat is $[M^0L^2T^{-2}]$

Electron volt is a unit of energy.

12 Consider the following statements.

(Chap 1, Class-XI, NCERT)

1. Dimensional formula of work and heat are $[MLT^{-2}]$ and $[ML^2T^{-2}]$, respectively.
2. Dimensional formula of potential energy and kinetic energy is same.

Which of the statement(s) given above is/are correct?

(a) Only 1
(b) Only 2
(c) Both 1 and 2
(d) Neither 1 nor 2

Ans. (b)

Exp. Statement (2) is correct.

Potential energy $(U) = mgh$

$$= [M][LT^{-2}][L] = [ML^2T^{-2}].$$

Similarly, kinetic energy $= \frac{1}{2}mv^2$

$$= [M][LT^{-1}]^2 = [ML^2T^{-2}]$$

Hence, the dimension of potential energy and kinetic energy is same.

Statement (1) is incorrect.

Work = Force (F) × Displacement (d)
= Mass (m) × Acceleration (a) × Displacement (d)
$= [M][LT^{-2}][L] = [ML^2T^{-2}]$

Heat is a form of energy and all forms of energy have same dimension as that of work done.

Heat $= [ML^2T^{-2}]$

13 Consider the following statements.

(Chap 1, Class-XI, NCERT)

1. Number of significant digits is unaffected by changing the place of decimal point.
2. Precision of measuring scale is greater for smaller least count of the scale.
3. If smaller will be error of measurement, then smaller will be the accuracy of measurement.

Which of the statement (s) given above is/are correct?

(a) Only 1 (b) 1 and 2
(c) 2 and 3 (d) 1, 2 and 3

Ans. (b)

Exp. Statements (1) and (2) are correct.

The first two zeroes in 0.058000 (five significant digits) are insignificant because they are before the first non-zero digit and the last three zeroes are significant because they are after the first non-zero digit. When the position of decimal is changed i.e. 00.58000, it also has five significant figures. Hence, the position of decimal does not affect the significant number.

The least count of an instrument is inversely proportional to the precision of the instrument. Hence, precision of measuring scale is greater for smaller least count of the scale.

Statement (3) is incorrect because accuracy and error are inversely proportional to each other. As the accuracy of a value increases, its deviation from the true value or error decreases.

Chapter 2

Motion

Motion

Types of Motion and Equation of Motion

Rectilinear Motion

- The motion in which object moves along straight line.
  e.g., Motion of sliding body on an inclined plane.

Circular Motion

- The motion in which object moves along circular path.
  e.g., A string whirled in a circular loop.

Rotational Motion

- The motion in which object rotates about a fixed axis.
  e.g., Motion of top.

Oscillatory Motion

- The motion in which object moves to and fro motion about its fixed position.
  e.g., Simple pendulum

Equations of Motion for Uniformly Accelerated Body

- The three equations of motion,
  (i) $v = u + at$ (ii) $s = ut + 1/2\, at^2$
  (iii) $2as = v^2 - u^2$
- where, u = initial velocity,
  v = final velocity,
  a = acceleration,
  t = time
  and s = distance.

Equations of Motion Due to Action of Gravity

- When the velocity of an object changes due to gravity, then the equation of motion are written as
  (i) $v = u + gt$ (ii) $h = ut + 1/2\, gt^2$
  (iii) $v^2 = u^2 + 2gh$
  where, g is the acceleration due to gravity.

Terms Related of Motion

Distance

- The actual length of the path covered by a moving body.
- Its SI unit is metre. It is always positive

Displacement

- The shortest distance between the initial and final position of the body.
- Its SI unit is metre.
- It can be positive, negative or zero.

Speed

- The distance travelled by the body in unit time.
- It is a scalar quantity. Its SI unit is m/s.
- Speed of body is always positive.

Velocity

- The displacement of an object or the distance travelled by an object in a particular direction in unit interval of time.
- Its SI unit is m/s or ms^{-1}.
- Its magnitude can be positive, zero or negative.

Acceleration

- The rate of change of velocity of the body with time.
- It is a vector quantity and SI unit is ms^{-2}.

Relative Velocity

- The velocity of an object with respect to another
  $v_{AB} = v_A \pm v_B$ and $v_{BA} = v_B \pm v_A$

Circular and Projectile Motion

Circular Motion

- The motion in which object moves along the circumference of a circle
- The speed of the body moving in a circular path is $v = 2\pi r/t$.
- Uniform circular motion is accelerated motion.

Angular Displacement (θ)

- The angle traced out by the radius vector at the centre of the circular path in a given time.
  $$\theta = \frac{\text{Arc}}{\text{Radius}}$$

Angular Velocity

- The time rate of change of angular displacement of the body.
- Its SI unit is rad/s.

Angular Acceleration

- The time rate of change of angular velocity of the body.
- Its SI unit is rad/s^2.

Centripetal Acceleration

- An acceleration which acts radially inwards in a uniform circular motion.
- It is expressed as $a = \frac{v^2}{r}$

Projectile Motion

- The motion in which the object moves along the parabolic path under the gravity.
- Height, $H = \frac{(u^2 \sin^2\theta)}{2g}$
- Time of flight, $T = \frac{2u \sin\theta}{g}$
- Horizontal range, $R = \frac{(u^2 \sin 2\theta)}{g}$

SOURCE New NCERT Class VI Chap 7 (Motion and Measurement of Distance), New NCERT Class IX Chap 7 (Motion), New NCERT Class XI Chap 2 (Motion in a Straight Line), Chap 3 (Motion in a Plane)

1 **Which of the following statement(s) is/are incorrect for displacement?** *(Chap 7, Class-IX, NCERT)*

1. It cannot be zero.
2. Its magnitude is greater than the distance travelled by the object.

Codes

(a) Only 1 (b) Only 2
(c) Both 1 and 2 (d) Neither 1 nor 2

Ans. (c)

Exp. Both the statements are incorrect for displacement as, displacement is the length of the shortest path measured in the direction from the initial position to the final position of the object.

If the initial and final position of the object is same, then in this case displacement is zero.

The magnitude of displacement of a moving object can never be greater than the distance travelled by it. It is always less than or equal to distance.

2 **Consider the following statements.** *(Chap 2, Class-XI, NCERT)*

Statement I A body may not posses displacement without distance covered.

Statement II Displacement depends on the path traced by the particle.

Which one of the following is correct in respect of the above statements?

(a) Both Statement I and Statement II are correct and Statement II is the correct explanation for Statement I.
(b) Both Statement I and Statement II are correct but Statement II is not the correct explanation for Statement I.
(c) Statement I is correct but Statement II is incorrect.
(d) Statement I is incorrect but Statement II is correct.

Ans. (c)

Exp. Statement I is correct but Statement II is incorrect.

The change in position of an object in a particular direction is termed as displacement.

Displacement does not depend on the path travelled. But it depends on the starting point and the finishing point.

3 **A vehicle covers half the distance with uniform speed v_1 and the other half with uniform speed v_2. The average speed of the vehicle is** *(Chap 2, Class-XI, NCERT)*

(a) $\frac{v_1 + v_2}{2}$ (b) $\frac{v_1 + v_2}{v_1 v_2}$ (c) $\frac{v_1 v_2}{v_1 + v_2}$ (d) $\frac{2v_1 v_2}{v_1 + v_2}$

Ans. (d)

Exp. A vehicle covers half the distance with uniform speed v_1 and the other half with uniform speed v_2, then the average speed of the vehicle is $\frac{2v_1 v_2}{v_1 + v_2}$.

Let t_1 and t_2 be the time taken by the vehicle to cover the first half distance $(d/2)$ and next half distance $(d/2)$.

A —d/2— —d/2— B ($t_1 v_1$, $t_2 v_2$)

$$\therefore \quad t_1 = \frac{d/2}{v_1} = \frac{d}{2v_1}$$

and
$$t_2 = \frac{d/2}{v_2} = \frac{d}{2v_2}$$

$$\therefore \text{Average speed, } v = \frac{\text{Total distance}}{\text{Total time}} = \frac{d}{\frac{d}{2v_1} + \frac{d}{2v_2}}$$

$$= \frac{d}{\frac{d}{2}\left(\frac{v_1 + v_2}{v_1 v_2}\right)} = \frac{2v_1 v_2}{v_1 + v_2}$$

4 **Match List-I with List-II and select the correct answer from the codes given below.** *(Chap 7, Class-IX, NCERT)*

List-I	List-II
A. Rate of change of velocity	1. Uniformly accelerated
B. Free fall motion	2. Uniformly decelerated
C. Car moving on the crowded street	3. Acceleration
D. Stone thrown upwards	4. Non-uniform acceleration

Codes

	A	B	C	D		A	B	C	D
(a)	3	1	4	2	(b)	1	2	3	4
(c)	2	4	1	3	(d)	3	2	4	1

Ans. (a)

Exp. The correct matching is A-3, B-1, C-4, D-2.

The rate of change of velocity is known as acceleration. Acceleration can be positive, zero and negative. If the magnitude of velocity of object is increasing with time, then the acceleration of the object is positive. If the magnitude of the velocity is decreasing, then the acceleration is negative. When a body is moving with a constant velocity, then the acceleration is zero.

The motion of freely falling body and the motion of a ball rolling down on an inclined plane are examples of uniformly accelerated motion because the velocity of body changes by equal amount in equal intervals of time.

A car moving on the crowded street is said to be moving with non-uniform acceleration because its velocity changes by unequal amounts in equal interval of time.

Similarly, the motion of a stone which is thrown upwards is uniformly decelerated.

5 **Consider the following statements about a particle performing uniform circular motion.** *(Chap 3, Class-XI, NCERT)*

1. magnitude of particle velocity (speed) remains constant.
2. particle velocity remains directed perpendicular to radius vector.

3. Direction of acceleration keeps changing as particle moves.
4. Angular momentum is constant in magnitude but direction keeps changing.

Which of the statement(s) given above is/are correct?

(a) 1, 2 and 3 (b) 2, 3 and 4 (c) 1, 2 and 4 (d) 1, 3 and 4

Ans. (a)

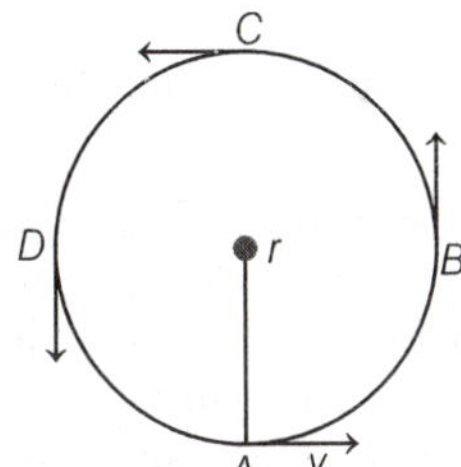

Exp. While a particle is in uniform circular motion, then

(i) speed will be always constant throughout.

(ii) velocity will be always tangential in the direction of motion at a particular point.

(iii) the centripetal acceleration, $a = \frac{v^2}{r}$ and its direction continuously changes and remains perpendicular to the direction of the velocity of the particle.

(iv) angular momentum (mvr) is constant in magnitude and direction. And its direction is perpendicular to the plane containing r and v.

6 Which of the following statement is correct? *(Chap 7, Class-IX, NCERT)*

(a) Average velocity is distance divided by time interval.

(b) Speed is always greater than the magnitude of the velocity.

(c) A particle with non-zero velocity can have zero speed.

(d) Average velocity can be equal to average speed.

Ans. (d)

Exp. Statement (d) is correct as, if a body is moving in a straight line, then the average speed and average velocity will be equal.

Statements (a), (b) and (c) are incorrect.

Average velocity is defined as the ratio of total displacement to total time taken by the body.

Speed can be equal to or greater than the magnitude of the velocity.

When a particle is having a non-zero velocity, its speed cannot be zero because speed is equal to the ratio of total distance travelled to the total time taken and distance can never be negative and zero.

7 Consider the following Assertion (A) and Reason (R) and choose the correct code. *(Chap 7, Class-IX, NCERT)*

Assertion (A) In case the velocity of the object is changing at a uniform rate, then average velocity is the arithmetic mean of initial and final velocity for a given period of time.

Reason (R) The change in velocity of the object during any time interval is always non-zero.

Codes

(a) Both A and R are true and R is correct explanation of A.

(b) Both A and R are true, but R is not correct explanation of A.

(c) A is true, but R is false.

(d) A is false, but R is true.

Ans. (c)

Exp. Assertion (A) is true but Reason (R) is false.

If the velocity of an object changes at a uniform rate, then average velocity is given by the arithmetic mean of the initial velocity and final velocity for a given time.

During uniform motion of an object along a straight line, the velocity remains constant with time. In this case, the change in velocity of the object for any time interval is zero. However, in non-uniform motion, velocity varies with time.

8 What is the correct equation for finding the acceleration? *(Chap 7, Class-IX, NCERT) (UPPSC Pre 2003)*

(a) $a = \frac{v-u}{t}$ (b) $a = u + vt$

(c) $a = \frac{v+u}{t}$ (d) $a = \frac{v+u}{2}$

Ans. (a)

Exp. Equation given in option (a) is correct for finding the acceleration. Acceleration of a body is defined as the rate of change of its velocity with time.

$$\text{Acceleration} = \frac{\text{Change in velocity}}{\text{Time taken}}$$

$$a = \frac{v-u}{t}$$

where, v = final velocity of the body

and u = initial velocity of the body.

9 Match the items of List-I with the items of List-II and choose the correct codes given below. *(Chap 7, Class-IX, NCERT)*

List-I (Types of relation)	List-II (Equation)
A. Equation for velocity-time relation	1. $v = \frac{s}{t}$
B. Equation for position-time relation	2. $v - u = at$
C. Equation for position-velocity relation	3. $s = ut + \frac{1}{2}at^2$
D. Equation for distance-time relation	4. $\frac{v^2 - u^2}{2a} = s$

Codes

	A	B	C	D
(a)	1	2	3	4
(b)	4	3	2	1
(c)	3	2	1	4
(d)	2	3	4	1

Ans. (d)

Exp. The correct matching is A-2, B-3, C-4, D-1.
The equation for velocity-time relation is given by the equation,

$$v = u + at$$

This is the first equation of motion. It gives the velocity acquired by a body in time t. The equation for position-time relation is given by the equation,

$$s = ut + \frac{1}{2}at^2$$

This is the second equation of motion. It gives the distance travelled by a body in time t.
The equation for position-velocity relation is given by the equation,

$$v^2 - u^2 = 2as$$

This is the third equation of motion. It gives the velocity acquired by a body in travelling distance s.
The equation for distance-time relation is given by the equation,

$$v = \frac{s}{t}$$

10 Consider the following statements. *(Chap 2, Class-XI, NCERT)*

1. Position-time graph of a stationary object is a straight line parallel to time axis.
2. In uniform motion of an object, velocity increases as the square of time elapsed.
3. The average velocity of the object over an interval of time is either smaller than or equal to the average speed of the object over the same interval.

How many of the above statements are correct?
(a) Only one (b) Only two
(c) All three (d) None of these

Ans. (b)

Exp. Only two statements (1 and 3) are correct but one statement (2) is incorrect.
Statement 1 Position-time graph for a stationary object is a straight line parallel to the time axis showing that there is no change is position with time.
Statement 2 The object moves with uniform velocity, the magnitude of its velocity at different instant will always be constant. Thus, velocity-time graph for an object in uniform motion along a straight path is a straight line parallel to time axis.
Statement 3 Because displacement $\leq$ distance and so, average velocity $\leq$ average speed.

11 Which of the following statements with reference to uniform linear motion and uniform circular motion is/are true? *(Chap 1, Class-IX, NCERT) (HPSC Pre 2023)*

1. In a uniform linear motion, a body moves in the same direction with a constant speed but in uniform circular motion, the speed of the body remains constant and the direction of the motion changes continuously.
2. In a uniform linear motion, here is instantaneous change in velocity but in uniform circular motion, the velocity remains the same.
3. A uniform linear motion is an accelerated motion but a uniform circular motion is not an accelerated motion.

Choose the correct answer from the options given below.
(a) 2 and 3 (b) Only 3 (c) Only 1 (d) 1 and 3

Ans. (c)

Exp. Statement (1) is true whereas Statement (2) and (3) are false. In uniform linear motion, body travels equal distances in equal intervals of time, hence its speed remains constant. It is not an accelerated motion. In uniform circular motion, the speed of the body remains constant and the directions of the motion changes continuously. Thus, in uniform circular motion, velocity changes continuously due to change in its direction. Hence, due to change in velocity, an acceleration acts on the body towards the centre of circular path called centripetal acceleration.

12 If a body moving with non-uniform velocity and uniform acceleration, then *(Chap 7, Class-IX, NCERT)*

(a) displacement-time graph is linear
(b) displacement-time graph is non-linear
(c) velocity-time graph is non-linear
(d) velocity-time graph is linear

Ans. (b)

Exp. If a body is moving with non-uniform velocity and uniform acceleration, then the displacement-time graph is non-linear. Linear motion is the motion of an object along a straight line. It is of two types

(i) uniform linear motion with constant velocity or zero acceleration
(ii) non-uniform linear motion with variable velocity or non-zero acceleration.

13 It is possible for an object to accelerate but not to change its speed if it *(Chap 7, Class-IX, NCERT)*

1. moves on a circular track.
2. moves on a straight path.
3. moves on a sloppy hill.
4. moves to and fro.

Which one of the statement(s) given above is/are correct?
(a) Only 1 (b) 2 and 3 (c) 2 and 4 (d) Only 3

Ans. (a)

Exp. Statement (1) is correct as when an object moves on a circular track, then at every point its velocity changes continuously due to continuous change in direction but the speed of the object doesn't change because it is a scalar quantity. Hence, motion of the object will be accelerated.
Statements (2), (3) and (4) are not correct because if the object moves on the straight path, on a sloppy hill and to and fro, then its speed changes.

14 **Consider the following statements.**

(Chap 7, Class-IX, NCERT)

1. The motion of the athlete moving along a circular path is an accelerated motion.
2. When a person throws a discus, he holds the discus in his hand and gives it a circular motion by rotating his own body.

Which of the statement(s) given above is/are correct?

(a) Only 1 (b) Only 2
(c) Both 1 and 2 (d) Neither 1 nor 2

Ans. (c)

Exp. Both the statements are correct.

If the athlete moves with a velocity of constant magnitude along the circular path, the only change in his velocity is due to the change in the direction of motion. Hence, the motion of athlete moving along a circular path is an accelerated motion. An athlete is throwing a discus in a sports event. He holds the discus in his hand and gives it a circular motion by rotating his own body. Then, he releases the discus in the desired direction and the discus moves along a straight line.

15 **A stone tied to a string is whirled in a circle. As it is revolving, the rope suddenly breaks, then the**

1. stone flies tangentially. *(Chap 7, Class-IX, NCERT)*
2. stone moves radially inward.
3. stone moves radially outward.
4. motion of the stone depends upon its velocity.

Which of the statement(s) given above is/are correct?

(a) Only 1 (b) 1 and 4 (c) 2 and 4 (d) 3 and 4

Ans. (a)

Exp. Statement (1) is correct as when the rope suddenly breaks, the stone moves along a straight line tangential to the circular path. This is because, once the stone is released, it continues to move along the direction it has been moving at that instant.

Statements (2), (3) and (4) are incorrect. In this case stone does not move radially inward or outward and the motion of the stone does not depend upon its velocity.

16 **Consider the following statements.**

(Chap 2, Class XI, NCERT)

Statement I For one dimensional motion, the angle between acceleration and velocity must be zero.

Statement II One dimensional motion is always on straight line.

Which one of the following is correct in respect of the above statements?

(a) Both Statement I and Statement II are correct and Statement II is the correct explanation for Statement I.
(b) Both Statement I and Statement II are correct but Statement II is not the correct explanation for Statement I.
(c) Statement I is correct but Statement II is incorrect.
(d) Statement I is incorrect but Statement II is correct.

Ans. (d)

Exp. Statement I is incorrect but Statement II is correct.

In one dimensional motion the object moves along a straight line. But acceleration may be opposite of velocity and so, angle between them will be 180°.

Chapter 3

Force and Newton's Laws of Motion

Force and Newton's Laws of Motion

Force and Inertia

Force

- An external effort in the form of pushing, pulling, stretching, etc.
- It is a vector quantity.
- Its SI unit is newton & CGS unit is dyne.

Effect of Force

- It can start or stop a motion.
- It can change speed of an object,
- It can change the direction of motion of an object.
- It can change the shape of an object.

Types of Force

Forces are of following types

- **Balanced Forces** When the net effect produced by a number of forces acting on a body is zero. Then forces are called Balanced forces.
- **Unbalanced Forces** When the net effect produced by a number of forces acting on a body is non-zero. Then forces are called unbalanced forces.

Inertia

Inertia are of three types

- **Inertia of Rest** The tendency of a body to resist (oppose) any change in its state of rest.
- **Inertia of Motion** The tendency of a body to resists (oppose) any change in its state of uniform motion.
- **Inertia of Direction** The tendency of a body to oppose any change in its direction of motion.

Newton's Laws of Motion and Friction

Newton's First Law of Motion

- A body remains in the state of rest or uniform motion in a straight line until an external force acts on it.
- **Momentum**
  - The product of its mass and velocity of the body.
    i.e. $p = m \times v$
  - It is a vector quantity and its SI unit is kg-ms^{-1}.

Newton's Second Law of Motion

- According to this law, the rate of change of momentum of an object is proportional to the applied unbalanced force in the direction of force.

  i.e., $F \propto \dfrac{\Delta p}{\Delta t}$ or $F = ma$

- **Impulse** The product of the force and the time interval.
- Its SI unit is newton-second.

Newton's Third Law of Motion

- It states that, whenever one object exerts a force on another object, then the second object exerts an equal and opposite force on the first object, i.e., to every action, there is a equal and opposite reaction.
- **Friction** The force generated by two surfaces of two objects when they come in contact and slide against each other.

Centripetal and Centrifugal Force

Centripetal Force

- A body performing circular motion is acted upon by a force which is always directed towards the centre of the circle. This force is called centripetal force.

  F = Mass x Acceleration

  $F = \dfrac{mv^2}{r}$

  $[\because a = \dfrac{v^2}{r}$, centripetal acceleration$]$

- The earth moves round the sun under a centripetal force directed towards the sun. This force is provided by gravitational attraction on the earth by the sun.

Centrifugal Force

- The outward radial force which is experienced by a body.
- When body moves along a circular path.

Apparatus Based on Centrifugal Force

- **Dryer of Washing Machine** It is based upon centrifugal force. It is a long and perpendicular cylindrical drum with hole in its walls. Wet cloths are dried inside this

Centrifuge

- A device which is used to separate the particles of different masses present in a liquid.

SOURCE New NCERT Class VIII Chap 8 *(Force and Pressure)*, New NCERT Class VIII Chap 9 *(Friction)*, New NCERT Class IX Chap 8 *(Force and Laws of Motion)*, New NCERT Class XI Chap 4 *(Laws of Motion)*, Tamil Nadu Board Class IX *(Motion)*

1 **Consider the following statements.**

(Chap 8, Class-VIII, NCERT)

1. Force may make an object move from rest.
2. Force does not change the direction of the motion of an object.
3. Force may not bring about a change in the shape of an object.
4. Force may change the speed of an object, if it is moving.

Which of the statement(s) given above are correct?

(a) 1 and 2 (b) 1 and 4 (c) 1 and 3 (d) 3 and 4

Ans. (b)

Exp. Statements (1) and (4) are correct as if the position of an object does not change w.r.t its surrounding with the passage of time, it is said to be at rest e.g. book lying on the table. Force can start or stop a motion and it can also change speed of an object.

Statements (2) and (3) are incorrect because, when a force applied to an object, it may also change the direction of the motion of an object.

Many time, force may also bring about change in the shape of an object.

2 **Consider the following statements.**

(Chap 4, Class-XI, NCERT)

Statement I Force is an external effort in the form of push and pull which either changes or tend to change the state of rest or of uniform motion of a body.

Statement II Every body continues in the state of rest or of uniform motion in a straight line, unless an internal force acts on it to change the state.

Which one of the following is correct in respect of the above statements?

(a) Both Statement I and Statement II are correct and Statement II is the correct explanation for Statement I.
(b) Both Statement I and Statement II are correct but Statement II is not the correct explanation for Statement I.
(c) Statement I is correct but Statement II is incorrect.
(d) Statement I is incorrect but Statement II is correct.

Ans. (c)

Exp. Statement I is correct but Statement II is incorrect.

Force is defined as a push or pull that changes or tend to change the state of rest or uniform motion of an object or changes the direction or shape of an object. It causes the object to accelerate or add to their overall pressure. Newton's first law of motion states that, a body at rest will remain at rest and body at motion will remain in uniform motion, unless an external force acts on it to change its state of rest or of uniform motion. Therefore, if no external force is acting on a body, a body will either remain in state of rest or uniform motion.

3 **A bus is moving along a straight path and takes a sharp turn to the right side suddenly. The passengers sitting in the bus will**

(Chap 8, Class-IX, NCERT) (BPSC Pre 2023)

(a) fall in the forward direction
(b) bent towards left side
(c) bent towards right side
(d) More than one of the above

Ans. (b)

Exp. When a bus moving along a straight path takes a sharp turn to the right suddenly, then passenger sitting in the bus bend towards left side. Initially, the passenger and the bus, both are moving in the same direction. When the bus suddenly takes a right turn, the lower portion of passengers who are in contact with the bus tends to move in that direction but upper portion of passengers will be thrown toward the left due to inertia.

4 **Which of the following statement is incorrect about inertia?** *(Chap 8, Class-IX, NCERT)*

(a) Inertia means resistance to change.
(b) A body does not change its state of rest or uniform motion, unless an external force compels it to change that state.
(c) Newton's first law of motion is also known as Law of inertia.
(d) An object remains in state of motion because inertia is applied on it.

Ans. (d)

Exp. Statement (d) is incorrect about inertia because, inertia can never be applied on any object. Inertia is the natural tendency of an object to resist a change in its state of motion or of rest.

Due to inertia, a body remains in a state of rest or of uniform motion in a straight line unless compelled to change that state by applying a force. This is Newton's first law of motion, which is also known as law of inertia.

5 **Consider the following statements, choose the correct option given below.** *(Chap 8, Class-IX, NCERT)*

Statement I A passenger standing in a bus fall in the forward direction when the stationary bus begins to move suddenly.

Statement II Every body continue in its state of rest or of uniform motion in a straight line, until and unless, it is compelled by some unbalanced force to change that state and passenger fall in the backward.

(a) Statement I is correct but Statement II is incorrect.
(b) Statement I is incorrect but Statement II is correct.
(c) Both statement I and II are correct.
(d) Both statement I and II are incorrect.

Ans. (b)

Exp. Statement I is incorrect but Statement II is correct.

A passenger standing in a bus fall in the backward direction not in forward direction. But when the running bus stops suddenly, the passengers are forced forward because of inertial of motion. The passenger tends of remain in their state of motion even though the bus has come to rest.

6 **Consider the following statements.** *(Chap 4, Class-XI, NCERT)*

1. Newton's second law gives the measure of force.
2. An object will continue moving uniformly until the resultant force on it is zero.
3. A particle is moving with a constant speed along a straight line path, a force is not required to keep it moving with uniform acceleration.

How many of the above statements are correct?

(a) Only one
(b) Only two
(c) All three
(d) None of the above

Ans. (b)

Exp. Only two statements (1 and 2) are correct, but one statement (3) is incorrect.

Statement 1 According to Newton's second law of motion, force is directly proportional to the rate of change of momentum.

Statement 2 A body will retain its state of inertia, until and unless, an external force is applied on it. Hence, a body will continue moving uniformly, i.e. with same speed and in same direction until an external force is applied to stop or the resultant force is zero.

Statement 3 Newton's first law states that, if a body is at rest or moving at a constant speed in a straight line, it will remain at rest or keep moving in a straight line at constant speed unless it is acted upon by a force. This postulate is known as the law of inertia.

Hence, a force is not required to keep the particle moving with uniform speed.

7 **Consider the following statements.** *(Chap 4, Class-XI, NCERT)*

Statement I The impulse of the force is defined as the product of the force and its time of action.

Statement II The impulse of the force is equal to the total change in momentum of the body.

Which one of the following is correct in respect of the above statements?

(a) Both Statement I and Statement II are correct and Statement II is the correct explanation for Statement I.
(b) Both Statement I and Statement II are correct but Statement II is not the correct explanation for Statement I.
(c) Statement I is correct but Statement II is incorrect.
(d) Statement I is incorrect but Statement II is correct.

Ans. (b)

Exp. Both Statement I and Statement II are correct but Statement II is not the correct explanation for Statement I.

The measure of the action of a large force acting for a duration of time to produce a finite change in the momentum is called an impulse and the product of the average force and the time interval for which the force acts on the body.

Thus, impulse = average force × time.

8 **According to Newton's third law of motion, consider the following statements.** *(Chap 8, Class-IX, NCERT)*

1. The stone exerts a force on the earth.
2. A billiard ball strikes a rigid wall and gets reflected without any change in speed.
3. Action and reaction forces act on the same body.

Which statement(s) is/are incorrect about the same?

(a) Only 1 (b) 1 and 2
(c) Only 3 (d) 2 and 3

Ans. (c)

Exp. Statement (3) is incorrect because whenever one body exerts a force on another body, the second body exerts an equal and opposite force on the first body.

The force exerted by the first body on the second body is known as action and the force exerted by the second body on the first body is known as reaction.

Thus, action and reaction forces act on two different bodies.

9 **Which of the following statement is incorrect about frictional force?** *(Chap 8, Class-VIII, NCERT)*

(a) It always acts on all the moving objects.
(b) Its direction is always opposite to the direction of motion.
(c) Friction between water and the boat brings it to a stop, once rowing is stopped.
(d) Friction cannot change the state of motion.

Ans. (d)

Exp. Statement (d) is incorrect about frictional force as this force can change the state of motion because an object moving on the ground stops after some time. In this case, the force of friction of ground stops the moving object.

10 **With the reference of friction, consider the following statements.** *(Chap 9, Class-VIII, NCERT)*

1. The force of friction always opposes the applied force.
2. The force of friction will increase, if the two surfaces are pressed harder.
3. Friction is caused by the irregularities of two surfaces in contact.

Which of the statements given above are correct?

(a) 1 and 2 (b) 2 and 3
(c) 1, 2 and 3 (d) None of these

Ans. (c)

Exp. All the given statements are correct about the frictional force.

The force of friction always opposes the applied force. It depends on the smoothness of the contact surfaces. Friction is caused by the irregularities of two surfaces in contact.

Even those surfaces which appear very smooth have large number of minute irregularities on them. Interlocking of these irregularities gives rise to the friction. So, if the two surfaces are pressed harder, these irregularities interlock each other more strongly and as a result, force of friction will increase.

11 Which of the following arrangements correctly represents the decreasing order of different types of frictions involved? *(Chap 9, Class-VIII, NCERT)*

(a) Rolling, static, sliding (b) Rolling, sliding, static
(c) Static, sliding, rolling (d) Sliding, static, rolling

Ans. (c)

Exp. The correct arrangement of frictions in a decreasing order is static > sliding > rolling.

Rolling friction comes into play when an object rolls over the other surface and the point of contact does not have enough time to interlock, hence the friction is the least.

Sliding friction comes into play when one object slides over the other. This friction is more than rolling friction but less than static friction because the body is already in motion. When we try to move an object from rest, static friction acts on the object which is the strongest among all.

12 Consider the following Assertion (A) and Reason (R) and choose the correct code. *(Chap 9, Class-VIII, NCERT)*

Assertion (A) Friction can never be entirely eliminated.

Reason (R) No surface is perfectly smooth.

Codes

(a) Both A and R are true and R is the correct explanation of A.
(b) Both A and R are true but R is not the correct explanation of A.
(c) A is true, but R is false.
(d) A is false, but R is true.

Ans. (a)

Exp. Both Assertion (A) and Reason (R) are true and Reason (R) is the correct explanation of Assertion (A).

As we know, friction is caused by the irregularities on the two surfaces in contact.

Even those surfaces which appear very smooth have a large number of minute irregularities on them.

Irregularities on the two surfaces lock into one another and we have to apply force to overcome it. Therefore, it is correct that friction can never be entirely eliminated because no surface is perfectly smooth.

13 Ball bearings are used to convert static friction into *(Chap 4, Class-XI, NCERT) (BPSC Pre 2023)*

(a) drag
(b) sliding friction
(c) rolling friction
(d) More than one of the above

Ans. (c)

Exp. Ball bearings are used to convert static friction into rolling friction. It is used to prevent sliding by forcing a machine's moving elements to roll over one another. Thus, static friction is changed into rolling friction.

14 With reference to fluid friction, consider the following statements. *(Chap 9, Class-VIII, NCERT)*

1. The fluid friction is also called drag.
2. The frictional force on an object in a fluid depends on its speed with respect to fluid.
3. It also depends on the nature of the fluid.

Which of the statements given above are correct?

(a) 1 and 2 (b) 2 and 3
(c) 1 and 3 (d) 1, 2 and 3

Ans. (d)

Exp. All the given statements are correct with reference to fluid friction. As we know, the fluids exert force of friction on objects in motion through them which is known as drag.

The frictional force on an object in a fluid depends on its speed with respect to fluid. The frictional force also depends on the shape of the object and the nature of the fluid. That's why, all vehicles are designed to have special shapes which reduce fluid friction.

15 Cycle and cars use ball bearing because *(Chap 4, Class-XI, NCERT) (IAS Pre 2013)*

(a) the actual area of contact between the wheel and axle is increased.
(b) the effective area of contact between the wheel and axle is increased.
(c) the effective area of contact between the wheel and axle is reduced.
(d) None of the above

Ans. (c)

Exp. Cycle and cars use ball bearing because the effective area of contact between the wheel and axle is reduced. Since, the frictional force is directly proportional to the effective area of contact, so it also gets reduced.

16 A person is sitting in a car which is at rest. The friction from the road at each of the four wheels of the car is *R*. When the car runs on a straight level road, how will the friction at either of the front wheels vary? *(Chap 5, Class-X, NCERT) (IAS Pre 2008)*

(a) It will be greater than *R*.
(b) It will be less than *R*. (c) It will be equal to *R*.
(d) It shall depend on the material of the road.

Ans. (b)

Exp. When the car is at rest, static friction R acts on the wheels of the car. And as we know, friction is a self-adjusting force in nature. So, when the car runs on a straight level road, the friction that acts on the wheels is kinetic friction which is less than the static friction R.

17 A batsman hits a cricket ball which then rolls on a level ground. After covering a short distance, the ball comes to rest. The ball slows to a stop because

(Chap 8, Class-IX, NCERT) (MPPSC Pre 2017)

(a) the batsman did not hit the ball hard enough.
(b) velocity is proportional to the force exerted on the ball.
(c) there is a force on the ball opposing the motion.
(d) there is no unbalanced force on the ball, so the ball would try to come to rest.

Ans. (c)

Exp. When a batsman hits a cricket ball which then rolls on a level ground. After covering a short distance, the ball comes to rest because there is an external force i.e., frictional force acting on the moving ball opposing its motion. If there is no frictional force, then the ball will roll continuously.

18 Consider the following statements.

(Chap 4, Class-XI, NCERT)

Statement I Linear momentum of a body is the amount of motion contained in the body and is measured as the product of its velocity and acceleration.

Statement II Linear momentum of a body is directly proportional to increase in its velocity.

Which one of the following is correct in respect of the above statements?

(a) Both Statement I and Statement II are correct and Statement II is the correct explanation for Statement I.
(b) Both Statement I and Statement II are correct but Statement II is not the correct explanation for Statement I.
(c) Statement I is correct but Statement II is incorrect.
(d) Statement I is incorrect but Statement II is correct.

Ans. (d)

Exp. Statement I is incorrect but Statement II is correct. As we know, $p = mv$ and from the equation, linear momentum is directly proportional to the object's mass m and velocity v. Therefore, the greater an object's mass or the greater its velocity, the greater its momentum.

19 Consider the following statements.

(Chap 4, Class-XI, NCERT)

Statement I When the speed of a moving body is doubled, its momentum is doubled.

Statement II In doubling the mass and acceleration of the mass, the force acting on the mass with respect to the previous value increases four times.

Which one of the following is correct in respect of the above statements?

(a) Both Statement I and Statement II are correct and Statement II is the correct explanation for Statement I.
(b) Both Statement I and Statement II are correct but Statement II is not the correct explanation for Statement I.
(c) Statement I is correct but Statement II is incorrect.
(d) Statement I is incorrect but Statement II is correct.

Ans. (b)

Exp. Both Statement I and Statement II are correct but Statement II is not the correct explanation for Statement I. Linear momentum is the product of mass and velocity of body (i.e. $P = mv$). So when the speed of moving body is doubled, its momentum is also doubled.

$$\text{Force} = \text{Mass} \times \text{Acceleration}$$

If mass and acceleration both are doubled, then force will become four times.

20 The working principle of a washing machine is

(Unit 2, Class-IX, Tamil Nadu Board)

(a) centrifugation
(b) dialysis,
(c) reverse osmosis
(d) diffusion

Ans. (a)

Exp. The working principle of a washing machine is centrifugation. Centrifugation is a separation process that uses the action of centrifugal force to promote accelerated settling of particles in a solid-liquid mixture.

Chapter 4

Work, Energy and Power

Work, Energy and Power

Work and Energy

Work

- Work is said to be done, when a body is displaced by applying a force on it.
- The SI unit of work is newton-metre, which is also called joule.

Types of Work

There are three types of work

- **Positive Work** Angle between force and displacement lies between 0° and 90°, then work done will be positive.
- **Negative Work** Angle between force and displacement lies between 90° and 270°, then work done will be negative.
- **Zero Work** The force and displacement are in perpendicular direction (angle between direction of force and displacement is 90°), work done is zero.

Energy

- The capacity or ability of a body to do work.
- The SI unit of energy is joule.
- **Kinetic Energy** The energy possessed by it due a body its state of motion.
- **Potential Energy** The energy possessed by a body due to change in its position or shape.
- Heat energy, chemical energy, light energy are the other forms of energy

Law of Conservation of Energy and Power

Law of Conservation of Energy

- According to this law, energy can neither be created nor be destroyed.
- It can only be transformed from one form to another.
- When a body is thrown upwards, its kinetic energy continuously converts into potential energy. The total energy before and after transformation always remains constant.

Transformation of Energy

- The conversion of energy from one form to other form.
- **Conversion of Muscular Energy into Kinetic Energy** When we throw a ball, the muscular energy which is stored in our body, gets converted into kinetic energy of the ball.

Power

- The rate of doing work.

$$\text{Power} = \frac{\text{Work}}{\text{Time}} \quad P = \frac{W}{t}$$

- The unit of power is watt (W).

$$1\text{ W} = 1\text{ Js}^{-1}$$

- We express larger rate of energy transfer in kilowatt (kW).

Sources of Energy

Sources of Energy

- Any system which is capable of providing energy in a convenient form at a steady rate over a long period of time.

Conventional Sources of Energy

- The sources of energy which have been accumulated in nature over a long time.
- These sources cannot be quickly replaced and will be exhausted one day.
- These sources are called non-renewable sources of energy.
  e.g., Fossil fuels such as coal, natural gas etc.
- **Coal** It is a naturally occurring material which is a mixture of carbon and compounds of carbon containing hydrogen, nitrogen, oxygen and sulphur.
- **Natural gas** It is the cleanest burning fossil fuel as it gives off 50% of carbon dioxide released by coal and 25% less carbon dioxide than oil for the same amount of energy produced.

Non-Conventional Sources of Energy

- The sources of energy which are being produced continuously in nature and are inexhaustible. These sources are called renewable sources of energy.
  e.g., Wind energy, Tidal energy etc.
- **Wind Energy** The energy possessed by the wind is due to its high speed.
- **Tidal Energy** Energy possessed by rising and falling water tides .

SOURCE New NCERT Class IX Chap 10 (Work and Energy), Old NCERT Class X Chap 14 (Source of Energy), New NCERT Class XI Chap 5 (Work, Energy and Power)

1 **Consider the following statements.** *(Chap 5, Class-XI, NCERT)*

Statement I When the body is projected up, the force of gravity is opposite to the motion and the kinetic energy of the body decreases.

Statement II When the body falls down, the force of gravity is in the direction of motion and the kinetic energy of the body decreases.

Which one of the following is correct in respect of the above statements?

(a) Both Statement I and Statement II are correct and Statement II is the correct explanation for Statement I.
(b) Both Statement I and Statement II are correct but Statement II is not the correct explanation for Statement I.
(c) Statement I is correct but Statement II is incorrect.
(d) Statement I is incorrect but Statement II is correct.

Ans. (c)

Exp. Statement I is correct but Statement II is incorrect.

The motion of the body and the direction of gravitational force will be in the opposite direction. So, work done will be negative. As the body moves upward, its velocity decreases hence, the kinetic energy too.

When the body falls from a height, then its potential energy changes into kinetic energy progressively. A decrease in the potential energy is equal to an increase in the kinetic energy of the body. During the process, total mechanical energy of the body remains conserved.

2 **Which of the following statement is incorrect about work?** *(Chap 5, Class-XI, NCERT)*

(a) Positive work is done by a man lifting a bucket with the help of a rope.
(b) Work done by friction on a body sliding down an inclined plane is negative.
(c) Negative work is done by an applied force on a body moving on a rough horizontal plane with uniform velocity.
(d) Negative work done is by the resistive force of air on a vibrating pendulum in bringing it to rest.

Ans. (c)

Exp. Statement (c) is incorrect about work because when a force is applied on a body moving on a rough horizontal plane with uniform velocity, the positive work is done on it.

3 **Consider the following statements.** *(Chap 5, Class-XI, NCERT)*

Statement I The work done is measured by the product of the force exerted on the body and the distance that the body travels in the direction of force.

Statement II Work done is said to be one joule if a force of one newton displaces a body through one metre in the opposite direction of force.

Which one of the following is correct in respect of the above statements?

(a) Both Statement I and Statement II are correct. Statement II is the correct explanation for Statement I.
(b) Both Statement I and Statement II are correct but Statement II is not the correct explanation for Statement I.
(c) Statement I is correct but Statement II is incorrect.
(d) Statement I is incorrect but Statement II is correct.

Ans. (c)

Exp. Statement I is correct but Statement II is incorrect.

As we know, work done is the product of the force exerted on body and direction of force applied.

$$W = F.d \cos \theta$$

whereas, one joule is said, when a force of one newton applied and body displace to one metre in same direction.

4 **Consider the following statements.** *(Chap 10, Class-IX, NCERT)*

1. Work done is negative when the force acts opposite to the direction of displacement.
2. Work done is positive when the force is in the direction of displacement.

Which of the statement(s) given above is/are correct?

(a) Only 1 (b) Only 2
(c) Both 1 and 2 (d) Neither 1 nor 2

Ans. (c)

Exp. Both the statements (1) and (2) are correct. Work done is negative when the force acts opposite to the direction of displacement. A body moving on the ground slows down gradually and ultimately stops. This is because a force due to friction acts on the body. The force of friction acts in a direction opposite to the direction of motion of body. So, the work done by the force of friction on the body is negative.

Work done is positive when the force is in the direction of displacement. If we kick a football lying on the ground, then it starts moving. The force of our kick has moved the football. We have applied the force in the direction of motion of football. So, the work done on the body is positive.

5 **Which of the following statement is incorrect about kinetic energy of an object?** *(Chap 5, Class-XI, NCERT)*

(a) The kinetic energy of an object increases with its speed.
(b) Kinetic energy is a vector quantity.
(c) The work done is equal to the change in kinetic energy of an object.
(d) None of the above

Ans. (b)

Exp. Statement (b) is incorrect about kinetic energy of an object, because kinetic energy is a scalar quantity. The kinetic energy of an object is a measure of the work an object can do by the virtue of its motion.

6 **Consider the following Assertion (A) and Reason (R) and choose the correct code.** *(Chap 10, Class-IX, NCERT)*

Assertion (A) The potential energy of an object at a height depends on the ground level or the zero level we choose.

Reason (R) The work done by gravity is independent of path followed.

Codes

(a) Both A and R are true, and R is the correct explanation of A.
(b) Both A and R are true, but R is not the correct explanation of A.
(c) A is true, but R is false.
(d) A is false but R is true.

Ans. (b)

Exp. Both Assertion (A) and Reason (R) are true, but Reason (R) is not the correct explanation of Assertion (A).

The potential energy of an object at a height depends on the ground level or the zero level we choose. An object in a given position can have a certain potential energy with respect to one level and a different value of potential energy with respect to another level.

The work done by gravity depends on the difference in vertical heights of the initial and final positions of the object and not on the path along which the object is moved.

7 **Match the items of List-I with items of List-II and choose the correct code from given below.** *(Chap 5, Class-XI, NCERT)*

List-I (Unit)	**List-II** (Values)
A. Erg	1. $3.6 \times 10^{+6}$ J
B. Electron volt (eV)	2. 4.186 J
C. Calorie (cal)	3. 10^{-7}J
D. Kilowatt hour (kWh)	4. 1.6×10^{-19} J

Codes

	A	B	C	D		A	B	C	D
(a)	3	4	2	1	(b)	1	2	3	4
(c)	2	3	4	1	(d)	1	4	2	3

Ans. (a)

Exp. The correct matching is A-3, B-4, C-2, D-1.

In CGS system, the absolute unit of work is erg.

$$1 \text{ Erg} = 10^{-7} \text{ joule}$$

Electron volt is very small unit of work (or energy), which is used in atomic physics. One electron volt is the energy which an electron acquires when accelerated through a potential difference of 1 volt.

$$1 \text{ electron volt} = 1.6 \times 10^{-19} \text{ joule}$$

Calorie is the unit of heat. The calorie is defined as the amount of heat required to raise the temperature of 1 g of water from 14.5° C to 15.5° C.

$$1 \text{ calorie} = 4.186 \text{ joule}$$

The commercial unit of energy is kilo-watt-hour. One kilowatt hour is the amount of electrical energy consumed when an electrical appliance having a power rating of 1 kilowatt is used for 1 hour.

$$1 \text{ kilowatt-hour} = 3.6 \times 10^{6} \text{ joule}$$

8 **Which of the following statement about energy is correct?** *(Chap 10, Class-IX, NCERT)*

(a) An object having a capability to do work is said to possess energy.
(b) The object which does the work, loses energy.
(c) The object on which the work is done, gains energy.
(d) All of the above statements are correct.

Ans. (d)

Exp. All the given statements are correct about energy. When an object having a capability to do work is said to possess energy. A body which possesses energy can exert a force on another body. Due to this process, some of the energy is transferred to the another body. So, the object which does the work, loses energy and the object on which the work is done, gains energy.

9 **Consider the following statements.** *(Chap 5, Class-XI, NCERT)*

Statement I Kinetic energy of a system can be increased or decreased without applying any external force on the system.

Statement II This is because KE $= \frac{1}{2}mv^3$, so it is independent of any external forces.

Which one of the following is correct in respect of the above statements?

(a) Both Statement I and Statement II are correct and Statement II is the correct explanation for Statement I.
(b) Both Statement I and Statement II are correct but Statement II is not the correct explanation for Statement I.
(c) Statement I is correct but Statement II is incorrect.
(d) Statement I is incorrect but Statement II is correct.

Ans. (c)

Exp. Statement I is correct but Statement II is incorrect.

KE can be increased or decreased without applying any external force, as internal forces can do work, e.g., explosion of a bomb. The kinetic energy of body is given by $K = \frac{1}{2}mv^2$.

10 **Which of the following energy changes involves frictional force?** *(Chap 5, Class-XI, NCERT) (BPSC Pre 2023)*

(a) Potential energy to sound energy
(b) Chemical energy to heat energy
(c) Kinetic energy to heat energy
(d) More than one of the above

Ans. (c)

Exp. The frictional force is involved to change the kinetic energy to heat energy. The objects which are in motion, stops due to friction force. In this process, kinetic energy of object is lost and converted into heat energy.

11 When a ball is projected upwards, there is an increase in its *(Chap 10, Class-IX, NCERT), (Tamil Nadu PCS Pre 2022)*

1. Potential energy 2. Momentum
3. Kinetic energy

Codes

(a) Only 1 (b) 1 and 2
(c) Only 2 (d) 2 and 3

Ans. (a)

Exp. When a ball is projected upwards, there is an increase in its potential energy.
According to law of conservation, energy can only be transformed from one form to another, it can neither be created not be destroyed, e.g. when an object is thrown upwards, its kinetic energy continuously converts into potential energy. Therefore, kinetic energy and momentum of object decrease, but total energy always remains constant.

12 Consider the following statements with reference to law of conservation of energy. *(Chap 5, Class-XI, NCERT)*

1. Conservation of energy is not valid in all situations and for all kinds of transformations.
2. The total mechanical energy of a system is conserved if the forces, doing work on it, are conservative.

Which of the statement(s) given above is/are incorrect?

(a) Only 1 (b) Only 2
(c) Both 1 and 2 (d) Neither 1 nor 2

Ans. (a)

Exp. Statement (1) is incorrect because according to law of conservation of energy, the total energy before and after the transformation remains the same. This law is valid in all situations and for all kinds of transformations.
Statement (2) is correct, when a body is released from a height, then the potential energy of the body is gradually transformed into kinetic energy. So, the total mechanical energy of a system is conserved if the forces, doing work on it are conserved.

13 Consider the following statements. *(Chap 5, Class-XI, NCERT)*

1. A force is conservative, if the work done by it on a body in moving it from one position to another depends only on the initial and final positions of the body and not on the path followed by it between the two positions.
2. A force is conservative if the work done by it on a body in moving it from one position to another depends on the path followed by the body between the two positions.
3. When a conservative force does positive work, the potential energy of the system decreases.

How many of the above statements are correct?

(a) Only one
(b) Only two
(c) All three
(d) None of the above

Ans. (b)

Exp. Only two statements (1 and 3) are correct but one statement (2) is incorrect because a force is said to be non-conservative if work done by or against the force in moving a body from one position to another position, depends on the path followed between these two positions. e.g., frictional force, viscous force, air drag, etc.

14 Consider the following statements. *(Chap 5, Class-XI, NCERT)*

1. All forces are conservative.
2. Magnetic force is a conservative force.
3. Spring force is a conservative force.

Which of the statements given above are correct?

(a) 1 and 3 (b) 1 and 2 (c) 2 and 3 (d) 1, 2 and 3

Ans. (c)

Exp. Statements (2) and (3) are correct.
A force is said to be conservative if the work done by the force in moving a body depends only upon the initial and final positions of the body and is independent of the path followed between the initial and final positions. Elastic of spring force, magnetic force and gravitational force are conservative forces.
Statement (1) is incorrect because, all forces are not conservative. Frictional force is a non-conservative force because friction depends on the path followed by the object.

15 Consider the following statements. *(Chap 12, Module 4, NIOS)*

1. Wood and cow dung are non bio-mass energy source, only gobar-gas is an example of bio-mass energy source.
2. Anything out of which usable energy can be extracted is a source of energy.
3. Energy obtained from coal is called ultimate source of energy.

Which of the statement(s) given above is/are incorrect?

(a) 1 and 2
(b) 2 and 3
(c) 1 and 3
(d) None of the above

Ans. (c)

Exp. Statements (1) and (3) are incorrect.
Wood, bio-gas or gobar-gas and cow dung are bio-mass energy sources.
Energy obtained from the sun is called ultimate source of energy.

16 In wind power, which form of energy is converted into electrical energy?

(Chap 14, Class-X, NCERT) (UPPSC Pre 2016)

(a) Kinetic energy (b) Potential energy
(c) Solar energy (d) Radiant energy

Ans. (a)

Exp. In wind power, kinetic energy of wind is converted into electrical energy. The wind is used to generate mechanical power or electricity. Wind turbines convert the kinetic energy of the wind into mechanical power. This mechanical power can be used for specific tasks such as pumping water.

17 In a hydro power plant, *(Chap 14, Class-X, NCERT)*

(a) kinetic energy possessed by stored water is converted into potential energy.
(b) potential energy is converted into electricity by falling water.
(c) electricity is extracted from water.
(d) water is converted into steam to produce electricity.

Ans. (b)

Exp. In hydro power plant, potential energy is converted into electricity by falling water and this potential energy stored in water at a height is converted into kinetic energy of flowing water and kinetic energy converts into the electricity. Electricity produced by hydro power plants is called hydroelectricity.

18 Most of the sources of energy we use represented stored solar energy. Which of the following is not ultimately obtained from the sun's energy?

(Chap 12, Module 4, NIOS)

(a) Nuclear energy
(b) Geothermal energy
(c) Biomass energy
(d) Wind energy

Ans. (a)

Exp. Nuclear energy is a form of energy released from nucleus. This source of energy can be produced in two ways.

Fission $\rightarrow$ when nuclei of atoms split into several parts or
Fusion $\rightarrow$ when nuclei of atoms fuse together.

Biomass energy and wind energy are ultimately derived from the sun's energy.

Geothermal energy comes directly and indirectly from the sun. Geothermal energy is the form of heat energy stored inside the crust of earth. This is formed when water molecules or any other substances that get heated and get trapped inside the crust of earth. The molecules absorb energy from the sun to get heated. Hence, geothermal energy is derived from the sunlight.

19 Which of these natural resources is considered as non-renewable resources? *(Chap 14, Class-X, NCERT) (RAS/RTS Pre 2023)*

(a) Timber (b) Fossil fuels
(c) Solar energy (d) Wind energy

Ans. (b)

Exp. Fossil fuels such as coal, petroleum, natural gas, fissionable materials are considered as non-renewable resources.

These sources of energy which have accumulated in nature over a long time and cannot be quickly replaced.

Renewable sources of energy are the sources which are being produced continuously in nature. Solar energy, wind energy, hydro energy and bio fuels (timber, bio gas and alcohol).

20 Consider the following statements.

(Class-XI, NCERT)

1. In a nuclear fission reaction, the energy stored in the nuclei of atom can be released by breaking a heavy nucleus into two lighter nuclei.
2. The fission reaction is carried out in a controlled and regulated manner in nuclear reactors by using control rods made of zinc/nickel.

Which of the statement(s) given above is/are correct?

(a) 1 and 2 (b) Only 1
(c) Only 2 (d) None of these

Ans. (b)

Exp. As we know, in fission, the energy stored in the nuclei of atom only released by breaking a heavy nuclei into daughter lighter. The fission reaction is controlled in nuclear reactor by using control rods made of boron/cadmium.

21 Consider the following statements.

(Chap 5, Class-XI, NCERT)

1. Unit of power is horse power (HP), which is equal to 740 watt.
2. Our electricity bill carry the energy consumption in unit of watt.

Which of the statement(s) given above is/are correct?

(a) 1 and 2 (b) Only 1
(c) Only 2 (d) None of these

Ans. (d)

Exp. Both statements (1) and (2) are incorrect. 1 HP is equal to 746 W. Our electricity bill carry the energy consumption in unit of kWh.

kWh is a unit of energy and not of power. One kilowatt hour is the amount of electrical energy consumed, when an electrical appliance of 1000 W is used for 1 h.

Chapter 5

Gravitation

Gravitation

Gravitation Law and Escape Speed

Universal Law of Gravitation

- Every object in the universe attracts every other object with a force which is proportional to the product of their masses and inversely proportional to the square of the distance between them. $F = \frac{Gm_1m_2}{r^2}$

Importance of Universal Law of Gravitation

- The force that binds us to the earth.
- The motion of the moon around the earth.
- The occurrence tides is due to the gravitational force of attraction of the moon.

Gravity

- The force by which the earth attracts a body towards its centre.
- **Acceleration Due to Gravity**
  - The rate of increase of velocity of a body falling towards the earth.
  - Its SI unit is m/s^2.

Escape Speed

- The minimum speed with which a body must be projected vertically upwards in order that it may just escape the gravitational field of earth.
- It depends on the mass and radius of the planet from the surface of which the body is projected.

Gravitational Field and Potential, Mass and Weight

Gravitational Field

- The space around an object in which its gravitational force of attraction can be experienced.
- It is a vector quantity.
- It is measured in newton per kilogram (N/kg).

Gravitational Potential

- The amount of work done in bringing the object of unit mass from infinity to a particular point in the gravitational field.
- Its is a scalar quantity.
- Its SI unit is J/kg.
- **Gravitational Potential Energy**
  - The work obtained in bringing a body from infinity to a point in a gravitational field.
  - It is given by $U = -\frac{GMm}{r}$

Mass

- The total content of the body which measures the inertia of a body.
- It is a scalar quantity.
- Its SI unit is kilogram (kg).

Weight

- The force with which body is attracted towards the earth.
- Weight = Mass × Acceleration due to gravity.
- It is a vector quantity.

Planetary Motion and Satellites

Kepler's Laws of Planetary Motion

- **Kepler's First Law** It states that the path of any planet in an orbit around the Sun follows the shape of an ellipse with the Sun at one of the foci.
- **Kepler's Second law** It states that an imaginary line from the Sun to the planet sweeps out equal areas in equal intervals of time.
- **Kepler's Third law** It states that the cube of the mean distance of a planet from the Sun is directly proportional to the square of its orbital period *T*.

Satellites

- A body which continuously revolves in an orbit around a comparatively much larger body or planets.
- Moon is the natural satellite of earth.
- **Geostationary Satellite**
  - A satellite which revolves from west to east with a time period of 24 hours in a circular orbit concentric and coplanar with the equatorial plane of the earth.
- **Polar Satellite**
  - A satellite which revoles in a polar orbit.
  - Its orbit is about 500 to 800 km above the surface of earth.
  - They revolve around the earth in a North-South direction.

SOURCE *New NCERT Class IX Chap 9* (Gravitation), *New NCERT Class XI Chap 7* (Gravitation), *Tamil Nadu Board Class IX* (Universe)

1 **With reference to Kepler's laws, consider the following statements.** *(Chap 7, Class-XI, NCERT)*

1. According to law of areas, the line joining the planet and the sun sweeps unequal areas in equal interval of time.
2. The cube of the mean distance of a planet from the sun is proportional to the square of its orbital period.
3. Law of orbits states that, all planets move in elliptical orbits with sun situated at one of the foci.

Which of the statements given above are correct?

(a) 1 and 3 (b) 2 and 3
(c) 1 and 2 (d) 1, 2 and 3

Ans. (b)

Exp. Statements (2) and (3) are correct. According to Kepler's law of planetary motion, the planets revolve around the sun in an elliptical orbit with the sun situated at one of the foci. The cube of the mean distance of a planet from the sun is directly proportional to the square of its orbital time period.

Statement (1) is incorrect because according to Kepler's law, the line joining the planet and the sun sweeps equal areas in equal interval of time.

2 **A falling apple is attracted towards the earth but earth does not move towards the apple. This is due to which law of motion?** *(Chap 9, Class-IX, NCERT)*

(a) Newton's first law
(b) Newton's second law
(c) Newton's third law
(d) Law of gravitation

Ans. (b)

Exp. A falling apple is attracted towards the earth but earth does not move towards the apple due to Newton's second law of motion.

The force of attraction on apple due to earth is equal to the force of attraction on earth due to apple but the change in momentum for the corresponding force is much greater in apple, therefore apple is attracted towards the earth.

3 **Which of the following statement is incorrect about law of gravitation?** *(Chap 9, Class-IX, NCERT)*

(a) The gravitational force between two objects is inversely proportional to the distance between them.
(b) The SI unit of gravitational constant is $\text{N-m}^2\ \text{kg}^{-2}$.
(c) The accepted value of constant of proportionality in law of gravitation is $6.673 \times 10^{-11}\ \text{N-m}^2/\text{kg}^2$.
(d) None of the above

Ans. (a)

Exp. Statement (a) is incorrect about law of gravitation because the gravitational force between two objects is inversely proportional to the square of the distance between them.

4 **Which of the following statements highlight the important consequences of the universal law of gravitation?** *(Chap 9, Class-IX, NCERT)*

(a) The motion of planets around the sun.
(b) The tides due to the moon and the earth.
(c) The force that binds us to the earth.
(d) All of the above are correct.

Ans. (d)

Exp. All the given statements highlight the important consequences of universal law of gravitation.

The motion of planets around the sun, the force binding us to the earth and the tides forming in the ocean due to gravitational pull of moon is a direct consequence of universal law of gravitation.

5 **Consider the following Assertion (A) and Reason (R) and choose the correct code.** *(Chap 9, Class-IX, NCERT)*

Assertion (A) Whenever an object falls towards the earth under gravitational force, the object is said to be in state of free fall.

Reason (R) Whenever an object falls towards the earth, a uniform acceleration is involved.

Codes

(a) Both A and R are true and R is the correct explanation of A.
(b) Both A and R are true, but R is not the correct explanation of A.
(c) A is true, but R is false.
(d) A is false, but R is true.

Ans. (a)

Exp. Both Assertion (A) and Reason (R) are true and Reason (R) is the correct explanation of Assertion (A).

When an object is subjected to only earth's gravitational force and other forces on the body are zero, this state is called free fall.

In this state of free fall, a uniform acceleration $g = 9.8\ \text{m/s}^2$ acts towards the centre of earth.

6 **Consider the following statements.** *(Chap 7, Class-XI, NCERT)*

Statement I Universal constant of gravitation is equal to the force of attraction between two unit masses placed at unit distance apart.

Statement II The gravitational force of repulsion between two bodies is affected by other bodies present nearby.

Which one of the following is correct in respect of the above statements?

(a) Both Statement I and Statement II are correct and Statement II is the correct explanation for Statement I.
(b) Both Statement I and Statement II are correct but Statement II is not the correct explanation for Statement I.
(c) Statement I is correct but Statement II is incorrect.
(d) Statement I is incorrect but Statement II is correct.

Ans. (c)

Exp. Statement I is correct but Statement II is incorrect. The gravitational force of attraction between two bodies is not affected by other bodies because gravitational force depends upon the product of two masses and the square of the distance between them

$$F \propto \frac{m_1 m_2}{r^2} \Rightarrow F = \frac{G\, m_1\, m_2}{r^2}$$

where, F is gravitational force and G is gravitational constant.
If $m_1 = m_2 = 1$ kg and $r = 1$ m, then $F = G$.

7 **Consider the following statements.** *(Chap 9, Class-IX, NCERT) (JKPSC Pre 2023)*

Statement I The universal gravitational constant G is important because it determines the strength of one of the four forces in nature.

Statement II By knowing G, an accurate value for earth's mass could finally be obtained.

From the above statements, choose the correct answer from the options given below.

(a) Both Statement I and Statement II are true.
(b) Statement I is correct but Statement II is false.
(c) Both Statement I and Statement II are false.
(d) Statement I is incorrect but Statement II is true.

Ans. (a)

Exp. Both Statement I and Statement II are true.
The universal gravitational constant G is important because it determines the strength of one of the four forces in nature.
From Newton's law of gravitation, we have

$$F = G\frac{mM_E}{R_E^2} \Rightarrow mg = G\frac{mM_E}{R_E^2}$$

$$M_E = \frac{gR_E^2}{G}$$

Hence, by knowing G an accurate value for earth's mass could finally be obtained by this formula.

8 **Amit buys few grams of gold at the poles and hand over the same to his friend at the equator. The weight of gold he brought comes out to be different, this is because** *(Chap 9, Class-IX, NCERT)*

(a) he travels a large distance from poles to the equator
(b) gravitational force becomes slightly less
(c) the value of g is greater at the poles than at the equator
(d) mass of gold becomes different at poles than at the equator

Ans. (c)

Exp. The weight of the gold he bought comes out to be different because the value of g is greater at the poles than at the equator.
Weight is the product of mass and acceleration due to gravity.
The value of acceleration due to gravity is not constant. It varies place to place and according to height and depth. Therefore, weight of the gold becomes less at equator due to lower value of g at equator.

9 **If a sheet of paper and a stone drop simultaneously from the first floor of a building, then** *(Chap 9, Class-IX, NCERT)*

(a) they reach the ground (earth) at the same time
(b) paper reaches the ground little faster than the stone
(c) stone reaches the ground first while paper reaches little later
(d) None of the above

Ans. (c)

Exp. If a sheet of paper and a stone dropped simultaneously from the first floor of building, then stone will reach the ground first while paper will reach a little later. It is due to the resistance offered by the air. The resistance offered by air to the paper is more than resistance offered to the stone.
Both stone and paper will reach ground at the same time, if there is an absence of air (or atmosphere).

10 **Consider the following statements.** *(Chap 7, Class-XI, NCERT)*

1. Acceleration due to gravity decreases with increasing altitude.
2. Acceleration due to gravity decreases with increasing depth.
3. Acceleration due to gravity is independent of mass of the earth.
4. Acceleration due to gravity is independent of mass of the body.

Which of the statements given above are correct?

(a) 2 and 4 (b) 1 and 4
(c) 1 and 3 (d) 1, 2 and 4

Ans. (d)

Exp. Statements (1), (2) and (4) are correct.
The acceleration produced in a free falling body due to the gravitational force of the earth is known as acceleration due to gravity. The acceleration due to gravity does not depend on the mass of the body.
The value of acceleration due to gravity is maximum on the surface of the earth. It decreases with increasing altitude and with increasing depth.
Statement (3) is incorrect because the acceleration due to gravity depends upon the mass of earth.

11 **Consider the following statements.** *(Chap 7, Class-XI, NCERT)*

1. There is no effect on the value of g due to the rotation of earth at poles.
2. The value of g increases as we go away from the surface of the earth.
3. The acceleration due to gravity at the centre of the earth is zero.

How many of the above statements are correct?

(a) Only one (b) Only two
(c) All three (d) None of these

Ans. (b)

Exp. Only two statements (1 and 3) are correct but one statement (2) is incorrect because as the height of an object from the surface of the earth increases, the distance between the object and the centre of the earth (r) increases. But acceleration due to gravity (g) at distance r from the centre of earth is given as, $g = \frac{GM}{r^2}$

therefore, acceleration due to gravity (g) dereases with the increase in r.

As a result, the value of gravitational acceleration (g) decreases as we go away from the surface of the earth.

12 **Consider the following Assertion (A) and Reason (R) and choose the correct code.** *(Chap 9, Class-IX, NCERT)*

Assertion (A) The weight of any body is maximum at equator.

Reason (R) The weight of the body depends upon the acceleration due to gravity.

In the light of the above statements, choose the correct answer from the options given below.

Codes

(a) Both A and R are true and R is the correct explanation of A.
(b) Both A and R are true but R is not the correct explanation of A.
(c) A is true but R is false.
(d) A is false but R is true.

Ans. (*d*)

Exp. A is false but R is true.

The weight of any body is maximum at poles because weight depends upon the acceleration due to gravity and acceleration due to gravity is maximum at the poles of the earth.

13 **If the spinning speed of the earth increases, then the weight of the body at the equator will** *(Chap 9, Class-IX, NCERT)*

(a) increase (b) decrease (c) remain same (d) be doubled

Ans. (*b*)

Exp. When the spinning speed of the earth increases, then the weight of the body at the equator will decrease. It is because, acceleration due to gravity decreases due to the increase of spinning speed of the earth. Hence, due to decrease, the value of gravitational acceleration, weight of the body a the equator is decreased.

14 **If suddenly, the gravitational force of attraction between the earth and a satellite revolving around it becomes zero, then the satellite will** *(Chap 7, Class-XI, NCERT)*

(a) continue to move in this orbit with same velocity.
(b) move tangentially to the original orbit with the same velocity.
(c) become stationary in its orbit.
(d) move towards the earth.

Ans. (*b*)

Exp. If suddenly, the gravitational force of attraction between the earth and a satellite revolving around it becomes zero, then the satellite will move tangentially to the original orbit with the same velocity.

The gravitational force provides the necessary centripetal force for the revolution of satellite around the earth. When this force becomes zero, the satellite will move along the tangential direction at that point.

15 **Consider the following statements.** *(Chap 7, Class-XI, NCERT)*

1. Satellites in a circular orbits around the earth in the equatorial plane with time period of 24 hours are called geostationary satellites.
2. Polar satellites has a time-period of around 100 min

Which of the statement(s) given above is/are correct?

(a) Only 1
(b) Only 2
(c) Both 1 and 2
(d) None of the above

Ans. (*c*)

Exp. Both the statements (1) and (2) are correct.

A geostationary satellite revolves around the earth from West to East in an orbit coplanar with equatorial plane at a height of about 36000 km above the surface of the earth.

Such a satellite will always appear to be over the same place relative to an observer on the earth. Its time period of revolution is exactly 24 h. It is used in radio transmission and telecommunication.

Polar satellites revolve around the earth in a North-South direction around the earth. The time period of revolution of polar satellite is around 100 min. These satellites are used to record the land and sea temperature.

16 **Satellites used for telecommunication relay are kept in a geostationary orbit. A satellite is said to be in such an orbit when** *(Chap 7, Class-XI, NCERT)*

1. the orbit is geosynchronous.
2. the orbit is circular.
3. the orbit lies in the place of the earth's equator.
4. the orbit is at an altitude of 22236 km.

Which of the above statements are correct for a geostationary satellite orbit?

(a) 1, 2 and 3 (b) 1, 3 and 4
(c) 2 and 4 (d) All of these

Ans. (*a*)

Exp. Statements (1), (2) and (3) are correct for a geostationary satellite orbit.

A geostationary or geosynchronous orbit is the circular orbit that is directly above the equator of the earth and its rotational period is equal to that of the earth. It lies at an altitude of 22236 miles or 35786 km.

17 Consider the following statements.

(Chap 7, Class-XI, NCERT)

Statement I The time period of earth's satellite in circular orbit is independent of the mass of the satellite.

Statement II Average density of the earth is inversely proportional to acceleration due to gravity.

Which one of the following is correct in respect of the above statements?

(a) Both Statement I and Statement II are correct and Statement II is the correct explanation for Statement I.

(b) Both Statement I and Statement-II are correct but Statement II is not the correct explanation for Statement I.

(c) Statement I is correct but Statement II is incorrect.

(d) Statement I is incorrect but Statement II is correct.

Ans. (c)

Exp. Statement I is correct but Statement II is incorrect.

The time period of the satellite depends only upon its height above the earth surface.

The volume of the earth is equal to the volume of the sphere which is equal to the $4/3\ \pi r^3$. Mass of the earth is given by gR^2/G. By equating both volume and mass into density, the average density comes out to be directly proportional to g.

18 Consider the following statements.

(Chap 7, Class-XI, NCERT)

1. The gravitational field strength at any point varies inversely as the square of the distance from the mass m.
2. The escape velocity depends on the mass of the body.
3. The potential energy of a satellite is equal to the total energy.

How many of the above statements are correct?

(a) Only one (b) Only two

(c) All three (d) None of these

Ans. (a)

Exp. Only one statement (1) is correct, but two statements (2 and 3) are incorrect.

Statement 1 The gravitational attraction force between two point masses is directly proportional to the product of their masses and inversely proportional to the square of their separation distance.

This force is always attractive and acts along the line joining them.

Statement 2 Escape velocity does not depend on mass of the body as well as the direction of projection of the body.

It only depends on the mass and radius of the planet or earth from where the body is to be projected.

The potential energy of a satellite is equal to the twice of total energy of its.

19 Which of the following describes the Geostationary Orbit (GEO) correctly? *(Unit 9, Class-IX, Tamil Nadu Board), (UPPSC Pre 2011), (MPSC Pre 2018)*

(a) Altitude of 20000 km above the sea level and the orbital period is 12 h.

(b) Altitude of 36000 km above the sea level and the orbital period is 24 h.

(c) Altitude of 400 km above the sea level and the orbital period is 90 min.

(d) None of the above

Ans. (b)

Exp. Statement (b) describes the Geostationary Orbit (GEO) correctly. The Geostationary Orbit (GEO) is at an altitude of 36000 km above the sea level and the orbital period is 24 h.

If the height of an artificial satellite above Earth's surface be such that its period of revolution is exactly equal to the period revolution (24 h) of the axial motion of the earth, then the satellite would appear stationary over point on earth's equator.

It would be synchronous with earth's spin. Such a satellite is known as geostationary satellite or geosynchronous satellite.

It is used to reflect TV signals and telecast TV programs from one part of the world to another.

Chapter 06

Mechanical Properties of Matter

Mechanical Properties of Matter

Elasticity Pressure, And Pascal's Law

Elasticity
- The property of the body by virtue of which it tends to regain its original shape and size after removal of applied forces.

Stress
- The internal restoring force acting per unit area of deforming body.

Strain
- The ratio of change in configuration to the original configuration of a body. when a deforming force acts on a body.

Hooke's Law
- It states that for small deformation the stress and strain are proportional to each other.

Modulus of Elasticity
- The ratio of stress and strain is called modulus of elasticity.

Thurst
- The force acting on an object perpendicular to its surface. The effect of depends on area on which it acts.

Pressure
- The force acting perpendicular on a unit area of an object.

Pascal's Law
- It states that, in an enclosed fluid , if pressure is change in any part of the fluid, then this change of pressure is transmitted undiminished to all the other parts of the fluid.

Archimedes' Principle and Flow of Liquid

Archimedes' Principle
- According to this principle, when an object is fully or partially in a fluid, it experiences an upward force that is equal to the weight of the fluid displaced by the object.

Applications of Archimedes's Principle
- Designing ships and submarines.
- Lactometer (a device used to determine the purity of milk).
- Hydrometer (a device used for determining the density of liquid).
- In determinig relative density of a substance.

Flow of Liquids
- **Streamline Flow** The flow in which every particle of the liquid follows exactly the same path and has the same velocity as its predecessor.
- **Turbulent Flow** The flow in which the path and velocity of the particles of liquid change continuously with time.

Viscosity ,Stoke's Law, Surface Tension

Viscosity
- The property of liquids due to which they oppose the relative motion between their different layers.

Stoke's Law
- According to Stoke's law, the backward viscous force acting on small spherical body of radius (r) moving with uniform velocity (η) is given by $F = 6\eta\pi rv$

Terminal Velocity
- The maximum constant velocity acquired by a body while failing through a viscous medium.

Surface Tension
- The property by virtue of which the free surface of a liquid at rest behaves like an elastic stretched membrane tending to contract so as to occupy minimum surface area.
- The surface tension of a liquid becomes zero at a particular temperature, called critical temperature of that liquid.

Surface Energy
- The potential energy per unit area of the surface film.

Capillarity
- The phenomena of rise or fall of liquid in capillary tube.

SOURCE *New NCERT Class VIII Chap 8* (Force and Pressure), *New NCERT Class IX Chap 9* (Gravitation), *New NCERT Class XI Chap 8* (Mechanical Properties of Solids), *Chap 9* (Mechanical Properties of Liquids)

1 Consider the following statements regarding the properties of solids. *(Chap 8, Class-XI, NCERT)*

1. The property of a body by virtue of which it tends to regain its original size and shape is called elasticity.
2. Plasticity is the property in which material has no gross tendency to regain its previous shape.

Which of the statement(s) given above is/are correct?

(a) Only 1 (b) Only 2
(c) Both 1 and 2 (d) Neither 1 nor 2

Ans. (c)

Exp. Both the statements (1) and (2) are correct.
As elasticity is the property of a body by virtue of which it regains its original shape and size and plasticity is the property in which material does not have gross tendency to regain its previous shape and size.
We may consider quartz as almost perfectly elastic and wax or wet clay as almost perfectly plastic.

2 Consider the following statements and select the correct code. *(Chap 8, Class-XI, NCERT)*

1. Stress and strain are proportional to each other for small deformations.
2. Hooke's law is found to be valid for all materials.
3. Every object in our surrounding has property of elasticity.

Which of the statement(s) given below is/are correct?

(a) 1, 2 and 3 (b) Only 1
(c) Only 2 (d) None of these

Ans. (b)

Exp. Statement (1) is correct. Stress and strain are proportional to each other for small deformations
Statement (2) and (3) are incorrect Hooke's law is found to be valid for most of materials. However, there are some materials which do not exhibit this linear relationship of Hooke's law.

$$\text{Stress} = k \times \text{strain}$$

where, k is the proportionality constant.
Every object in our surrounding has not property of elasticity, e.g., Putty and mud are close to ideal plastics.

3 Consider the following statements and select the correct code. *(Chap 8, Class-XI, NCERT)*

1. For a given stress, the strain produced in glass is much less than that in rubber.
2. In plastic materials, the force of cohesion are very small.
3. Elastic limit is the smallest stress, which results in permanent distortion.

Which of the statement(s) given above is/are correct?

(a) 1, 2 and 3 (b) 1 and 2
(c) 2 and 3 (d) 1 and 3

Ans. (a)

Exp. All the given statements (1), (2) and (3) are correct.
As rubber has lower elastic modulus, so strain produced is higher as compared to glass.
In plastics, intermolecular forces or cohesive forces are very small.
Elastic limit is the smallest stress, beyond which the material suffers permanent distortion.

4 Which of the following is not a way in which a solid may change its dimensions when an external force acts on it? *(Chap 8, Class-XI, NCERT)*

(a) Tensile stress (b) Compressive stress
(c) Longitudinal stress (d) Tangential stress

Ans. (d)

Exp. When two forces are applied in opposite directions on the body, a tangential stress is developed in parallel to surface (horizontal direction), it may change the shape of the object but it does not change the dimensions.

5 While designing a building, the structural design of the columns, beams and supports require knowledge of *(Chap 8, Class-XI, NCERT)*

(a) density of material used
(b) temperature under which material is used
(c) strength of material used
(d) None of the above

Ans. (c)

Exp. While designing a building, the structural design of the columns, beams and supports require knowledge of strength of material used.
The structural integrity of a building is maintained by the different materials used in the construction process. The knowledge of the strength of these materials is very crucial while designing the building.

6 Consider the following statements regarding the strength of materials. *(Chap 8, Class-XI, NCERT)*

1. Pillars and columns are commonly used in buildings and bridges to distribute the load.
2. The ropes are always made of a number of thin wires braided together.

Which of the statement(s) given above is/are incorrect?

(a) Only 1
(b) Only 2
(c) Both 1 and 2
(d) Neither 1 nor 2

Ans. (a)

Exp. Statement (1) is incorrect, because pillars and columns are commonly used in buildings to support or bearing the load. While wires and ropes are used with pillars in different kinds of bridges to support and distribute the load.

7 **A person stands on a loose sand and his feet go deep into the sand but when he lies down on the sand, his body will not go that deep in the sand. This is due to** *(Chap 9, Class-IX, NCERT)*

(a) force (b) thrust
(c) pressure (d) area

Ans. (c)

Exp. A person stands on a loose sand and his feet go deep into the sand but when he lies down on the sand, his body does not go that deep in the sand because of pressure.

The weight of the body is constant when the person stands on loose sand, then pressure (force per unit area) is maximum as area in contact with sand is minimum whereas when he lies down, then pressure (force per unit area) is minimum because area in contact with soft sand increases. Therefore, pressure in second case is less and he does not go that deep in loose sand.

8 **Consider the following Assertion (A) and Reason (R) and choose the correct code.** *(Chap 9, Class-IX, NCERT)*

Assertion (A) The density of iron is more than that of mercury therefore nail of iron sinks in mercury.

Reason (R) The relative density is a ratio of similar quantities, so it has no unit.

Codes

(a) Both A and R are true and R is the correct explanation of A.
(b) Both A and R are true, but R is not the correct explanation of A.
(c) A is true, but R is false.
(d) A is false, but R is true.

Ans. (d)

Exp. Assertion (A) is false, but Reason (R) is true.

The density of a substance is defined as mass of the substance per unit volume. The density of iron is less than that of mercury, therefore, a nail of iron floats in mercury. The relative density of a substance is the ratio of its density to that of water. Therefore, the relative density is a ratio of similar quantities (density), so it has no units and dimensions.

9 **Pressure exerted in any confined mass of fluid is** *(Chap 9, Class-IX, NCERT)*

(a) transmitted undiminished in all directions.
(b) transmitted undiminished in a particular direction.
(c) absorbed partially in all directions.
(d) absorbed completely in a particular direction.

Ans. (a)

Exp. Pressure exerted in any confined mass of fluid is transmitted undiminished in all directions. The molecules of the liquid are in constant motion and can move in any direction.

These particles exert pressure (momentum) on every wall of the container or vessel equally.

10 **Which of the following statements is/are not true about pressure?** *(Chap 8, Class-VIII, NCERT)*

1. Forces act parallel to the surface on which the pressure is to be computed.
2. Pressure exerted by water at the bottom of the container depends on the height of its column.
3. A liquid exerts pressure on the walls of the container.
4. Liquids exert equal pressure at the same depth.

Codes

(a) Only 1 (b) 1 and 4 (c) 2 and 4 (d) 2, 3 and 4

Ans. (a)

Exp. Statement (1) is not true about the pressure.

Only those forces which act perpendicular to the surface on which the pressure is to be computed. Due to this reason, porters place a round piece of cloth on their heads, when they have to carry heavy loads. If force acts parallel to the area of contact, no pressure will be experienced.

11 **Consider the following statements.** *(Chap 8, Class-VIII, NCERT)*

1. Atmospheric pressure is the weight of air in a column of unit area.
2. It would be impossible to pull the sucker off the surface, if there were no air at all between the sucker and the surface.

Which of the statement(s) given above is/are correct?

(a) Only 2
(b) Only 1
(c) Both 1 and 2
(d) Neither 1 nor 2

Ans. (c)

Exp. Both the statements (1) and (2) are correct.

The envelope of air is known as atmosphere and the pressure exerted by this atmosphere is called atmospheric pressure which is technically defined as the weight of air in a column of unit area.

Due to this atmospheric pressure, it would not be possible to pull the sucker off the surface, if there were no air at all between the sucker and the surface.

12 **Consider the following statements regarding the Hooke's law.** *(Chap 8, Class-XI, NCERT)*

1. Elastic limit is the upper limit of deforming force up to which, if deforming force is removed, the body regains its original form completely.
2. Within the elastic limit, the extension of an elastic body is directly proportional to the force is proportional to strain.

Which of the statement(s) given above is/are correct?

(a) Only 1 (b) Only 2
(c) Both 1 and 2 (d) Neither 1 nor 2

Ans. (c)

Exp. Both statements (1) and (2) are correct.
If deforming force is removed, the body will regains its original form completely and beyond which if deforming force is increased, the body loses its property of elasticity.
stress ∝ strain or stress = $E \times$ strain.

13 Which one of the following options is incorrect about pressure? *(Chap 9, Class XI, NCERT)*

1. The smaller the area, larger the pressure on the surface for the same force.
2. We don't feel atmospheric pressure as it is negligible in quantity.
3. Air exerts atmospheric pressure on us.

Codes

(a) Only one (b) Only two
(c) Only three (d) None of these

Ans. (b)

Exp. Only two statements (1 and 3) are correct, but one statement (2) is incorrect. Pressure is the quantity which is defined as the force acting per unit of area,

$$p = \frac{F}{A}$$

Pressure by liquid, is liquid exerts pressure on the walls of its container and equal pressure distributed in all sides of the container. So, smaller the area, the larger the pressure on a surface for same force. Air exerts atmospheric pressure on us.

Statement (2) is incorrect because, we don't feel atmosphere pressure because our blood exerts a pressure slightly more than that of the atmosphere. Atmosphere pressure is not negligible in quantity. Its value is 1.013×10^5 pascal.

14 An empty plastic bottle is pushed into the water. The force (s) experienced by bottle is/are *(Chap 9, Class-IX, NCERT)*

1. gravitational force
2. buoyant force
3. upthrust

Which of the above given force(s) is/are experienced by plastic bottle?

(a) Only 1
(b) 2 and 3
(c) 1 and 3
(d) All of the above

Ans. (d)

Exp. When an empty bottle is pushed into the water, all the given forces i.e., gravitational force, buoyant force and upthrust will be experienced by the bottle.

Gravitational force is acting on the bottle, whether it is pushed into the water or outside.

When empty bottle is pushed into the water, the buoyant force acts on the bottle which opposes the motion and at a certain point, it pushes the bottle in upward direction which is called upthrust.

15 While lifting a bucket of water from a well, we feel that the bucket *(Chap 9, Class-IX, NCERT)*

(a) becomes heavier above the surface of water.
(b) becomes lighter above the surface of water.
(c) loses stability on coming out of the water.
(d) has gained mass on coming out of water.

Ans. (a)

Exp. While lifting a bucket of water from a well, we feel that the bucket becomes heavier above the surface of water.

It is because water exerts an upward force on the objects immersed in it. This reduction is equal to the weight of the fluid that body displaces.

16 Which of the following statements is incorrect about an iron nail that sinks and a cork that floats when placed on the surface of water? *(Chap 9, Class-IX, NCERT)*

(a) The downward force acting on the nail is greater than the upthrust of water on the nail.
(b) The upthrust of water on the cork is greater than the weight of the cork.
(c) The objects of density greater than that of a liquid, sink in the liquid.
(d) The density of iron nail is less than the density of water.

Ans. (d)

Exp. Statement (d) is incorrect, as density of iron nail is greater than the density of water and density of cork is less than the water. Therefore, iron nail sinks and a cork floats on the surface of water.

17 Match the following items of List-I with the items of List-II and choose the correct code. *(Chap 9, Class-IX, NCERT)*

	List-I (Substance)		List-II (Density)
A.	Water	1.	10.8×10^3 kg/m^3
B.	Silver	2.	1.2 kg/m^3
C.	Gold	3.	1×10^3 kg/m^3
D.	Air	4.	19.3×10^3 kg/m^3

Codes

	A	B	C	D
(a)	3	4	1	2
(b)	3	1	4	2
(c)	2	1	4	3
(d)	2	4	1	3

Ans. (b)

Exp. The correct matching is A-3, B-1, C-4, D-2.
The density of a substance is one of its characteristic properties.
The density of water is 1×10^3 kg/m^3.
The density of silver is 10.8×10^3 kg/m^3.
The density of gold is 19.3×10^3 kg/m^3.
The density of air is 1.2 kg/m^3.

18 **Which of the following is not based on the application of Pascal's law?** *(Chap 9, Class-IX, NCERT)*

(a) Hydraulic brakes in trucks and cranes.
(b) Hydraulic lift in multistoried buildings.
(c) Hydraulic press in punching machines.
(d) Aerodynamic lift in cars.

Ans. (d)

Exp. Aerodynamic lifts in cars is not based on the application of Pascal's law. It is based on the Bernoulli's principle which states that an increase in the speed of a fluid occurs simultaneously with a decrease in pressure or a decrease in fluid's potential energy.

19 **A piece of stone is tied to one end of a rubber string and suspended freely. Now, stone is slowly dipped in the water. The conclusions from this observation are** *(Chap 9, Class-IX, NCERT)*

1. the elongation of the string decreases as the stone is gradually lowered in the water.
2. the upward force exerted by water on the stone is called pressure.
3. the elongation produced in string is due to the force exerted by water in upward direction.

Which of the above given conclusion(s) is/are correct?

(a) Only 1 (b) 1 and 2 (c) 2 and 3 (d) All of these

Ans. (a)

Exp. Statement (1) is correct as liquid applies a buoyant force on the stone, as it is lowered in the liquid. So, the elongation of the string decreases.

Statements (2) and (3) are incorrect. The upward force acting on an object (stone) immersed in a liquid is called buoyant force. The force is also known as upthrust.

The force exerted by water acts in the opposite direction of motion of stone therefore tension in the string decreases and hence, elongation of the rubber string is not produced by this force.

20 **Consider the following Assertion (A) and Reason (R) and choose the correct code.** *(Chap 9, Class-IX, NCERT)*

Assertion (A) All objects experience a force of buoyancy when they are immersed in a fluid.

Reason (R) When a body is immersed partially or fully in a fluid, it experiences an upward force that is equal to the weight of fluid displaced by it.

Codes

(a) Both A and R are true and R is the correct explanation of A.
(b) Both A and R are true, but R is not the correct explanation of A.
(c) A is true, but R is false.
(d) A is false, but R is true.

Ans. (a)

Exp. Both Assertion (A) and Reason (R) are true and Reason (R) is the correct explanation of Assertion (A). All objects experience a force of buoyancy when they are immersed in a fluid.

When a body is partially or fully immersed in a liquid, it experiences an upward force that is equal to the weight of the fluid displaced by it and this force is called buoyant force.

21 **Pressure applied to an enclosed fluid is transmitted undiminished to every portion of the fluid and the walls of the containing vessel. This law was first formulated by** *(Chap 9, Class-XI, NCERT)*

(a) Bernoulli's (b) Archimedes
(c) Boyle (d) Pascal

Ans. (d)

Exp. The pressure applied to an enclosed fluid will be transmitted without a change in magnitude to every point of the fluid and the walls of the container called Pascal's law.

Bernoulli's principle states that, an increase in the speed of the fluid occurs simultaneously with a decrease in static pressure or the fluid's potential energy called Bernoulli's principle.

An object immersed in a fluid experiences a buoyant force that is equal in magnitude to the force of gravity on the displaced fluid called Archimedes.

The volume of a gas at constant temperature varies inversely with the Pressure, called Boyle's law.

22 **Consider the following statements regarding a streamline.** *(Chap 9, Class-XI, NCERT)*

1. Along a streamline, the velocity of all fluid particles crossing a given position is constant.
2. Streamline flow is a curve whose tangent at any point is in the opposite direction of the fluid velocity at that point.
3. The velocity of all fluid particles at a given instant is constant.

Which of the statement(s) given above is/are incorrect?

(a) Only 1
(b) 1 and 2
(c) 2 and 3
(d) 1 and 3

Ans. (c)

Exp. Statements (2 and 3) are incorrect. For a streamline flow, velocity of each particle at a particular cross-section is constant because $Av =$ constant (law of continuity) between two cross-section of a tube of flow.

Streamline flow curve tangent at any point is in the direction of the fluid velocity at that point.

So, we can say that along a streamline, the velocity of every fluid particle while crossing a given position is the same.

23 Consider the following statements.
(Chap 9, Class-XI, NCERT)

1. The coefficient of viscosity is the only parameter through which the viscosity of the fluid is measured.
2. Negative sign of coefficient of viscosity indicates that the viscous force opposes the relative motion.
3. The SI unit of viscosity is N-sm^{-2}.
4. 1 Poise = 0.1 N-sm^{-2}.

Which of the statements given above are correct?

(a) 1, 2 and 3
(b) 1, 2 and 4
(c) 2, 3 and 4
(d) 1, 2, 3 and 4

Ans. (d)

Exp. All given statements (1), (2), (3) and (4) are correct.
The coefficient of viscosity is the only parameter through which the viscosity or resistance to flow of liquid is measured.
The negative sign of coefficient of viscosity indicates that the viscous force opposes the relative motion between different layers of fluid. Its SI unit is N-sm^{-2}. Poise of the unit of dynamic viscosity and it is equal to 0.1 N-sm^{-2}.

24 Consider the following statements about viscosity.
(Chap 9, Class-XI, NCERT)

1. With increase in temperature, viscosity of gases also increases.
2. The viscosity of liquids decreases with increase in temperature.

Which of the statement(s) given above is/are correct?

(a) Only 1
(b) Only 2
(c) Both 1 and 2
(d) Neither 1 nor 2

Ans. (c)

Exp. Both the statements (1) and (2) are correct about viscosity. With increase in temperature, the average kinetic energy of the gases increases and therefore, the collision between the molecules occurs more frequently.
Therefore, the viscosity of gases increases with increase in temperature. With increase in temperature, the relative force between layers of liquid decreases, therefore the viscosity of liquid decreases with increase in temperature.

25 Which of the following is not based on the phenomenon of surface tension?

(a) Mercury wets a glass. *(Chap 9, Class-XI, NCERT)*
(b) Soap and water rise up to the top of the leaves of the tree.
(c) Oil and water do not mix.
(d) Oil rises up a cotton wick.

Ans. (a)

Exp. Mercury wets a glass is not an example of surface tension because mercury does not wet a glass surface. The cohesive force between drops of mercury are stronger than the adhesive force between the drops and glass.

26 If there were no phenomenon of capillarity, then
(Chap 9, Class-XI, NCERT)

1. it would be difficult to use a kerosene lamp.
2. one would not be able to use a straw to consume a soft drink.
3. the blotting paper would fail to function.
4. the big trees that we see around would not have grown on the earth.

Which of the statements given above are correct?

(a) 1, 2 and 3
(b) 1, 3 and 4
(c) 2 and 4
(d) All of these

Ans. (b)

Exp. Statements (1), (3) and (4) are correct. If there were no phenomenon of capillarity, then
It would be difficult to use a kerosene lamp, because the kerosene oil in lanterns rise in the capillaries formed in cotton wick and burns.
The blotting paper would fail to function because blotting paper has large number of pores on its surface which acts like a capillary tube.
The big trees that we see around would not have grown on the earth because the fine roots of trees act as capillary tubes which provide them useful nutrients and water.
Statement (2) does not depend upon the capillarity because if a person wants to consume the soft drink, he needs to apply some external force by his mouth.

Chapter 07

Heat and Thermodynamics

Heat and Thermodynamics

Temperature and Heat

Temperature

- The measure of degree of the hotness or coldness of a body.
- Its SI unit is kelvin.

Thermometer

- A device which is used to measure temperature.

Liquid Thermometer

- It is a contact type of thermometer which measures temperature from changes in the volume of liquid.

Heat

- The form of energy which flows from hotter body to colder body by virtue of temperature difference.
- It is measured in joule.

Thermal Expansion

- The phenomenon of change in dimensions of an object due to heat supplied. There are three types of thermal expansion
  - **Linear Expansion** The expansion in length of a body due to increase in its temperature.
  - **Superficial Expansion** The expansion in the area of a surface of body due to increase in its temperature.
  - **Volume Expansion** The expansion in the volume of body due to increase in its temperature.

Heat Transfer

Heat Transfer

There are three modes of heat transfer

- **Conduction** The process of transfer of heat taking place due to molecular vibrations.
- **Convection** The process in which heat is transferred from one point to another by the actual motion of matter from a region of high temperature to a region of lower temperature.
- **Radiation** The mode of heat transfer from one place to another without heating the intervening medium.

Kirchhoff's Law

- According to this law, at any temperature and for a particular wavelength.
- The ratio of emissive power to the absorptive power of all substances is same and it is equal to the emissive power of a perfectly black body.

Wein's Displacement Law

- The wavelength of maximum intensity of emission of black body radiations is inversely proportional to the absolute temperature of the black body.

Thermodynamics

Zeroth Law of Thermodynamics

- The zeroth law of thermodynamics states that if two systems A and B are separately in thermal equilibrium with a third system C, then A and B are in thermal equilibrium with each other.

First Law of Thermodynamics

- It states that heat is given to a system used in doing external work and it increases the internal energy of the system.
  i.e, Heat supplied, $\Delta Q = \Delta U + \Delta W$
  where, ΔU= change in internal energy
  ΔW= work done by the system on the surroundings

Second Law of Thermodynamics

- **Kelvin-Planck's Statement** No process is possible whose sole result is the absorption of heat from a reservoir and the complete conversion of the heat into work.
- **Clausius Statement** No process is possible whose sole result is the transfer of heat from a colder object to a hotter object.

Carnot Engine

- The reversible engine which operates between two temperatures of source and sink.

SOURCE *New NCERT Class VII Class 3* (Heat), *New NCERT Class XI Chap 10* (Thermal Properties of Matter), *Chap 11* (Thermodynamics)

1 Consider the following statements.

(Chap 10, Class-XI, NCERT)

1. In glass tumbler of ice-cold water, heat flows from the environment to the glass tumbler.
2. Heat can be expressed in kelvin.

Which of the statement(s) given above is/are correct?

(a) Only 1 (b) Only 2
(c) Both 1 and 2 (d) Neither 1 nor 2

Ans. (a)

Exp. Among the given statements, only statement (1) is correct. Heat is a form of energy which flows from higher temperature region (called hotter body) to low temperature region (called colder body).

When an ice-cold water is poured in glass tumbler, the heat flows from the environment to the glass-tumbler because ice-cold water has lower temperature than environment.

Statement (2) is incorrect because heat is measured in joule (J) in SI unit and calorie in CGS unit.

2 Consider the following statements.

(Chap 3, Class-VIII, NCERT)

1. Mercury and alcohol are used in liquid-in-glass thermometers which is suitable for using in cold places.
2. Celsius temperature scale can be converted into Fahrenheit temperature scale.
3. By measuring temperature, any heat can also be measured.

Which one of the following is incorrect in respect of the above statements?

(a) Only 1 (b) 1 and 2
(c) Only 3 (d) All of these

Ans. (c)

Exp. Statement (3) is incorrect because by measuring temperature only, heat cannot be measured as heat is a form of energy transferred between two systems or a system and its surrounding medium by virtue of temperature difference.

3 Which of the following statement is incorrect?

(Chap 3, Class-VII, NCERT)

(a) A clinical thermometer reads temperature from 35°C to 42°C.
(b) The range of a laboratory thermometer is generally from −10°C to 110°C.
(c) Laboratory thermometer can be used to measure temperature of human body.
(d) Digital thermometers do not use mercury.

Ans. (c)

Exp. Statement (c) is incorrect because laboratory thermometer cannot be used to measure temperature of human body. The reading by laboratory thermometer should be taken while its bulb is still in touch with the substance whose temperature is being measured.

4 In cold countries, alcohol is preferred to mercury as a thermometric liquid because

(Chap 10, Class-XI, NCERT) (UPPSC Pre 1997)

(a) alcohol has a lower freezing point
(b) alcohol is a better conductor of heat
(c) alcohol is cheaper than mercury
(d) the production of alcohol is more than that of mercury

Ans. (a)

Exp. In cold countries lying near polar regions, alcohol is preferred as a thermometric liquid because alcohol has lower freezing point than that of mercury. It remains in liquid form even at very low polar temperatures.

5 Consider the following Assertion (A) and Reason (R) and choose the correct code.

(Chap 10, Class-XI, NCERT) (IAS Pre 2001)

Assertion (A) The boiling point of water decreases as the altitude increases.

Reason (R) The atmospheric pressure increases with altitude.

Codes

(a) Both A and R are true and R is the correct explanation of A.
(b) Both A and R are true, but R is not the correct explanation of A.
(c) A is true, but R is false.
(d) A is false, but R is true.

Ans. (c)

Exp. Assertion (A) is true but Reason (R) is false.

Boiling is the process by which a liquid turns into vapour at a fixed temperature called boiling point.

The boiling point of water decreases as the altitude increases because at higher altitude, the atmospheric pressure decreases.

6 Consider the following statements.

(Chap 10, Class-XI, NCERT)

Statement I The rate of cooling is directly proportional to the excess of temperature.

Statement II The total radiant energy E emitted per sec from unit surface area of a black body is proportional to the second power of its absolute temperature T.

Which one of the following is correct in respect of the above statements?

(a) Both Statement I and Statement II are correct and Statement II is the correct explanation for Statement I.
(b) Both Statement I and Statement II are correct and Statement II is not the correct explanation for Statement I.
(c) Statement I is correct but Statement II is incorrect.
(d) Statement I is incorrect but Statement II is correct.

Ans. (c)

Exp. Statement I is correct but Statement II is incorrect. The rate at which an exposed body changes temperature through radiation, which is approximately proportional to the difference between the object's temperature and its surroundings.

The constant is based on Stefan Boltzmann's law, which states that the radiant heat energy emitted from a unit area of the black body in one second (E) is directly proportional to the fourth power of its absolute temperature.

$$E \propto T^4 \text{ or, } E = \sigma T^4$$

7 Consider the following statements.

(Chap 10, Class-XI, NCERT)

Statement I In the range of 0°C to 4°C, water contracts on heating and expands on cooling.

Statement II At 4°C, density of water is minimum while its specific volume is maximum.

Which one of the following is correct in respect of the above statements?

(a) Both Statement I and Statement II are correct and Statement II is the correct explanation for Statement I.
(b) Both Statement I and Statement II are correct but Statement II is not the correct explanation for Statement I.
(c) Statement I is correct but Statement II is incorrect.
(d) Statement I is incorrect but Statement II is correct.

Ans. (c)

Exp. Statement I is correct but Statement II is incorrect.

At 4°C, density of water is maximum while its specific volume is minimum because, when temperature is increased from 0°C to 4°C some of the H-bonds breaks and molecules come and density increases till 4°C because volume decreases.

8 Water has the highest specific heat capacity. Which of the following statement is/are correct about it?

(Chap 10, Class-XI, NCERT)

1. Water is used as a coolant in automobile radiators.
2. Water warms up more slowly than land during summer.
3. During the night, the land cools slowly than the sea.

Codes

(a) 1 and 2 (b) 2 and 3
(c) 1 and 3 (d) Only 2

Ans. (a)

Exp. Here, statements (1) and (2) are correct.

Specific heat capacity is the measure of heat required to raise the temperature of the unit mass of substance by 1°C. Since, water has highest specific heat, it warms slowly and cools slowly. Hence, it is used in radiators as coolant.

Statement (3) is not the reason because during the night land loses heat faster than sea and become cooler quickly.

9 Consider the following statements.

(Chap 10, Class-XI, NCERT)

1. The temperature at which the solid and the liquid states of the substance are in thermal equilibrium with each other is called its melting point.
2. The change of state from vapour to liquid is called vaporisation.
3. The change from solid state to vapour state without passing through the liquid state is called sublimation.

Which of the statement(s) given above is/are incorrect?

(a) Only 1 (b) Only 2
(c) 1 and 3 (d) 1 and 2

Ans. (b)

Exp. Statement (2) is incorrect because during condensation, the molecules of vapour coalesce to form bigger droplets of the liquid.

The change of state from vapour to liquid is called liquefaction or condensation. The change of state from liquid to vapour is called vaporisation.

10 The temperature point at which solid, liquid and gaseous states may stay together is known as

(Chap 10, Class-XI, NCERT) (BPSC Pre 2022)

(a) Boiling point (b) Melting point
(c) Freezing point (d) Triple point

Ans. (d)

Exp. The temperature point at which solid, liquid and gaseous states may stay together is known as triple point. Triple point is a specific temperature and pressure point at which all three states of a substance can exist simultaneously.

Scientists use the triple point of water as the basis for defining the kelvin temperature scale.

11 Consider the following statements.

(Chap 10, Class-XI, NCERT) (UPPSC Pre 2023)

Statement I The temperature contrast between continents and oceans is greater during summer than in winter.

Statement II The specific heat of water is more than that of land surface.

Which one of the following is correct in respect of the above statements?

(a) Both Statement I and Statement II are correct and Statement II is the correct explanation for Statement I.
(b) Both Statement I and Statement II are correct but Statement II is not the correct explanation for Statement I.
(c) Statement I is correct, but Statement II is incorrect.
(d) Statement I is incorrect, but Statement II is correct.

Ans. (a)

Exp. Both Statement I and Statement II are correct and Statement II is the correct explanation Statement I. The temperature contrast between continents and oceans is greater during summer than in winter because the specific heat capacity of water is much greater than the land as the relative density of water is much lower than that of the land surface. It means more heat is required to raise the temperature of one gram of water by one degree than one gram of land.

12 Consider the following statements about cooking food. *(Chap 8, Class-VII, NCERT)*

1. Food is cooked faster in pressure cooker due to the boiling point of water increases with increase pressure.
2. The food is cooked faster in a pressure cooker due to water boils at constant temperature.
3. In daily, the food is cooked quickly by steam due to temperature increases and pressure will also decrease.

(a) Only 2 (b) Only 1
(c) Only 3 (d) None of these

Ans. (b)

Exp. Statement (1) is correct but statements (2) and (3) are incorrect.

Food is cooked faster in pressure cooker because the boiling point of water increases with increase in pressure. Pressure cooker is an isolated system in which steam generated due to boiling is not allowed to escape. The steam of water vapour increases the overall boiling point of the system. Hence, the heat required to cook food is maintained in the cooker and thus food is cooked faster in the pressure cooker.

13 A fan produces a feeling of comfort during hot weather, because *(Chap 8, Class-VII, NCERT) (BPSC Pre 2022)*

(a) our body radiates more heat in air
(b) fan supplies cool air
(c) conductivity of air increases
(d) our perspiration evaporates rapidly

Ans. (d)

Exp. A fan produces a feeling of comfort during hot weather because our perspiration evaporates rapidly. As, when we feel hot, our body perspires. The sweat comes out of the body through tiny pores, which then comes in contact with wind being produced by various sources like fan. Due to which, sweat starts to evaporate. Thus, as the sweat evaporates, it thereby, takes away the body heat.

14 Which of the following statement(s) is/are correct? *(Chap 8, Class-VII, NCERT)*

1. In hot tea, heat flows from the cup of hot tea to the environment.
2. The process by which heat is transferred from the hotter end to the colder end of an object is known as conduction.
3. Convection is a mode of heat transfer by actual motion of matter in fluids.
4. Land breeze is the cool air which moves from the sea towards the land.

Codes

(a) Only 1 (b) Both 2 and 3 (c) 1, 2 and 3 (d) 1, 2 and 4

Ans. (c)

Exp. Statements (1), (2) and (3) are correct.

In hot tea, heat flows from the cup of hot tea to the environment because heat flows from an object at higher temperature to another object which is at lower temperature.

The mode of transfer of heat from hotter part of a material to its colder part or from a hot material to a cold material in contact with it, without the movement of material is known as conduction. In all the solids, heat is transferred by the process of conduction.

Convection is a mode of heat transfer by actual motion of matter in fluids. The transfer of heat by convection cannot take place in solid because the particles in the solid are fixed at a place and cannot move freely.

Statement (4) is incorrect because during the night, when sea water and land both lose heat, specific heat capacity of land being very low as compared to that of sea water, land loses heat energy fast and cools more rapidly as compared to sea. Thus, cool air from the land moving towards sea is called land breeze.

15 Consider the following statements. *(Chap 10, Class-XI, NCERT)*

1. In conduction, molecules of the body transfer heat from a place of higher temperature to a place of lower temperature without actually moving in the body.
2. In convection, when a liquid contained in a vessel is heated, the molecules at the bottom receive heat energy first and density is lowered. These lighter molecules now rise up to the surface and heavier molecules come down.
3. Radiation is the process in which heat is transferred indirectly from one body to another without affecting the inverting medium.

How many of the above statements are correct?

(a) Only one (b) Only two
(c) Only three (d) None of these

Ans. (b)

Exp. Only two statements (1 and 2) are correct but one statement (3) is incorrect.

Heat conduction is a process in which heat is transferred from the hotter part to the colder part in a body without involving any actual movement of the molecules of the body. Heat transfer takes place from one molecule to another molecule as a result of the vibratory motion of the molecules.

Heat transfer in fluids generally takes place via convection. Convection currents are set up in the fluid because the hotter part of the fluid is not as dense as the cooler part, so there is an upward buoyant force on the hotter fluid, making it rise, while the cooler denser fluid sinks.

Statement (3) is incorrect. Radiation is the process of heat transfer in which heat is directly passed from one body at higher temperature to another body at lower temperature without affecting the medium. No medium is required for the transfer of heat by radiation process.

16 Consider the following statements.

(Chap 10, Class-XI, NCERT)

Statement I In the transmission of heat by radiation, the radiant energy is transported by electromagnetic waves because these waves can travel through vacuum.

Statement II Thermal radiation travels through empty space without the speed of light.

Which one of the following is correct in respect of the above statements?

(a) Both Statement I and Statement II are correct and Statement II is the correct explanation for Statement I.
(b) Both Statement I and Statement II are correct but Statement II is not the correct explanation for Statement I.
(c) Statement I is correct but Statement II is incorrect.
(d) Statement I is incorrect but Statement II is correct.

Ans. (c)

Exp. Statement I is correct but Statement II is incorrect. As there are no particles in a vacuum, heat transfer can only occur through radiation. This is because radiation involves electromagnetic waves, not particles, and is therefore, able to transmit heat across a vacuum.

Thermal radiations are electromagnetic in nature and fall into infrared range of frequencies. These are radiated by all bodies having a non-zero absolute temperature. As these are electromagnetic, thermal radiations can reflect and refract, and travel with speed of light in free space.

17 Consider the following statements.

(Chap 10, Class-XI, NCERT)

Statement I A body which is capable of absorbing radiation must also be capable of emitting all possible wavelengths.

Statement II The wavelength of emitted radiation by a black body independs only on its temperature.

Which one of the following is correct in respect of the above statements?

(a) Both Statement I and Statement II are correct and Statement II is the correct explanation for Statement I.
(b) Both Statement I and Statement II are correct but Statement II is not the correct explanation for Statement I.
(c) Statement I is correct but Statement II is incorrect.
(d) Statement I is incorrect but Statement II is correct.

Ans. (c)

Exp. Statement I is correct but Statement II is incorrect. It would emit at every wavelength of light as it must be able to absorb every wavelength to be sure of absorbing all incoming radiation.

It has a specific, continuous spectrum of wavelengths inversely related to intensity, that depend only on the body's temperature, which is assumed for the sake of calculations and theory, to be uniform and constant.

18 Consider the following Assertion (A) and Reason (R) and choose the correct code.

(Chap 3, Class-VII, NCERT) (UKPSC Pre 2012)

Assertion (A) Mostly people prefer the white outfit in winters, while absorb light.

Reason (R) White dresses are good reflectors of heat.

Codes

(a) Both A and R are true and R is the correct explanation of A.
(b) Both A and R are true, but R is not the correct explanation of A.
(c) A is true, but R is false.
(d) A is false, but R is true.

Ans. (d)

Exp. Assertion (A) is false, but Reason (R) is true.

White dresses or light coloured objects are good reflectors of heat. Thus, they are preferred in summer. Whereas black clothes absorb heat radiation and they are preferred in winters.

19 With reference to radiation, consider the following statements. *(Chap 10, Class-XI, NCERT)*

1. Heat transfer by radiation does not need any medium.
2. All bodies emit radiant energy, whether they are solid, liquid or gas.
3. Heat is transferred to the earth from the sun through empty space.
4. Speed of electromagnetic waves is less than the speed of light in vacuum.

Which of the statements given above are correct?

(a) 1 and 3 (b) 1 and 4 (c) 1, 2 and 3 (d) 1, 2 and 4

Ans. (c)

Exp. Statements (1), (2) and (3) are correct with reference to radiation. Radiation is the process by which heat is transmitted from one place to another without heating intervening medium. Therefore, heat transfer by radiation does not need any medium.

The heat from the sun reaches the earth by the process of radiation after travelling through millions of kilometres of vacuum. Due to the absence of material medium, the transmission of heat by conductor and convection is impossible. Properties of heat radiation are similar to those of light. The energy of heat radiation is called radiant energy. All bodies emit radiant energy, whether they are solid, liquid or gas.

Statement (4) is incorrect because speed of electromagnetic waves is equal to the speed of light in vacuum. Light is also an electromagnetic wave and all electromagnetic waves slow down while travelling through a denser medium.

20 Stainless steel pans are usually provided with copper bottoms. The reason for this could be that

(Chap 3, Class-VII, NCERT)

(a) radiation of heat through copper bottom is more than stainless steel.
(b) stainless steel bottoms get easily cracked while heating.
(c) copper conduct heat more readily than stainless steel.
(d) convection of heat in stainless bottom is more than copper.

Ans. (c)

Exp. Stainless steel pans are usually provided with copper bottoms because copper is a good conductor of heat. It conducts heat more readily than stainless steel and stainless steel retains the heat for a longer time.

21 Consider the following statement regarding thermal radiation which one is not correctly explain?

(Chap 10, Class-XI, NCERT)

1. Black body radiation depends on the temperature, size, shape and material of the object.
2. When thermal radiation falls on body, it is partly reflected and partly absorbed.

(a) Only 1 (b) Only 2
(c) Both 1 and 2 (d) None of these

Ans. (a)

Exp. Statement (1) is incorrect because the black body radiation depends only on the temperature and not on the size, shape or material of the black body.

A perfect black body is a perfect absorber and it will also be a perfect radiator. By Kirchhoff's law, when a perfectly black body is heated to high temperature, it emits radiation of all possible wavelengths.

22 Which one of the following is the general law of conservation of energy in which energy transfer from or to the surroundings is taken into account?

(Chap 11, Class-XI, NCERT)

(a) Zeroth Law of Thermodynamics
(b) First Law of Thermodynamics
(c) Second Law of Thermodynamics
(d) None of the above

Ans. (b)

Exp. First Law of Thermodynamics is a consequence of conservation of energy. The heat exchanged in a thermodynamic process is equal to the sum of work done and internal energy changed in the system.

23 Match the items of List-I with the item of List-II and choose the correct code from given below.

(Chap 11, Class-XI, NCERT)

List-I	List-II
A. Isothermal process	1. Constant pressure
B. Isobaric process	2. Constant temperature
C. Isochoric process	3. No heat flow
D. Adiabatic process	4. Constant volume

Codes

	A	B	C	D		A	B	C	D
(a)	4	3	1	2	(b)	1	2	4	3
(c)	1	4	2	3	(d)	2	1	4	3

Ans. (d)

Exp. The correct matching is A-2, B-1, C-4, D-3.

Isothermal process It is a thermodynamical process in which temperature remains constant.

Isobaric process It is a thermodynamical process in which pressure remains constant. The boiling of water to steam taking place at a constant pressure is isobaric process.

Isochoric process It is a thermodynamical process in which volume remains constant.

Adiabatic process It is a thermodynamical process in which no heat is exchanged from the surroundings. When a motor cycle tyre bursts, the sudden expansion of air into the atmosphere is an adiabatic process in which the tyre is cooled down.

24 Consider the following statements.

(Chap 11, Class-XI, NCERT)

1. Heat engine is a device by which heat is converted into work.
2. There is a fundamental limit on the efficiency of a heat engine set by an independent principle of nature.
3. Working of a refrigerator is same as that of a heat engine.

Which of the statement(s) given above is/are correct?

(a) 1 and 2 (b) 2 and 3 (c) Only 2 (d) Only 3

Ans. (a)

Exp. Statements (1) and (2) are correct. A heat engine is a device, which convert heat into mechanical work. There is a fundamental limit on the efficiency of a heat engine set by an independent principle of nature. Gasoline, diesel engines, jet engines and steam turbines are there generate electricity.

Statement (3) is incorrect because working of a refrigerator is not same as that of heat engine. Working of refrigerator is based on second law of thermodynamics.

25 Irreversibility is a rule rather an exception in nature. The example(s) of this is/are *(Chap 3, Class-VII, NCERT)*

(a) combustion reaction of a mixture of petrol
(b) air ignited by a spark
(c) cooking gas leaking from a gas cylinder
(d) All of the above

Ans. (d)

Exp. All the given options are examples of irreversibility. Combustion reactions are generally irreversible in nature as new bonds are formed during combustion and a lot of heat is evolved.

Air ignited by spark, ionises the air within its vicinity which is also an irreversible process. Cooking gas leaking from a gas cylinder is irreversible process because the molecules of the gas spread in the environment very rapidly which cannot be reversed.

Chapter 08

Oscillations

Oscillations

Periodic, Vibratory and Simple Harmonic Motion

Periodic Motion

- A motion in which a particle repeats its motion continuously on a definite path in a regular internal of time.

Oscillatory or Vibratory Motion

- A motion in which body moves to and fro repeatedly about its fixed position. e.g., vibrating strings.

Simple Harmonic Motion

- A special type of periodic motion, in which a particle moves to and fro repeatedly on straight path about a mean position under a restoring force which is always directed towards the mean position.
- e.g. Vibrations of tuning fork.

Conditions of Simple Harmonic Motion

- The motion of particles should be to and fro about its mean position.
- The direction of restoring force should be towards the mean position.
- Restoring force acting on the particle should always be proportional to its displacement from the mean position.

Terms Related to SHM and Simple Pendulum

Terms Related to SHM

- **Displacement (x)**
  The distance of the oscillating particle from its mean position at any instant
- **Amplitude (A)**
  The maximum displacement of the oscillating particle on either side of its mean position.
- **Time Period (T)**
  The time taken by a particle to complete on oscillation.
- **Frequency (ν)**
  The number of oscillations completed per unit time by a particle.
- **Phase (ϕ)**
  The phase of a vibrating particle at any instant gives the state of the particle as regards its position and the direction of motion at that instant.

Simple Pendulum

- A small metallic bob suspended by a light inextensible string from a rigid support, such that it is free to oscillate without friction about a point.

Vibrations

Damped Vibrations

- The periodic vibrations of a body with diminshing amplitude in the presence of a resistive force.
  e.g., The vibration of loaded spring in air.

Forced Vibrations

- The vibrations of a body under the action of an external periodic force in which the body vibrates with a frequency equal to the frequency of an external periodic force (driving frequency) other than natural frequency.
  e.g., When the wire of a sitar or a guitar is plucked, its board and wind box make forced vibrations.

Free Vibrations

- The vibrations of a body with constant amplitude and constant frequency.
  e.g., when a tuning fork is struck against a hard rubber pad, vibrates with its natural frequency.

SOURCE *New NCERT Class XI Chap 13* (*Oscillations*)

1 **Consider the following statements.**

(Chap 13, Class-XI, NCERT)

1. When a simple pendulum is made to oscillate on the surface of moon, its time period increases.
2. In SHM, kinetic energy is zero, when the potential energy is maximum.

Which one of the above statement(s) is/are correct?

(a) Only 1 (b) Only 2 (c) Both 1 and 2 (d) None of these

Ans. (c)

Exp. Both Statements 1 and 2 are correct. The value of acceleration due to gravity on the surface of moon is $\frac{1}{6}$th times of the value of acceleration due to gravity on the surface of earth and time period of pendulum is given as

$$T = 2\pi\sqrt{\frac{l}{g}} \Rightarrow T \propto \frac{1}{\sqrt{g}}$$

As g decreases, T increases.
In S.H.M, kinetic energy is maximum at mean position and zero at the extreme positions while potential energy is zero at mean position and maximum of extreme positions. hence kinetic energy is zero, when the potential energy is maximum.

2 **Consider the following statements.**

(Chap 13, Class-XI, NCERT)

Statement I Acceleration is proportional to the displacement of the particle. This condition is not sufficient for motion in simple harmonic motion.

Statement II In simple harmonic motion, the direction of displacement is also important.

Which one of the following is correct in respect of the above statements?

(a) Both Statement I and Statement II are correct and Statement II is the correct explanation for Statement I.
(b) Both Statement I and Statement II are correct but Statement II is not the correct explanation for Statement I.
(c) Statement I is correct but Statement II is incorrect.
(d) Statement I is incorrect but Statement II is correct.

Ans. (a)

Exp. Both Statement I and Statement II are correct and Statement II is the correct explanation for Statement I.
In simple harmonic motion, acceleration is directly proportional to the displacement of the particle from mean position and direction of displacement is always directed towards the mean position.

3 **Consider the following statements.**

(Chap 13, Class-XI, NCERT)

1. The time period of a pendulum depends on the weight of the bob.
2. The length of the string decides the time period of pendulum.
3. Acceleration due to gravity determine the time period of pendulum.

Which of the statement(s) given above is/are correct?

(a) 1 and 2 (b) 2 and 3 (c) 1 and 3 (d) 1, 2 and 3

Ans. (b)

Exp. Statements (2) and (3) are correct and statement (1) is incorrect.

As we know that time period of pendulum $T = 2\pi\sqrt{\frac{l}{g}}$.

Hence, the time period of a pendulum depends on the length and acceleration due to gravity.

4 **Consider the following statements.**

(Chap 13, Class-XI, NCERT)

Statement I Resonance is a special case of forced vibration in which the natural frequency of vibration of the body is the same as the impressed frequency of external periodic force and the amplitude of forced vibration is maximum.

Statement II The amplitude of forced vibrations of a body increases with an increase in the frequency of the externally impressed periodic force.

Which one of the following is correct in respect of the above statements?

(a) Both Statement I and Statement II are correct and Statement II is the correct explanation for Statement I.
(b) Both Statement I and Statement II are correct but Statement II is not the correct explanation for Statement I.
(c) Statement I is correct but Statement II is incorrect.
(d) Statement I is incorrect but Statement II is correct.

Ans. (c)

Exp. Statement I is correct but Statement II is incorrect.
When the frequency of an externally applied periodic force on a body is equal to the natural frequency of the body, the body readily begins to vibrate or free to vibrate with an increased amplitude. This phenomenon is known as resonance.
If the frequency of the externally impressed periodic force is increased, the amplitude of the force vibration does not increases but it decreases.

5 **A ball is thrown up with a velocity of 2.5 m/s. It collides elastically with the ground. Find the frequency of this periodic motion.** *(Chap 13, Class-XI, NCERT)*

(a) 1 Hz (b) 2 Hz (c) 3 Hz (d) 0.5 Hz

Ans. (b)

Exp. The motion will repeat itself after the ball hits the ground every time. The time taken for the ball to reach the top most position is $t = \frac{u}{g}$.

This will also be the time to reach the ground.

Thus, total time, $T = \frac{2u}{g}$

This will be the time period

$$\text{Frequency} = \frac{1}{T} = \frac{g}{2u} \Rightarrow \frac{10}{5} = 2\,\text{Hz}$$

6 **For a particle executing SHM, the displacement x is given, $x = A\cos\omega t$. Identify the graph which represent the variation of potential energy (PE) as a function of time t and displacement x.** *(Chap 13, Class-XI, NCERT)*

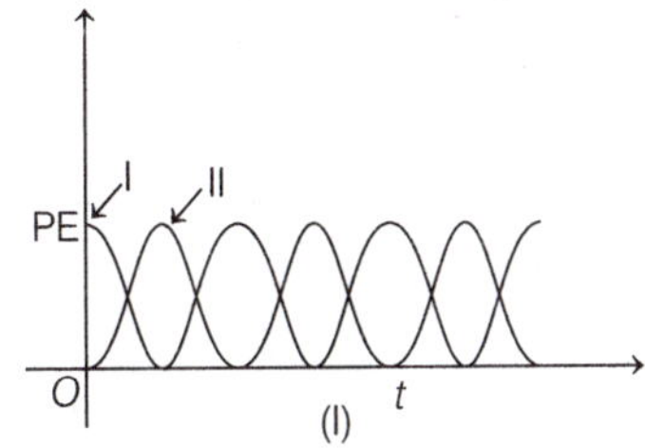

(I)

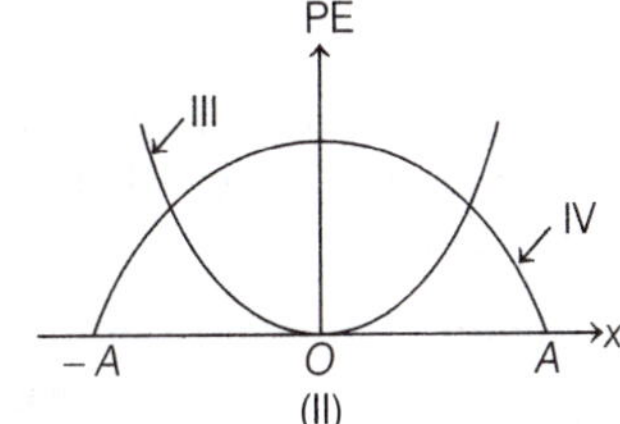

(II)

(a) I, III (b) II, IV (c) II, III (d) I, IV

Ans. (a)

Exp. At $t = 0$, $x = A\cos(\omega t) = A$, the particle is at extreme position and its PE must be maximum. Further in graph III, PE is minimum at $x = 0$. Hence, the correct options are I and III.

7 **The period of oscillations of simple pendulum of length l is suspended from the roof of a vehicle which moves without friction down an inclined plane of inclination α, is given by** *(Chap 13, Class-XI, NCERT)*

(a) $2\pi\sqrt{\frac{L}{g\cos\alpha}}$ (b) $\sqrt{\frac{L}{g\sin\alpha}}$ (c) $2\pi\sqrt{\frac{L}{g}}$ (d) $2\pi\sqrt{\frac{L}{g\tan\alpha}}$

Ans. (a)

Exp. The effective value of g will be equal to the component of g normal to the inclined plane which is

$$g' = g\cos\alpha \;\therefore T = 2\pi\sqrt{\frac{L}{g'}} = 2\pi\sqrt{\frac{L}{g\cos\alpha}}$$

8 **A simple pendulum is oscillating without damping. When the displacement of the bob is less than maximum, its acceleration vector is a correctly shown is** *(Chap 13, Class-XI, NCERT)*

(a) 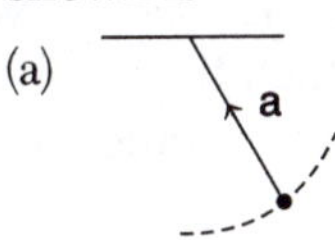

(b) 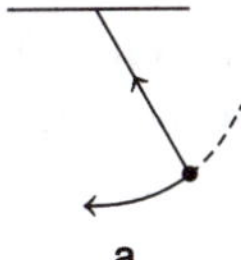

(c) 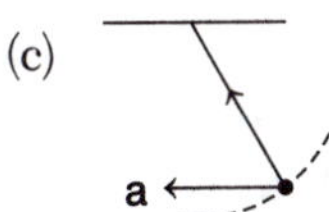

(d) 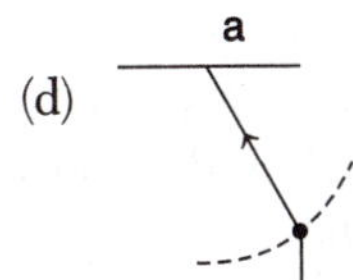

Ans. (c)

Exp. When the displacement of the bob is less than maximum, there will be two component acceleration of the bob and the resultant acceleration is always directed towards the mean position.

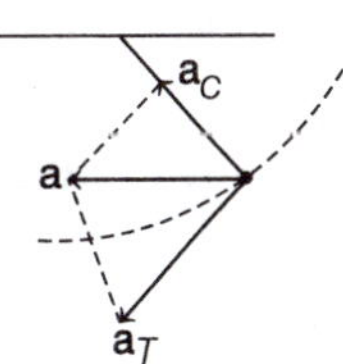

Transverse component = $\mathbf{a}_T$

Centripetal or radial component = $\mathbf{a}_C$

The resultant acceleration **a** will be along the diagonal of the parallelogram.

9 **A particle executes simple harmonic motion with a frequency f. The frequency with which its kinetic energy oscillates is** *(Chap 13, Class-XI, NCERT)*

(a) $\frac{f}{2}$ (b) f

(c) $2f$ (d) $4f$

Ans. (c)

Exp. During one complete oscillation, the kinetic energy will become maximum two times.

Thus, the frequency of kinetic energy will be $2f$

For SHM $x = A\sin\omega t$; $v = A\omega\cos(\omega t)$

i.e., kinetic energy, $K = \frac{1}{2}mv^2$

$$= \frac{1}{2}ma^2\omega^2\cos^2(\omega t)$$

$$= \frac{1}{4}m\omega^2a^2(1+\cos 2\omega t)$$

$$= \frac{1}{4}m\omega^2a^2 \qquad [1+\cos 2(2f)\pi t]$$

Hence, Frequency of KE is $2f$.

10 **Consider the following statements.** *(Chap 13, Class-XI, NCERT)*

Statement I Every oscillatory motion is periodic but every periodic motion need not be oscillatory.

Statement II Circular motion is not a periodic motion, but it is oscillatory.

Which one of the following is correct in respect of the above statements?

(a) Both Statement I and Statement II are correct and Statement II is the correct explanations for Statement I.

(b) Both Statement I and Statement II are correct but Statement II is not the correct explanations for Statement I.

(c) Statement I is correct but Statement II is incorrect.

(d) Statement I is incorrect but Statement II is correct.

Ans. (c)

Exp. Statement I is correct but Statement II is incorrect. Circular motion is only periodic and not oscillatory because the wheels do not move to and for about a mean position, whereas every oscillatory motion is periodic but every periodic motion never will be a oscillatory is a correct statement.

11 Consider the following statements.

(Chap 13, Class-XI, NCERT)

1. When a body is displaced from its equilibrium positions by doing work upon it, it acquires potential energy.
2. The potential energy of particle is maximum at the mean position and zero at the extreme position.
3. The total mechanical energy of a particle in SHM is dependent of time and displacement.

How many of the above statements are correct?

(a) Only one (b) Only two
(c) All three (d) None of these

Ans. (a)

Exp. Only one Statement (1) is correct but two Statements (2 and 3) are incorrect.

Statement 1 When a body displace from its equilibrium position by doing work upon it, it acquires potential energy because when body is released, it begins to move back with velocity, thus acquiring kinetic energy. Both kinetic energy and potential energy of a particle varies between zero and maximum values.

Statement 2 In SHM, kinetic energy is maximum at mean position and zero at the extreme position, while potential energy is zero at mean position and maximum at the extreme positions.

Statement 3 The total mechanical energy is always constant is equal to $\frac{1}{2}m\omega^2a^2$. Hence total energy is independent of time and displacement.

12 Consider the following statements.

(Chap 13, Class-XI, NCERT)

Statement I The graph of total energy of a particle in SHM with respect to position is a straight line with zero slope.

Statement II Total energy of particle in SHM remains constant throughout its motion.

Which one of the following is correct in respect of the above statements?

(a) Both Statement I and Statement II are correct and Statement II is the correct explanation for Statement I.
(b) Both Statement I and Statement II are correct but Statement II is not the correct explanation for Statement I.
(c) Statement I is correct but Statement II is incorrect.
(d) Statement I is incorrect but Statement II is correct.

Ans. (a)

Exp. Both Statement I and Statement II are correct and Statement II is the correct explanation for Statement I.

The total energy of SHM = kinetic energy of particle + potential energy of particle.

The variation of total energy of the particle in SHM with time is shown in graph.

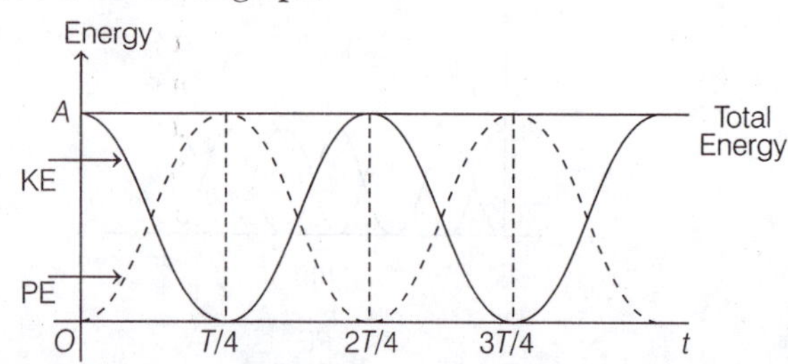

Solid line for kinetic energy and dotted line for potential energy. From graph, it is clear that total energy remains constant throughout.

13 Consider the following statements.

(Chap 13, Class-XI, NCERT)

Statement I The periodic time of a hard spring is less as compared to that of a soft spring.

Statement II The periodic time depends upon the spring constant is large for hard spring.

Which one of the following is correct in respect of the above statements?

(a) Both Statement I and Statement II are correct and Statement II is the correct explanation for Statement I.
(b) Both Statement I and Statement II are correct but Statement II is not the correct explanation for Statement I.
(c) Statement I is correct but Statement II is incorrect.
(d) Statement I is incorrect but Statement II is correct.

Ans. (a)

Exp. Both Statement I and Statement II are correct and Statement II is the correct explanation for Statement I.

The time period of a oscillating spring is given by,

$$T = 2\pi\sqrt{\frac{m}{k}} = T \propto \frac{1}{\sqrt{k}}$$

Since, the spring constant is large for hard spring, therefore hard spring has a less periodic time as compared to soft spring.

14 Consider the following statements.

(Chap 13, Class-XI, NCERT)

Statement 1 The oscillations in which the amplitude decreases gradually with the passage of time are called damped oscillation.

Statement 2 In free oscillations the frequency with which a body oscillates is called a natural frequency.

Which of the above statement(s) is/are correct?

(a) Only 1 (b) Only 2
(c) Both 1 and 2 (d) None of them

Ans. (c)

Exp. Both statements 1 and 2 are correct.

In damped oscillations, the amplitude decreases gradually with the passage of time. The energy of a real oscillator decreases because a part of its mechanical energy is used in doing work against the frictional forces and is lost as heat.

If a body, capable of oscillation is slightly displaced from its position of equilibrium and then released, it starts oscillating with a frequency of its own.

Such oscillations are called free oscillations. The frequency with which a body oscillates is called natural frequency and is given by

$$\nu_0 = \frac{1}{2\pi}\sqrt{\frac{k}{m}}$$

Here, a body continues to oscillate with constant amplitude and fixed frequency.

15 **Consider the following statements.**

(Chap 13, Class-XI, NCERT)

Statement I In SHM, acceleration always acts towards mean position.

Statement II In extreme position of a particle executing SHM, both velocity and acceleration are zero.

Which one of the following is correct in respect of the above statements?

(a) Both Statement I and Statement II are correct and Statement II is the correct explanation for Statement I.
(b) Both Statement I and Statement II are correct but Statement II is not the correct explanation for Statement I.
(c) Statement I is correct but Statement II is incorrect.
(d) Statement I is incorrect but Statement II is correct.

Ans. (c)

Exp. Statement I is correct but Statement II is incorrect. In simple harmonic motion, the velocity is given by $v = \omega\sqrt{a^2 - y^2}$ at extreme position, $y = a$.

$\therefore v = 0$. But acceleration $A = -\omega^2 a$, which is maximum at extreme position. Direction towards the mean position.

16 **Consider the following statements.**

(Chap 13, Class-XI, NCERT)

1. To and fro motion about a mean position is called simple harmonic motion. In which the restoring force is directly proportional to its displacement from mean position.
2. Army troops march in steps while crossing a bridge.

Which one of the above statement(s) is/are correct?

(a) Only 1
(b) Only 2
(c) Both 1 and 2
(d) None of the above

Ans. (a)

Exp. Statement (1) is correct as a particle is said to execute simple harmonic motion, if it moves to and fro about a mean position under the action of a restoring force which is directly proportional to its displacement from the mean position and is always directed towards the mean position.

Statement (2) is incorrect because army troops are not allowed to march in steps while crossing a bridge because it is quite likely that the frequency of the foot steps may match with the natural frequency of the bridge and due to resonance, the bridge may pick up large amplitude and break.

Chapter 09

Wave Motion

Wave Motion

Wave and Its Types

Waves

- A disturbance which is produced in a material medium and advancing with a definite speed in the medium without changing its form.
- Sound waves, radio waves, electromagnetic waves, etc. are the example of waves.

Types of Waves

- **Mechanical or Elastic Waves** The waves which require a material medium for their propagation. Such waves are also called elastic waves because their propagation depends on the elastic properties of the medium.
- **Transverse Waves** The waves in which the individual particles of the medium oscillate perpendicular to the direction of wave propagation.
- **Longitudinal Waves** The waves in which the individual particles of the medium oscillate along the direction of wave propagation.
- **Electromagnetic Waves** The waves which travel in the form of

Electromagnetic Spectrum

- Electromagnetic waves include visible light waves, X-rays, gamma rays, radio-waves, micro-waves, ultraviolet and infrared waves.

Progressive, Stationary and Sound Waves

Progressive Waves

- The wave which originates from a source and travels forward in a medium.

Stationary Waves

- The wave which is produced by superposition of two progressive waves of equal amplitude and frequency, travelling with the same speed in opposite directions.

Sound Wave

A form of energy which produces a sensation of hearing in our ears. It is produced by vibrating objects.

- Vibration means a rapid to and fro motion of an object.

Characteristics of Sound

- **Loudness** It is the measure of the sound energy reaching the ear per second. The loudness of sound depends on the amplitude of vibrations of the source producing the sound.
- **Pitch** The characteristic of sound by which we can distinguish between different sounds of the same loudness.
- **Quality** The quality or timbre of sound enables us to distinguish one sound from another having the same pitch and loudness.

Speed of Sound and Range of Hearing

Speed of Sound

- The speed of sound depends on the elasticity of medium through which it travels and the density of the medium.

Effect of Physical Parameters on Speed of Sound

Speed of sound is affected by the following physical parameters

- **Effect of Temperature** The speed of sound in a gas is directly proportional to the square root of absolute temperature of the gas.

Effect of pressure

- If temperature remains constant, then there is no effect of change in pressure on the velocity of sound.

Range of Hearing

- **Audible Sound** Sound waves having frequencies lying between 20 Hz - 20000 Hz are called audible sound.
- **Infrasonic Sound** The sound of frequencies lower than 20 Hz are known as infrasonic sounds or infrasound, which cannot be heard by human beings.
- **Ultrasonic Sound** The sounds of frequencies higher than 20000 Hz are called ultrasonic sounds or ultrasounds which, cannot be heard by human beings.

SOURCE *New NCERT Class VIII Chap 10* (Sound), *New NCERT Class IX Chap 11* (Sound)
New NCERT Class XI Chap 14 (Waves), *New NCERT Class XII Chap 8* (Electronmagnetic Waves)

1 Consider the following statements. *(Chap 11, Class- IX, NCERT)*

1. Sound waves are longitudinal waves.
2. Waves seen on the surface of water are transverse waves.
3. Light waves are longitudinal waves.

Which of the statements given above are correct?

(a) 1 and 2 (b) 2 and 3 (c) 1 and 3 (d) 1, 2 and 3

Ans. (a)

Exp. Statements (1) and (2) are correct as sound waves are longitudinal waves. In longitudinal waves, the individual particles of the medium move in a direction parallel to the direction of propagation of the disturbance. Longitudinal waves can be produced in all the three media such as solids, liquids and gases.

The wave on the surface of water are transverse wave. In transverse wave, the individual particles of the medium move about its mean position in a direction perpendicular to the direction of wave propagation.

Transverse waves can be produced only in solids which have rigidity. Transverse wave cannot be formed in the interior of liquids.

Statement (3) is incorrect because light waves are transverse waves not longitudinal i.e., it does not require a medium for its propagation.

2 Two astronauts cannot hear each other on the moon's surface, because *(Chap 11, Class- IX, NCERT)*

(a) their ears have stopped working on the moon.
(b) there is no atmosphere on the moon.
(c) they wear special space suits on the moon.
(d) the sound travels much more slowly on moon.

Ans. (b)

Exp. Two astronauts cannot hear each other on the moon's surface because, there is no atmosphere on the moon. In order for sound to propagate from one place to another, it requires a medium to move through. The air on the earth allows sound waves to move from one point to another. However, there is vacuum on the surface of moon. Thus, there is no sound on the moon.

3 When the same tone is played on a sitar and a flute, the sound produced can be distinguished from each other because of the difference in *(Chap 11, Class- IX, NCERT) (IAS Pre 1995)*

(a) pitch, loudness, and quality
(b) pitch and loudness
(c) quality only
(d) loudness only

Ans. (c)

Exp. When the same tone is played on a sitar and flute, the sound produced can be distinguished from each other because of the difference in quality only.

Quality refers to the sound of the same pitch and loudness produced by two different musical instruments or people which can be distinguished.

4 Heinrich Rudolph Hertz discovered which of the following achievements? *(Chap 8, Class-XII, NCERT)*

1. Confirmation of Maxwell's electromagnetic theory.
2. Photoelectric effect.
3. Foundation for future development of radio and television.

Codes

(a) 1 and 2 (b) 2 and 3
(c) 1 and 3 (d) All of these

Ans. (d)

Exp. All of the given statements are correct.

Heinrich Rudolph Hertz confirmed Maxwell's electromagnetic theory by a famous experiment called 'Frank and Hertz' experiment; which discovered the origin of electromagnetic waves. This led the foundation of future development of radio and television.

Hertz also discovered photoelectric effect (the interaction of electromagnetic wave with particles).

5 Consider the following pairs. *(Chap 11, Class- IX, NCERT)*

1. Tone	A sound of single frequency
2. Note	Sound produced due to a mixture of several frequencies
3. Intensity of sound	Amount of sound energy passing each second through unit area

Which of the pairs given above are correctly matched?

(a) 1 and 2 (b) 2 and 3
(c) 1 and 3 (d) 1, 2 and 3

Ans. (d)

Exp. All the given pairs are correctly matched.

Tone is a sound of single frequency. Note is the sound produced due to a mixture of several frequencies.

Intensity of sound is the amount of sound energy (amplitude) passing through a unit area per unit time.

Loudness and intensity are not same terms.

Loudness is a measure of the response of the ear to the sound. Even when two sounds are of equal intensity, we may hear one as louder than the other, simply because our ear detects it in a better way.

6 When a sound wave travels from one medium to another medium, then which of the following property will not change? *(Chap 11, Class- IX, NCERT)*

1. Speed 2. Wavelength
3. Frequency

Codes

(a) Only 2 (b) Only 3 (c) 1 and 2 (d) 1, 2 and 3

Ans. (b)

Exp. When sound wave travels from one medium to another medium, its frequency does not change. Frequency is an intrinsic characteristic of the wave. The momentum, energy, speed and wavelength may change but frequency remains constant.

7 With reference to speed of sound, consider the following statements. *(Chap 11, Class- IX, NCERT)*

1. In any medium, the speed of sound depends on the temperature of medium.
2. As compared to liquids and gases, sound travels slower in solids.
3. Speed of sound is less than the speed of light.

Which of the statement (s) given above is/are correct?

(a) 1 and 2 (b) Only 2
(c) 1 and 3 (d) 2 and 3

Ans. (c)

Exp. Statements (1) and (3) are correct with reference to speed of sound. The speed of sound depends on the temperature of medium. The speed of sound will increase with increase in temperature of medium.

The speed of sound is less than the speed of light.

The speed of sound in air is 331 m/s at 0°C and the speed of light in air is 3×10^8 m/s. Thus, speed of light is very high as compared to the speed of sound.

This is the reason why in the rainy season, the flash of lightning is seen first and the sound of thunder is heard little later, though both are produced at the same time in clouds.

Statement (2) is incorrect because the medium through which sound propagates can be a solid substance, a liquid or a gas. The speed of sound depends on the properties of medium through which it travels. The speed of sound decreases from solid to gaseous state. Therefore, as compared to liquids and gases, sound travels faster in solids.

8 Consider the following statements about sonic boom. *(Chap 11, Class- IX, NCERT)*

1. Sonic boom occurs when the speed of any object exceeds the speed of sound.
2. It is produced by shock waves in liquid.
3. It produces a very sharp and loud sound with air pressure variation.

Which of the statements given above is/are correct?

(a) Only 1 (b) Only 2
(c) 2 and 3 (d) 1 and 3

Ans. (d)

Exp. Statements (1) and (3) are correct about sonic boom. Sonic boom is produced when the speed of any object exceeds the speed of sound. Sonic boom produces a very sharp and loud sound with air pressure variation. When the speed of any object exceeds the speed of sound, it is said to have supersonic speed.

Supersonic speed of object produces shock waves in air, which carry a large amount of energy. The tremendous air pressure variations caused by the shock waves produced a loud burst of sound is known as sonic boom.

Statement (2) is incorrect because sonic boom is produced by shock waves in air.

9 Which of the following statement is incorrect? *(Chap 11, Class- IX, NCERT)*

(a) Sound bounces off a solid or a liquid like a rubber ball bounces off a wall.
(b) To hear a distinct echo, the time interval between the original sound and the reflected one must be atleast 0.1 s.
(c) For hearing echoes, the minimum distance between source and obstacle must be 17.2 m.
(d) Speed of sound in water is less than that in air.

Ans. (d)

Exp. Statement (d) is incorrect because the speed of sound in water is more than that in air. Sound travels faster in water than air. The speed of sound in water is 1480 metres per second.

10 Consider the following Assertion (A) and Reason (R) and choose the correct code. *(Chap 11, Class- IX, NCERT)*

Assertion (A) In summers, speed of sound is more than that of in winters.

Reason (R) The speed of sound depends on the temperature of the surrounding medium.

Codes

(a) Both A and R are true, and R is the correct explanation of A.
(b) Both A and R are true, but R is not the correct explanation of A.
(c) A is true, but R is false.
(d) A is false, but R is true.

Ans. (a)

Exp. Both Assertion (A) and Reason (R) are true, and R is the correct explanation of Assertion (A).

As molecules at higher temperature have more energy, thus they can vibrate faster and since the molecules vibrate faster, so sound waves can travel more quickly. Thus, the speed of sound is more in summer than that of in winters as speed of sound depends on the temperature of the surrounding medium.

11 Consider the following statements. *(Chap 11, Class- IX, NCERT)*

1. Reverberation is the repeated reflection that results in persistence of sound.
2. The roof and walls of auditorium are covered with sound-absorbent materials to reduce reverberation.
3. Reverberation can be increased with the help of fibreboard, rough plaster or draperies.
4. In stethoscopes, the sound of patient's heartbeat reaches the doctor's ears by multiple reflections.

Which of the statement(s) given above is/are correct?

(a) 1 and 4 (b) 1, 2 and 4
(c) 1, 2 and 3 (d) Only 4

Ans. (b)

Exp. Statements (1), (2) and (4) are correct.

The persistence of sound in a big hall due to repeated reflections from the wall, ceiling and floor of the hall is known as reverberation. This occurs when original sound and reflected sound overlaps. For reverberation to occur, reflection occurs at less than 17 m distance. To reduce reverberation, the roof and walls of the auditorium are covered with sound absorbent materials.

In stethoscopes, the sound of patient's heart beat reaches the doctor's ears by multiple reflections. The reflection of sound is used in the working of devices such as megaphone, horns, stethoscope and sound board.

Statement (3) is incorrect because reverberation is reduced by the help of fibreboard, rough plaster or draperies.

12 Consider the following statements. *(Chap 11, Class- IX, NCERT)*

1. Rhinoceroses and whales communicate using infrasound frequency.
2. Earthquake produces high frequency infrasonic sound before the main shock waves.

Which of the statement (s) given above is/are correct?

(a) Only 1 (b) Only 2
(c) Both 1 and 2 (d) Neither 1 nor 2

Ans. (a)

Exp. Statement (1) is correct. As rhinoceroses and whales communicate using infrasound frequency which is lower than the human audible range.

Statement (2) is incorrect because earthquake also produces low frequency infrasonic sound waves before the main shock waves which can be detected by octopus and dolphins. The sound of frequencies lower than 20 Hz are known as infrasonic sound which cannot be heard by human being.

13 With reference to human ear, consider the following statements. *(Chap 11, Class- IX, NCERT)*

1. Pinna collects the sound from the surroundings.
2. In the inner ear, the pressure variations are turned into electrical signals by the cochlea.
3. Hammer reduces the vibrations in the middle ear, so that ear can be protected.

Which of the statement(s) given above is/are correct?

(a) 1 and 2 (b) 2 and 3 (c) Only 3 (d) Only 2

Ans. (a)

Exp. Statements (1) and (2) are correct with reference to human ear. Pinna is the part of human ears which collects sound from the surroundings. These collected sound waves pass through the ear canal and fall on the ear drum. In the inner ear, the pressure variations are turned into electrical signal by the cochlea, so that the signals are transmitted to the brain. The brain interprets them as sound and we get the sensation of hearing.

Statement (3) is incorrect because the bones i.e., hammer, anvil and stirrup amplify the vibrations in the middle ear.

14 Consider the following statements. *(Chap 11, Class-IX, NCERT)*

Statement I Children under the age of 5 can hear upto 25000 Hz.

Statement II As people grow older, their ears become less sensitive to higher and lower frequencies.

Which one of the following is correct in respect of the above statements?

(a) Both Statement I and Statement II are correct and Statement II is the correct explanation for Statement I.
(b) Both Statement I and Statement II are correct but Statement II is not the correct explanation for Statement I.
(c) Statement I is correct but Statement II is incorrect.
(d) Statement I is incorrect but Statement II is correct.

Ans. (a)

Exp. Both Statement I and Statement II are correct and Statement II is the correct explanation for Statement I.

The audible range of sound for human being is from 20 Hz to 20000 Hz.

Children eardrums are more sensitive, so they can near upto 25000 Hz.

As people grow older, structure inside the ear start to change and their function decline. Thus, ability to pick up sounds decreases.

15 Consider the following statements about ultrasonic waves. *(Chap 11, Class- IX, NCERT)*

1. They can destroy insects.
2. They can clean clothes by removing dust.
3. They can be used to treat diseases.
4. They can control automatic doors.

Which of the statement (s) given above is/are correct?

(a) 1 and 2 (b) 3 and 4
(c) 1, 2 and 3 (d) All of these

Ans. (d)

Exp. All the given statements about ultrasonic waves are correct. As ultrasonic waves kill insects, and can clean clothes.

They are used to treat diseases and used to control automatic devices like doors or windows.

Ultrasonic waves or ultrasounds are high frequency waves. They travel in straight line without bending around the corners.

They penetrate into matter to a large extent. Due to these properties, ultrasound is used in industry and in hospitals for medical purposes.

16 Consider the following statements.

Statement I Sound waves cannot propagate through vacuum but light waves can.

Statement II Sound waves cannot be polarised but light waves can be polarised.

Which one of the following is correct in respect of the above statements? *(Chap 14, Class-XI, NCERT)*

(a) Both Statement I and Statement II are correct and Statement II is the correct explanation for Statement I.
(b) Both Statement I and Statement II are correct but Statement II is not the correct explanation but Statement I.
(c) Statement I is correct but Statement II is incorrect.
(d) Statement I is incorrect but Statement II is correct.

Ans. (b)

Exp. Both Statement I and Statement II are correct but Statement II is not the correct explanation of Statement I. Sound waves cannot propagate through vacuum because sound waves are mechanical waves. Light waves can propagate through vacuum because light waves are electromagnetic waves.

Since, sound waves are longitudinal waves, the particle moves in the direction of propagation, therefore these waves cannot be polarised.

17 **Consider the following statements.** *(Chap 14, Class-XI, NCERT)*

Statement I Compression and rarefaction involve changes in density and pressure.

Statement II When particles are compressed, density of medium increases and when they are rarefied, density of medium decreases.

Which one of the following is correct in respect of the above statements?

(a) Both Statement I and Statement II are correct and Statement II is the correct explanation for Statement I.
(b) Both Statement I and Statement II are correct but Statement II is not the correct explanation for Statement I.
(c) Statement I is correct but Statement II is incorrect.
(d) Statement I is incorrect but Statement II is correct.

Ans. (a)

Exp. Both Statement I and Statement II are correct and Statement II is the correct explanation of Statement I. A compression is a region of medium in which particles come closer, i.e., distance between the particles becomes less than the normal distance between them.

Thus, there is a temporary decrease in volume and a consequent increase in rarefaction, particle get farther apart and a consequent decrease in density.

18 **Consider the following statements.** *(Chap 11, Class IX, NCERT)*

Statement I Ultrasound waves penetrate into matter to a large extent.

Statement II Ultrasound wave is used in industry and in hospital for medical purposes.

Which one of the following is correct in respect of the above statements?

(a) Both Statement I and Statement II are correct and Statement II is the correct explanation for Statement I.
(b) Both Statement I and Statement II are correct but Statement II is not the correct explanation for Statement I.
(c) Statement I is correct but Statement II is incorrect.
(d) Statement I is incorrect but Statement II is correct.

Ans. (a)

Exp. The ultrasound waves have a much greater penetrating power than ordinary sound because they have very high amplitude frequency wave length. Therefore, ultrasound wave is used in industry and in hospitals for medical purposes.

19 **Consider the following statements.** *(Chap 11, Class- IX, NCERT)*

1. Sonar uses ultrasonic waves to measure the distance, direction and speed of underwater objects.
2. In echocardiography, infrasonic waves are used.
3. Ultrasonography is used to examine the foetus during pregnancy.

Which of the statement(s) given above is/are correct?

(a) 1 and 2 (b) 1 and 3
(c) Only 2 (d) Only 3

Ans. (b)

Exp. Statements (1) and (3) are correct.

The word SONAR stands for sound navigation and ranging. SONAR is an apparatus used to find the depth of a sea or to locate the underwater things like shoals of fish, shipwrecks and enemy submarines. It uses ultrasonic waves to measure and detect the distance, direction and speed of underwater objects.

Ultrasound helps us to see inside the human body and to give pictures of the inner organs by converting into electrical signals. These pictures or images are then displayed on a monitor or printed on a film. This technique is called ultrasonography.

Ultrasonography is used for the examination of foetus during pregnancy to detect any growth abnormalities, which helps in taking the necessary action to rectify the abnormalities.

Statement (2) is incorrect because ultrasound is also used for diagnosing heart diseases by scanning the heart from inside. This technique is called echocardiography.

20 **Frequency range of audible sound for humans is 20 Hz and 20000 Hz. Find the corresponding time period for these audible sound.** *(Chap11, Class-IX, NCERT)*

(a) 0.05 s to 5×10^{-5} s (b) 0.5 s to 5×10^{-5} s
(c) 5 s to 5×10^{-3} s (d) 5 s to 5×10^{-5} s

Ans. (a)

Exp. The frequency of a wave is the number of full waveform generated per second. This is same as the number of repetitions per second or the number of oscillations per second.
Time period is reciprocal of frequency. In this case, frequency range of audible sound is 20 Hz to 20,000 Hz.

Time period for 20,000 Hz $= \frac{1}{f} = \frac{1}{20,000} = 5 \times 10^{-5}$ s.

Time period for 20 Hz $= \frac{1}{f} = \frac{1}{20} = 0.05$ s.

21 **The waves used in common TV remote control are**

(Chap 8, Class-XII, NCERT) (UPPSC Pre 2013)

(a) X-rays
(b) Ultraviolet rays
(c) Infrared rays
(d) Gamma rays

Ans. (c)

Exp. The waves used in common TV remote control are infrared rays. Remote control can be used to operate devices such as television set, DVD player or other home appliances. X-rays are used for studying structures of inner atomic electron shells and crystals and detection of fractures, diseased organ.
Ultraviolet rays are used to destroy bacteria and in detection of invisible writing. Gamma rays are used to provide the information about structure of atomic nuclei.

22 **Consider the following statements.**

(Chap 10, Class-VIII, NCERT)

1. A stretched rubber band when plucked, vibrates and produces sound.
2. The sound of the human voice is produced due to vibrations in the vocal cords.

Which of the statement(s) given above is/are correct?

(a) Only 1
(b) Only 2
(c) Both 1 and 2
(d) Neither 1 nor 2

Ans. (c)

Exp. Both statements (1) and (2) are correct.
A stretched rubber band when plucked, vibrates and this vibration produces sound. Similarly, the sound of the human voice is produced due to vibrations in the vocal cords.
When we are silent, then the muscles of vocal cords are completely relaxed due to which the vocal cords are separated. When we are speaking, the muscles of vocal cords contract due to which the two vocal cords become stretched and close together leaving only a narrow slit between them. When the lungs release the air through slit, the vocal cords start vibrating and produce sound.

Chapter 10

Electricity

Electricity

Electric Charge, Potential and Capacitance

Electric Charge

- A physical entity which is defined by excess or deficiency of electrons on a body. The SI unit is coulomb (C).

Basic Properties of Electric Charge

- Unlike charges i.e., opposite charges always attract each other while like charges i.e., similar charges always repel each other.

Coulomb's Law

- The force of attraction or repulsion between two stationary charges is directly proportional to the product of the magnitudes of the two charges and inversely proportional to the square of the distance between them.

Electric Potential

- The work done by an external agent in carrying a unit positive test charge from infinity to a point in the electric field.
- The SI unit of electric potential is Volt.
- **Electric Potential Difference** The electric potential difference between two points in an electric circuit carrying some current is equal to the work done to move a unit charge from one point to the another.

Capacitance

- The ratio of charge given to the conductor to its potential. due to the given charge.
- Its SI unit is farad.

Electric Current and Resistance

Electric Current

- The amount of charge flowing through a particular area in unit time. In other words, it is the rate of flow of electric charges.

Ohm's law

- The electric current flowing through a conductor is directly proportional to the potential difference applied across its ends.

Electric Resistance

- Electric resistance is that property of a conductor by virtue of which it opposes or resists the flow of charges through it.
- Its SI unit is ohm.

Factors on which Resistance Depends

- **Length of the conductor** The resistance of a conductor is directly proportional to its length.
- **Area of Cross-Section of The Conductor** The resistance of a conductor is inversely proportional to its area of cross-section.
- **Nature of the Material of The Conductor** The resistance of a conductor depends on the nature of the material of which it is made. Some materials have low resistance, whereas others have high resistance.

Kirchhoff's Laws

- **Junction Law** This is based upon the conservation of charge.
- **Loop Law** This is based upon the conservation of energy.

Magnetic Effect of Current and Galvanometer

Magnetic Field Effect of Current

- The phenomena in which a magnetic field is generated around a conductor when an electric current flow through it.

Magnetic Field due to a Current a Straight Conductor

- The magnetic field lines around a current carrying straight conductor are concentric circles whose centres lie on the wire.
- The magnitude of magnetic field produced by a straight current carrying-wire at a given point is :
  - **Directly Proportional** to the current passing through the wire.
  - **Inversely Proportional** to the distance from the wire.

Galvanometer

- An instrument that can detect the presence of current in a circuit.
- **Conversion of Galvanometer into an Ammeter and Voltmeter**
- An Ammeter is a device used to measure current through a circuit element.
- A galvanometer is converted into an ammeter by connecting a low resistance in parallel with the galvanometer.
- Voltmeter is an instrument used to measure potential difference across any two points in a circuit.
- A galvanometer can be converted into a voltmeter by connecting a high resistance in series connection within it.

SOURCE *Old NCERT Class VI Chap 9* (Electricity and Circuits), *New NCERT Class VIII Chap 11* (Chemical Effects of Electric Current), *New NCERT Class X Chap 11* (Electricity), *Chap 12* (Magnetic Effect of Current), *New NCERT Class XII Chap 1* (Electric Charges and Fields), *Chap 3* (Current Electricity) *Chap 4* (Moving Charges and Magnetism),

1 Which of the following statement(s) is/are correct? *(Chap 1, Class-XII, NCERT)*

1. Like charges attract each other while unlike charges repel each other.
2. When a body loses electrons, then it attains positive charge.

Codes

(a) Only 1 (b) Only 2
(c) Both 1 and 2 (d) Neither 1 nor 2

Ans. (b)

Exp. Only statement (2) is correct. When a body loses electrons, then it attains positive charge. Since, charge on electron is negative, therefore, when a body loses electrons, then amount of negative charge on the body will decrease which means that amount of positive charge on the body will increase.

Statement (1) is incorrect because like charges repel each other while unlike charges attract each other.

2 If mass of a neutral body increases due to giving charge to it. Then given charge may be *(Chap 1, Class-XII, NCERT)*

(a) negative charge (b) positive charge
(c) Both 'a' and 'b' (d) Neither 'a' nor 'b'

Ans. (a)

Exp. If mass of a neutral body increases due to giving charge to it, then given charge will be negative. It is because negatively charged body means addition of some extra electrons inside the body. Due to addition of electrons inside the body, mass of the neutral body increases.

3 A body is positively charged, it implies that *(Chap 1, Class-XII, NCERT)*

(a) there is equal positive and negative charge in the body but positive charge lies in the outer region.
(b) there is positive as well as negative charge in the body but the positive charge is more than the negative charge.
(c) there is only positive charge in the body.
(d) there is only negative charge in the body.

Ans. (b)

Exp. A body is positively charged, it implies that there is positive as well as negative charge in the body but the positive charge is more than the negative charge.

A charge is a physical entity which is defined by excess or deficiency of electron on a body.

4 Which of the following statements are correct? *(Chap 1, Class XII, NCERT)*

1. Electric lines of forces are closed curves.
2. Electric lines of forces emerge from positive charge and enter into negative charge.
3. Two electric lines of forces do not intersect each other.

Codes

(a) 1 and 2 (b) 2 and 3
(c) 3 and 1 (d) 1, 2 and 3

Ans. (b)

Exp. Statements (2) and (3) are correct.

Electric lines of forces emerge out from positive charge, going to infinity and enter into negative charge, coming from infinity.

Two electric lines of forces do not intersect each other, because if they intersect, then at the intersection point, there will be two directions of electric field, which is not possible.

Statement (1) is incorrect because electric lines of forces are not closed curves, these are open curves.

5 The direction of flow of current through the conductor is taken *(Chap 3, Class-XII, NCERT)*

(a) in the direction of flow of electron.
(b) in the opposite direction of flow of electron.
(c) Both 'a' and 'b'
(d) Neither 'a' nor 'b'

Ans. (b)

Exp. The direction of flow of current through the conductor is taken in opposite direction of flow of electron.

The flow of electric charges through a conductor constitutes an electric current. The electric current is measured by a device called ammeter.

6 Consider the following statements. *(Chap 9, Class-VI, NCERT)*

1. A simple device which is used to either break the electric circuit or to complete it, is known as an electric switch.
2. Our body is good conductor of electricity.

Which of the statement(s) given above is/are correct?

(a) Only 1 (b) Only 2
(c) Both 1 and 2 (d) Neither 1 nor 2

Ans. (c)

Exp. Both statements (1) and (2) are correct.

A simple device which is used to either break the electric circuit or to complete it, is known as an electric switch. An electric circuit is a circuit which contains all the components such as electric bulb, electric switch and cell. Our body is good conductor of electricity.

7 On increasing the temperature of a conductor, its *(Chap 3, Class-XII, NCERT)*

(a) resistance increases.
(b) resistivity increases.
(c) resistance and resistivity will increase.
(d) None of the above

Ans. (c)

Exp. On increasing the temperature of a conductor, its resistance and resistivity will increase.

Resistance is that property of a conductor by virtue of which it opposes/resists flow of current through it. Resistivity is defined as the resistance of a conductor of unit length and unit area of cross-section. Its unit is ohm-metre (Ω - m).

8 **The electric current does not flow between two properly connected charged bodies, if they are having same** *(Chap 11, Class-X, NCERT) (UPPSC Pre 2014)*

(a) charge (b) resistance
(c) resistivity (d) potential

Ans. (d)

Exp. The electric current does not flow between two properly connected charged bodies, if they are having same potential.

According to Ohm's law, we know that without a potential difference between any two points in the conductor, current can not flow. Hence, if both charged bodies have same potential, then potential difference will be zero, hence no current flow through the properly connected charged bodies.

9 **Of the two bulbs in a house, one glows brighter than the other. Which of the two will have a larger resistance?** *(Chap 3, Class-XII, NCERT) (UPPSC Mains 2013)*

(a) The dim bulb
(b) The brighter bulb
(c) Both have the same resistance
(d) The brightness does not depend on the resistance

Ans. (a)

Exp. The dim bulb will have a larger resistance. If the bulb is dim, then it has less power, therefore, the dim bulb has larger resistance. On the other hand, if the bulb is brighter, then it has more power and therefore, it has less resistance.

10 **Consider the following statements.** *(Chap 3, Class-XII, NCERT)*

Statement I Two resistances r_1 and r_2 $(r_1 < r_2)$ are joined in parallel. The equivalent R is $r_1 < R < r_2$.

Statement II The region between two concentric spheres of radii r_1 and r_2 is filled with a conducting material of resistivity ρ. The resistance between two spheres R is $\frac{\rho(r_2 - r_1)}{4\pi r_1 r_2}$.

Which one of the following is correct in respect of the above statements?

(a) Both Statement I and Statement II are correct and Statement II is the correct explanation for Statement I.
(b) Both Statement I and Statement II are correct but Statement II is not the correct explanation for Statement I.
(c) Statement I is correct but Statement II is incorrect.
(d) Statement I is incorrect but Statement II is correct.

Ans. (d)

Exp. Statement I is incorrect but Statement II is correct.

r_1 and r_2 are joined in parallel, then equivalent resistance is

$$\frac{1}{R} = \frac{1}{r_1} + \frac{1}{r_2}$$

$$R = \frac{r_1 r_2}{r_1 + r_2}$$

The value of R should be less (smaller) than the smallest value

$$R < r_1$$

11 **Consider the following statements.** *(Chap 3, Class-XII, NCERT)*

Statement I The specific resistance of a wire does not depend upon its length, cross-section and mass.

Statement II If a piece of aluminium wire of finite length is drawn through a series of dyes to reduce its diameter to half its original value, then its resistance will become four times.

Which one of the following is correct in respect of the above statements?

(a) Both Statement I and Statement II are correct and Statement II is the correct explanation for Statement I.
(b) Both Statement I and Statement II are correct but Statement II is not the correct explanation for Statement I.
(c) Statement I is correct but Statement II is incorrect.
(d) Statement I is incorrect but Statement II is correct.

Ans. (c)

Exp. Statement I is correct but Statement II is incorrect.

ρ is independent of length, mass and area of cross-section and depends on material.

Diameter is reduced to half, length increases 4 times as mass of the material remains the same.

$$R = \rho\frac{l}{A} = 4\rho\frac{l}{\pi D^2} \qquad \left[\because A = \frac{\pi d^2}{4}\right]$$

$$\therefore \quad R' = \frac{4\rho \times 4l}{\pi\left(\frac{D}{2}\right)^2} = 16R$$

12 **Consider the following statements.** *(Chap 11, Class-X, NCERT)*

Statement I The equivalent resistance in a series combination is greater than the highest of the individual resistances.

Statement II The equivalent resistance in a parallel combination is greater than the lowest of the individual resistances.

Which one of the following is correct in respect of the above statements?

(a) Statement I is correct but, Statement II is incorrect.
(b) Statement II is correct but, Statement I is incorrect.
(c) Both Statement I and II are correct.
(d) Both Statement I and II are incorrect.

Ans. (a)

Exp. Statement I is correct but Statement II is incorrect. In series combination, the equivalent resistance is greater because the current in the circuit is not distributed in different wire connection.

13 **Consider the following statements.** *(Chap 4, Class-XII, NCERT)*

Statement I An electric charge in uniform motion produces both electric and magnetic field.

Statement II Protons are shot perpendicular to a magnetic field, then magnetic field will have no influence on the motion of protons.

Which one of the following is correct in respect of the above statements?

(a) Both Statement I and Statement II are correct and Statement II is the correct explanation for Statement I.
(b) Both Statement I and Statement II are correct but Statement II is not the correct explanation for Statement I.
(c) Statement I is correct but Statement II is incorrect.
(d) Statement I is incorrect but Statement II is correct.

Ans. (c)

Exp. Statement I is correct but Statement II is incorrect.

When a electric charge in uniform motion will produced electric and magnetic field. Angle between the directions of motion of protons and magnetic field $\theta = 90°$. The magnetic force on protons is given by,

$$F = qvB\sin\theta = qvB\sin 90° = qvB$$

So, there will be a centripetal force on protons.

$\therefore$ The proton will bend in an arc of a circle.

14 **Consider the following Assertion (A) and Reason (R) and choose the correct code.** *(Chap 3, Class-XII, NCERT)*

Assertion (A) The temperature of a metal wire rises when an electric current is passed through it.

Reason (R) Collision of metal atoms with each other releases heat energy.

Codes

(a) Both A and R are true, and R is the correct explanation of A.
(b) Both A and R are true, but R is not the correct explanation of A.
(c) A is true, but R is false.
(d) A is false, but R is true.

Ans. (a)

Exp. Both Assertion (A) and Reason (R) are true and Reason (R) is the correct explanation of Assertion (A). The heating effect of an electric current is caused by the collision of electrons with atoms of material as they move along the conductor.

In these collisions, the energy of the electrons is lost to the positive ions and they begin to vibrate more vigorously. The greater vibrations of the atoms manifest in the form of increased temperature and heat is produced.

15 **Consider the following Assertion (A) and Reason (R) and choose the correct code.** *(Chap 11, Class-VIII, NCERT)*

Assertion (A) Tin cans used for storing food are made by electroplating tin onto iron.

Reason (R) Tin is less reactive than iron.

Codes

(a) Both A and R are true, and R is the correct explanation of A.
(b) Both A and R are true, but R is not the correct explanation of A.
(c) A is true, but R is false.
(d) A is false, but R is true.

Ans. (a)

Exp. Both Assertion (A) and Reason (R) are true and Reason (R) is the correct explanation of Assertion (A).

Tin cans used for storing food are made by electroplating tin onto iron.

Tin is less reactive than iron. Thus, by electroplating the iron with tin, the food does not come into contact with iron and is protected from getting spoiled.

16 **Which of the following statement(s) is/are correct?** *(Chap 12, Class-X, NCERT)*

1. A current carrying conductor produces magnetic field around it.
2. Magnetic field has only magnitude.
3. On increasing the current, through the conductor, no effect occurs on the intensity of magnetic field around it.

Codes

(a) Only 1
(b) 1 and 2
(c) Only 2
(d) 1, 2 and 3

Ans. (a)

Exp. Statement (1) is correct as a current carrying conductor produces magnetic field around it. The pattern of magnetic field produced by a current carrying conductor depends on its shape.

Statements (2) and (3) are incorrect. Magnetic field is a vector quantity, hence it has both magnitude and direction. On increasing the magnitude of current through the conductor, magnetic field intensity around the conductor increases.

17 Which of the following statements is true according to right hand thumb rule? *(Chap 12, Class-X, NCERT)*

(a) Thumb represents the direction of current.
(b) Thumb represents the direction of magnetic field.
(c) Curling of fingers except thumb around the conductor represents the direction of magnetic field.
(d) Both 'a' and 'c'

Ans. (d)

Exp. Statements (a) and (c) are correct according to right hand thumb rule.

According to this rule, if we hold the current carrying conductor such that the thumb points in the direction of the flow of current, then curling of fingers except thumb around the conductor represents the direction of magnetic field.

18 A straight horizontal conductor carries a steady electric current from South to North. Which one of the following events would happen if a small magnetic compass is placed just above the wire? *(Chap 12, Class-X, NCERT)*

(a) The needle remains perpendicular to the conductor.
(b) The needle remains parallel to the conductor.
(c) The North pole of the needle is deflected towards East.
(d) The North pole of the needle is deflected towards West.

Ans. (c)

Exp. If the current is moving from South to North, then the needle will point East. The current will cause a magnetic field around the East direction. The magnetic dipole of compass needle place above wire will deflected in towards East.

19 The strength of magnetic field inside a long current carrying straight solenoid is *(Chap 12, Class-X, NCERT)*

(a) more at the ends than at the centre
(b) minimum in the middle
(c) same at all points
(d) found to increase from one end to the other

Ans. (c)

Exp. The strength of magnetic field lines inside a long current carrying straight solenoid is same at all points because the magnetic field lines are straight, equi-spaced and parallel to the axis of solenoid and hence, uniform magnetic field exists inside the solenoid.

20 Which type of charge particle can experience a magnetic force in magnetic field? *(Chap 4, Class-XII, NCERT)*

(a) A moving charge
(b) A static charge
(c) Both 'a' and 'b'
(d) Neither 'a' nor 'b'

Ans. (a)

Exp. Only a moving charge can experience a magnetic force (Lorentz force) in magnetic field. A static charge does not experience any force inside the magnetic field.

21 Which of the following statement(s) is/are incorrect? *(Chap 4, Class-XII, NCERT)*

1. Two parallel current carrying conductors attract each other, if both have currents in the opposite directions.
2. Two parallel current carrying conductors repel each other, if both have currents in the opposite directions.

Codes

(a) Only 1 (b) Only 2
(c) Both 1 and 2 (d) Neither 1 nor 2

Ans. (a)

Exp. Statement (1) is incorrect as two parallel current carrying conductors having currents in same direction, attract each other and those having currents in opposite directions repel each other.

22 Consider the following statements. *(Chap 4, Class-XII, NCERT)*

1. A current carrying loop is placed in a uniform magnetic field. The torque acting on it does not depend upon shape of the loop.
2. Two parallel beams of positrons moving in the opposite direction will attract each other.
3. If a long hollow copper pipe carries a direct current, the magnetic field associated with the current will be only outside the pipe.

How many of the above statements are correct?

(a) Only one (b) Only two
(c) All three (d) None of these

Ans. (b)

Exp. Only two statements (1 and 3) are correct but one statement (2) is incorrect.

Statement 1 When current carrying torp is placed in a uniform magnetic field/torque will be $\tau = BIA \sin \theta$.

Statements 2 and 3 Two parallel beams of positions moving in the same direction will attract each other inside of hollow conductor, the current is zero.

So Magnetic field $B = 0$

But, out side hollow conductor, the current is not zero.

So Magnetic field $B \neq 0$

Hence the magnetic field associated with the current will be only out side the hollow pipe.

23 In a three-pin electrical plug, longest pin should be connected to *(Chap 11, Class-X, NCERT) (UPPSC Pre 2007)*

(a) line terminal (b) ground terminal
(c) neutral terminal (d) None of these

Ans. (b)

Exp. In a three-pin electrical plug, longest pin should be connected to ground terminal. In three terminal plug, the earth terminal on a plug is longer than the line and neutral terminals. This means the ground terminal or earthed terminal provides an alternative and easy path for leakage or fault current flow.

24 **Match List-I with List-II and select the correct answer from the codes given below.**

(Chap 11, Class-X, NCERT)

List-I	List-II
A. Electric fuse	1. Copper
B. Heater wire	2. Tungsten
C. Filament wire	3. Nichrome
D. Conducting wire	4. Lead and tin

Codes

	A	B	C	D
(a)	4	3	1	2
(b)	4	3	2	1
(c)	3	4	2	1
(d)	4	2	3	1

Ans. (b)

Exp. The correct matching is A-4, B-3, C-2 and D-1.

Electric fuse It consists of an alloy of lead and tin which has appropriate melting point. It is connected in series with the mains supply.

Heater wire It is made up of nichrome which is the most common resistance wire used for heating purpose. It is because it has high resistivity and resistance to oxidation at high temperature.

Filament wire An electric bulb has a filament made of tungsten. It has high resistivity and high melting point. Tungsten retains as much of heat generated, so that it becomes very hot and emits light. That's why tungsten is used as filament of electric lamps.

Conducting wire It is made up of copper because current can pass easily through it and it is cheaper. Copper and aluminium wires are used for transmission of electricity because they have low resistivity. So, they conduct the electric current without heavy heat loses.

25 **A fuse is used in main electric supply as a safety device. Which one of the following statements about the fuse is correct?** *(Chap 11, Class-X, NCERT) (IAS Pre 1998)*

(a) It is connected in parallel with the main switch.
(b) It is made mainly from silver alloys.
(c) It must have a low melting point.
(d) It must have a very high resistance.

Ans. (c)

Exp. A fuse is used in main electric supply as a safety device to prevent damage to an electrical circuit when excessive current flows through it.

It works on the principle of heating effect of current. It is made up of alloy of lead and tin of low melting point.

When excessive current flows through the fuse, then it melts due to the production of excessive heat and hence, circuit connection breaks off. The circuit is broken and current stops flowing through it.

26 **Consider the following statements.**

(Chap 11, Class-X, NCERT)

Statement I Tungsten metal is used in bulbs, but not in fuse wires.

Statement II Overloading happens when a large number of appliances are connected in parallel to the different source of electric power.

Which one of the following is correct in respect of the above statements?

(a) Statement I is correct but, Statement II is incorrect.
(b) Statement II is correct but, Statement I is incorrect.
(c) Both Statement I and II are correct.
(d) Both Statement I and II are incorrect.

Ans. (a)

Exp. Statement I is correct but statement II is incorrect. Overloading happens when a large number of appliances are connected in parallel to the same source of electric power. This leads to flow of excess current in the electric circuit.

Chapter 11

Magnetism and Electromagnetic Induction

Magnetism and Electromagnetic Induction

Magnet, Magnetic Field and Magnetic Field Lines

Magnet

- A material that produces a magnetic field. The magnetic field is invisible but is responsible for most notable property of a magnet.
- **Natural Magnets** It is an ore of iron (Fe_3O_4) Natural magnets are also known as lodestone.
- **Artificial Magnets** These magnets have desired shape and strength. They are stronger than natural magnets.

Magnetic Field

- The space in the surrounding of a magnet in which its magnetic influence can be experienced.
- It is a vector quantity. The SI unit of magnetic field is Tesla (T) or weber/metre^2 .

Magnetic Field Lines

- The magnetic field lines in a magnetic field are those imaginary lines which continuously represent the direction of the magnetic field.
- The magnetic field lines of force originate from North pole of a magnet and end its South pole.
- A magnetic field line is a closed and continuous curve. The magnetic field lines never intersect each other.
- The tangent at any point on the field line gives the direction of force at that point.

Earth's Magnetism and Magnetic Substance

Earth's Magnetism

- The earth is a natural source of magnetic field where the magnetic field is present everywhere near the surface of the earth.

Elements of Earth's Magnetic Field

There are three elements of the Earth's magnetic field.

- **Magnetic Declination** The angle between the geographical meridian and the magnet meridian at a place.
- **Angle of Dip** The angle made by the total magnetic field *B* of the Earth with the horizontal direction in the magnetic meridian.

Horizontal Component of Earth's Magnetic Field

- The component of earth's magnetic field in the horizontal direction in the magnetic meridian.

Magnetic Substance

- **Diamagnetic Substances** Those substances which are feebly magnetised opposite to the direction of the magnetic field. e.g. gold, etc.
- **Paramagnetic Substances** Those substances which are feebly magnetised in the direction of magnetic field. e.g. aluminium, etc.
- **Ferromagnetic Substances** Those substances which strongly magnetised in the direction of magnetic field. e.g. cobalt etc.

Electromagnetic Induction

Electromagnetic Induction

- The phenomenon of production of induced emf due to a change of magnetic flux linked with a closed circuit.
- **Self-Induction** The phenomenon of Production of induced emf in coil when a changing current passes through it.
- **Mutual-Induction** The phenomenon of production of induced emf in one coil due to a change of current in the neighbouring coil.

Electric Generator

- A device which is used to convert mechanical energy to electrical energy.
- An electric generator is based on the

Transformer

- A device which is used to increase or decrease the alternating voltage. It is based on the principle of mutual induction.
- If the transformer increases the input voltage, is called step-up transformer and if it decreases the input voltage, it is called step-down transformer.
- A transformer is used in voltage regulations for TV, refrigerator, computer etc.
- A transformer is used in the induction furnaces.

SOURCE New NCERT Class VI Chap 10 (*Fun with Magnets*), New NCERT Class X Chap 12 (*Magnetic Effects of Electric Current*), New NCERT Class XII Chap 5 (*Magnetism and Matter*), Chap 6 (*Electromagnetic induction*), Chap 7 (*Alternating Current*), Tamil Nadu Board Class IX (*Magnetism and Electromagnetism*)

1 **Consider the following Assertion (A) and Reason (R) and choose the correct code.** *(Chap 5, Class-XII, NCERT)*

Assertion (A) Like poles of two bar magnet attract each other when they are kept closer.

Reason (R) When a bar magnet is freely suspended, then it always points in North-South direction.

Codes

(a) Both A and R are true, and R is the correct explanation of A.
(b) Both A and R are true, but R is not the correct explanation of A.
(c) A is true, but R is false.
(d) A is false, but R is true.

Ans. (d)

Exp. Assertion (A) is false but Reason (R) is true.
When two bar magnets are kept closer, then like poles of bar magnets repel each other while unlike poles of bar magnets attract each other.
When a bar magnet is freely suspended in air, then it always points in North-South direction.

2 **Consider the following statements.** *(Chap 5, Class-XII, NCERT)*

1. The magnetic moment of atomic neon is equal to $3/2\ \mu_B$.
2. At magnetic poles, the angle of dip is 90°.
3. A magnetic needle is kept in a non-uniform magnetic field. It experiences a force and a torque.

How many of the above statements are correct?

(a) Only one (b) Only two (c) All three (d) None

Ans. (b)

Exp. Only two statements (2 and 3) are correct but statement (1) is incorrect.
Statement (1) is incorrect. The magnetic dipole moment of atomic neon is zero, since it has noble gas configuration and does not have any unpaired electron. Therefore, magnetic moment of atomic neon is equal to zero.
At magnetic poles, the magnetic needle points vertical.

$\therefore \quad \delta = 90°$

In a non-uniform magnetic field, a magnetic needle experiences a force and a torque.

3 **Magnetic Resonance Imaging (MRI) is used in medical diagnosis to obtain images of our internal body organs. This is primarily possible, because** *(Chap 12, Class-X, NCERT) (IAS Pre 2004)*

(a) our body possesses a permanent magnet
(b) MRI uses an external magnet to generate a magnetic field in our body
(c) MRI uses an external electric field to generate magnetic field in our body
(d) ions motion along our nerve cells generates magnetic fields

Ans. (d)

Exp. Magnetic Resonance Imaging (MRI) is used in medical diagnosis to obtain image of our internal body organs.
This is primarily possible because the ions motion along our nerve cells generates magnetic field. to generate image of organs in body and MRI scanner uses strong magnetic field.

4 **Consider the following statements.** *(Chap 12, Class-X, NCERT)*

1. Magnetic lines of forces are always closed curves.
2. Magnetic lines of forces do not intersect each other.

Which of the statement (s) given above is/are correct?

(a) Only 1
(b) Only 2
(c) Both 1 and 2
(d) Neither 1 nor 2

Ans. (c)

Exp. Both the statements (1) and (2) are correct.
Magnetic lines of forces emerge out from North pole and enter into South pole and again passes from South pole to North pole inside the magnet.
Thus, magnetic lines of forces are always closed curves whereas magnetic lines of forces do not intersect each other, because if they intersect, then at intersection point, there will be two directions of magnetic field which is impossible.

5 **Consider the following statements.** *(Chap 5, Class-XII, NCERT)*

Statement I For a paramagnetic material, the dependence of the magnetic susceptibility χ on the absolute temperature T is $\chi \propto \frac{1}{T}$.

Statement II If the magnetic flux is expressed in weber, then magnetic induction can be expressed in weber.

Which one of the following is correct in respect of the above statements?

(a) Both Statement I and Statement II are correct and Statement II is the correct explanation for Statement I.
(b) Both Statement I and Statement II are correct but Statement II is not the correct explanation for Statement I.
(c) Statement I is correct but Statement II is incorrect.
(d) Statement I is incorrect but Statement II is correct.

Ans. (c)

Exp. Statement I is correct but Statement II is incorrect. For a paramagnetic material, the dependence of magnetic susceptibility χ is inversely proportional to absolute temperature T or $\chi \propto \frac{1}{T}$.

Magnetic induction = Magnetic flux per unit area = weber/m^2.

6 Consider the following statements.

(Chap 5, Class-XII, NCERT)

Statement I In a ferromagnetic material, number of atoms in a domain is 10^{17} to 10^{21}.

Statement II Earth's magnetic field always has a vertical component except at magnetic pole.

Which one of the following is correct in respect of the above statements?

(a) Both Statement I and Statement II are correct and Statement II is the correct explanation for Statement I.
(b) Both Statement I and Statement II are correct but Statement II is not the correct explanation for Statement I.
(c) Statement I is correct but Statement II is incorrect.
(d) Statement I is incorrect but Statement II is correct.

Ans. (c)

Exp. Statement I is correct but Statement II is incorrect.

Earth's magnetic field always has a horizontal component except at poles, where there is only vertical component of field.

7 Retentivity and coercivity of a permanent magnet should be, respectively *(Chap 5, Class-XII, NCERT)*

(a) high, high (b) low, low
(c) high, low (d) low, high

Ans. (a)

Exp. Retentivity and coercivity of a permanent magnet, both should be high. High value of retentivity signifies that magnet is strong and high value of coercivity signifies that its magnetisation is not wiped out by stray magnetic fields.

8 Consider the following statements.

(Chap 6, Class-XII, NCERT)

Statement I Lenz's law violates the principle of conservation of energy.

Statement II Induced emf always opposes the change in magnetic flux responsible for its production.

Which one of the following is correct in respect of the above statements?

(a) Both Statement I and Statement II are correct and Statement II is the correct explanation for Statement I.
(b) Both Statement I and Statement II are correct but Statement II is not the correct explanation for Statement I.
(c) Statement I is correct but Statement II is incorrect.
(d) Statement I is incorrect but Statement II is correct.

Ans. (a)

Exp. Both Statement I and Statement II are correct and Statement II is the correct explanation for Statement I. Lenz's law (that the direction of induced emf is always such as to oppose the change that cause it) is direct consequence of the law of conservation of energy.

9 Consider the following statements.

(Chap 6, Class-XII, NCERT)

Statement I Faraday's laws are consequence of conservation of energy.

Statement II In a purely resistive AC circuit, the current and emf are in the same phase.

Which one of the following is correct in respect of the above statements?

(a) Both Statement I and Statement II are correct and Statement II is the correct explanation for Statement I.
(b) Both Statement I and Statement II are correct but Statement II is not the correct explanation for Statement I.
(c) Statement I is correct but Statement II is incorrect.
(d) Statement I is incorrect but Statement II is correct.

Ans. (b)

Exp. Statement I and Statement II are correct but Statement II is not the correct explanation for statement I. Faraday's laws are consequence of conservation of energy. In purely resistive circuit, the current and emf are in the same phase.

10 Consider the following statements.

(Chap 7, Class-XII, NCERT)

Statement I Choke coil is preferred over a resistor to adjust current in an AC circuit.

Statement II Power factor for inductance is zero.

Which one of the following is correct in respect of the above statements?

(a) Both Statement I and Statement II are correct and Statement II is the correct explanation for Statement I.
(b) Both Statement I and Statement II are correct but Statement II is not the correct explanation for Statement I.
(c) Statement I is correct but Statement II is incorrect.
(d) Statement I is incorrect but Statement II is correct.

Ans. (a)

Exp. Both Statement I and Statement II are correct and Statement II is the correct explanation for Statement I. A Choke Coil is preferred over resistor in AC circuit because a choke coil has large value of Inductance and hence power dissipation is zero for choke coil.

11 Consider the following statements.

(Chap 7, Class-XII, NCERT)

Statement I The root mean square value of AC is equivalent to that of DC producing same average power loss as AC.

Statement II The root mean square value of alternating voltage is $V_{rms} = \frac{V_0}{\sqrt{3}}$.

Which one of the following is correct in respect of the above statements?

(a) Both Statement I and Statement II are correct and Statement II is the correct explanation for Statement I.
(b) Both Statement I and Statement II are correct but Statement II is not the correct explanation for Statement I.
(c) Statement I is correct but Statement II is incorrect.
(d) Statement I is incorrect but Statement II is correct.

Ans. (c)

Exp. Statement I is correct but Statement II is incorrect.

The value of voltage rms is $\frac{V_0}{\sqrt{2}}$ or $0.707\ V_0$.

12 The essential difference between AC generator and DC generator is that

(Chap 13, Class-X, NCERT) (CGPSC Pre 2018)

(a) AC generator has electromagnet while DC generator has permanent magnet
(b) DC generator generates higher voltage
(c) AC generator generates higher voltage
(d) AC generator has slip rings while DC generator has commutator

Ans. (d)

Exp. The essential difference between AC generator and DC generator is that AC generator has slip rings while DC generator has slip rings as commutator.

Due to slip rings the current produced by AC generator flows in both directions while current produced by DC generator flows in single direction.

13 Consider the following Assertion (A) and Reason (R) and choose the correct code.

(Chap 7, Class-XII, NCERT) (IAS Pre 1996)

Assertion (A) Transformation is useful for stepping up or stepping down voltages.

Reason (R) Transformation is used in DC circuits.

Codes

(a) Both A and R are true and R is the correct explanation of A.
(b) Both A and R are true but R is not the correct explanation of A.
(c) A is true but R is false.
(d) A is false but R is true.

Ans. (c)

Exp. Assertion (A) is true and Reason (R) is false.

A transformer transfers electric energy between two or more interconnected circuits through electromagnetic induction. It converts the high voltage to low voltage (stepping down) and low voltage to high (stepping up) and transmits it. Transformation can only function with Alternating Current (AC). It cannot work with Direct Current (DC).

14 Consider the following statements.

(Chap 7, Class-XII, NCERT)

Statement I A transformer is employed to obtain a suitable DC voltage.

Statement II The average power dissipation in pure inductance is 0.

Statement III The natural frequency of a L-C circuit is equal to $\sqrt{\frac{LC}{2\pi}}$.

How many of the above statements are correct?

(a) Only one (b) Only two (c) All three (d) None of these

Ans. (a)

Exp. Only one statement (2) is correct but two statements (1 and 3) are incorrect.

Statement I Transformer converts low voltage AC into high voltage AC and *vice-versa.*

Statement II P_{av} (in inductor) $= E_v \cdot i_v \cos 90° = 0$

Statement III The natural frequency of a L - C circuit is equal to $f = \frac{1}{2\pi\sqrt{LC}}$.

15 Consider the following statements.

(Chap 7, Class-XII, NCERT)

Statement I In general, an alternating current circuit the average value of current is zero.

Statement II A set-up transformer converts low voltage, low current into high voltage and high current.

Which one of the following is correct in respect of the above statements?

(a) Both Statement I and Statement II are correct and Statement II is the correct explanation for Statement I.
(b) Both Statement I and Statement II are correct but Statement II is not the correct explanation for Statement I.
(c) Statement I is correct but Statement II is incorrect.
(d) Statement I is incorrect but Statement II is correct.

Ans. (c)

Exp. Statement I is correct but Statement II is incorrect.

As in the set-up transformer, the number of coils is more than in the primary coil. So, the electrical potential increases. A set-up transformer converts low voltage at high current into a high voltage at low current.

16 The main cause/causes for energy loss in transformer is/are *(Chap 6, Class-XII, NCERT)*

1. copper loss
2. eddy current loss
3. hysteresis loss

Codes

(a) 1 and 3
(b) Only 1
(c) 2 and 3
(d) 1, 2 and 3

Ans. *(d)*

Exp. The main causes for energy loss in transformer are copper loss, eddy current loss and hysteresis loss.

Copper loss It is the energy loss in the form of heat in the copper coils of transformer. This is due to joule heating of conducting wires.

Eddy current loss The alternating magnetic flux induces eddy current in the iron core which leads to some energy loss in the form of heat.

Hysteresis loss The alternating current carries the iron core through cycles of magnetisation and demagnetisation. Work done in each of these cycles is lost as heat. This is called hysteresis loss.

17 Consider the following statements. *(Chap 6, Class-XII, NCERT)*

Statement I When the current through a solenoid increases at a constant rate, the induced current increases with time and is in the direction of the inducing current.

Statement II In a series, *L-C-R* circuit (AC circuit) the current becomes maximum when $X_L = X_C$.

Which one of the following is correct in respect of the above statements?

(a) Both Statement I and Statement II are correct and Statement II is the correct explanation for Statement I.
(b) Both Statement I and Statement II are correct but Statement II is not the correct explanation for Statement I.
(c) Statement I is correct but Statement II is incorrect.
(d) Statement I is incorrect but Statement II is correct.

Ans. *(d)*

Exp. Statement I is incorrect but Statement II is correct. When a current through a solenoid increases at a constant rate, the induced current is constant and is opposite to the direction of inducing current.

When reactance inductance equal to reactance capacitance the impedance of the AC circuit becomes minimum and the current becomes maximum.

18 Some pairs of devices and associated energy changes are given below. *(Unit 5, Class-IX, Tamil Nadu Board), (RAS/RTS Pre 2013)*

1. Electric generator – Mechanical to electrical
2. Electric Motor – Electrical to mechanical
3. Diesel engine – Light to electrical
4. Solar cell – Chemical to mechanical

Which of the above pairs is/are correctly matched?

(a) 1 and 2
(b) 1 and 3
(c) 2 and 4
(d) 3 and 4

Ans. *(a)*

Exp. Only Pairs (1 and 2) are correctly matched. Electric generator converts mechanical energy to electrical energy. Electric motor converts electrical energy to mechanical energy.

Pairs (3 and 4) are incorrectly matched. Diesel engine converts chemical energy to mechanical energy.

Solar cell converts light energy to electrical energy.

Chapter 12

Light

Light

Light and Mirror

Light

- A form of energy which produces sensation of vision to our eye and makes objects visible. An object reflects the light rays that fall on it.
- **Light Sources** An object from which light is given out. Some sources of light are natural like Sun, Stars and some are man made like oil lamp, a candle, an electric bulb.
- **Properties of Light**
  - The speed of light in vacuum is 3×10^8 m/s.
  - Light travels in a straight line and the straight line path along which light travels is called ray of light.

Mirror

- A smooth and polished surface which reflects almost all the light incident on it.
- Silver metal is one of the best reflectors of light.
- **Types of Mirror**
  - **Plane Mirror** A mirror whose reflecting surface is plane.
  - **Spherical Mirror** A mirror whose reflecting surface is curved inwards or outwards.
- **Types of Spherical Mirror**
  - **Concave Mirror** The spherical mirror whose reflecting surface is inwards.
  - **Convex Mirror** The spherical mirror whose reflecting surface is outwards

Refraction, Total Internal Reflection and Human Eye

Refraction of Light

- The phenomena of change in path of a light ray as it passes from one medium to another medium.

Total Internal Reflection (TIR)

- When a ray of light travelling from denser medium to rarer medium, is incident at the interface of two media at an angle greater than the critical angle for the two media, the ray is totally reflected back to denser medium. This phenomenon is called Total Internal Reflection (TIR).
- **Optical Fibres** A thin tube of transparent material that allows light to pass through, without being refracted into the air or another external medium. Optical fibres are based upon the total internal reflection.

Human Eye

- A one of the most valuable and sensitive sense organ in the human body. It enables us to see the world.
- The human eye is like a camera. The eye lens is a convex lens made of a transparent soft and flexible material like a jelly made of proteins.
- They eye lens forms an inverted real image of the object on the retina.
- The retina is a delicate membrane having enormaus number of light sensitive cells.

Lens and Prism

Lens

- A transparent medium which is bounded by two surfaces and its one or both surfaces are spherical.
- **Convex or Converging Lens** A lens which is thicker at the centre and thinner at its ends.
- **Concave or Diverging lens** A lens which is thinner at the centre and thicker at its ends.
- **Power of a Lens** The ability of a lens to converge or diverge light rays. It is defined as the reciprocal of focal length.

Prism

- A transparent refracting medium which is bounded by atleast two lateral surfaces, inclined to each other at a certain angle.

Rainbow

- A natural spectrum which appears in the sky after a rain shower. It is caused by dispersion of sunlight by tiny water droplets present in the

Dispersion of Light

- The phenomena of splitting of white light into its constituent colours, when it passes through a prism.
- Red light has maximum wavelength and violet light has the minimum wavelength.

SOURCE **New NCERT Class VI Chap 8** *(Light, Shadows and Reflections)*, **New NCERT Class VII Chap 11** *(Light)*, **New NCERT Class VIII Chap 13** *(Light)*, **New NCERT Class X Chap 9** *(Light-Reflection and Refraction)*, **Chap 10** *(The Human Eye and the Colourful World)*, **New NCERT Class XII Chap 9** *(Ray Optics and Optical Instruments)*, **Chap 10** *(Wave Optics)*

1 **Consider the following statements.** *(Chap 9, Class-X, NCERT)*

Statement I The image formed by a pin hole camera is big in size as compared to the object.

Statement II A pin hole camera works on the principle that light travels in a straight line.

Which one of the following is correct in respect of the above statements?

(a) Both Statement I and Statement II are correct and Statement II is the correct explanation for Statement I.

(b) Both Statement I and Statement II are correct but Statement II is not the correct explanation for Statement I.

(c) Statement I is correct but Statement II is incorrect.

(d) Statement I is incorrect but Statement II is correct.

Ans. *(d)*

Exp. Statement I is incorrect but Statement II is correct.

Image formed by a pin hole camera is not enlarge as compare to the object.

2 **Consider the following statements.** *(Chap 9, Class-XII, NCERT)*

1. The nature of light is transverse.
2. Speed of light is maximum in vacuum.

Which of the statement(s) given above is/are correct?

(a) Only 1 (b) Only 2

(c) Both 1 and 2 (d) Neither 1 nor 2

Ans. *(c)*

Exp. Both the statements (1) and (2) are correct.

The nature of light is transverse because its electric field vector and magnetic field vector both vibrate perpendicular to the direction of propagation of light.

Since, refractive index of vacuum or air is minimum. Therefore, speed of light is maximum in vacuum.

3 **A full length image of a distant tall building can definitely be seen by using** *(Chap 9, Class-X, NCERT)*

(a) a concave mirror

(b) a convex mirror

(c) a plane mirror

(d) Both concave as well as plane mirror

Ans. *(b)*

Exp. The convex mirror forms virtual, erect and diminished image of the objects. So, it can form full length image of a distant tall building.

4 **The image formed by concave mirror is real, inverted and of the same size as that of the object. The position of the object should be** *(Chap 9, Class-X, NCERT), (BPSC Pre 2023)*

(a) at the focus

(b) at the centre of curvature

(c) between the focus and centre of curvature

(d) beyond the centre of curvature

Ans. *(b)*

Exp. The image formed by concave mirror is real, inverted and of the same size as that of the object. The position of the object should be at the centre of curvature.

Concave mirrors are commonly used in torches, search lights and vehicles headlights to get powerful parallel beams of light.

5 **Which of the following mirror is used by a dentist to examine a small cavity?** *(Chap 9, Class-X, NCERT)*

(a) Convex mirror

(b) Plane mirror

(c) Concave mirror

(d) Combination of convex and concave mirror.

Ans. *(c)*

Exp. Concave mirror forms erect and enlarged image when held close to the cavity.

Convex mirrors are used, to magnification of image.

Plane mirrors are used in solar cookers. They are also used in constructing periscope which is used in submarines.

6 **A person standing in front of a mirror finds his image larger than himself. This implies that the mirror is** *(Chap 9, Class-X, NCERT) (BPSC Pre 2022)*

(a) concave

(b) plane

(c) convex

(d) cylindrical with bulging side outwards

Ans. *(a)*

Exp. A person standing in front of a concave mirror finds his image larger than himself.

Convex mirror gives diminished image and plane mirror gives image of equal size of object.

7 **In torches, search lights and headlights of vehicles, the bulb is placed** *(Chap 9, Class-X, NCERT)*

(a) between the pole and the focus of the reflector.

(b) very near to the focus of the reflector.

(c) between the focus and centre of curvature of the reflector.

(d) at the centre of curvature of the reflector.

Ans. *(b)*

Exp. The bulb is placed very near to the focus of the reflector as the incident rays, which pass through the focus of concave mirror, after reflection become parallel to the principal axis of the mirror.

Concave mirrors are commonly used in torches, search lights and vehicles headlights to get powerful parallel beams of light.

8 **Consider the following statements.** *(Chap 9, Class-XII, NCERT)*

1. The speed of light is higher in a rarer medium than in a denser medium.
2. When a ray of light travels from air to water, it speeds up.

Which of the statement(s) given above is/are correct?

(a) Only 1 (b) Only 2
(c) Both 1 and 2 (d) Neither 1 nor 2

Ans. (a)

Exp. Among the given statements, Statement (1) is correct. Speed of light is higher in a rarer medium than in a denser medium because refractive index of rarer medium is less than the refractive index of denser medium.

Statement (2) is incorrect because when a ray of light travels from air (rarer medium) to water (denser medium), then speed of light decreases.

9 **The speed of light will be minimum while passing through** *(Chap 9, Class-XII, NCERT) (BPSC (Pre) Re-exam 2022)*

(a) glass (b) vacuum
(c) water (d) air

Ans. (a)

Exp. The speed of light will be minimum while passing through glass because, it has highest refractive index among water, air and vacuum.

The speed of light in a vacuum is approximately 3×10^8 m/s. However, when light travels through different media, such as air, water or glass, its speed changes due to the interaction between light and atoms or molecules in the medium, which can slow down light.

In denser medium like glass, light typically travels at a slower speed than it does in rarer medium, such as air.

10 **Consider the following statements.**

(Chap 9, Class-XII, NCERT) (JKPSC Pre 2023)

1. When a ray of light travelling from a rarer medium to a denser medium slows down and bends towards the normal.
2. When it travels from a denser medium to a rarer medium, it speeds up and bends away from the normal.

The correct statement(s) is/are

(a) Only 1 (b) Only 2
(c) Both 1 and 2 (d) Neither 1 nor 2

Ans. (c)

Exp. Both statements (1 and 2) are correct. When a ray of light travelling from a rarer medium to denser medium slows down and bends towards the normal. When a ray of light travels from a denser medium to a rarer medium, it speeds up and bends away from the normal.

11 **Consider the following Assertion (A) and Reason (R) and choose the correct code.** *(Chap 9, Class-XII, NCERT)*

Assertion (A) Light bends from its path, when it goes from one medium to another medium.

Reason (R) Speed of light changes, when it goes from one medium to another medium.

Codes

(a) Both A and R are true, and R is the correct explanation of A.
(b) Both A and R are true, but R is not the correct explanation of A.
(c) A is true, but R is false.
(d) A is false, but R is true.

Ans. (a)

Exp. Both Assertion (A) and Reason (R) are true, and Reason (R) is the correct explanation of Assertion (A). When light goes from one medium to another medium, then it bends (deviates) from its path because speed of light is different in different medium due to variation of their refractive index.

12 **Consider the following statements.**

(Chap 9, Class-XII, NCERT)

1. Endoscope is based on the phenomenon of reflection of light while twinkling of stars is based on the phenomenon of principle of reversibility.
2. Mirage is an optical illusion and mirage is based on the phenomenon of total internal reflection.

Which of the statement(s) given above is/are correct?

(a) Only 1 (b) Only 2 (c) Both 1 and 2 (d) None of these

Ans. (b)

Exp. Statement (2) is correct but statement (1) is incorrect.

Mirage and endoscope are based on the phenomenon of total internal reflection while twinkling of stars is based on the phenomenon of refraction of light. Mirage is an optical illusion occuring in deserts and colter roads on hot summer days. An object, such as a tree, appears inverted to a distant observer who gets the wrong impression of a part of water in which the tree is reflected.

13 **Consider the following statements.**

(Chap 9, Class-XII, NCERT)

Statement I Higher is the refractive index of a medium or denser the medium, lesser is the velocity of light in that medium.

Statement II Refractive index is inversely proportional to velocity.

Which one of the following is correct in respect of the above statements?

(a) Both Statement I and Statement II are correct and Statement II is the correct explanation for Statement I.
(b) Both Statement I and Statement II are correct but Statement II is not the correct explanation for Statement I.
(c) Statement I is correct but Statement II is incorrect.
(d) Statement I is incorrect but Statement II is correct.

Ans. (b)

Exp. Both Statement I and Statement II are correct but Statement II is not the correct explanation for Statement I.

The refractive index of a medium,

$$n_m = \frac{\text{speed of light in the vacuum}}{\text{speed of light in the medium}} = \frac{c}{v}$$

⇒ Refractive index of a medium is inversely proportional to velocity of light in that medium.

∴ Higher the refractive index of a medium, lesser will be the velocity of the light in that medium.

14 Consider the following Assertion (A) and Reason (R) and choose the correct code.

(Chap 9, Class-XII, NCERT) (IAS Pre 2001)

Assertion (A) A stick is dipped in water in slanting position. If observed sideways, the stick appears short and bent at the surface of the water.

Reason (R) A light coming from the stick undergoes scattering from water molecules giving the stick a short and bent appearance.

Codes

(a) Both A and R are true, and R is the correct explanation of A.
(b) Both A and R are true, but R is not the correct explanation of A.
(c) A is true, but R is false.
(d) A is false, but R is true.

Ans. (c)

Exp. Assertion (A) is true, but Reason (R) is false.

When stick is dipped in water in slanting position. It appears short and bent at the surface of water. It is caused by the phenomenon of refraction of light.

Change in path of a light ray as it passes from one transparent medium to another transparent medium is called refraction of light.

15 Which one of the following statement is not correct?

(Chap 9, Class-XII, NCERT) (UPPSC Mains 2010)

(a) Mirage is an optical illusion arising due to total internal reflection of light.
(b) Concave mirrors are used in searchlights.
(c) In summer, white or light coloured clothes are preferred to dark coloured clothes generally.
(d) Convex mirror with a small aperture is used by doctors to examine, ear, nose or throat of a patient.

Ans. (d)

Exp. Among the given statements, statement in option (d) is incorrect.

Concave mirrors are used by ENT doctors to examine ear, nose and throat. They illuminate these organs by convergent beam of light reflected from a concave mirror and look them through a hole at the centre of the mirror.

16 The twinkling of a star is due to ...... of starlight.

(Chap 10, Class-X, NCERT) (BPSC Pre 2022)

(a) Tyndall effect
(b) atmospheric refraction
(c) Sonar
(d) dispersion

Ans. (b)

Exp. The twinkling of stars is due to atmospheric refraction of starlight. As, the light from the star enters the earth's atmosphere, it undergoes atmospheric refraction. Thus, the continuously changing atmosphere refracts the light by different amounts. In this way, the starlight reaching our eyes increases and decreases continuously and the star appears to twinkle at night .

17 Which of the following phenomena of light are involved in the formation of a rainbow?

(Chap 10, Class-X, NCERT)

(a) Reflection, refraction and dispersion
(b) Refraction, scattering and total internal reflection
(c) Refraction, dispersion and internal reflection
(d) Dispersion, scattering and total internal reflection

Ans. (c)

Exp. A rainbow is caused by dispersion, refraction and internal reflection of sunlight by tiny water droplets, present in the atmosphere and it is always formed in a direction opposite to that of the sun. The water droplets act like small prisms.

They refract and disperse the incident sunlight, then reflect it internally and finally refract it again when it comes out of the raindrop.

18 When light passes through a prism, it splits into its component colours. This phenomenon is called

(Chap 10, Class-X, NCERT) (Tripura PCS Pre 2023)

(a) spectrum
(b) reflection
(c) refraction
(d) dispersion

Ans. (d)

Exp. When white light passes through a prism, it splits into its component colour. This phenomenon is called dispersion.

In dispersion, white light splits into seven colours as violet, indigo, blue, green, yellow, orange and red.

19 Which of the following statement is correct regarding the propagation of light of different colours of white light in air? *(Chap 10, Class-X, NCERT)*

(a) Red light moves fastest.
(b) Blue light moves faster than green light.
(c) All the colours of the white light move with the same speed.
(d) Yellow light moves with the mean speed as that of the red and the violet light.

Ans. (c)

Exp. The propagation of light of different colours of white light in air or vacuum moves with the same speed but they have different wavelengths and frequencies. If light travels in any other medium, they travel with different speeds and bend thought different angles, which leads to the dispersion of light.

20 Consider the following Assertion (A) and Reason (R) and choose the correct code. *(Chap 9, Class-XII, NCERT)*

Assertion (A) The sky would appear black in the absence of atmosphere.

Reason (R) The colour of sky is blue due to scattering of light in atmosphere.

Codes
(a) Both A and R are true, and R is the correct explanation of A.
(b) Both A and R are true, but R is not the correct explanation of A.
(c) A is true, but R is false.
(d) A is false, but R is true.

Ans. (b)

Exp. Both Assertion (A) and Reason (R) are true, but Reason (R) is not the correct explanation of Assertion (A). The dust and air particles in the atmosphere are responsible for the scattering of light. Since, blue colour of light has least wavelength, so it is scattered the most and the sky appears blue. In the absence of atmosphere, no scattering will occur and hence sky will appear black.

21 A thin film of oil is spread over the surface of water. In sunlight beautiful colours are seen on the film due to *(Chap 10, Class-X, NCERT)*

(a) dispersion of light (b) polarisation of light
(c) interference of light (d) diffractions of light

Ans. (c)

Exp. A thin film of oil is spread over the surface of water. In sunlight beautiful colours are seen on the film due to interference of light.
The re-distribution of light intensity due to the superposition of two light waves is called interference of light.

22 Match the following List-I with List-II and choose the correct code given below. *(Chap 9, Class-XII, NCERT)*

	List-I (Object)		List-II (Nature of Power)
A.	Convex lens	1.	Zero
B.	Concave lens	2.	Positive
C.	Plane mirror	3.	Negative

Codes

	A	B	C		A	B	C
(a)	1	2	3	(b)	3	2	1
(c)	2	3	1	(d)	2	1	3

Ans. (c)

Exp. The correct matching is A-2, B-3, C-1.

Power of lens, $\text{Power} = \dfrac{1}{\text{Focal length}}$

Since, focal length of convex mirror is positive, hence power of convex lens is positive.
Since, focal length of concave mirror is negative, hence its power is negative. Since, focal length of plane mirror is infinite, hence its power will be zero.

23 A student is using a magnifying glass to burn paper in the school group. What type of lens is used in magnifying glass? *(Chap 9, Class-X, NCERT)*

(a) Concave lens (b) Plano-concave lens
(c) Convex lens (d) Convex mirror

Ans. (c)

Exp. Convex lens is used in magnifying glass because, using this, we can see an object much larger than it's actual size. When object is placed between focus and optical centre.

24 When an object is kept at infinity, the nature of the image formed by the convex lens is
(Class-XII, NCERT) (JKPSC Pre 2023)

1. Real
2. Inverted
3. Virtual
4. Upright

The correct answer(s) is/are
(a) 1 and 2 (b) 2 and 3
(c) 3 and 4 (d) All of these

Ans. (a)

Exp. When an object is kept at infinity, the nature of the image formed by the convex lens is real, inverted and very small in size.
The image formed by convex lens depends on the position of object, while the image formed by a concave lens is always virtual, erect and diminished.

25 Consider the following statements.
(Chap 9, Class-XII, NCERT)

1. A reflecting telescope utilises a convex mirror.
2. Large aperture of telescope is used for greater resolution.
3. In the human eye, the focusing is done by change in the convexity of the lens.

How many of the above statements are correct?
(a) Only one
(b) Only two
(c) All three
(d) None of the above

Ans. (b)

Exp. Only two Statements (2 and 3) are correct but one Statement (1) is incorrect.
Statement 1 In a reflecting telescope, only a concave mirror is used instead of the objective lens, because it helps to gather large amount of light coming from the object, due to which a sharper and clearer image of the distant object is formed.
Statement 2 Telescopes objective lenses have large apertures so that more number of light rays coming from object should enter and have greater resolution.
Statement 3 Due to change in refractive index of the eye, fluids eye can focus objects at different distances as focal length of a lens depends upon. Hence in the human eye, the focusing is done by change in the convexity of the lens.

26 Consider the following statements.
(Chap 9, Class-XII, NCERT)

Statement I In an astronomical telescope, the final image for normal vision is formed at infinity.

Statement II The magnifying power of telescope can be increased by increasing focal length of eye piece.

Which one of the following is correct in respect of the above statements?

(a) Both Statement I and Statement II are correct and Statement II is the correct explanation for Statement I.
(b) Both Statement I and Statement II are correct but Statement II is not the correct explanation for Statement I.
(c) Statement I is correct but Statement II is incorrect.
(d) Statement I is incorrect but Statement II is correct.

Ans. (c)

Exp. Statement I is correct but Statement II is incorrect.

The magnifying power of telescope

$$\therefore \quad M = \frac{f_0}{f_e}$$

M is increased by either by increasing f_0 or decreasing f_e or increasing power of eye piece.

27 **Consider the following statements.** ***(Chap 9, Class-XII, NCERT)***

Statement I When the object is close to the eye, the sharp image of the object is formed on the retina with decrease in the focal length of the eye lens.

Statement II In ciliary muscles, when the muscles contracts, the focal length of the eye lens increases.

Which one of the following is correct in respect of the above statements?

(a) Both Statement I and Statement II are correct and Statement II is the correct explanation for Statement I.
(b) Both Statement I and Statement II are correct but Statement II is not the correct explanation for Statement I.
(c) Statement I is correct but Statement II is incorrect.
(d) Statement I is incorrect but Statement II is correct.

Ans. (c)

Exp. Statement I is correct but Statement II is incorrect. When the ciliary muscles contracts, the eye lens becomes thick and therefore, decreases its focal length.

28 **Presbyopia occurs due to the** ***(Chap 9, Class-X, NCERT) (JKPSC Pre 2023)***

(a) Eyeball has become too small.
(b) elongation of the eyeball.
(c) gradual weakening of the ciliary muscles.
(d) excessive curvature of the eye lens.

Ans. (c)

Exp. Presbyopia occurs due to the gradual weakening of the ciliary muscles. In this defect, both near and far objects are not clearly visible. It is an old age disease and it is due to the loosing power of accommodation. It can be removed by using bifocal lens.

29 **Myopia and hypermetropia can be respectively corrected by** ***(Class-XII, NCERT) (RAS/RTS Pre 2023)***

(a) plano-concave and cylindrical lens
(b) convex and concave lens
(c) concave and convex lens
(d) concave and cylindrical lens

Ans. (c)

Exp. Myopia and hypermetropia can be respectively corrected by concave and convex lens.

In myopia, person can see only nearer objects but distant objects are not see clearly. In this defect, focal length or radius of curvature of eye lens decreases.

In hypermetropia, person can see distant objects clearly but nearer object are not clearly visible.

In this defect, the focal length or radius of curvature of eye lens increase.

30 **Which of the following defect can be removed by using a convex lens?** ***(Chap 10, Class-X, NCERT)***

(a) Myopia
(b) Hypermetropia
(c) Cataract
(d) None of the above

Ans. (b)

Exp. Hypermetropia can be removed by using a convex lens.

In hypermetropic defect, a person can see distant object but cannot see nearby object.

This defect arises due to following reasons

- Focal length of eye lens becomes large.
- Eyeball becomes too short, so that the image is formed behind retina.

31 **Consider the following statements.** ***(Chap 9, Class-XII, NCERT)***

1. To see the image with relaxed eye, the image must be formed at infinity.
2. For clear vision, the image must form at the distance of distinct vision, i.e. the near point.
3. A human eye which cannot see the far objects clearly, is said to suffer from a defect known as Myopia.

How many of the above statements is/are correct?

(a) Only one
(b) Only two
(c) All three
(d) None of these

Ans. (b)

Exp. Only two Statements (1 and 3) are correct but one Statement (2) is incorrect.

Statement 1 Although, the most comfortable distance for viewing an image is when it is at near point, it causes strain in the eye. So, the image formed at infinity is considered the most suitable distance for viewing an image by the relaxed eye.

Statement 2 For a clear vision, the image must be on the retina. The image distance is fixed for clear vision and it equals the distance of retina form eye lens.

Statement 3 A human eye which can not see distant objects clearly, is said to suffer from a defect known Myopia.

Chapter 13

Dual Nature of Radiation and Matter

Dual Nature of Radiation and Matter

Electron Emission

Dual Nature of Light

- Light behaves sometimes as a wave and sometimes as a particle. This behaviour of light is known as its dual nature of light.

Work Function

- The minimum energy required by an electron to escape from the metal surface.

Electron Emission

- The phenomenon of emission of electrons from the surface of metals.

Types of Electron Emission

- **Thermionic Emission** The process in which energy is supplied as heat to emit electron from metal surface. The emitted electrons are called thermions or thermal electrons.
- **Field Emission or Cold Cathode Emission** The process in which energy is supplied by applying an electric field to accelerate the electrons.
- **Photoelectric Emission** The process in which energy is supplied as light to emit the electrons.

Photoelectric Effect

Photoelectric Effect

- The phenomenon of emission of electrons from surface of metal, when radiations of suitable frequency fall on it.
- **Photoelectric Current**
  - The current which is produced due to the emission of electrons in photoelectric effect.
  - The photocurrent is directly proportional to the number of photoelectrons emitted per second.
- **Threshold Frequency** The minimum frequency of light which can emit photoelectrons from a material.

Einstein's Photoelectric Equation

- In photoelectric effect, an electron absorbs a quantum of energy ($h\nu$) of radiation. If this quantum of energy absorbed exceeds the minimum energy needed for the electron to escape from the metal surface, the electron is emitted with maximum kinetic energy which is given by

$$K_{max} = h\nu - \phi$$

- This called Einstein's photoelectric equation.

Photon and Photocell

Photon : Particle Nature of Light

- Photoelectric effect, gave evidence that light consists of packets-of energy. These packets of energy are called light quantum that are associated with particles named as photons.

Wave Nature of Matter

- The French scientist, Louis Victor de-Broglie suggested that the particles like electrons, protons, neutrons, etc. have dual nature that is they can have particle as well as wave nature.
- According to de-Broglie, the wave associated with moving particle is called matter wave or de-Broglie wave. These waves can travel in vacuum hence, they are not mechanical waves.

Photocell

- A device which converts light energy into electrical energy. As, the photoelectric current sets up in the photoelectric cell corresponding to incident light, it provides the information about the objects.

SOURCE *New NCERT Class XII Chap 11* (*Dual Nature of Radiation and Matter*)

1 **Electron emission from a metallic surface is possible only, when a frequency of the incident light is** *(Chap 11, Class-XII, NCERT)*

(a) half of the threshold frequency.
(b) one-third of the threshold frequency.
(c) slightly smaller than threshold frequency.
(d) greater than the threshold frequency.

Ans. (d)

Exp. Electron emission from a metallic surface is possible only, when a frequency of the incident light is greater than the threshold frequency.
The minimum frequency of light which can emit photoelectrons from a material is called the threshold frequency of that material.

2 **Consider the following statements.** *(Chap 11, Class-XII, NCERT)*

1. The phenomena of interference, diffraction and polarisation can be best explained by wave nature of light.
2. The photoelectric effect and compton effect can be understand by the particle nature of light.
3. Light has dual nature, whether a particle or wave description is best suited for understanding an experiment depends on the nature of the experiment.

How many of the above statement(s) is/are correct?
(a) Only one (b) Only two
(c) All three (d) None of these

Ans. (c)

Exp. All three statements (1, 2 and 3) are correct.
The wave nature of light shows up in the phenomena of interference, diffraction and polarisation. On the other hand, in photoelectric effect and compton effect which involve energy and momentum transfer, light behaves as if it is made up of a bunch of particles i.e., the photons. So, we can say light has a dual nature but it depends on the nature of the experiment, whether a particle or wave description is best suited for understanding an experiment.

3 **Due to temperature variation along a conductor, potential variation occurs along it. This phenomenon is known as** *(Chap 11, Class-XII, NCERT)* *(BPSC (Pre) Re-exam 2022)*

(a) Thomson effect
(b) Joule effect
(c) Seebeck effect
(d) Peltier effect

Ans. (a)

Exp. When a current flows through an unequal heated conductor, heat is evolved or absorbed along the length of the conductor, depending on the direction of flow of current. This effect is called the Thomson effect. This effect is reversible.

4 **Consider the following statements.** *(Chap 11, Class-XII, NCERT)*

1. Photo-cell can be used for the reproduction of sound.
2. Photo-cell can be used as a counting device.
3. Photo-cell can be used in burglar's alarm.

Which of the statements given above are correct?
(a) 1 and 2 (b) 2 and 3 (c) 1 and 3 (d) 1, 2 and 3

Ans. (d)

Exp. All the statements (1), (2) and (3) are correct.
In cinematography, photo-cells are used for the reproduction of sound. Photo-cells can be used in counting devices. It can also be used in burglar's alarm. When a person approaching a doorway interrupts the beam of invisible UV light falling on a photo-cell, the sudden change in photoelectric current starts a device which opens the door or rings an alarm.

5 **Consider the following statements.** *(Chap 11, Class-XII, NCERT)*

1. Photoelectrons are emitted from an emitter surface. only if, the frequency of the incident light is greater than the threshold frequency.
2. Photoelectric current is directly proportional to the intensity of the incident radiations.
3. Photoelectric current is measure with microammeter which is connected in parallel.

How many of the above statements are correct?
(a) Only one
(b) Only two
(c) Only three
(d) None of the above

Ans. (b)

Exp. Only two statements (1 and 2) are correct but one statement (3) is incorrect.
The phenomenon of emission of the electrons from a material caused by the light (electromagnetic radiation). Electrons emitted in this manner are called photoelectrons and the surface on which light falls is emitter surface.
These photelectrons are emitted from an emitter surface, only if, the frequency of the incident light is greater than the threshold frequency. Flow of photoelectrons constitutes photoelectric current which is directly proportional to the intensity of the incident light and this current is measured with microammeter, connected in series.

6 **Consider the following statements.** *(Chap 11, Class-XII, NCERT)*

Statement I The process of photoelectric emission is instantaneous.

Statement II Photoelectric current does not depends upon the intensity of incident light.

Which one of the following is correct in respect of the above statements?

(a) Both Statement I and Statement II are correct and Statement II is the correct explanation for Statement I.
(b) Both Statement I and Statement II are correct but Statement II is not the correct explanation for Statement I.
(c) Statement I is correct but Statement II is incorrect.
(d) Statement I is incorrect but Statement II is correct.

Ans. (c)

Exp. Statement I is correct but Statement II is incorrect. The photoelectric effect is an instantaneous phenomenon. There is no time delay between the incidence of light and emission of photoelectrons from the emitter surface i.e., metal surface.

The number of photoelectrons emitted is proportional to the intensity of incident light. These photoelectrons emitted from the metal surface constitutes photoelectric current. Thus, this current depends upon the intensity of incident light.

7 In the photoelectric effect, electrons are emitted

(Class 11, Class-XII, NCERT)

(a) at a rate that is independent of the emitter.
(b) at a rate that is proportional to the square of the amplitude of the incident radiation.
(c) with a maximum velocity proportional to the frequency of the incident radiation.
(d) only if, the frequency of the incident radiation is above a certain threshold value.

Ans. (d)

Exp. The work function of metal surface is a property that determines the rate of emission of electrons and the rate of emission is dependent on the frequency of incident radiation. The velocity of the photoelectrons is dependent on the energy of photon that falls on the metal surface. And electrons will be emitted only if, the frequency of the incident radiation is above a certain threshold value called threshold frequency.

8 A photon of frequency ν has a momentum associated with it. If c is the velocity of light, this momentum is

(Chap 11, Class -XII, NCERT)

(a) $\frac{h\nu}{c^2}$ (b) $\frac{h\nu}{c}$ (c) $\frac{\nu}{c}$ (d) $h\nu c$

Ans. (b)

Exp. The energy of photon is given by, $E = h\nu$ ...(i)

($h \rightarrow$ Planck's constant, $\nu \rightarrow$ frequency of wave)

We have also the relation between energy and momentum.

$$E = pc$$

($p \rightarrow$ momentum of photon, $c \rightarrow$ speed of light)

Combining the two equations, we get

$$h\nu = pc$$

$$\Rightarrow \quad p = \frac{h\nu}{c}$$

9 The maximum kinetic energy of the emitted photoelectrons depends upon

(Chap 11, Class-XII, NCERT)

(a) the frequency of the incident light
(b) the velocity of incident light photon
(c) the intensity of incident light
(d) the voltage applied between the electrodes of photo cell

Ans. (a)

Exp. Einstein's photoelectric effect equation is

$$E = w_0 + (\text{kinetic energy})_{\text{max}} \quad ...(i)$$

where, $E = h\nu_{\text{photon}}$ = energy of incident photon

$w_0 = h\nu_0$ = energy required to eject an electron.

We can see in Eq. (i), that kinetic energy (KE) is dependent on the frequency of the incident light.

10 Consider the following statements.

(Chap 11, Class-XII, NCERT)

Statement I Photolelectric effect gave evidence that light consists of packets of energy.

Statement II Photons can deflected by electric and magnetic fields.

Which one of the following is correct in respect of the above statements?

(a) Both Statement I and Statement II are correct and Statement II is the correct explanation for Statement I.
(b) Both Statement I and Statement II are correct but Statement II is not the correct explanation for Statement I.
(c) Statement I is correct but Statement II is incorrect.
(d) Statement I is incorrect but Statement II is correct.

Ans. (c)

Exp. Statement I is correct but Statement II is incorrect.

Photons cannot deflected by electric and magnetic fields because if you connect one of the photon lines to a real electron, you get the diagram that describes the splitting of a photon due to interaction with a charge.

11 Consider the following statements.

(Chap 11, Class-XII, NCERT)

1. In photoelectric effect, an electron absorbs a quantum of energy ($h\nu$) of radiation.
2. Each photon has energy $E(= h\nu)$ and momentum $p = \left(\frac{h\nu}{c}\right)$
3. In a photon-particle, the total energy and momentum are not conserved.

How many of the above statements are incorrect?

(a) Only one (b) Only two
(c) All three (d) None of these

Ans. (b)

Exp. Only one statement (3) is incorrect because in a photon-particle, the total energy and momentum are conserved.

12 Consider the following statements.
(Chap 11, Class-XII, NCERT)

Statement I The photocurrent is directly proportional to the number of photoelectrons emitted per second.

Statement II Above the threshold frequency, the maximum kinetic energy of the emitted photoelectrons does not depend upon frequency of the incident light.

Which one of the following is correct in respect of the above statements?

(a) Both Statement I and Statement II are correct and Statement II is the correct explanation for Statement I.
(b) Both Statement I and Statement II are correct but Statement II is not the correct explanation for Statement I.
(c) Statement I is correct but Statement II is incorrect.
(d) Statement I is incorrect but Statement II is correct.

Ans. (c)

Exp. Statement I is correct but Statement II is incorrect. The maximum kinetic energy depends upon frequency of the incident light.

Photoelectric current is directly proportional to the number of photoelectrons emitted per second. So, the number of photoelectrons emitted per second is directly proportional to the intensity of the incident radiations.

13 In the phenomenon of electric discharge through gases at low pressure, the coloured glow in the tube appears as a result of *(Chap 11, Class-XII, NCERT)*

(a) excitation of electrons in the atoms
(b) collision between the atoms of the gas
(c) collision between the changed particles emitted from the cathode and the atoms of the gas
(d) collision between different electrons of the atoms of the gas

Ans. (c)

Exp. Collisions between the charged particles emitted from the cathode and the atoms of the gas.

When a sufficient voltage is applied in a discharged tube, the gas dissipates and becomes conducting. In the discharge tube collision between charged particles emitted from the cathode and atoms of the gas takes place and form cathode rays which on striking on the walls give a fluorescence effect.

14 Consider the following statements.
(Chap 11, Class-XII, NCERT)

1. As the intensity of incident light increases photo electric current decreases.
2. The stopping potential (v_0) is independent of the intensity of the incident light.
3. When light falls on a metal surface the maximum kinetic energy of the emitted photo- electrons depends upon frequency of the incident light

How many of the above statement(s) is/ are correct?

(a) Only one (b) Only two (c) All three (d) None of these

Ans. (b)

Exp. Only two statements (2 and 3) are correct but one statement (1) is incorrect.

Statement 1 Intensity increases means more photons of same energy will emit more electrons of the same energy, hence only photoelectric current increases.

Statement 2 Stopping potential is independent of the intansity of the incident light.

Statement 3 When light falls on metal surface, the maximum kinetic energy of the emitted photo-electrons depends upon the frequency of the incident light.

As we know, $K_{max} = (h\nu - Wo)$

ν = frequency of incident light

15 If an electron and a photon propagate in the form of waves having the same wavelength, it implies that they have the same *(Chap 11, Class-XII, NCERT)*

(a) energy (b) momentum
(c) velocity (d) angular momentum

Ans. (b)

Exp. The de-Broglie wavelength of a particle or a photon is given by $\lambda = h/p$, where h is the planck's constant and p is the momentum.

As the electron and the photon are having the same wavelength the momentum of both of them will be the same.

16 When the kinetic energy of an electron is increased, the wavelength of the associated wave will?

(a) Increase *(Chap 11, Class-XII, NCERT)*
(b) Decrease
(c) Wavelength does not depend on the kinetic energy
(d) None of the above

Ans. (b)

Exp. We know that

$$\lambda = \frac{h}{p} = \frac{h}{\sqrt{2mE}}$$

$$\therefore \quad \lambda \propto \frac{1}{E} \text{ (as } h \text{ and } m \text{ will be constants)}$$

So, when the kinetic energy of electron increases the wavelength associated with it decreases.

17 According to de-Broglie, the de-Broglie wavelength for electron in an orbit of hydrogen atom is 10^{-9} m. The principle quantum number for this electron is *(Chap 11, Class-XII, NCERT)*

(a) 1 (b) 2 (c) 3 (d) 4

Ans. (c)

Exp. As we know,

$$2\pi rn = \lambda$$

$$n = \frac{\lambda}{2\pi r} = \frac{10^{-9}}{2\times 3.14\times 5.13\times 10^{-11}} = 3$$

18 **Statement I** Photo electrons are emitted from an emitter surface only if the frequency of the incident light is greater than the threshold frequency.

Statement II The intensity of incident radiation affect the stopping potential. *(Chap 11, Class-XII, NCERT)*

Which one of the following is correct in respect of the above statements?

(a) Both Statement I and Statement II are correct and statement II is the correct explanation for Statement I.

(b) Both Statement I and Statement II are correct but Statement II is not the correct explanation for statement I.

(c) Statement I is correct but Statement II is incorrect.

(d) Statement I is incorrect but Statement II is correct.

Ans. (c)

Exp. Statement I is correct but Statement II is incorrect. The stopping potential does not depends upon the intensity of the incident light.

Changing the intensity of incident radiation does not affect the stopping potential.

19 **According to Einstein's photoelectric equation the graph between the kinetic energy of photoelectrons ejected and the frequency of incident radiation is** *(Chap 11, Class-XII, NCERT)*

(a) 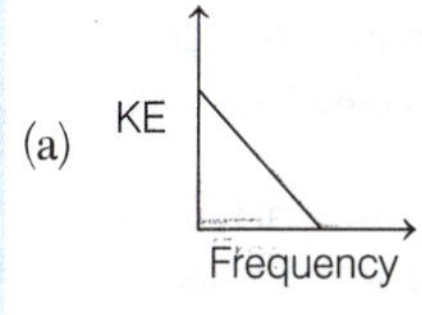

(b) KE Frequency

(c) 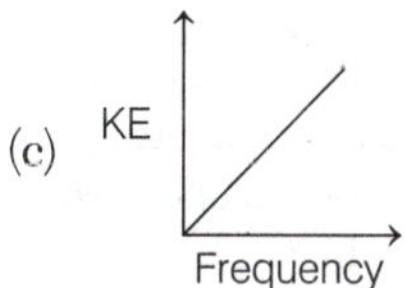

(d) KE Frequency

Ans. (d)

Exp. from Eienstein's photoelectric equation

$$hv = W + \text{KE}$$

$$hv - W = \text{KE}$$

above equation is in the form of $\gamma = mx - c$

Hence, straight line with negative λ – intercept

20 **Statement I** The minimum wavelength of X-rays produced by electrons accelerated through a potential difference of V volt is directly proportional to $1/V$

Statement II In an X-rays tube, the intensity of the emitted X-rays beam is decreased by increasing the filament current. *(Chap 11, Class-XII, NCERT)*

Which one the following is correct in respect of the above statement?

(a) Both Statement I and Statement II are correct and statement II is the correct explanation for Statement I.

(b) Both Statement I and Statement II are correct but Statement II is not the correct explanation for statement I.

(c) Statement I is correct but Statement II is incorrect.

(d) Statement I is incorrect but Statement II is correct.

Ans. (c)

Exp. Statement I is correct but Statement II is incorrect. In an X-rays tube, the intensity of the emitted X-rays beam in increased by increasing the filament current because if we increase the filament current, the temperature of the filament rises and so the number of thermionic electrons emitted per second increases.

21 **The shortest wavelength of X-rays emitted from an x-ray tube depends on the** *(Chap 11, Class-XII, NCERT)*

(a) current in the tube

(b) voltage applied to the tube

(c) nature of gas in the tube

(d) atomic number of target material

Ans. (b)

Exp. Shortest wavelength or cut off wavelength depends only open the voltage applied in the Coolidge tube

22 **Statement I** The energy E and momentum p of a photon are related by $p = E/c$ *(Chap 11, Class-XII, NCERT)*

Statement II The photon behaves like a particle

Which one of the following is correct in respect of the above statement?

(a) Both Statement I and Statement II are correct and statement II is the correct explanation for Statement I.

(b) Both Statement I and Statement II are correct but Statement II is not the correct explanation for statement I.

(c) Statement I is correct but Statement II is incorrect.

(d) Statement I is incorrect but Statement II is correct.

Ans. (a)

Exp. Both Statement I and Statement II are correct and statement II is the correct explanation for Statement I.

Momentum of a photon is given by

$$p = \frac{h}{\lambda}$$

Also the photon is a form of energy pack etc, behave as a particle having energy

$$E = \frac{hc}{\lambda}$$

So, $$p = \frac{E}{c}$$

Chapter 14

Semiconductor Electronics

Semiconductor Electronics

Energy Band and Types of Solids

Solid

- A solid object has the tendency of maintaining a defined shape and volume due to strong intermolecular force.

Energy Band

- The energy band are the set of energy levels in the solids which are formed due to the informing of atoms.
- The energy band, which includes the energy levels of the valence electrons is called valence band.
- The energy band above the valence band is called conduction band.
- The minimum energy required for shifting electrons from valence band to conduction band is called energy band gap.

Types of Solids

- **Conductor** The substance in which the electrons can easily flow. e.g. Silver, gold etc.
- **Insulator** These substances in which electrical conduction is not possible. e.g. Rubber, ebonite, glass etc.
- **Semiconductor** The material whose conductivity lie between metals and insulator. e.g. Silicon and Germanium

Types of Semiconductors

Intrinsic Semiconductors

- A pure semiconductor without an significant presence of dopant species.
- This type of semiconductor is also called an undoped semiconductor.
- Pure germanium silicon in their nature state are intrinsic semiconductor.

Extrinsic Semiconductor

A semiconductor which is doped with a suitable impurity to increases its conductivity.

- ***n*-type semiconductors** Extrinsic semiconductor which is doped with pentavalent impurity like antimony, phosphorus or arsenic in which negatively charged electrons work as charge carrier.
  - Every pentavalent impurity atoms donates one electron into the crystal, therefore it is called a donar atom.
- ***p*-type semiconductors** Extrinsic semiconductor which is doped with trivalent impurity like boron, aluminium, gallium or indium in which positively charged work as charge carrier.
  - Every trivalent impurity atom has a tendency to accept one electron, therefore it is called an accepter atom.

Semiconductor Diode

Semiconductor Diode

- A semiconductor diode is basically a *p-n* junction with metallic contacts provided at the ends for the application of an external voltage.
- **Zener Diode** It is a highly doped *p-n* junction diode which is not damaged by high reverse current.
- It is designed to operate under reverse bias in the breakdown region and used as a voltage regulator.
- **Photodiode** A special type of junction diode which is used for detecting optical signals.
  - A photodiode fabricated with a transparent cover to allow light to fall on the diode and operated under reverse bias.
- **Light-Emitting Diode (LED)** A heavily doped *p-n* junction which under forward bias emits spontaneous radiation. The diode is covered with a transparent cover, so that emitted light can come out. It converts electrical energy into light energy.

SOURCE *New NCERT Class XII Chap 14 (Semiconductor Electronics : Materials, Devices and Simple Circuits)*

1 **Consider the following statements.**

(Chap 14, Class-XII, NCERT)

Statement I If Arsenic is doped to Silicon, then its conductivity increases.

Statement II In an intrinsic semiconductor, number of electrons and holes at room temperature are zero.

Which one of the following is correct in respect of the above statements?

(a) Both Statement I and Statement II are correct and Statement II is the correct explanation for Statement I.
(b) Both Statement I and Statement II are correct but Statement II is not the correct explanation for Statement I.
(c) Statement I is correct but Statement II is incorrect.
(d) Statement I is incorrect but Statement II is correct.

Ans. (c)

Exp. Statement I is correct but Statement II is incorrect.
At room temperature, due to thermal vibrations, the few bonds of intrinsic semiconductor are broken and producing equal number of electrons and holes in the semiconductor.

2 **Which one of the following metals is used as semiconductor in transistors?**

(Chap 14, Class-XII, NCERT) (BPSC Pre 2000)

(a) Copper (b) Germanium (c) Graphite (d) Silver

Ans. (b)

Exp. Germanium and silicon are the main elements which are used as a semiconductor in transistors. Their conductivity at the room temperature (normal) lies between the conductivity of conductors and insulators.

3 **Germanium is better conductor than silicon in terms of performance but still silicon is largely used because** *(Chap 14, Class-XII, NCERT)*

(a) it has small size.
(b) silicon required low processing.
(c) silicon has high electron density.
(d) silicon is readily available.

Ans. (d)

Exp. Germanium is better conductor than silicon in terms of performance but still silicon is largely used because silicon is readily available. Therefore, manufacturing and processing cost of silicon is lower than germanium.

4 **Read the following statements regarding semiconductors.** *(Chap 14, Class-XII, NCERT)*

1. Conductivity of semiconductor increases upon increasing temperature.
2. Resistivity of semiconductor increases upon increasing temperature.

Which of the statements given above is/are incorrect?

(a) Only 1 (b) Only 2
(c) Both 1 and 2 (d) None of these

Ans. (b)

Exp. Statement (2) is incorrect regarding semiconductors because resistivity of semiconductor decreases upon increasing temperature.
and semiconductors have negative temperature coefficient.
A pure semiconductor is an insulator because the valence band is full and there are no free electrons in the conduction band.

5 **Consider the following statements.**

(Chap 14, Class-XII, NCERT)

Statement I If the temperature of a semiconductor is increased, then its resistance decreases.

Statement II The energy gap between conduction band and valence band is very small.

Which one of the following is correct in respect of the above statements?

(a) Both Statement I and Statement II are correct and Statement II is the correct explanation for Statement I.
(b) Both Statement I and Statement II are correct but Statement II is not the correct explanation for Statement I.
(c) Statement I is correct but Statement II is incorrect.
(d) Statement I is incorrect but Statement II is correct.

Ans. (a)

Exp. Both Statement I and Statement II are correct and Statement II is the correct explanation for Statement I.
In semiconductors, the energy gap between conduction band and valence band is small (1 eV). Due to temperature rise, electrons in the valence band gain thermal energy and may jump across the small energy gap. Thus, conductivity increases and hence, resistance increases.

6 **Electric conduction in a semiconductor takes place due to** *(Chap 14, Class-XII, NCERT) (UKPSC Pre 2016)*

(a) electrons only
(b) holes only
(c) Both electrons and holes
(d) Neither electron nor holes

Ans. (c)

Exp. Electric conduction in a semiconductor takes place due to both electrons and holes.
Higher the temperature, larger is the number of electron-hole-pairs produced. When an electric field is applied to the crystal, the free electrons in the conduction band move in a direction opposite to the field , and the holes in the valence band move in a direction opposite to the field, both giving rise to electric currents. Thus, in a semiconductor, electrons and holes both constitute currents.

7 **The conductivity of a semiconductor at zero kelvin is**

(Chap 14, Class-XII, NCERT)

(a) 10^5 ohm (b) 10^{-1} ohm
(c) 10^{-5} ohm (d) zero

Ans. (d)

Exp. The conductivity of a semiconductor at zero kelvin is zero. The materials (Germanium, Silicon) whose electrical conductivity vary between conductors and dielectric are called semiconductors. At absolute zero temperature, a semiconductor behaves like a perfect dielectric.

8 Consider the following statements. *(Chap 14, Class-XII, NCERT)*

1. In a semiconductor, the uppermost band is the valence band.
2. All semiconductors are electrically neutral.
3. With increase of temperature, the resistivity of a semiconductor decreases.
4. Addition of a small amount of impurity of a III or V group elements to a pure semiconductor increases its resistivity.

Which of the statements given above are correct?

(a) 1 and 2 (b) 2 and 3
(c) 3 and 4 (d) 1 and 4

Ans. (b)

Exp. Statements (2) and (3) are correct.

All semiconductors are electrically neutral and with rise in temperature, number of electrons jump to conduction band which increases in conductivity and thus, decreases resistivity.

Statements (1) and (4) are incorrect.

In a semiconductor, uppermost band is the conduction band. Addition of small amount of impurity of a III or V group elements to a pure semiconductor decreases its resistivity.

9 Which of the following is an example of inorganic semiconductor? *(Chap 14, Class-XII, NCERT)*

(a) Gallium arsenide
(b) Polypyrrole
(c) Anthracene
(d) All of the above

Ans. (a)

Exp. Gallium arsenide is an example of inorganic semiconductor, with a zinc blende crystal structure. It has various applications and used for fast electronics, solar cells and LEDs.

10 Holes are majority charge carriers in *(Chap 14, Class-XII, NCERT)*

(a) intrinsic semiconductor
(b) *n*-type semiconductor
(c) *p*-type semiconductor
(d) diode

Ans. (c)

Exp. In a *p*-type semiconductor, the holes are majority carriers and *p*-type semiconductor is the one that is formed by doping trivalent impurity (boron, aluminium, gallium or indium) in pure semiconductor.

In the *p*-type semiconductor, holes are majority charge carriers and electrons are minority charge carriers.

11 The charge carriers in an *n*-type semiconductor are *(Chap 14, Class-XII, NCERT)*

(a) electrons only.
(b) equal number of electrons and holes.
(c) large number of electrons and smaller number of holes.
(d) large number of holes and smaller number of electrons.

Ans. (c)

Exp. The charge carriers in an *n*-type semiconductor are large number of electrons and smaller number of holes. *n*-type semiconductor is the one that is formed by doping pentavalent impurity (antimony, phosphorus and arsenic) in pure semiconductor.

12 Consider the following Assertion (A) and Reason (R) and choose the correct code. *(Chap 14, Class-XII, NCERT)*

Assertion (A) An *n*-type semiconductor is negatively charged.

Reason (R) Atoms are electrically neutral and addition of two different atoms are also electrically neutral.

Codes

(a) Both A and R are true and R is the correct explanation of A.
(b) Both A and R are true, but R is not the correct explanation of A.
(c) A is true, but R is false.
(d) A is false, but R is true.

Ans. (d)

Exp. Assertion (A) is false, but Reason (R) is true.

As atoms are electrically neutral and addition of two atoms also electrically neutral. Therefore, in doping process both *p*-type and *n*-type semiconductors are electrically neutral.

13 Match the following lists and choose the correct code. *(Chap 14, Class-XII, NCERT)*

List I	List II
A. Germanium at 0K	1. *n*-type semiconductor
B. Germanium at room temperature	2. *p*-type semiconductor
C. Germanium doped with indium	3. Insulator
D. Germanium doped with arsenic	4. Intrinsic semiconductor

Codes

	A	B	C	D		A	B	C	D
(a)	1	2	3	4	(b)	4	3	2	1
(c)	3	4	2	1	(d)	4	3	1	2

Ans. (c)

Exp. The correct matching is A-3, B-4, C-2, D-1.

Germanium at 0K is an insulator as there is no change in carriers present for conduction. But at room temperature, some bonds break and it becomes intrinsic semiconductor.

Doping of germanium with indium (trivalent) atom makes it a *p*-type semiconductor while doping with arsenic (pentavalent) atom makes it *n*-type semiconductor.

14 **Consider the following statements.**

(Chap 14, Class-XII, NCERT)

1. The depletion layer in the *p-n* junction region is caused by diffusion of charge carriers.
2. The function diode offers a high resistance for the current to flow in reverse bias.
3. In insulators, the conduction band is empty and the valence band is filled with electrons.

How many of the above statements are correct?

(a) Only one (b) Only two
(c) All three (d) None of these

Ans. (c)

Exp. All three statements (1, 2 and 3) are correct.

Statement 1 The depletion layer in the p-n junction region is caused by diffusion of carriers because depletion layer is formed due to the diffusion of electrons and holes in a *p-n* junction diode.

Statement 2 The function diode offers a high resistance for the current to flow in reverse bias.

Statement 3 In an insulator, there exists a large band gap between the conduction band and valence band. The valence band is fully filled with electrons. There are no electrons in the conduction band, and therefore, no electrical conduction is possible.

15 **Consider the following statements.**

(Chap 14, Class-XII, NCERT)

1. Conductivity of a semiconductor increases with the increase in temperature.
2. Resistance of a semiconductor increases with the increase in temperature.
3. Conductivity of a conductor increase with the decrease in temperature.

How many of the above statements are correct?

(a) Only one
(b) Only two
(c) All three
(d) None of the above

Ans. (a)

Exp. Only one statement (1) is correct but two statements (2 and 3) are incorrect.

Statement 1 The electrical conductivity of semiconductors increases with increasing temperature because with increase in temperature, number of electrons from the valence bond can jump to the conduction band in semiconductors.

Statement 2 In a semiconductor, as the temperature increases, the electrons get excited and jump from the valence band into the conduction band and thereby, increases conductance resulting in the decrease of the resistance.

Hence, on increasing temperature, the resistance of semiconductor decreases.

Statement 3 The conductivity of semiconductors increases (or resistance decreases) with rise in temperature.

16 **Consider the following statements.**

(Chap 14, Class-XII, NCERT)

Statement I When two semiconductors of *p*-type and *n*-type are brought in contact, they form *p-n* junction which act like a rectifier.

Statement II A rectifier is used to convert alternating current into direct current.

Which one of the following is correct in respect of the above statements?

(a) Both Statement I and Statement II are correct and Statement II is the correct explanation for Statement I.
(b) Both Statement I and Statement II are correct but Statement II is not the correct explanation for Statement I.
(c) Statement I is correct but Statement II is incorrect.
(d) Statement I is incorrect but Statement II is correct.

Ans. (b)

Exp. Both Statement I and Statement II are correct but Statement II is not the correct explanation for Statement I.

Study of junction diode characteristics shows that the junction diode offers a low resistance path, when forward biased and high resistance path when reverse biased. This feature of the junction diode enables it to be used as a rectifier.

17 **Consider the following statements about difference between a CFL and an LED lamp.**

(Chap 14, Class-XII, NCERT) (IAS Pre 2011)

1. To produce light, a CFL used mercury vapour and phosphor while an LED lamp uses semiconductor material.
2. The average life span of a CFL is much longer than that of an LED lamp.
3. A CFL is less energy-efficient as compared to an LED lamp.

Which of the statement (s) given above is/are correct?

(a) Only 1 (b) 2 and 3 (c) 1 and 3 (d) 1, 2 and 3

Ans. (c)

Exp. Statements (1) and (3) are correct about difference between a CFL and an LED lamp. CFL uses mercury vapour and phosphor to produce light. The gases become excited by electricity and when combined with mercury particles, produces invisible ultraviolet light. The UV light then hits the white phosphor coating inside the bulb causing it to fluorescence and emit white light.

LED lamps use semiconductor material to produce light. LED lamps are more energy efficient as compared to CFL.

LED is an important light source used in optical communication and it is based on the principle of conservation of biasing electricity into light.

Statement (2) is incorrect because the average life span of an LED lamp is much longer than that of a CFL. CFLs have a life of about 6000 to 10000 h, while LED has a life span of about 50000 hours.

Chapter 15

Stars and Solar System

Stars and Solar System

Celestial Bodies and Constellations

Celestial Bodies

- The bodies that are found in the universe. These include planets, moons, satellites, meteoroids, stars, galaxies etc.
- **Moon** is a natural satellite of Earth. It revolves around the Earth on a regular path.
  - The gravitational attraction between the Earth and the natural satellite holds it in its orbit even as the Moon revolves around the Earth.
- **The Stars** Celestial objects that are extremely hot and have light of their own. Stars emit heat and light continuously.
- The sun is also a star which is nearest to the earth.
- The sun appears much bigger and brighter because it is much nearer to us than only other star.

Constellations

- The stars forming a group that has a recognisable shape of animals, human beings or other objects.
- Each constellation is signified by an animal, a human being or some other object which it appears to resemble.
- Constellations seem to move in the sky from East to West.

Solar System

Solar System

- The Sun and the celestial bodies which revolve around it from the solar system.
- It consists of large number of bodies such as planets, comets, asteroids and meteors.
  - **Sun** The sun is the nearest star from us. It is continuously emitting huge amounts of heat and light.
  - **Mercury (Budh)** The planet mercury is nearest to the sun. It is the smallest planet of our solar system.
  - **Venus (Shukra)** Venus is Earth's nearest planetary neighbour, it is the brightest planet in the night sky.
  - **The Earth (Prithvi)** The earth is the only planet in the solar system on which life is known to exist.
  - **Mars (Mangal)** The next planet, the first outside the orbit of the earth is mars, it appears slightly reddish.
  - **Jupiter (Brihaspati)** Jupiter is the largest planet of the solar system. It is so large that about 1300 earth can be placed inside this giant planet.
  - **Saturn (Shani)** The sixth planet from the sun is saturn which is the second largest planet of the solar system.
  - **Uranus (Indra)** Uranus is the seventh planet from the sun.
  - **Neptune (Varun)** Neptune is the eighth planet from the sun.

Other Members of the Solar System

Asteroids

- There is a large gap in between the orbits of mars and jupiter.
- This gap is occupied by a large number of small objects that revolve around the Sun.
- Asteroids can only be seen through large telescopes.

Meteors and Meteorites

- A meteor is usually a small object that occasionally enters the earth's atmosphere. At that time it has a very high speed.
- The friction due to the atmosphere heats it up. It glows and evaporates quickly.
- That is why, the bright steak lasts for a very short time.
- Some meteors are large and so they can reach the earth before they evaporate completely.
- The body that reaches the earth is called the meteorite.
- Meteorites help scientists in investigating the nature of the material from which the

SOURCE *Old NCERT Class VIII (Stars and the Solar system)*

1 Consider the following statements.
(Chap 17, Class-VIII, NCERT)

1. Asteroids are rocky debris of varying sizes orbiting the sun.
2. Most of the asteroids are small but some have diameter as large as 1000 km.
3. The orbit of asteroids lies between orbits of Jupiter and Saturn.

How many of the above statements are correct?

(a) Only one (b) Only two
(c) All three (d) None of these

Ans. (b)

Exp. Only two statements (1 and 2) are correct but only one statement (3) is incorrect.

Statement 1 As asteroids are indeed rocky debris of varying sizes that orbit the sun. They are remnants from the early solar system and can range in size.

Statement 2 While most of the asteroids are small, some of them can indeed be large with diameters up to 1000 km.

Statement 3 The main region where asteroids are found is not between the orbits of Jupiter and Saturn, but mostly situated in an area of space called the asteroid belt, which lies between the orbits of Mars and Jupiter.

2 Usually sky of big cities is not so clear as village's sky in the night because *(Chap 17, Class-VIII, NCERT)*

(a) big cities have more energy consumption.
(b) big cities have bright light smoke and dust.
(c) big cities have less trees.
(d) area of big cities is larger than the area of village.

Ans. (b)

Exp. Sky of big cities is not so clear as village's sky in the night because big cities have bright light smoke and dust. These circumstances produce light pollution and therefore, less stars are visible in big cities.

3 Consider the following statements.
(Chap 17, Class-VIII, NCERT)

1. The day on which the whole disc of the moon is visible is known as the new moon day.
2. After full moon day, every light the size of the bright part of the moon appears to become thinner and thinner.
3. The various shapes of the bright part of the moon as seen during a month are called phases of the moon.

Which of the above statement (s) is/are correct?

(a) Only 1 (b) Both 2 and 3 (c) Only 3 (d) Both 1 and 2

Ans (b)

Exp. Statement (1) is incorrect and Statements (2) and (3) are correct. We know that, the day on which the whole disc of the moon is visible is known as the full moon day. Thereafter, the size of the bright part of the moon appears to become thinner and thinner. On the fifteenth day, the moon is not visible to us. This day is known as the new moon day. It is a fact that various shapes of the bright part of the moon as seen during a month are called phases of the moon.

4 The phases of moon we see every night differ from each other. They are due to *(Chap 17, Class-VIII, NCERT)*

(a) revolution of the Moon around the Earth.
(b) rotation of the moon on its own axis.
(c) the amount of light it receives from the Sun.
(d) All of thc abovc

Ans. (a)

Exp. The phases of the moon we see every night differ from each other due to revolution of the moon around the Earth. The various shapes of the bright part of the moon as seen during a month are called phases of the moon. As the moon has no light of its own, so it shines and becomes visible to us because it reflects sunlight falling on it towards the Earth.

Since, the moon revolves around the Earth and the Earth revolves around the Sun, so we cannot see all of the sunlit surface of moon from the Earth all the time. That is why we only able to see that part of the sunlit surface of moon which is towards us.

5 Which of the following statement(s) is/are correct?
(Chap 17, Class-VIII, NCERT)

1. The size of the illuminated part of the moon visible from the Earth increases each day after the new moon day.
2. After the full moon day, the sunlit part of the moon visible from the Earth decreases in size every day.
3. We can never see the back side of the moon from the Earth.

Codes

(a) Only 1
(b) Only 2
(c) 1 and 2
(d) 1, 2 and 3

Ans. (d)

Exp. All the statements (1), (2) and (3) are correct.

As moon's revolution and rotation periods are same, therefore only the part of the moon is always visible to us. The illuminated portion of the moon increases and decreases periodically.

The size of illuminated part of the moon visible from the Earth increases each day after the new moon day. On new moon day, the whole disc of the moon is not visible.

After the full moon day, the sunlit part of the moon visible from the Earth decreases in size every day. We can never see the back side of the moon from the Earth.

6 Which of the following planets has the least density?
(Chap 17, Class-VIII, NCERT) (BPSC Pre 2022)

(a) Earth (b) Mars
(c) Venus (d) Saturn

Ans. (d)

Exp. Saturn has the least density, whereas mercury and earth are the densest planets in the solar system.

7 **The time period between one full moon to the next full moon is approximately** *(Chap 17, Class-VIII, NCERT)*

(a) 20 days (b) 30 days
(c) 15 days (d) 60 days

Ans. (b)

Exp. The time period between one full moon to the next but moon is slightly longer than 29 days. From the above option, 30 days is close to 29 days.

8 **All stars appear to move from East to West because the** *(Chap 17, Class-VIII, NCERT)*

(a) Earth is revolving around the sun.
(b) Earth rotates from West to East on its axis.
(c) Stars move from East to West.
(d) None of the above

Ans. (b)

Exp. All stars appear to move from East to West because the Earth rotates from West to East on its axis.
Earth takes 24 h to complete one rotation on its own axis.

9 **When entire Northern sky moves around, one star does not change its positions. The name of the star is** *(Chap 17, Class-VIII, NCERT)*

(a) Alpha centuari (b) Red star
(c) North star (d) None of these

Ans. (c)

Exp. When entire Northern sky moves around, one star does not change its position. It is known as North star or pole star or polaris.
It was used for navigation in ancient times.
It appears to be at rest because it lies on the axis of rotation of the Earth and the axis of the Earth is fixed and does not vary with time.

10 **A constellation is used to identify the North star's position. The hindi translation of the constellation is** *(Chap 17, Class-VIII, NCERT)*

(a) Saptrishi (b) Brahmos
(c) Makar (d) Mesh

Ans. (a)

Exp. A constellation used to identify the North star's position is called Ursa Major. It is also known as Saptrishi.
The stars forming a group that has a recognisable shape is called a constellation.
The Ursa Major constellation consists of seven bright stars. It appears like a big-ladle or a question mark. There are three stars in the handle of the ladle and four in its bowl. During the summer, the Ursa Major constellation is visible in the early part of the night sky.

11 **Arrange the planets in the correct ascending order based on their orbital period** *(Chap 17, Class-VIII, NCERT)*

1. Venus 2. Jupiter
3. Earth 4. Mars

Choose the correct answer from the codes given below.

(a) 1, 3, 4, 2
(b) 1, 2, 3, 4
(c) 1, 2, 4, 3
(d) None of these

Ans. (a)

Exp.

Planet	Orbital period
Mercury	88 days
Venus	225 days
Earth	365 days
Mars	687 days
Jupiter	12 years
Saturn	29 years
Uranus	84 years
Neptune	165 years

12 **Consider the following statements.** *(Chap 17, Class-VIII, NCERT)*

1. Sirius is the brightest star in the sky.
2. The stars which make up a constellation are same distance apart.
3. Cassiopeia is another prominent constellation in Northern sky.

Which of the statement(s) given above is/are incorrect?

(a) Only 1 (b) Only 2
(c) Only 3 (d) 1 and 3

Ans. (b)

Exp. Among the given statements, statement (2) is incorrect because the stars which make up constellation are not the same distance apart, they just appear to be in the same line of sight.

13 **Consider the following statements.** *(Chap 17, Class-VIII, NCERT)*

Statement I The Earth's equatorial plane and orbital plane inclined at 23.5°.

Statement II The earth have a lower density than Mercury.

Which one of the following is correct in respect of the above statements?

(a) Both Statement I and Statement II are correct and Statement II is the correct explanation for Statement I.
(b) Both Statement I and Statement II are correct but Statement II is not the correct explanation for Statement I.
(c) Statement I is correct but Statement II is incorrect.
(d) Statement I is incorrect but Statement II is correct.

Ans. (c)

Exp. Statement I is correct but Statement II is incorrect.

The earth's equatorial plane and orbital plane are inclined to each other as on angle of 23.5°. This means that the axis of the earth is inclined to its orbital plane as on angle of 66.5°.

Mercury is a terrestrial planet like Earth, but it is much smaller in size. The average density of Earth is approximately 5.51 grams per cubic centimetre (g/cm^3), while the average density of mercury is about 5.43 g/cm^3. Therefore, earth is denser due to its larger mass and volume.

14 **In the vast universe, our solar system have many planets, which planet is least dense?**

(Chap 17, Class-VIII, NCERT)

(a) Mars (b) Venus
(c) Saturn (d) Neptune

Ans. (c)

Exp. Saturn is the least dense planet in our solar system. It is lighter than water and hence, it can float on water. Saturn is the sixth planet from the Sun which is the second biggest planet of the solar system.

The system of colourful rings which surround it, is the most distinguishing feature of Saturn. Saturn is the only planet with a system of well-developed rings encircling it. The rings of Saturn can be observed only with the help of a telescope.

15 **Which of the following is/are name of artificial satellite?** *(Chap 17, Class-VIII, NCERT)*

1. INSAT
2. IRS
3. EDUSAT
4. Kalpana-1

Coeds

(a) 1 and 2
(b) 2 and 4
(c) 1, 2 and 3
(d) All of the above

Ans. (d)

Exp. INSAT, IRS, EDUSAT and Kalpana-1 are the name of few artificial satellites launched by India. Aryabhatt was the first satellite launched by India in April 1975.

Artificial satellite is man-made spacecraft placed in orbit around the Earth with the help of a launch vehicle called rocket. These satellites carry a large variety of equipment and instruments like cameras, infrared sensors, telescope etc.

16 **Consider the following statements.**

(Chap 17, Class-VIII, NCERT)

1. Venus is Earth's nearest planetary neighbour. It is the brightest planet in the night sky.
2. Venus has one moon or satellite of its own.
3. Venus rotates from East to West while the Earth rotates from West to East.

Which of the statements(s) given above is/are correct?

(a) Only 1 (b) Only 2
(c) 1 and 3 (d) 1, 2 and 3

Ans. (c)

Exp. Statements (1) and (3) are correct. Venus is Earth's nearest planetary neighbour. It is the brightest planet in the night sky.

Sometimes, the Venus appears in the Eastern sky before sunrise. Sometimes, it appears in the Western sky just after sunset. It rotates from East to West while the Earth rotates from West to East.

Statement (2) is incorrect because Venus has no moon or satellite of its own.

17 **Consider the following statements.**

(Chap 17, Class-VIII, NCERT)

Statement I Radio waves are used to carry satellite signals.

Statement II The electromagnetic waves require medium. They can move through air as well as the vacuum of space.

Which one of the following is correct in respect of the above statements?

(a) Both Statement I and Statement II are correct and Statement II is the correct explanation for Statement I.
(b) Both Statement I and Statement II are correct but Statement II is not the correct explanation for Statement I.
(c) Statement I is correct but Statement II is incorrect.
(d) Statement I is incorrect but Statement II is correct.

Ans. (c)

Exp. Statement I is correct but Statement II is incorrect. Radio waves are used to carry satellite signals. These waves travel at 30000 km/s (the speed of light). This means that a signal sent to a satellite 38000 km away takes 0.13s to reach the satellite and another 0.13S for the return signal to be received back on Earth.

For most waves, they require a medium to transmit energy. But Electromagnetic waves differ from mechanical moves in that they do not need a medium to propagate as they are composed of electric and magnetic fields, which means they can travel in a vacuum.

18 Consider the following statements.

(Chap 17, Class-VIII, NCERT)

Statement I A black hole is an extremely dense object in space from which no light can escape.

Statement II When hydrogen fuel ends up in a star, then it will expand.

Which one of the following is correct in respect of the above statements?

(a) Both Statement I and Statement II are correct and Statement II is the correct explanation for Statement I.

(b) Both Statement I and Statement II are correct but Statement II is not the correct explanation for Statement I.

(c) Statement I is correct but Statement II is incorrect.

(d) Statement I is incorrect but Statement II is correct.

Ans. (c)

Exp. Statement I is correct but Statement II is incorrect. A black hole is so dense that gravity just beneath its surface, the event horizon is strong enough that nothing, not even light can escape. The event horizon isn't a surface like earth's or even the Sun's. It is a boundary that contains all the matter that makes up the black hole.

As the main sequence star glows, hydrogen in its core is converted into helium by nuclear fusion. When the hydrogen supply in the core begins to run out, and the star is no longer generating heat by nuclear fusion, the core becomes unstable and contracts.

19 The tail of a comet is directed away from the Sun because *(Chap 17, Class-VIII, NCERT)*

(a) as the comet rotates around the sun, the lighter mass of the comet is pushed away due to the centrifugal force alone.

(b) as the comet rotates, the lighter mass of the comet is attracted by some stars situated in the direction of its tail.

(c) the radiation emitted by the Sun exerts a radial pressure on the comet throwing its tail away from the Sun.

(d) the tail of the comet always exists in the same orientation.

Ans. (a)

Exp. The tail of a comet is directed away from the Sun because of centrifugal force alone. When a body moves along a circular path, due to inertia. the body experiences a force along the radius but away from the centre.

Comets are also members of our solar system. They revolve around the Sun in highly elliptical orbits. However, their period of revolution round the Sun is usually very long. A comet appears generally as a bright head with a long tail.

20 Consider the following statements.

(Chap 17, Class-VIII, NCERT)

Statement I Comets are the members of our solar system and revolve around the sun in highly elliptical orbit.

Statement II Venus is the third planet in our solar system and brightest planet in the might sky.

Which one of the following is correct in respect of the above statements?

(a) Both Statement I and Statement II are correct and Statement II is the correct explanation for Statement I.

(b) Both Statement I and Statement II are correct but Statement II is not the correct explanation for Statement I.

(c) Statement I is correct but Statement II is incorrect.

(d) Statement I is incorrect but Statement II is correct.

Ans. (c)

Exp. Statement I is correct but Statement II is incorrect. Here, comets are the members of our solar system. They revolve around the sun in highly elliptical orbit as a bright head with a long tail whereas venus is the second planet in our solar system and brightest planet in the night sky.

Atomic Structure and Radioactivity

Atomic Structure and Radioactivity

Atomic Theory

Dalton's Atomic Theory

- Atoms are indivisible.
- Atoms of same element are identical in mass as well as in chemical properties.
- Atoms combine in the ratio of small whole numbers forming compounds.
- **Subatomic Particles** Particles from which an atom is made.
  - **Electrons** Negatively charged particle Discovered by J J Thomson Mass = 9.1×10^{-31} kg Charge = -1.602×10^{-19} C
  - **Protons** Positively charged particle Discovered by E. Goldstein Mass = -1.6×10^{-27}kg Charge = 1.602176×10^{-19} C
  - **Neutrons** Neutral particles Discovered by J Chadwick Mass = 1.6×10^{-27} kg Charge = 0

Atomic Models

- Arrangement of sub-atomic particles within an atom.
- **Thomson's Model**
  - Atom like Christmas pudding.
  - Electrons well embedded in a sphere of positive charge.
  - Failed to explain stability of an atom.
- **Rutherford's Model**
  - α-particle scattering experiment on thin sheet of gold foil.
  - Discovery of nucleus.
  - Electron revolves around nucleus.
- **Bohr's Model**
  - Only certain special orbits called discrete orbits or energy levels of electrons are allowed inside the atom.
  - While revolving in discrete orbits, the electrons do not radiate energy.

Characteristics and Structural Features of the Atom

Characteristic of an Atom

- **Atomic Number (Z)** = No. of protons = No. of electrons
- **Mass Number (A)** = No. of protons + No. of neutrons

Types of Atomic Species

- isotopes, isobars, isotones and isoelectronic.
- **Valency** Lost or gain of electron to make stable octet.

Structural Features of the Atom

- **Shells** Circular path in which electrons move.
- **Subshells** One or more subshells, orbitals denoted by *s, p, d, f*.
- **Orbitals** 3D-space present around the nucleus.

Rules for Filling Electrons in the Orbitals

- **Aufbau Principle** Orbitals are filled in increasing order of energies.
- **Pauli Exclusion Principle** No two electrons in an atom.
- **Hund's Rule of Maximum Multiplicity** Pairing of electrons in the orbitals does not take place until each orbital of subshell are singly occupied.
- **Quantum Numbers**
  - **Principal Quantum Number** (n) Identify the shell or orbit number of an electrons.
  - **Azimuthal Quantum Number** (l) Subshell or angular momentum of revolving electrons.
  - **Magnetic Quantum Number** (m) Determine the orientation of orbitals.
  - **Spin Quantum Number** (s) Spin of an electron in an orbital.

Molecular Mass/ Mole Concept/Radioactivity

Molecular Mass

- Sum of atomic masses of all the elements present in a molecule.
- It is obtained by multiplying the atomic mass of each element by the number of its atoms and adding them together.
- **Formula Unit Mass** Sum of atomic masses of all the atoms in a formula unit of a compound.

Mole Concept

- One mole of any species is that quantity in number having a mass equal to its atomic or molecular mass in gram.
- The number of particles present in 1 mole is equal to 6.022×10^{23}.

Radioactivity

- It is a spontaneous process by which a nucleus disintegrate with the emission of some particle or electromagnetic radiation.
- Radioactivity of a substance is measured by an instrument called Geiger Muller counter which is based on the ionisation of gases.
  - **Radioactive or Becquerel Rays** Radiation distributed in three parts
  - **α-rays** (positively charged) moves toward negative plate.
  - **β-rays** (negatively charged) moves toward positive plate.
  - **γ-rays** (neutral) remain unaffected by electric and magnetic field.

SOURCE *New NCERT Class IX Chap 3* (Atoms and Molecules), *Chap 4* (Structure of the Atom), *New NCERT Class XI Chap 2* (Structure of Atom)

1 Consider the following statements.

(Chap 3, Class-IX, NCERT)

1. Matter can neither be created nor be destroyed in a chemical reaction.
2. Total mass of reactants are always equal to the total mass of products.
3. Atoms are the smallest unit of matter.

How many statements given above is/are correct?

(a) Only one (b) Only two
(c) All three (d) None of these

Ans. (c)

Exp. All three Statements (1, 2 and 3) are correct.
According to law of conservation of mass, "matter can neither be created nor be destroyed in a chemical reaction". For example, when wood burns, the mass of the shoot, ashes and gases equals to the original mass of the charcoal and the oxygen.
It also suggested that total mass of reactants are always equal to the total mass of product. Dalton concluded that atoms are the smallest unit of matter.

2 Which of the following statement is not true about an atom? *(Chap 3, Class-IX, NCERT)*

(a) Atoms are not able to exist independently.
(b) These are the basic units from which molecules and ions are formed.
(c) These are always neutral in nature.
(d) These can aggregate in large numbers to form the matter that we can see, feel or touch.

Ans. (a)

Exp. Statement (a) is not true about an atom because atoms of noble gases can exist independently as their octet is completely filled and they don't need extra electrons to become stable. An atom is the smallest unit of ordinary matter that forms a chemical element. Every solid, liquid, gas and plasma is composed of neutral or ionized atoms.

3 Which of the following statement is correct according to Dalton's Atomic Theory?

(Chap 4, Class-IX, NCERT)

(a) Atoms of same element are identical in mass and chemical properties.
(b) Atoms of different elements have same chemical properties.
(c) These are divisible particles.
(d) These can combine in the ratio of any whole number to form a compound.

Ans. (a)

Exp. Statement (a) is correct according to Dalton's Atomic Theory. This theory states that the atoms of same element are identical in mass and chemical properties as the number of protons and electrons are same.
Statements (b), (c) and (d) are incorrect.
Atoms of different elements differ in number of protons and electrons. So, they do not have same chemical properties.
Atoms cannot be divided further.
Dalton also concluded that an atom is a smallest and indivisible part of matter. An atom should combine in simple whole number ratio to form a compound.

4 Consider the following statements, before the discovery of electrons, E. Goldstein in 1886 discovered the presence of canal rays. These rays

(Chap 4, Class-IX, NCERT)

1. were positively charged radiations which ultimately led to the discovery of another sub-atomic particle.
2. travel in straight line and get deflected in electric and magnetic field.
3. have electromagnetic ratio which does not depend upon the nature of gas, taken in discharge tube.

How many of the above statement(s) is/are correct?

(a) Only one (b) Only two (c) All three (d) None

Ans. (b)

Exp. Only two statements (1 and 2) are correct but one statement (3) is incorrect as, in canal rays, electromagnetic ratio depends upon the nature of gas, taken in discharge tube.
Goldstein discovered positive particles by using a tube filled with hydrogen gas. The positive particle had a charge equal and opposite to the electron. The positive particle was named as proton.

5 Consider the following statements

(Chap 4, Class-IX, NCERT)

Statement I Sub atomic particles are present inside an atom which is responsible to forming as structure of an atom.

Statement II Deutron is a sub-atomic particle.

Which of the above statements is correct?

(a) Both Statement I and Statement II are correct.
(b) Statement I is correct but Statement II is incorrect.
(c) Both Statement I and Statement II are incorrect.
(d) Statement I is incorrect but Statement II is correct.

Ans. (b)

Exp. Statement I is correct but Statement II is incorrect. Deutron is not a sub-atomic particle. It is an isotope of hydrogen consisting one proton and one neutron.

6 Match the following lists correctly and choose the correct codes. *(Chap 4, Class-IX, NCERT)*

List-I (Scientist)	**List-II** (Discovery)
A. E. Goldstein	1. Atomic theory
B. J. Chadwick	2. Proton
C. J. J. Thomson	3. Neutron
D. John Dalton	4. Electron

Codes

	A	B	C	D		A	B	C	D
(a)	2	3	4	1	(b)	2	4	3	1
(c)	1	4	3	2	(d)	1	3	4	2

Ans. (a)

Exp. The correct matching is A-2, B-3, C-4, D-1.

Goldstein Discovered proton using cathode ray experiment in 1886.

J Chadwick Discovered neutron in 1932. This experiment resulted that the positive particles protons had a charge equal and opposite to the electron. He was awarded in 1935 with Noble Prize in Physics for this discovery.

JJ Thomson Discovered electrons using cathode ray tube experiment in 1897.

John Dalton Proposed atomic theory in 1804 which includes all matter is composed of extremely small particles called atoms.

7 The number of portons in a negatively charged atom (anion) is *(Chap 3, Class-IX, NCERT)*

(a) more than the atomic number of the element.
(b) less than the atomic number of electrons in the atom.
(c) less than the number of electrons in the atom.
(d) more than the number of electrons in the atom.

Ans. (c)

Exp. The number of protons in a negatively charged atom i.e anion is less than the number of electrons in the atom. As in neutral atom, number of electrons and protons are equal but when an atom gains electrons to form an anion than number of electrons increases.

8 Among the following, which elements are isoelectronic? *(Chap 2, Class-XI, NCERT)*

1. $^{39}_{18}Ar$ 2. $^{40}_{19}K^+$ 3. $^{40}_{20}Ca^{2+}$ 4. $^{35}_{17}Cl$

Codes

(a) 1 and 2 (b) 2 and 4
(c) 3 and 4 (d) 1, 2 and 3

Ans. (d)

Exp. $^{39}_{18}Ar$, $^{40}_{19}K^+$ and $^{40}_{20}Ca^{2+}$ are isoelectronic as they contain same number of electrons. Isoelectronic species have same number of electrons and differ in other sub-atomic particles.

9 Which of the following properties of atom could be explained correctly by Thomson model of atom? *(Chap 2, Class-XI, NCERT)* *(MPSC Pre 2020)*

(a) Overall neutrality of atom
(b) Spectra of hydrogen atom
(c) Position of electrons, protons and neutrons in atom
(d) Stability of atom

Ans. (a)

Exp. Overall neutrality of atom could be explained correctly by Thomson model of atom. As this model states that the positive charge (protons) is uniformly distributed in the atom and the negative charge (electrons) are embeded such that atom possess the most stable electrostatic arrangement.

10 Consider the following properties of an atom explained correctly by Rutherford model. *(Chap 4, Class-IX, NCERT)*

1. Stability of an atom.
2. Overall neutrality of an atom.
3. Charged particle radiate energy during acceleration.
4. Size of nucleus is very small as compared to the size of atom.

(a) Only 1 (b) Only 2
(c) 3 and 4 (d) None of the above

Ans. (c)

Exp. Among the given properties (1) and (2) are incorrect.

As overall neutrality of an atom could be explained correctly by Thomson model of atom. Since, the positive and negative charges are equal in magnitude, they cancel each other's effect and thus, the atom become neutral.

Rutherford model of an atom, could not explain the stability of an atom, where charged electrons are moving under the attractive force of positively charged nucleus.

11 Consider the following statements. *(Chap 4, Class-IX, NCERT)*

1. Atom consists of nucleus and shell.
2. Nucleus consists of protons and electrons.
3. Neutrons are present in atoms.

Which of the statements given above are correct?

(a) 1 and 2
(b) 1 and 3
(c) Only 2
(d) 1, 2 and 3

Ans. (b)

Exp. Statements (1) and (3) are correct. An atom consists of nucleus and surrounded by shells. Its sub-atomic particles are neutron, proton and electron.

Statement (2) is incorrect because in atomic nucleus, neutrons and protons are present while electrons are present around nucleus in the orbits.

12 The alpha (α) particle carries two positive charges. Its mass is very nearly equal to that of *(Chap 4, Class-IX, NCERT) (IAS Pre 1996)*

(a) two protons
(b) nucleus of a helium atom
(c) sum of masses of two positrons and two neutrons
(d) two positrons, as each positron carries a single positive charge

Ans. (b)

Exp. An alpha (α) particle is a fast moving particle containing two protons and two neutrons similar to a helium nucleus. So, the mass of an alpha (α) particle is equal to that of nucleus of a helium atom.

13 Which one among the following is correct regarding ^{20}Ne, $^{23}Na^{+}$, $^{19}F^{-}$ and $^{24}Mg^{2+}$? *(Chap 4, Class-IX, NCERT)*

(a) They are isomers of each other.
(b) They are isotopes of each other.
(c) They are isoelectronic of each other.
(d) All of the above

Ans. (c)

Exp. ^{20}Ne, $^{23}Na^{+}$, $^{19}F^{-}$ and $^{24}Mg^{2+}$ are isoelectronic of each other. As isoelectronic species are those in which there are same number of electrons present.

14 Rutherford performed the α-particle scattering experiment, which led to the birth of the nuclear model of an atom. What were their observations? *(Chap 4, Class-IX, NCERT) (Chap 5, Module 2, NIOS)*

1. Most of the α-particles passed straight through the gold foil.
2. Most of the mass of an atom was contained by nucleus.
3. Volume occupied by the nucleus is large as compared to the total volume of the atom.

Which of the statement(s) given above is/are correct?

(a) Only 1
(b) Only 3
(c) 1 and 2
(d) All of the above

Ans. (c)

Exp. Among the given statements (1) and (2) are correct, while (3) statement is incorrect. Its corrected form is ; the volume occupied by the nucleus is negligibly small as compared to the total volume of the atom. The radius of the atom is about 10^{-10} m, while that of nucleus is 10^{-15} m.

15 Consider the following statements about Bohr's model of atom *(Chap 4, Class-IX, NCERT)*

1. The electrons move in definite circular paths of fixed energy around a central nucleus.
2. The electron can change its shells or energy level by absorbing or releasing energy.
3. The negatively charged electrons revolve in circular orbits around the positively charged nucleus.

Which of the statement(s) given above is/are correct?

(a) Only 3
(b) 1 and 2
(c) 1 and 3
(d) All of the above

Ans. (b)

Exp. Among the given statements, only (1) and (2) are correct regarding Bohr's model of an atom. Statement (3) is given by Rutherford. He proposed that the negatively charged electrons surround the nucleus of an atom i.e., electrons revolve in circular orbits around the positively charged nucleus.

16 An atom consists of nucleus surrounded by electrons moving in circular path called orbits.

Which of the following model supports the above statement? *(Chap 4, Class-IX, NCERT)*

(a) Dalton's atomic model
(b) Thomson's atomic model
(c) Rutherford's nuclear model of an atom
(d) Millikan's Oil drop method

Ans. (c)

Exp. Rutherford's nuclear model of an atom suggests about the orbits.

According to his model, the positive charge and most of the mass of the atom was densely concentrated in extremely small region, called the nucleus.

The nucleus is surrounded by electrons that move around the nucleus with a very high speed in circular paths called orbits. Also the electrons and the nucleus are held together by electrostatic forces of attraction.

17 Consider the following Assertion (A) and Reason (R) and choose the correct code. *(Chap 4, Class-IX, NCERT) (Unit 11, Class-IX, Tamil Nadu Borad)*

Assertion (A) In Rutherford's gold foil experiment, very few α-particles are deflected back.

Reason (R) Nucleus present inside the atom is heavy but very small.

Codes

(a) Both A and R are true and R is the correct explanation of A.
(b) Both A and R are true but R is not the correct explanation of A.
(c) A is true but R is false.
(d) R is true but A is false.

Ans. (a)

Exp. Both Assertion (A) and Reason (R) are true and Reason (R) is the correct explanation of Assertion (A). In Rutherford's gold foil experiment, very few alpha (α) particles are deflected back. This is because in an atom, nucleus is positively charged and have very small in size which repels the positively charged alpha (α) particles which make them deflected back.

18 When β- particles are sent through a tin metal foil, most of them go straight through the foil as

Codes *(Chap 4, Class-IX, NCERT)*

(a) β-particles are much heavier than electrons .
(b) β-particles are positively charged.
(c) most part of the atom is empty space.
(d) β-particles move with high velocity.

Ans. (c)

Exp. As β-particles are positively charged, when sent through the foil. most of them go straight because a positively charged nucleus is concentrated in very less space and most of the space in the atom is empty.

19 Consider the following Assertion (A) and Reason (R) and choose the correct code. *(Chap 2, Class-XI, NCERT)*

Assertion (A) Bohr's orbits are called stationary orbits.

Reason (R) Electrons remain stationary in these orbits for some time.

Codes

(a) Both A and R are true and R is the correct explanation of A.
(b) Both A and R are true, but R is not the correct explanation of A.
(c) A is true but R is false.
(d) R is true but A is false.

Ans. (c)

Exp. Assertion (A) is true but Reason (R) is false.

Bohr's orbits are called stationary orbit because each orbit has its constant energy respectively. Also, electrons continuously move along the orbits and they never remain stationary.

20 Using which of the following parameters, we can calculate atomic mass number of an atom? *(Chap 2, Class-XI, NCERT)*

(a) By neutron and electron number of that atom.
(b) Using proton and electron number of that atom.
(c) Using neutron and proton number of that atom.
(d) Using atomic number and electron number of that atom.

Ans. (c)

Exp. Atomic mass number of an atom can be calculated by using neutron and proton number of that atom. Atomic mass is basically the mass of nucleus of an atom as electrons have very negligible mass. It is the sum of number of neutrons and number of protons present in an atom.

∴ Mass number = No. of neutrons + No. of protons.

21 Regarding the atom of a chemical element, the magnetic quantum number refers to *(Chap 2, Class-XI, NCERT) (IAS Pre 2003)*

(a) orientation (b) shape (c) size (d) spin

Ans. (a)

Exp. The magnetic quantum number refers to orientation of electrons. It is denoted by '*m*'.

Rest of the three quantum numbers are as follows:

(i) Principal quantum number refers to energy level of an electron and it is denoted by '*n*'.
(ii) Azimuthal quantum number refers to shape of an orbital and it is denoted by '*l*'.
(iii) Spin quantum number refers to spin of an electron and it is denoted by '*s*'.

22 Which of the following is an isotonic species? *(Chap 2, Class-XI, NCERT)*

(a) $^{16}_{8}O$, $^{19}_{9}F$ (b) $^{40}_{18}Ar$, $^{14}_{7}N$
(c) $^{30}_{14}Si$, $^{31}_{15}P$ (d) $^{52}_{24}Cr$, $^{39}_{19}K$

Ans. (c)

Exp. Among the given pairs of elements, $^{30}_{14}Si$, $^{31}_{15}P$ is isotonic species, because both have same number of neutrons while others have different number of neutron.

23 Isotope of which of the following element is used in the treatment of cancer? *(Chap 4, Class-IX, NCERT)*

(a) Potassium (b) Cobalt (c) Uranium (d) Chlorine

Ans. (b)

Exp. Among the given elements, isotope of cobalt is used in the treatment of cancer. Cobalt therapy is the medical use of gamma (γ) rays from the radioisotope cobalt-60. It is used as an external source of radiation exposure.

24 Isobars are those atoms of the same element which have *(Chap 4, Class-IX, NCERT)*

(a) same atomic mass but different atomic number.
(b) different atomic mass but same atomic number.
(c) atomic number and atomic mass both are same.
(d) None of the above.

Ans. (a)

Exp. Isobars are atomic species that have the same atomic mass but different atomic number.

$^{40}_{16}S$, $^{40}_{17}Cl$, $^{40}_{18}Ar$, $^{40}_{19}K$ and $^{40}_{20}Ca$ are examples of isobars which have same atomic mass, i.e. 40 but different atomic number.

25 Consider the following Assertion (A) and Reason (R) and choose the correct code. *(Chap 4, Class-IX, NCERT)*

Assertion (A) Isotopes are electrically neutral.

Reason (R) Isotopes are species with same mass number but different atomic number.

Codes

(a) Both A and R are true and R is the correct explanation of A.
(b) Both A and R are true, but R is not the correct explanation of A.
(c) A is true but R is false.
(d) R is true but A is false.

Ans. (c)

Exp. Assertion (A) is true but reason (R) is false.

Isotopes are electrically neutral as they differ in mass number, that is number of neutrons. They have same number of proton and electrons.

Isotopes are species with same atomic number and different mass number.

26 Consider the following statements. *(Chap 4, Class-IX, NCERT), (Chap 2, Class-XI, NCERT)*

1. Isotopes of an element have different atomic numbers.
2. Electrons have negligible mass and no charge.
3. The maximum number of electrons in *L*-shell is 8.

Which of the statements given above is/are correct?

(a) Only 1 (b) 1 and 2 (c) Only 3 (d) 2 and 3

Ans. (c)

Exp. Among the given statements only statement (3) is correct whereas statement (1) and (2) are incorrect.

As, isotopes of an element have same atomic number and different mass number. For example, ${}_6C^{12}$, ${}_6C^{13}$ and ${}_6C^{14}$ are three isotopes of the element carbon with mass number 12, 13 and 14 respectively.

Electrons have negligible mass but it has approximately 1 unit of negative charge. It is the smallest of the particles that make up an atom. The number of protons and electrons is equal in a neutral atom.

27 **Consider the following statement about atomic species.** *(Chap 4, Class-IX, NCERT)*

1. Chlorine have two isobars ${}^{35}_{17}Cl$ and ${}^{37}_{17}Cl$ in the ratio of 3 : 1. Then average atomic mass of chlorine will be 35.5 u.
2. ${}^{40}_{18}Ar$, ${}^{40}_{19}K$ are the example of isotopes.

Which of the statement(s) given above is/are correct?

(a) Only 1 (b) Only 2
(c) Both 1 and 2 (d) Neither 1 nor 2

Ans. (d)

Exp. Both statements (1) and (2) are incorrect.

${}^{35}_{17}Cl$ and ${}^{37}_{17}Cl$ are two isotopes of chlorine in the ratio 3 : 1.

$$\text{Average atomic mass of Cl} = \frac{35\times 3 + 37\times 1}{4} = 35.5 \text{ u.}$$

Atoms of different elements which have same mass number but different atomic number are called isobars. ${}^{40}_{18}Ar$ and ${}^{40}_{19}K$ are examples of isobar.

28 **Which among the following is an incorrect option?** *(Chap 4, Class-IX, NCERT), (Chap 2, Class-XI, NCERT)*

(a) Atom is electrically neutral due to presence of protons and electrons inside the nucleus.
(b) Electrons are negatively charged and have negligible mass.
(c) Atomic number is the number of protons in an atom of an element.
(d) Isotopes are useful as nuclear fuel, in medical field, in carbon dating, etc.
(e) None of the above/More than one of the above

Ans. (a)

Exp. Statement (a) is incorrect while statements (b), (c) and (d) are correct.

The corrected form of (a) is as, atom is electrically neutral as protons and neutrons embedded inside the nucleus and electrons spinning around the nucleus.

29 **Consider the following statements.** *(Chap 4, Class-IX, NCERT)*

1. The electronic configuration of Ne is 2, 8.
2. Valency of chlorine is 1.
3. Cobalt-60 isotope is used to cure cancer.

Which of the statements given above is/are correct?

(a) Only 1 (b) 1 and 2
(c) 2 and 3 (d) All of these

Ans. (d)

Exp. All the given statements are correct. The atomic number of Ne is 10, thus its electronic configuration is $\overset{K}{2}, \overset{L}{8}$.

The number of electrons in the outermost shell of chlorine is 7, thus its valency is 1.

Cobalt-60 is used in the treatment of cancer.

30 **Consider the following statements.** *(Chap 4, Class-IX, NCERT)*

1. ${}^{35}_{17}Cl$ and ${}^{37}_{17}Cl$ have different valencies.
2. Electrons are also known as planetary electrons.
3. Electrons, protons and neutrons do not have any colour.

How many statement(s) given above is/are correct?

(a) Only one (b) Only two (c) All three (d) None of these

Ans. (b)

Exp. Statements (2 and 3) are correct, while one Statement (1) is incorrect. ${}^{35}_{17}Cl$ and ${}^{37}_{17}Cl$ are the isotopes of chlorine, so they have same number of protons and electrons.

Rutherford suggested that his model of atom was similar to that of our solar system. In the solar system, the different planets are revolving around the Sun. In the same manner, in an atom the electrons are revolving around the nucleus. So, these electrons are also called Planetary electrons.

Electrons, protons and neutrons do not have any colour, since the wavelength of these particles is extremely small.

31 **In an atom, the order of filling up of the orbitals is governed by** *(Chap 2, Class-XI, NCERT) (IAS Pre 2001)*

(a) Aufbau's principle
(b) Heisenberg's uncertainty principle
(c) Hund's rule
(d) Pauli's exclusion principle

Ans. (a)

Exp. In an atom, order of filling up of the orbitals is governed by Aufbau's principle. It states that electrons fill lower energy atomic orbitals before filling higher energy ones. The electronic configuration can be easily predicated using this rule.

32 **Which of the following statement about molecular structure is correct?** *(Chap 4, Class-IX, NCERT) (RAS/RTS Pre 1992)*

(a) Neutrons and electrons are found inside the nucleus and protons revolve around the nucleus.
(b) Electrons and protons are found inside the nucleus and neutrons revolve around the nucleus.
(c) Protons and neutrons are found inside the nucleus and electrons revolve around the nucleus.
(d) Protons, neutrons and electrons all are inside the nucleus.

Ans. (c)

Exp. Statement (c) is correct about molecular structure. The protons and neutrons are found inside the nucleus of an atom, while the negatively charged electrons revolve around the nucleus. These are arranged in defined shells. Protons are positively charged while neutrons are neutral.

33 Consider the following statements.

(Chap 2, Class-XI, NCERT)

1. Alpha, beta and gamma are radioactive rays.
2. Radioactivity was discovered by Henri Becquerel.
3. Radium was discovered by Marie Curie and Pierre Curie.

Which of the statement(s) given above is/are correct?

(a) Only 1 (b) 1 and 2
(c) 2 and 3 (d) All of these

Ans. (d)

Exp. All of these statements are correct.

Alpha, beta and gamma are three most common type of radiation. These are called radioactive particle. The α and β rays can be deflected by electromagnetic field while γ rays remains undeflected by the electric and magnetic field as it is neutral.

Radioactivity was discovered by Henri Becquerel. He was awarded the Nobel Prize in 1903 and other half was given to Pierre Curie and Marie Curie. Radium was discovered by Marie Curie and Pierre Curie in 1898. She used radium, as the gamma ray source on X-ray machines which makes it more accurate.

34 Which of the following radio isotopes is used in the treatment of blood cancer (leukemia)?

(Chap 4, Class-IX, NCERT)
(Chap 3, Module-2, NIOS) (BPSC Pre 2017)

(a) Iodine-131 (b) Sodium-24
(c) Phosphorus-32 (d) Carbon-13

Ans. (c)

Exp. An unstable form of a chemical element that releases radiation when it breaks down and becomes more stable, is called radio isotopes. These radio isotopes may be occur in nature or can be made in a laboratory. In medical science they are used in imaging tests and in treatment.

Phosphorus-32 is used to treat blood cancer (leukemia). It is also used to detect tumors.

Iodine-131 is used to treat hyperthyroidism and thyroid cancer.

Sodium-24 is used as a tracer to diagnose various malfunctioning including heart disease.

Carbon-13 is widely used in physiological investigation and medical reasearch.

35 Which of the following statements is incorrect?

(Chap 2, Class-XI, NCERT)

(a) X-rays and gamma rays are electromagnetic in nature.
(b) The part of radiation that moves towards the positive plate is called α-rays.
(c) The part of the radiation that remains unaffected by the electric field and magnetic field is called γ-rays.
(d) Radioactivity of a substance is measured by Geiger Muller counter.

Ans. (b)

Exp. Among the given statement only (b) is incorrect.

The corrected form of statement (b) is, the part of radiation that moves towards the positive plate, is negatively charged and is called β-rays. It can be deflected by electromagnetic field.

Physical & Chemical Changes of Substances and Their Separation

Physical & Chemical Changes of Substances and Their Separation

Changes/Matter

Changes
- Due to involvement of one or more substances.
- **Physical Changes** Physical properties are affected and reversible, e.g. evaporation of water, melting of wax, etc.
- **Chemical Changes** Chemical composition is changed and a new compound is obtained e.g. rusting of iron, formation of curd in milk, etc.

Matter
- Have mass, occupy volume, physical resistance, inertia and can be realised by the sense organs.
- **Classification of Matter** On the basis of chemical composition or purity, matter can be classified as follows
  - **Pure Substances** Only single type of constituent particles.

(i) Elements Only one kind of atoms and cannot be broken down into simpler substances by chemical reactions. e.g. sodium, etc.

(ii) Compounds Two or more atoms combined together in fixed proportion, e.g. water (H_2O).

Impure Substances/Mixture Two or more substance in any proportion. e.g. sugar solution, etc.
- **Homogeneous Mixture** Uniform composition of mixture, e.g salt & water.
- **Heterogeneous Mixture** Non-uniform composition of mixture, e.g. milk.

- **Solution** Two or more substances e.g. soda water.
  - **Components** Solvent and Solute.
  - **Types of Solution** Basis of physical phase and concentration.

(i) On the Basis of Concentration
- **Dilute Solution** A solution having lesser amount of solute.
- **Concentrated Solution** A solution having higher amount of solution.
- **Saturated Solution** A solution in which no more amount of solute can be dissolved at a given temperature.
- **Unsaturated Solution** A solution in which the amount of solute is less than the saturation level.
- **Suspension** Solute particle remain suspended.
- **Colloidal** Particle are uniformly spread through the solutions.

Tyndall Effect
- Scattering of light by colloidal particle.
- **Emulsions** Dispersion of finely divided liquid droplets.

Separation of Substances

Separation the Components of a Mixture
- **Separation of Homogeneous Mixture**
  - **Evaporation** Liquid state to gaseous state; volatile solvent from non-volatile solute of separate the mixture, e.g. Common salt from sea water.
  - **Centrifugation** Difference in densities, e.g. Washing machine.
  - **Separation by using Separating Funnel** Separate two immiscible liquid, e.g. Oil & water.
  - **Sublimation** Separation of two solid mixture one sublime on heating.
  - **Chromatography** Separation of solutes in solvent.
  - **Distillation** Conversion of liquid into vapour followed by condensation of vapour back into liquid.
  - **Separation of Different Gases Present in Air** Gases get separated at different heights.
- **Separation of Heterogeneous Mixture**
  - **Handpicking** Separation slightly larged sized impurities.
  - **Evaporation** Conversion of water into vapour.
  - **Threshing** Separate grains from stalks.
  - **Winnowing** Separate heavier and lighter components of a mixture by wind.
  - **Sieving** Separate two components of mixture of different sizes.
  - **Sedimentation** Heavier component settle down.
  - **Decantation** Water is removed, after sedimentation.
  - **Filtration** Liquid or gaseous fluid are removed

SOURCE *New NCERT Class VI Chap 3* (Separation of Substances), *New NCERT Class VII Chap 5* (Physical and Chemical Changes), *New NCERT Class IX Chap 1* (Matter in Our Surroundings), *New NCERT Class IX Chap 2* (Is Matter Around Us Pure), *Old NCERT Class XI Chap 5* (States of Matter) *New NCERT Class XI Chap 8* (Organic Chemistry (Some Basic Principles and Techniques), *New NCERT Class XII Chap 1* (Solution)

1 **Consider the following statements and choose the incorrect one.** *(Chap 5, Class-VII, NCERT)*

(a) The ripening of fruits is a chemical change.
(b) The spoiling of cooked food is a harmful change.
(c) Heat is the cause of the change of state of ice from solid to liquid.
(d) Melting of wax is an irreversible change.

Ans. (d)

Exp. Statement (d) is incorrect because melting of wax is a reversible change. As upon cooling, it changes back to solid wax.

2 **Which of the following statement is correct?** *(Chap 5, Class-VII, NCERT)*

(a) Burning of candle is a reversible change.
(b) Boiling of water is an irreversible change.
(c) Bursting of balloon is a reversible change.
(d) Shaping of wet clay is a reversible change.

Ans. (d)

Exp. Statement (d) is correct as shaping of wet clay is a reversible change because the wet clay objects can be converted back into the original clay.

Statements (a), (b) and (c) are incorrect. Their corrected form are :

Burning of candle is an irreversible change.

Boiling of water is reversible change as on cooling, its changes back to its cooled state.

Bursting of balloon is an irreversible change as after bursting we cannot get that balloon back.

3 **Freezing, condensation and evaporation process are examples of** *(Chap 1, Class-IX, NCERT)*

(a) physical change (b) chemical change (c) Both 'a' & 'b'
(d) freezing is physical while condensation and evaporation are chemical change

Ans. (a)

Exp. Freezing, condensation and evaporation process are examples of physical change as in all cases only change of state takes place. Process in which matter changes between liquid and solid states are freezing and melting.

Process in which matter changes between liquid and gaseous state are vaporisation, evaporation & condensation.

4 **Which of the following statements is incorrect about physical changes?** *(Chap 5, Class-VII, NCERT)*

(a) There is no gain or loss of energy
(b) It is permanent and irreversible
(c) Composition of the substance remains same
(d) No new substance is formed

Ans. (b)

Exp. Statement (b) is incorrect because the physical change is temporary and can be easily reversed.

There is no change in mass of substance takes place as there is a change in its form only. There is no loss or gain of energy because the exact same amount of energy is released back during the reverse process. Also, during this process no new substance is formed.

5 **Consider the following statements.** *(Chap 1, Class-IX, NCERT)* *(Unit 10, Class-IX, Tamil Nadu Board)*

1. Process change of solid camphor into camphor vapour is a vaporisation process.
2. A sample of camphor disappears when exposed to air due to sublimation.
3. Dissolving of sugar in water is a physical change.

Which of the statement(s) given above is/are correct?

(a) 2 and 3 (b) 1 and 2
(c) 1 and 3 (d) Only 3

Ans. (a)

Exp. Among the given statements only (2) and (3) are correct while statement (3) is incorrect. The corrected form of statement (1) is, process of change of solid camphor into camphor vapour is a sublimation process. It is a process in which a solid changes directly into vapour.

6 **Adding salt to water makes it salty. Which of the following statements is true regarding this change?** *(Chap 5, Class-VII, NCERT)*

(a) It is a chemical change because a new substance is formed.
(b) It is a physical change because the original substances can be recovered.
(c) It is a chemical change because there is exchange of heat.
(d) It is a physical change because there is a slight change in colours.

Ans. (b)

Exp. Adding salt to water is a physical change as salt can be recovered back form its solution of the process of evaporation.

7 **Which of the following processes release heat?** *(Chap 1, Class-IX, NCERT)*

1. Condensation
2. Vaporisation
3. Freezing
4. Melting

Codes

(a) 1 and 2 (b) 1 and 3 (c) Only 2 (d) Only 4

Ans. (b)

Exp. Condensation and freezing are processes which release heat whereas in vaporisation and melting, heat is absorbed.

Condensation is a process by which water vapour turns into liquid water on coming in contact with cooler substance. This causes water vapour molecules to lose some energy.

Vaporisation and melting involves changing of physical state from liquid to vapour and solid to liquid respectively which results is decrease in interaction. Hence, energy consumed.

Freezing involves changing of state from liquid to solid. Hence, it releases energy.

8 Consider the following statements and choose the correct one. *(Chap 5, Class-VII, NCERT)*

(a) Melting of wax is reversible change.
(b) Bursting of balloon is a irreversible change.
(c) Shaping of wet clay is irreversible change.
(d) Physical change is permanent and irreversible.

Ans. (b)

Exp. Statement (b) is correct, while statement (a), (c) and (d) are incorrect.

Melting of ice is an irrversible change. Shaping of wet clay is a reversible change. The physical change is temporary and can be easily reversed.

9 If an unsaturated sugar solution is prepared by mixing 100 gm of sugar with half-litre of water. Which of the following physical quantities will not change? *(Chap 5, Class-VII, NCERT) (UPPSC Pre 2017)*

(a) Mass (b) Density
(c) Concentration (d) Volume

Ans. (d)

Exp. Volume of the solution will not change when unsaturated sugar solution is prepared by mixing 100 gm of sugar with half-litre of water. It is because, empty spaces are present between the molecules of liquid in unsaturated solution. So, the sugar molecules do not occupy new spaces instead they get dissolved and occupy those empty spaces.

10 Which of the following methods is most suitable for obtaining a pure sample of sodium chloride from a mixture of solid sodium chloride and sand? *(Chap 3, Class-VI, NCERT)*

(a) Shake the mixture with water, filter and evaporate the filtrate.
(b) Shake the mixture with water, filter and dry the residue on the filter paper.
(c) Heat the mixture gently and collect the substance with sublimes.
(d) Shake the mixture with water and filter it.

Ans. (a)

Exp. Mixture of sodium chloride and sand is added in water. Sodium chloride is soluble in water while sand is insoluble in water and can be removed by filtration. The filtrate obtained is evaporated in which water evaporate while salt is left behind.

11 When we put some crystals of potassium permanganate in a beaker containing water, we observe that after sometime whole water has turned pink. This is due to ? *(Chap 5, Class-VII, NCERT)*

(a) boiling
(b) melting of potassium permanganate crystals
(c) sublimation of crystals
(d) diffusion

Ans. (d)

Exp. Diffusion is the process of mixing of a substance with another substance due to the motion or movement of its particles.

When we put crystal of potassium permanganate in water, its particles mixed with the interparticles of water and changes its colour to pink.

12 Match the following lists correctly and choose the correct code. *(Chap 5, Class-VII, NCERT)*

	List-I (Chemical compounds)		List-II (Chemical formulae)
A.	Rust	1.	Sodium hydrogen carbonate ($NaHCO_3$)
B.	Vinegar	2.	Ferric oxide (Fe_2O_3)
C.	Baking soda	3.	Calcium hydroxide [$Ca(OH)_2$]
D.	Lime water	4.	Acetic acid (CH_3COOH)

Codes

	A	B	C	D		A	B	C	D
(a)	2	4	3	1	(b)	2	4	1	3
(c)	3	4	1	2	(d)	4	1	2	3

Ans. (b)

Exp. The correct matching is A-2, B-4, C-1, D-3.

Rust Chemically, rust is ferric oxide which is formed when iron and its alloy comes indirect contact with air for a long time. Its chemical formula is Fe_2O_3.

Vinegar Chemically, vinegar is acetic acid. It is also known as ethanoic acid. Its chemical formula is CH_3COOH. A dilute solution of acetic acid is vinegar.

Baking soda Chemically, baking soda is sodium hydrogen carbonate with formula $NaHCO_3$. It is the important constituent of baking powder.

Lime water It is the common name for a dilute aqueous solution of calcium hydroxide. Its chemical formula is $Ca(OH)_2$.

13 Which of the following is/are the examples of chemical change? *(Chap 5, Class-VII, NCERT)*

1. Crystallisation of sodium chloride
2. Melting of ice
3. Souring of milk

Codes

(a) 1 and 2 (b) Only 3
(c) 1, 2 and 3 (d) None of these

Ans. (b)

Exp. Statement (3) is an example of chemical change as it results in the formation of new product, that is lactic acid. Crystallisation of sodium chloride and melting of ice are not the examples of chemical change. They are physical changes. In crystallisation of sodium chloride, only change of physical state takes place and no new substance is formed. In melting of ice, only solid state of water is changed into liquid state.

14 Match the following lists correctly and choose the correct codes. *(Chap 5, Class-VII, NCERT)*

	List-I (Process)		List-II (Reactions)
A.	Crystallisation	1.	Burning of paper
B.	Galvanisation	2.	Reversible
C.	Chemical change	3.	Process of formation of crystals
D.	Physical change	4.	Zinc coating on iron

Codes

	A	B	C	D		A	B	C	D
(a)	4	1	2	3	(b)	3	4	2	1
(c)	4	3	1	2	(d)	3	4	1	2

Ans. (d)

Exp. The correct matching is A-3, B-4, C-1, D-2.

Crystallisation It is a process of formation of crystals of pure substances from their solutions.

Galvanisation It is a process in which iron is coated with zinc to prevent it from rusting .

Burning of paper It is a chemical change as it results in the formation of ash which is a new product.

Physical changes These are reversible in nature as it only effects the form or state but not its chemical composition.

15 What will happen, if carbon dioxide gas is passed through lime water? *(Chap 5, Class-VII, NCERT)*

(a) Calcium carbonate is formed (b) Lime water turns milky
(c) Both 'a' and 'b' (d) Neither 'a' nor 'b'

Ans. (c)

Exp. If carbon dioxide gas is passed through lime water, then calcium carbonate is formed which turns the lime water milky.

$$\underset{\text{Lime water}}{Ca(OH)_2} + \underset{\text{Carbon dioxide}}{CO_2} \longrightarrow \underset{\substack{\text{Calcium carbonate}\\\text{(White ppt.)}}}{CaCO_3 \downarrow} + \underset{\text{Water}}{H_2O}$$

16 Which of the following statement is incorrect for a chemical change? *(Chap 5, Class-VII, NCERT)*

(a) Heat may come out but never be absorbed.
(b) Sound may be produced.
(c) A colour change may take place.
(d) A gas may be evolved.

Ans. (a)

Exp. Statement (a) is incorrect for a chemical reaction because in chemical reaction, either heat may come out or may be absorbed. Those reactions in which heat is released are exothermic reactions whereas those reactions in which heat is absorbed are endothermic reactions.

17 Consider the following Assertion (A) and Reason (R) and choose the correct code. *(Chap 1, Class-IX, NCERT)*

Assertion (A) Smell of burning incense stick spreads all around due to the diffusion of its fumes into air.

Reason (R) Increased temperature results in increased kinetic energy of the molecules.

Codes

(a) Both A and R are true and R is the correct explanation of A.
(b) Both A and R are true, but R is not the correct explanation of A.
(c) A is true and R is false.
(d) R is true and A is false.

Ans. (a)

Exp. Both Assertion (A) and Reason (R) are true and Reason (R) is the correct explanation of Assertion (A).

As the temperature increases, velocity of particles increases, so rate of diffusion as well as kinetic energy increases. Also, gases show the property of diffusion. This is due to high speed of particles and large intermolecular spaces between their particles. Hence, fumes of burning incense stick spreads all around.

18 Which of the following is an example of chemical change? *(Chap 5, Class-VII, NCERT) (RAS/RTS Pre 2003)*

(a) Dispersion of white light into the light of 7 colours.
(b) Softening of vegetables when cooked.
(c) Wet soil lump, when dried, gets fragile.
(d) Dissolving of salt in water.

Ans. (b)

Exp. Softening of vegetables on cooking is an example of chemical change as it brings irreversible changes in the composition of vegetables.

A change which alters the specific properties of a material by bringing about a change in its molecular composition, followed by a change in state, is called a chemical change.

19 Consider the following Assertion (A) and Reason (R) and choose the correct code. *(Chap 1, Class-IX, NCERT)*

Assertion (A) A chemical reaction becomes faster at a higher temperature.

Reason (R) At higher temperature, molecular motion becomes more rapid.

Codes

(a) Both A and R are true and R is the correct explanation of A.
(b) Both A and R are true, but R is not the correct explanation of A.
(c) A is true and R is false.
(d) A is false and R is true.

Ans. (a)

Exp. Both Assertion (A) and Reason (R) are true and Reason (R) is the correct explanation of Assertion (A).

A chemical reaction generally becomes faster at a higher temperature because at higher temperature, molecular motion becomes more rapid i.e molecules have higher kinetic energy.

The process of a chemical reaction depends on the concentration, temperature and physical state of molecules and their nature. Generally, higher the temperature of molecules, faster would be the reaction.

20 Consider the following statements.
(Chap 5, Class-VII, NCERT) (Telangana PCS Pre 2022)

1. It is chemically named as iron oxide.
2. Rusting is considered as a chemical change.
3. Zinc is coated on iron articles to prevent them from rusting.

How many statement(s) given above is/are correct?
(a) Only one (b) Only two (c) All three (d) None of these

Ans. (c)

Exp. All three Statements (1, 2 and 3) are correct.
Rusting of iron is chemically named as ferric oxide (Fe_2O_3) or iron oxide.
Rusting is considered as a chemical change as a new substance i.e. iron oxide is formed.
Zinc is more reactive than iron, it is used to protect iron from corrosion. It forms an impermeable coating of zinc oxide which creates a physical barrier from further attack of air and moistures.

21 Which of the following is/are the example of chemical change? *(Chap 5, Class-VII, NCERT)*

1. Sunlight from the sun
2. Curdling of milk
3. Change of water into ice

Codes
(a) 1 and 2 (b) 1, 2 and 3 (c) 2 and 3 (d) 1 and 3

Ans. (a)

Exp. A chemical change brings a change in the chemical properties of a substance.
Sunlight from the sun, curdling of milk examples of chemical change. The change of water into ice is a physical change.

22 Which of the following statement is correct?
(Chap 5, Class-VII, NCERT)

(a) Cutting of paper is a physical change.
(b) Crystallisation of sodium chloride is a chemical change.
(c) Setting of cement is a physical change.
(d) Burning of coal is a physical change.

Ans. (a)

Exp. Among the given statement only (a) is correct. The corrected form of statements (b), (c) and (d) are as; crystallisation of sodium chloride is an example of physical change, since sodium chloride does not transform into some new chemical element after crystallisation.
Setting of cement is a chemical change, as some amount of heat is liberated due to hydration. Burning of coal is a chemical change as when coal is burnt, carbon changed to carbon dioxide. This process can not be reversed.

23 Which of the following statement is incorrect?
(Chap 1, Class-IX, NCERT)

(a) The particle of matter are very-very small.
(b) Particles of matter attract one another.
(c) The particles of all the matter have spaces between them.
(d) The particles of solids are not moving constantly.

Ans. (d)

Exp. Statement (d) is incorrect because the particles of matter of all three states - solid, liquid and gaseous are moving constantly. As the particles in solid state are fixed at their positions, but they vibrate constantly.

24 Which of the following is not a colloid?
(Chap 2, Class-IX, NCERT)

(a) Curd (b) Blood (c) Ice-cream (d) Honey

Ans. (d)

Exp. Among the given options, honey is not a colloid. At room temperature, honey is supercooled liquid, in which the glucose precipitates into solid granules.
This forms a semi-solid solution of precipitated glucose crystals in a solution of fructose and other ingredients. Milk, curd, blood and ice-cream are colloids.

25 Which of the following relations between kinetic energy and potential energy is true about solids?
(Chap 2, Class-IX, NCERT)

(a) Kinetic energy = Potential energy
(b) Kinetic energy > Potential energy
(c) Kinetic energy >> Potential energy
(d) Kinetic energy < Potential energy

Ans. (d)

Exp. In solids, kinetic energy is always less than the potential energy. As in solids, intermolecular spaces are very less due to which particles don't get space for the movement.

26 Which type of colloidal system is expressed in the fog? *(Chap 2, Class-IX, NCERT)*

(a) Liquid in a gas (b) Gas in a liquid
(c) Solid in a gas (d) Liquid in liquid

Ans. (a)

Exp. Liquid in a gas type of colloidal system is expressed as the fog. When the water vapour in the air condensed to form small droplets of water, the fog is formed. This can be explained as, when the temperature of air during winter season reaches new to dew point, the water vapour gets condensed around small particles of dust and remains suspended in the air because of their low weight.

27 Match the following lists correctly and choose the correct code. *(Chap 2, Class-IX, NCERT)*

List-I (Types of colloid)	List-II (Examples)
A. Gel	1. Rubber
B. Foam	2. Face cream
C. Emulsion	3. Coloured gemstone
D. Solid sol	4. Butter
E. Aerosol	5. Cloud

Codes

	A	B	C	D	E		A	B	C	D	E
(a)	1	2	4	5	3	(b)	2	1	3	4	5
(c)	4	1	2	3	5	(d)	3	4	5	1	2

Ans. (c)

Exp. The correct matching is A-4, B-1, C-2, D-3, E-5.
Gel It is liquid in solid type of colloid. Butter is an example of gel in which water molecules are trapped in between the fat.
Foam It is gas in solid type of colloid. Rubber is an example of foam in which gas is dispersed in rubber.
Emulsion It is liquid in liquid type of colloid. Face cream is an example of emulsion in which liquid is dispersed in liquid medium.
Solid sol It is solid in solid type of colloid. Coloured gemstone is an example of solid sol in which solid acts as the dispersed phase as well as the dispersion medium.
Aerosol It is liquid in gas type of colloid. Cloud is an example of aerosol in which water droplets are dispersed in gaseous medium.

28 **Match the following lists correctly and choose the correct code.** *(Chap 2, Class-IX, NCERT)*

List-I (Type of mixture)	List-II (Examples)
A. Colloid	1. Chalk in water
B. Suspension	2. Starch in water
C. Homogeneous mixture	3. A mixture of chalk and sand
D. Heterogeneous mixture	4. Air

Codes

	A	B	C	D		A	B	C	D
(a)	2	1	4	3	(b)	1	3	4	2
(c)	3	2	1	4	(d)	4	2	3	1

Ans. (a)

Exp. The correct matching is A-2, B-1, C-4, D-3.
Colloid Starch molecules have colloidal dimensions. Therefore, starch forms a colloidal solution in water.
Suspension It is a fluid with finely dispersed solid particles. Chalk powder is very little soluble in water, therefore, this will form an suspension.
Homogeneous In air all gases would have a uniform composition. Therefore, the air is an example of homogeneous mixture.
Heterogeneous Chalk and sand does not form uniform composition. Hence, mixture of chalk and sand is a heterogeneous mixture.

29 **Which one of the following is most likely to exhibit Tyndall effect?** *(Chap 2, Class-IX, NCERT)*
(a) Chalk powder and water mixture
(b) Potash alum and water mixture
(c) Sugar and water mixture
(d) Potassium permanganate and water mixture
Ans. (a)

Exp. Among the given options, chalk powder and water mixture are most likely to exhibit Tyndall effect because they form a colloidal solution.
A colloid is a kind of solution in which the size of solute particles is intermediate between those in true solutions and those in suspensions. The scattering of light by colloidal particle is known as Tyndall effect.

30 **During summer, water kept in an earthen pot becomes cool because of the phenomenon of** *(Chap 3, Class-VI, NCERT)*
(a) diffusion (b) transpiration
(c) osmosis (d) evaporation
Ans. (d)

Exp. During summer, water kept in an earthen pot becomes cool because of the phenomenon of evaporation.
Earthen pot has a large number of tiny pores in its walls and some of the water molecules continuously keep evaporating through these pores to outside the pot. This keeps the water inside the pot cool.

31 **Consider the following statements :** *(Chap 2, Class-IX, NCERT)*
1. Mixture of sand and naphthalene can be separated by distillation.
2. Distillation is useful for purification of solid impurities.
3. In chromatography, separation is based on differential partitioning between the mobile and stationary phase.

Which of the statement(s) given above is/are correct?
(a) Only 1 (b) 1 and 2
(c) Only 3 (d) 1 and 3
Ans. (c)

Exp. Among the given statements only (3) are correct. The corrected form of incorrect statement are as;
Mixture of sand and naphthalene can be separated by sublimation instead of distillation. On heating, naphthalene sublimes and is deposited on the edges of the flask while sand is left behind.
Distillation method is not useful for purification of solid impurities. It is generally used for purification of liquid impurities.

32 **Consider the following statements.** *(Chap 3, Class-VI, NCERT)*
1. Handpicking method is used for separating larger sized impurities.
2. Separating grains from stalks is threshing.
3. Winnowing is used to separate lighter and heavier components.

Which of the statements given above are correct?
(a) 1 and 2 (b) 1 and 3
(c) 1, 2 and 3 (d) None of these
Ans. (c)

Exp. All the given statements are correct.
Handpicking method involves separating slightly larger sized impurities like the pieces of dirt, stone and husk from wheat, rice or pulses.
Threshing is used to separate grain from stalks. It involves beaten of stalks to free the grain seeds.
Winnowing is used to separate heavier and lighter components of a mixture by wind or by blowing air.

33 **Match the following list correctly and choose the correct code.** *(Chap 3, Class-VI, NCERT)*

List-I	List-II
A. Sedimentation	1. Separation of common salt from water solution
B. Saturation	2. Conversion of water vapour into liquid
C. Evaporation	3. Setting of heavier components at bottom
D. Condensation	4. No more solute can be dissolved

Codes

	A	B	C	D		A	B	C	D
(a)	1	2	3	4	(b)	4	2	1	3
(c)	3	4	1	2	(d)	2	4	3	1

Ans. (c)

Exp. The correct matching is A-3, B-4, C-1, D-2.

Sedimentation The process of settling of heavier components at bottom in the solution when it is lest undisturbed is called sedimentation.

Saturation Solution in which no more solute can be dissolved is said to be saturated.

Evaporation The process of separation of common salt from water solution is evaporation. In this process, water is converted into its vapour and salt left in the vessel.

Condensation The process of conversion of water vapour into its liquid state, is known as condensation. In this process, water vapours are cooled and converted into liquid.

34 **Consider the following statements** *(Chap 3, Class-VI, NCERT) (Unit 10, Class-IX, Tamil Nadu Board)*

1. Oil and water are immiscible with each other.
2. Decantation method is used to separate two miscible liquids.
3. Pebbles and stones separated from sand by winnowing.

How many statement(s) given above is/are incorrect?

(a) Only one (b) Only two (c) All three (d) None of these

Ans. (b)

Exp. Only two Statements (2 and 3) are incorrect, while one Statement (1) is correct.

As decantation method is used to separate two immiscible liquids or a mixture of a solid and a gas.

Pebbles and stones separated from sand by sieving. It is a method of using a sieve to distinguish small particles from bigger particles.

35 **Consider the following statements for separation of components from a mixture.** *(Chap 3, Class-VI, NCERT)*

1. A mixture of sand and naphthalene can be separated by distillation.
2. Mixture of acetone and water is separated by evaporation.
3. Decantation method is used to separated two immiscible liquids.

Which of the statement(s) given above is/are correct?

(a) Only 3 (b) 1 and 2
(c) Only 1 (d) None of these

Ans. (a)

Exp. Only Statement (3) is correct. Rest two statements are incorrect. Mixture of sand and naphthalene can be separated by sublimation. It is because naphthalene displays the phenomenon of sublimation. Mixture of acetone and water is separated by distillation method. Since, both have large differences in their boiling point.

36 **Consider the following statements.** *(Chap 1, Class-XII, NCERT) (IAS Pre 2005)*

1. During the process of osmosis, the solvent travels from the concentrated solution to the dilute solution.
2. In the reverse osmosis, external pressure is applied to the dilute solution.

Which of the statement(s) given above is/are correct?

(a) Only 1 (b) Only 2
(c) Both 1 and 2 (d) Neither 1 nor 2

Ans. (d)

Exp. Neither statement (1) nor (2) is correct because in the process of osmosis, the solvent moves through a semipermeable membrane from a region of high concentration to a region of low concentration. While in reverse osmosis, we apply external pressure upon concentrated solution to reverse the movement of solvent. This technique is used to purify the solution by making it free from impurities.

37 **Which one of the following process is not useful for purification of solid?** *(Chap 5, Class-VII, NCERT) (Unit 10, Class-IX, Tamil Nadu Board) (UP RO/ARO Pre 2016)*

(a) Distillation (b) Sublimation
(c) Crystallisation (d) All of these

Ans. (a)

Exp. Distillation is not useful for purification of solid impurities. It is generally used for purification of liquid impurities. While sublimation and crystallisation are used for purification of solid impurities.

38 **The technique of chromatography is used to** *(Chap 8, Class-XI, NCERT) (BPSC Pre 1997)*

(a) identify colour substances
(b) determine the structure of substances
(c) dry distillation of colouring substances
(d) separate the substances from a mixture

Ans. (d)

Exp. The technique of chromatography is used to separate the substances from a mixture. The separation is based on differential partitioning between the mobile and stationary phases.

Chromatography may be preparative or analytical. The purpose of preparative chromatography is to separate the components of a mixture for more advanced use and thus it is a form of purification.

Chemical Reactions, Bonds and Chemical Equations

Chemical Reactions, Bonds and Chemical Equations

Chemical Reaction

Chemical Reaction

- Irrerversible atteration in chemical composition

$$2Mg + O_2 \rightarrow 2MgO$$

Types of Chemical Reactions

- Classified into different types depending upon the chemical changes taking place.
- **Combination Reaction** Two or more reactants react together to give single product. eg. burning of coal, $C(s) + O_2(g) \rightarrow CO_2(g)$
- **Decomposition Reaction** Single reactant breaks down into two or more simple products.
  - **Thermal Decomposition** Heat is used to decompose the substance. e.g. $CaCO_3(s) \xrightarrow{Heat} CaO(s)+CO_2(g)$
  - **Electrolysis** Electricity is used to decompose the substance e.g. $2H_2O(l) \xrightarrow[Current]{Electric} 2H_2(g)+O_2(g)$
  - **Photolysis** Decomposes by using light energy. e.g. $2AgCl(s) \xrightarrow{h\nu} 2Ag(s) + Cl_2(g)$
- **Displacement Reaction** One element displaces the other from its salt solution.
  - **Single Displacement Reactions** More reactive element displaces the less reactive one from its salt solution e.g. $Fe(s)+CuSO_4(aq) \longrightarrow FeSO_4(aq) + Cu(s)$
  - **Double Displacement Reactions** In two different ions in the reactant molecules are displaced by each other. e.g. $Na_2SO_4(aq) + BaCl_2(aq) \rightarrow BaSO_4(s)\downarrow + 2NaCl(aq)$
- **Neutralisation Reaction** Acid and base react to form salt & water $2NaOH + H_2SO_4 \rightarrow Na_2SO_4 + 2H_2O$ (acid) (base) (salt) (water)
- **Reversible Reaction (both direction)** $N_2 + H_2 \xrightleftharpoons{Fe, Mo} 2NH_3$
- **Irreversible Reaction (single direction)** $2NaOH + H_2SO_4 \rightarrow Na_2SO_4 + 2H_2O$
- **Exothermic & Endothermic Reaction**
  - Evolution of heat are called exothermic. e.g. Respiration
  - Occurring by the absorption of heat are called endothermic reaction e.g. Photosynthesis
- **Isomerisation or Rearrangement Reaction** Atoms of the molecule of a compound undergo rearrangement e.g. $NH_4CNO \xrightarrow{\Delta} NH_2CONH_2$ (Ammonium cyanate → Urea)
- **Hydrolysis Reaction** Reaction with salt of weak acid or weak base with water. $CH_3COONa + H_2O \rightarrow CH_3COOH + NaOH$
- **Photochemical Reaction** Presence of sunlight $6CO_2 + 12H_2O \xrightarrow{h\nu} C_6H_{12}O_6 + 6H_2O + 6O_2$
- **Oxidation and Reduction Reaction**
  - Oxidation (loss of electron) oxidant cause oxidation. reduction (gain of electron), reductant cause reduction.

Chemical Equation

Chemical Equation

- Reactants symbol/formula are written on the left and products symbol / formula were written on the right separated by an arrow.
- **Balanced Chemical Equations**
- Number of atoms of each element are equal on both sides of the equation, based on law of conservation of mass.

Steps Involved in Balancing Chemical Equation

- **Hit and Trial method** Can be used to balance a chemical equation
- Several steps are involved in balancing a chemical equation. These steps are follows.
  - **Step I** Write unbalanced equation and enclose the formulae in brackets.
  - **Step II** Make list of elements present in unbalanced or skeletal equation.
  - **Step III** Balance, first, second and successive elements.
  - **Step IV** Check the correctness of equation.
  - **Step V** Make the equation more informative by adding following parameters.

(i) Physical state of reactants and products.
(ii) Reaction conditions.
(iii) Concentration of reactants and products.

SOURCE *New NCERT Class X Chap 1 (Chemical Reactions and Equations), New NCERT Class XI Chap 7 (Redox Reactions)*

1 **Match the following lists correctly and choose the correct code.** *(Chap 1, Class-X, NCERT)*

List-I (Reaction)	List-II (Gas evolved)
A. Zinc granules are treated with dilute H_2SO_4.	1. Oxygen
B. Calcium carbonate on reaction with HCl.	2. Carbon dioxide
C. Lead nitrate is heated strongly.	3. Hydrogen
D. Decomposition of $KClO_3$.	4. Nitrogen dioxide

Codes

	A	B	C	D		A	B	C	D
(a)	3	2	4,1	1	(b)	3	2	1,4	4
(c)	2	3,1	4	1	(d)	2,3	1	4	3

Ans. (a)

Exp. The correct matching is A-3, B-2, C-4,1, D-1.

Zinc granules when treated with dilute sulphuric acid, it displaces hydrogen from the acid and forms zinc sulphate and hydrogen gas.

$$\underset{\text{Zinc}}{Zn} + \underset{\text{Sulphuric acid}}{H_2SO_4} \longrightarrow \underset{\text{Zinc sulphate}}{ZnSO_4} + \underset{\text{Hydrogen gas}}{H_2\uparrow}$$

Calcium carbonate on reacting with hydrochloric acid forms calcium chloride, carbon dioxide and water.

$$\underset{\text{Calcium carbonate}}{CaCO_3} + \underset{\text{Hydrochloric acid}}{2HCl(aq)} \longrightarrow \underset{\text{Calcium chloride}}{CaCl_2(aq)} + \underset{\text{Carbon dioxide}}{CO_2(g)} + \underset{\text{Water}}{H_2O}$$

Lead nitrate when heated strongly decomposes to form lead oxide, nitrogen dioxide and oxygen gas.

$$\underset{\text{Lead nitrate}}{2Pb(NO_3)_2} \xrightarrow{\Delta} \underset{\text{Lead oxide}}{2PbO} + \underset{\text{Nitrogen dioxide}}{4NO_2} + \underset{\text{Oxygen}}{O_2}$$

Potassium chlorate is decomposed on heating into potassium chloride and oxygen gas.

$$\underset{\text{Potassium chlorate}}{2KClO_3(s)} \xrightarrow{\Delta} \underset{\text{Potassium chloride}}{2KCl(s)} + \underset{\text{Oxygen}}{3O_2(g)}$$

2 **Assertion (A)** A chemical reaction becomes faster at higher temperatures.

Reason (R) At higher temperatures, molecular motion becomes more rapid.

(Chap 1, Class-X, NCERT) (UPPSC Pre 2001)

Codes

(a) Both A and R are individually true and R is the correct explanation of A.

(b) Both A and R are individually true but R is not a correct explanation of A.

(c) A is true but R is false.

(d) A is false but R is true.

Ans. (a)

Exp. Both A and R are true and R is the correct explanation of A.

A chemical reaction becomes faster at higher temperatures due to increase in motion of its interparticles. As when temperature is raised, the kinetic energy of the particles increases.

Due to the increase in kinetic energy, the particles start vibrating with greater speed. These particles colloid more frequently and hence, rate of chemical reaction increases.

3 **Match the following lists correctly and choose the correct code.** *(Chap 1, Class-X, NCERT)*

List-I (Compound)	List-II (Chemical formula)
A. Quick lime	1. $CaCO_3$
B. Lead nitrate	2. Na_2SO_4
C. Limestone	3. CaO
D. Sodium sulphate	4. $Pb(NO_3)_2$

Codes

	A	B	C	D		A	B	C	D
(a)	1	2	3	4	(b)	3	4	1	2
(c)	3	4	2	1	(d)	4	3	2	1

Ans. (b)

Exp. The correct matching is A-3, B-4, C-1, D-2.

Quick lime Its chemical name is calcium oxide with formula CaO. It is a white, caustic, alkaline and crystalline solid at room temperature.

Lead nitrate Its chemical formula is $Pb(NO_3)_2$. It commonly occurs as a colourless crystal or white powder.

Limestone It is chemically named as calcium carbonate having formula $CaCO_3$. It is composed mostly of the minerals calcite and aragonite, which are different crystal forms of calcium carbonate.

Sodium sulphate It is having formula Na_2SO_4. It is mainly used as a filler in the manufacture of powdered home laundry detergents.

4 **Which of the following compound is used in manufacturing of cement ?** *(Chap 1, Class-X, NCERT)*

(a) Quick lime

(b) Barium hydroxide

(c) Aqueous solution of ammonia

(d) Precipitate of silver chloride

Ans. (a)

Exp. Quick lime is used in manufacturing of cement. It can also be used as a drying or neutralising agent. Chemically, it is known as calcium oxide and it is usually made by burning of limestone.

5 **Which of the following is not an "element + element → compound" type reaction?** *(Chap 1 Class-X, NCERT)*

(a) $C(s) + O_2(g) \longrightarrow CO_2(g)$

(b) $2K(s) + Br_2(l) \longrightarrow 2KBr(s)$

(c) $2CO(g) + O_2(g) \longrightarrow 2CO_2(g)$

(d) $4Fe(s) + 3O_2(g) \longrightarrow 2Fe_2O_3(s)$

Ans. (c)

Exp. Among the given reactions, only (c) is not a element + element → compound, type reaction, In this type of combination reaction two elements react with one another to form a compound. While in reaction (c), CO_2 is a compound reacting with element O_2 to form carbon dioxide.

6 Reaction between carbon and oxygen is represented by

$$C(s)+O_2(g) \longrightarrow CO_2(g)+\text{Heat}$$

In which type, the above reaction can be classified? *(Chap 1, Class-X, NCERT)*

1. Combination reaction 2. Displacement reaction
3. Combustion reaction

Codes

(a) 1 and 3 (b) Only 1 (c) 1 and 2 (d) 2 and 3

Ans. (a)

Exp. In the given reaction, carbon is combining with oxygen to form CO_2, it is a combination reaction and the oxidation of carbon is also taking place in the presence of oxygen. So, it is also a combustion reaction.

7 Consider the following reaction. *(Chap 1, Class-X, NCERT)*

$$Fe_2O_3 + 2Al \longrightarrow Al_2O_3 + 2Fe$$

The above reaction is an example of

(a) combination reaction
(b) double displacement reaction
(c) decomposition reaction
(d) displacement reaction

Ans. (d)

Exp. The given reaction is a displacement reaction. It is also called as single replacement reaction. It is a kind of oxidation-reduction chemical reaction when an ion or element moves out of a compound, i.e. Fe_2O_3 is reduced to Fe and Al is oxidised to Al_2O_3.

Here, aluminium is more reactive than iron, so displaces iron from its oxide and forms aluminium oxide.

8 A single displacement reaction is represented by *(Chap 1, Class-X, NCERT)*

$$X(s)+2HCl(aq) \longrightarrow XCl_2(aq)+H_2(g).$$

Which of the following could be X.

1. Zn 2. Cu 3. Ag 4. Mg

Codes

(a) 1 and 2 (b) 2 and 3 (c) 3 and 4 (d) 1 and 4

Ans. (d)

Exp. X can be Zn or Mg. Displacement reaction is a chemical reaction in which a more reactive element displaces a less reactive element from its compound.

Among the given elements, Zn and Mg are more reactive than hydrogen thus, displaces it in the reaction.

9 Which among the following is an incorrect statement? *(Chap 1, Class-X, NCERT)*

(a) Copper displaces iron from the aqueous solution of its compound.
(b) Reaction between Na_2SO_4 and $BaCl_2$ is a precipitation reaction.
(c) Reaction between nitrogen and hydrogen proceeds in both directions.
(d) Decomposition of calcium carbonate is done in the presence of heat.

Ans. (a)

Exp. Among the given statements, only (a) is incorrect. The corrected form of statement (a) is, copper being less reactive than iron, can't displaces iron from the aqueous solution of its compound.

10 Which of the following statement(s) is/are correct? *(Chap 1, Class-X, NCERT)* *(Unit 10, Class-X, Tamil Nadu Board)*

1. Energy is absorbed in exothermic reactions.
2. Addition of water in quick lime is an exothermic reaction.
3. Barium hydroxide is used in manufacturing of cement.
4. Energy is released in endothermic reaction.

Codes

(a) 1 and 3 (b) 2 only
(c) 1 and 4 (d) 3 only

Ans. (b)

Exp. Among the given statements only (2) is correct. The corrected form of incorrect statements are energy is released in exothermic reactions because the total energy of the products is less than the total energy of the reactants.

Quick lime is used in manufacturing of cement instead of barium hydroxide and it is added to mortar.

Energy is absorbed in endothermic reactions because the total energy of the products is more than the total energy of reactants.

11 Which one of the following actions is related with evaporation of sweat? *(Chap 1, Class-X, NCERT) (UKPSC Pre 2011)*

(a) Exothermic action
(b) Endothermic action
(c) Chemical action
(d) Salty action

Ans. (b)

Exp. Endothermic action is related with evaporation of sweat. Sweating allows the body to regulate its temperature. When the external temperature reaches 37°C or above, body recognises that the temperature in the surrounding air is higher than the temperature of the body. So, it perspires. The sweat evaporates from the skin using the body heat and making our body a bit cooler.

12 Which of the following compound is used in black and white photography? *(Chap 1, Class-X, NCERT)*

(a) $Pb(NO_3)_2$
(b) AgBr
(c) $FeSO_4$
(d) $CaCO_3$

Ans. (b)

Exp. AgBr (Silver bromide) is used in black and white photography. It gets broken down into elemental bromine and metallic silver on exposure to light and loses its colour.

It is photosensitive due to which it is suspended into gelatin and creates a photographic emulsion.

13 Which of the following is not an exothermic reaction? *(Chap 1, Class-X, NCERT)*

(a) Addition of water in quick lime
(b) Melting of ice
(c) Burning of natural gas
(d) Respiration

Ans. (b)

Exp. Melting of ice is not an exothermic reaction. It changes its physical state from solid to liquid by absorbing heat from surroundings. Therefore, this is an endothermic process.

14 Match the following lists correctly and choose the correct code. *(Chap 7, Class-XI, NCERT) (IAS Pre 2002)*

List-I (Oxidation number)		List-II (Elements)
A. 2	1.	Oxidation number of Mn in MnO_2.
B. 3	2.	Oxidation number of S in H_2SO_4.
C. 4	3.	Oxidation number of Ca in CaO.
D. 6	4.	Oxidation number of Al in $NaAlH_4$.

Codes

	A	B	C	D		A	B	C	D
(a)	3	4	1	2	(b)	4	3	1	2
(c)	3	4	2	1	(d)	4	3	2	1

Ans. (a)

Exp. The correct matching is A-3, B-4, C-1, D-2.
The oxidation number of any neutral compound is always zero. This means that sum of the oxidation number of all the elements present in the compound is zero.
By this rule, we can now find the oxidation number of element given compounds as.
Suppose, the oxidation number of Mn in MnO_2 is x.
MnO_2 contains two oxygen ions, each with an oxidation number (–2).

$$\Rightarrow \quad x + 2\times(-2) = 0$$
$$x - 4 = 0 \Rightarrow x = 4$$

Suppose, the oxidation number of S in H_2SO_4 is x. H_2SO_4 contains two hydrogen ion, each with an oxidation number (+1) and oxidation number of oxygen (–2).

$$2(+1) + x + 4(-2) = 0$$
$$\Rightarrow \quad 2 + x - 8 = 0$$
$$\Rightarrow \quad x = 6$$

Suppose, the oxidation number of Ca in CaO when oxygen has oxidation number (–2).

$$\Rightarrow \quad x - 2 = 0$$
$$\Rightarrow \quad x = 2$$

Suppose, the oxidation number of Al in $NaAlH_4$ is x.
$NaAlH_4$ contains one Na which has oxidation number (+1) and four H which has oxidation number (–1).

$$\Rightarrow \quad (+1) + x + 4(-1) = 0$$
$$\Rightarrow \quad 1 + x - 4 = 0$$
$$\Rightarrow \quad x = 3$$

15 Consider the following statement. *(Chap 7, Class-XI, NCERT)*

$3Fe(s) + 4H_2O(g) \longrightarrow Fe_3O_4(s) + 4H_2(g)$

1. Iron metal is getting oxidised.
2. Water is getting reduced.
3. Water is acting as reducing agent.
4. In the oxidation of iron, there is the difference of 3 in the oxidation number.

Which of the above statements about the given reaction are correct ?

(a) 1, 2 and 3 (b) 3 and 4 (c) 1, 2 and 4 (d) 2 and 4

Ans. (c)

Exp. Statements (1), (2) and (4) are correct about the given reaction.

$$\underset{\text{Iron}}{3Fe(s)} + \underset{\text{Water}}{4H_2O(g)} \longrightarrow \underset{\text{Iron oxide}}{Fe_3O_4(s)} + \underset{\text{Hydrogen}}{4H_2(g)}$$

Iron metal is oxidised as the oxidation number of iron will change from 0 to +3. Water is getting reduced as oxidation number of hydrogen will change from +1 to 0. Statement (3) is incorrect as water itself gets reduced, so it will act as oxidising agent.

16 Consider the following statements about corrosion. *(Chap 1, Class-X, NCERT)*

1. Surface of copper acquires a green coating in moist air.
2. The rusting of iron can be prevented by painting, oiling and greasing.

Which of the statement(s) given above is/are correct?

(a) Both 1 and 2 (b) Only 1
(c) Only 2 (d) Neither 1 nor 2

Ans. (a)

Exp. Both statements (1) and (2) are correct about corrosion.
Copper when reacts with moist air forms a mixture of copper carbonate and copper hydroxide, this results in appearance of green coating on the surface which is an effect of corrosion.
Rusting of iron occurs when iron surface comes in contact with atmospheric oxygen and forms iron oxide. It results in deposition of reddish brown coating on metal.
Corrosion can be prevented by painting, oiling and greasing.

17 Due to corrosion, copper acquires coating of which colour ? *(Chap 1, Class-X, NCERT)*

(a) Gray (b) Black
(c) Green (d) Reddish brown

Ans. (c)

Exp. Due to corrosion, copper acquires coating of green colour. When copper is exposed to air in rainy season, it reacts with gases and moisture to form a mixture of copper carbonate and copper hydroxide which results in green coating.

18 Consider the following statements.

(Chap 1, Class-X, NCERT) (Chap 4, Module-2, NIOS)

1. Green coating on copper and black coating on silver is an example of corrosion.
2. Chips manufacturers usually flush bags of chips with nitrogen gas.
3. Most effective disinfectants are strong oxidizers.

How many of the above statement(s) is/are correct?

(a) Only one (b) Only two
(c) All three (d) None of these

Ans. (c)

Exp. All three Statements (1, 2 and 3) are correct.

When a metal is attacked by substances around it such as moisture, acid, etc., it gets damage slowly & this process is called corrosion.

Chips manufacturers usually flush bags of chips with nitrogen gas to prevent the chips from getting oxidised. A substance capable of destroying bacteria is called a disinfectant. Most effective disinfectants are strong oxidizers.

19 Fats and oils become rancid due to the process of

(Chap 1, Class-X, NCERT)

(a) oxidation (b) corrosion
(c) reduction (d) hydrogenation

Ans. (a)

Exp. Fats and oils become rancid due to the process of oxidation. This phenomenon is known as rancidity. It is produced by aerial oxidation of unsaturated fat present in foods and other products, marked by unpleasant odour or flavour.

20 Which gas is used to prevent chips from getting oxidised in packets ? *(Chap 1, Class-X, NCERT)*

(a) Oxygen (b) Carbon dioxide
(c) Helium (d) Nitrogen

Ans. (d)

Exp. Nitrogen gas is used to prevent chips from getting oxidised in packets. It is an inert gas and is used during the packaging process to remove air which cause oxidation.

Chapter 04

Periodic Classification of Elements

Periodic Classification of Elements

Development of Periodic Table

Development of Periodic Table

- At present, 118 elements are known, out of these 94 are naturally occurring.
- **Dobereiner's Traids (1817)** Order of increasing atomic masses, the atomic mass of the middle element was roughly the average of the atomic masses of the other two elements.
- **Newland's Law of Octaves (1866)** Order of increasing atomic masses and found that every eight element had properties similar to that of the first.
- **Limitations** Applicable only upto calcium. 56 elements existed in nature.

Mendeleev's Periodic Table (1869)

- The physical and chemical properties of elements are periodic function of their atomic mass.
- **Features**
  - 8 vertical columns called groups and 6 horizontal rows called periods.
  - Mendeleev's left gaps in his table for the element not discovered at that time.
  - An element with slightly greater atomic mass is placed before an element with slightly lower atomic mass.
- **Limitations**
  - Position of hydrogen, Position of isotopes. Uncertainty in Atomic masses. Placing of heavier element before the lighter one.

Modern Periodic Table

Modern Periodic Table (1913)

- Physical and chemical properties of the elements are periodic function of their atomic number.

Determining Atomic Number and Mass Number of an Element

- **For *s*-Block Elements**, atomic number = number of valence electrons.
- **For *p*-Block Elements** atomic number = 10 + number of valence electrons.
- **For *d*-Block Elements** atomic number = *ns* electrons + $(n-1)$ *d* elements.

Types of Elements

(i) *s*-Block Elements Group-1 and 2 (IA and IIA)
- Group-1 (IA) alkali metals.
- Group-2 (IIA) alkaline earth metals.

(ii) *p*-Block Elements Group-13 to 18 (IIIA to VIII A) metals. non-metals and metalloids.

(iii) *d*-Block Elements Group-3 to 12

(iv) *f*-Block Elements lanthanoids and actinoids of periodic table.

Features of Modern Periodic Table

- 18 groups and 7 rows.
- **Features of Groups** Not divided into sub-groups. Same number of valence electrons and valency.
- **Features of Periods** Elements of period do not have same number of shells Maximum electron in a shell is $2n^2$.

Trends in Modern Periodic Table

Periodic Properties

- **Periodic Properties** The properties which are repeated at regular intervals
- **Valency**
  - Combining capacity of an atom of an element to acquire noble gas configuration.
  - In a group, there are same number of valence electrons and valency.
- **Atomic Size**
  - Radius of an atom.
  - Moving along one period from left to right, atomic radius decreases.
  - On moving from top to bottom, atomic size increases.
- **Metallic and Non-metallic Properties**
  - Tendency of an element to form cation by the loss of electrons.
  - Metallic character decreases along a period and increases down a group.
- **Nature of Oxides**
  - Oxides of the metals are of basic nature while those of non-metals are acidic.
  - Along a period the basic character of the oxides of the elements decreases while their acidic character increases.
- **Electronegativity**
  - Relative electrons attracting tendency of an atom for a shared electron pair in a covalent bond with other atom.
  - The electronegativity of the elements increases along a period and decreases down the group.

SOURCE New NCERT Class XI Chap 3 (Classification of Elements and Periodicity in Properties)
Tamil Nadu Board Class X (Carbon and its Compounds), (Periodic classification of Elements)

1 **Which of the following will not represent Dobereiner's triad?** *(Chap 3, Class-XI, NCERT)*

(a) Li, Na, K (b) Be, Mg, Ca
(c) Cl, Br, I (d) N, P, As

Ans. (d)

Exp. Among the given triads, N, P and As will not represent the Dobereiner's triad because the average of atomic masses of nitrogen (N) and arsenic (As) is not equal to the atomic mass of phosphorus (P).

Atomic mass (N) = 14

Atomic mass (As) = 74.9

$$\text{Average} = \frac{74.9 + 14.0}{2} \simeq 44.45$$

which is not equal to the atomic mass of P (i.e. 31.0).

2 **Which statement is correct according to Mendeleev's periodic law?** *(Chap 3, Class-XI, NCERT)*

(a) The properties of element are the periodic function of their atomic number.
(b) The properties of the element are the periodic function of their atomic weights.
(c) The properties of elements are the periodic function of their atomic volume.
(d) None of the above

Ans. (b)

Exp. Statement (b) is correct. According to Mendeleev's periodic law, the properties of elements are the periodic function of their atomic weights. Mendeleev arranged 63 elements in his table.

3 **Consider the following statements regarding limitations of Mendeleev's periodic law;** *(Chap 3, Class-XI, NCERT)*

1. Position of isotopes could not be explained by this law.
2. This law was applicable only up to calcium.
3. The atomic masses do not increase in a regular manner in going from one element to the next.

How many statement(s) is/are correct?

(a) Only one (b) Onle two
(c) All three (d) None of these

Ans. (b)

Exp. Only two Statements (1 and 3) are correct reagrding the limitations of Mendeleev's periodic law. Whereas statement (2) is the limitations of Newland's law of octaves. Every eighth element did not show properties similar to that the first after calcium.

4 **Consider the following statements regarding modern periodic table.** *(Chap 3, Class XII, NCERT)*

1. The table is not divided into sub-groups.
2. The elements present in a group have the different valency.
3. Melting point and boiling point of the elements in a group vary gradually.

Which of the statements given above is/are correct.

(a) Only 1
(b) Only 2
(c) 1 and 3
(d) 2 and 3

Ans. (c)

Exp. Among the given statements only (1) and (3) are correct, whereas statement (2) is incorrect. The correct form of statement (2) is, the element present in a group have the same valency, because the number of valence electrons for all the elements in a group are same.

On moving from left to right in a period the number of valence electrons in a period increases, thus valence increases from + 1 to + 4, then goes from –3 to a noble element which has a valency of zero.

5 **Which of the following statement is incorrect according to modern periodic table?** *(Chap 3, Class-XI, NCERT)*

(a) Properties of elements are a periodic function of their atomic number.
(b) It consists of 18 vertical columns known as groups and 7 horizontal rows called periods.
(c) Elements in same group have different number of valence electrons.
(d) Number of shells increases on going down the group.

Ans. (c)

Exp. Statement (c) is incorrect according to modern periodic table because in this tabular form, elements are arranged in their increasing atomic number so that elements in same group have same number of valence electrons. Therefore, they have similar chemical properties.

6 **Identify the correct statement about the controversial issue for modern periodic table.** *(Chap 3, Class-XI, NCERT)*

(a) Placement of elements according to increasing order of atomic numbers.
(b) Position of hydrogen.
(c) Position of transition elements.
(d) Position of noble gases.

Ans. (b)

Exp. Statement (b) is correct according to controversial issue for modern periodic table.

Position of hydrogen is a big issue as its electronic configuration belongs to *s*-block elements but it shows properties like halogens or *p*-block elements.

7 **Consider the following Assertion (A) and Reason (R) and choose the correct codes.** *(Chap 3, Class-XI, NCERT)*

Assertion (A) The elements of the same group have similar chemical properties.

Reason (R) The elements of the same group have the different number of valence electrons.

Codes

(a) Both A and R are true and R is the correct explanation of A.
(b) Both A and R are true but R is not the correct explanation of A.
(c) A is true but R is false.
(d) A is false but R is true.

Ans. (c)

Exp. Assertion (A) is true but Reason (R) is false. According to modern periodic law, physical and chemical properties of the elements are periodic functions of their atomic number. The elements of same group have same chemical properties as the valence shell configuration is same for the elements of same group.

8 Correctly match the following.

(Chap 3, Class-XI, NCERT)
(Unit 11, Class-X, Tamil Nadu Board) (CGPSC Pre 2023)

Elements	Valency
A. Silicon	1. 1
B. Fluorine	2. 2
C. Aluminium	3. 3
D. Sulphur	4. 4

Codes

	A	B	C	D		A	B	C	D
(a)	4	3	2	1	(b)	4	1	3	2
(c)	3	4	1	2	(d)	3	4	2	1

Ans. (b)

Exp. The correct matching is A-4, B-1, C-3 D-2.
In a silicon atom, the outermost orbital contains 4 electrons, therefore its valency is 4.
Similarly, the valency of fluorine is 1, aluminium is 3 and sulphur is 2.

9 Match the following lists correctly and choose the correct code. *(Chap 3, Class-XI, NCERT)*

List-I (Properties)	List-II (Block)
A. Alkali and alkaline earth metals	1. *p* - block elements
B. Transition elements	2. *s* - block elements
C. Representative elements (except zero group)	3. *f*- block elements
D. Inner-transition elements	4. *d*- block elements

Codes

	A	B	C	D		A	B	C	D
(a)	3	4	2	1	(b)	2	4	1	3
(c)	2	4	3	1	(d)	2	3	4	1

Ans. (b)

Exp. The correct matching is A-2, B-4, C-1, D-3.
Alkali and alkaline earth metals It refers to *s*-block elements. Metals are present in this block are very reactive in nature.
Transition elements They refer to *d*-block elements as they are moderately reactive. They exhibit transitional behaviour between *s* and *p*-block.
Representative elements (except zero group) It refers to *p*-block elements and these are present in the right side of the periodic table. They require few electrons to fulfill their octet that's why have high electron affinity.
Inner-transition elements They refer to *f*-block elements due to their placement in periodic table and electronic configuration.

10 Consider the following statements

(Chap 3, Class-XI, NCERT)

Statement I Heavier members of *p*-block show inert pair effect.
Statement II +2 valency is more stable for Pb as compared to its +4 valency.

(a) Both Statement I and Statement II are correct.
(b) Statement I is correct but Statement II is incorrect.
(c) Both Statement I and Statement II are incorrect.
(d) Statement II is correct but Statement I is incorrect.

Ans. (a)

Exp. Both Statement I and Statement II are correct.
The inert pair effect is the tendency of the two electrons in the outermost atomic *s*-orbital to remain unshared in compounds of post-transition metals (In, Ga, Bi, etc).
Heavier members of *p*-block show inert pair effect. The Inert pair effect increases down the group hence, stability of Pb^{2+} ions increases and Pb^{4+} ions decreases down
the group.

11 In modern periodic table, which of the following statements about atomic radius are true?

(Chap-3, Class XI, NCERT),
(Unit 8, Class X, Tamil Nadu Board) (MPSC Pre 2020)

1. Increases from top to bottom
2. Decreases from top to bottom
3. Increases from left to right
4. Decreases from left to right

Find out the correct option.

(a) 1 and 4
(b) 1 and 3
(c) 2 and 4
(d) 2 and 3

Ans. (a)

Exp. With reference to atomic radius. Statements (1) and (4) are true.
The atomic radius decreases from left to right in a period because within the period, the outer electrons are in the same valence shell and the effective nuclear charge increases as the atomic number increases resulting in the increased attraction of electrons to the nucleus.
Hence, atomic radius decreases, whereas while moving down the group the electrons are added into new shells, hence atomic radius increases.

12 Consider the following statements.

(Chap 3, Class-XI, NCERT)

1. Atomic radius decreases on moving left to right along a period.
2. Atomic radius decreases on going down the group.
3. Non-metals are electronegative in nature.
4. Metalloids exhibit properties of both metals and non-metals.

Which of the statement(s) given above is/are correct?

(a) Only one (b) Only two
(c) Only three (d) All four

Ans. (c)

Exp. Only three Statements (1, 3 and 4) are correct.

In periodic table, atomic radius decreases on moving left to right along a period, as effective nuclear charge increases.

Non-metals have high electron affinity, so they are electronegative in nature.

Metalloids have properties of both metals and non-metals, so their oxides are amphoteric in nature.

One Statement (2) is incorrect because as we go down the group, number of shell increases and atomic radius also increases.

13 Consider the following Assertion (A) and Reason (R) and choose the correct code.

(Chap 3, Class-XI, NCERT) (IAS Pre 2003)

Assertion (A) In the periodic table of chemical elements, electron affinity is always found to increase from top to bottom in a group.

Reason (R) In a group, the atomic radii generally increases from top to bottom.

Codes

(a) Both A and R are true and R is the correct explanation of A.
(b) Both A and R are true, but R is not the correct explanation of A.
(c) A is true but R is false.
(d) A is false but R is true.

Ans. (d)

Exp. Assertion (A) is false but Reason (R) is true.

On moving top to bottom along a group in periodic table, size of an element increases, electronegativity decreases and effective nuclear charge also decreases. Therefore, electron affinity decreases down the group. In case of atomic radii, as the number of shells increases from top to bottom, atomic radii also increases.

14 Which of the following statements is incorrect about the trends when going from left to right across the periods of periodic table? *(Chap 3, Class-XI, NCERT)*

(a) The elements become less metallic in nature.
(b) The number of valence electrons increases.
(c) The atoms lose their electrons more easily.
(d) The oxides become more acidic.

Ans. (c)

Exp. Statement (c) is incorrect about the trends when going from left to right across the periods of periodic table, size of the atom decreases because effective nuclear charge increases. It results in increase in ionisation enthalpy which means atom will not lose electrons easily.

Chapter 05

Acids, Bases and Salts

Acids, Bases and Salts

Acids/Bases

Acids

- Sour taste and turn blue litmus red.
- According to Arrhenius, these furnish H^+ ions in the aqueous solution.
- **Types of Acids**
  - **Strong Acids** Ionise completely to furnish H^+ ion, e.g. H_2SO_4, HCl etc.
  - **Weak Acids** Ionise only partially to give less H^+ ion, e.g. CH_3COOH etc.
- **Properties of Acids**
  - **Reaction with Metals** Hydrogen gas is released which burns with 'pop' sound.
  - **Reaction with Metallic oxides** Salt and water are produced.
  - **Reaction with Carbonates and Hydrogen Carbonates** Carbon dioxide gas is produced, which turns lime water milky.

Bases

- Bitter taste and turn red litmus blue.
- According to Arrhenius, these furnish OH^- ions in aqueous solution.
- Water soluble bases are called alkali, e.g. NaOH.
- **Types of Bases**
  - **Strong Base** Completely dissociates in water, e.g. NaOH
  - **Weak Base** Partially dissociates in water, e.g. CuO.

Properties of Bases

- **Reaction with Metals** Strong bases produce hydrogen gas when react with active metals.
- **Reaction with Non-metallic Oxides** Salt and water are the products of such reaction. e.g. $CO_2 + Ca(OH)_2 \rightarrow CaCO_3 + H_2O$

Acid and Base Combinations

Indicators

Indicate presence of acid or base
- Natural e.g. turmeric
- Synthetic e.g phenophthalein
- Odorous e.g clone

Strength of Solutions of Acid or Base (pH scale)

- A scale which is used for measuring hydrogen ion concentration in solution is called pH scale.
- More H^+ ions strong acids, less H^+ ions be weak acids.

Importance of pH in Everyday Life

- pH change leads to tooth decay.
- Self defence by animals and plants through chemical warfare.

Buffer Solutions

- The change in its pH value on addition of a small amount of acid or
- **Acidic** $CH_3COOH + CH_3COONa$
- **Basic** $NH_4OH + NH_4Cl$

Effect of Dilution on an Acid or Base

- Acids are diluted by adding acid to water, as the reaction is highly exothermic.
- Mixing base with water is an exothermic process.

Aqueous solution of Acids or Bases

- Acids and bases conduct electricity due to the presence of free ions in their aqueous solution.

Reaction Between Acid and Base

- Acid react with base to produces salt and water with the evolution of heat, called neutralisation reaction.

Salts

Salts

- Products of neutralisation reaction between acids and bases.
- **Alkaline salt** Weak acid + strong base.
- **Neutral salt** Strong acid + strong base.
- **Types of Salts**
  - **Common Salts** Complete replacement of hydrogen atom from acid by metal. e.g. KCl, NaCl, etc.
  - **Acidic Salts** Incomplete neutralisation of a acids. e.g. $NaHCO_3$, NaN_2PO_4 etc.
  - **Basic Salts** Incomplete neutralisation of bases. e.g. Mg(OH)Cl, Zn(OH)Cl, etc.
  - **Double Salts** Mixture of two salts and exists only in solid state. e.g., $K_2SO_4.Al_2(SO_4)_3.24H_2O$, etc.
  - **Complex Salts** Contain complex ion and also exist in solutions. e.g., $K_4[Fe(CN)_6]$, etc.
  - **Mixed Salts** Given more than one cation or anion on dissolving in water. e.g. $CaOCl_2$,etc.

Uses of Some Common Compounds

- Common salt Cl_2, H_2 etc.
- Bleaching powder $CaOCl_2$
- Caustic soda NaOH.
- Baking soda $NaHCO_3$
- Washing soda $Na_2CO_3.10H_2O$.
- Plaster of Paris $CaSO_4.1/2H_2O$.
- Chloroform $CHCl_3$
- Dry ice CO_2 Magnesia MgO.
- Sand SiO_2
- Quicklime CaO.
- Potassium nitrate Glass industry.

SOURCE *New NCERT Class VII Chap 4* (*Acids, Bases and Salts*), *New NCERT Class X Chap 2* (*Acids, Bases and Salts*) *Tamil Nadu Board Class IX* (*Acids, Bases and Salts*)

1 Nettle sting is a natural source of which acid? *(Chap 2, Class-X, NCERT)*

(a) Methanoic acid (b) Lactic acid
(c) Citric acid (d) Tartaric acid

Ans. (a)

Exp. Nettle sting is a natural source of methanoic acid. In the sting of nettle leaf, methanoic or formic acid is present which is used to treat urinary problems due to enlarge prostrate. It is present along with histamine and acetylcholine.

2 Match the following lists correctly and choose the correct code. *(Chap 4, Class-VII, NCERT)*

List-I (Organic acids)	List-II (Natural sources)
A. Acetic acid	1. Curd
B. Lactic acid	2. Tamarind
C. Tartaric acid	3. Vinegar
D. Oxalic acid	4. Tomato

Codes

	A	B	C	D		A	B	C	D
(a)	3	1	2	4	(b)	4	3	2	1
(c)	3	1	4	2	(d)	4	2	1	3

Ans. (a)

Exp. The correct matching is A-3, B-1, C-2, D-4.

Acetic acid Vinegar is a dilute solution of acetic acid in water. It is 4% to 5% acetic acid by volume, making acetic acid, main component of vinegar apart from water.

Lactic acid It is present in sour milk or curd. It is formed during the process of preparation of curd.

Tartaric acid It is the major acid present in tamarind pulp which gives the pulp acidic taste.

Oxalic acid Tomato contains trace of oxalic acid along with maleic, citric and ascorbic acids.

3 Consider the following statements regarding acids. *(Chap 4, Class-VII, NCERT)*

1. H_2CO_3 ionise completely in water to produce H^+ ions.
2. Acids turns red litmus to blue.
3. Flow of electric current in acidic solution is done by the ions present in acid.

How many statement(s) given above is/are correct ?

(a) Only one (b) Only two (c) All three (d) None of these

Ans. (a)

Exp. Only one Statement (3) is correct, whereas two Statements (1 and 2) are incorrect. The corrected form of these statements are as,

H_2CO_3 ionise partially in water to produce small number of H^+ ions. It is a very weak acid that is formed when carbon dioxide dissolves in water.

Acids turn blue litmus to red, whereas bases turns red litmus to blue.

4 Which of the following statements is incorrect? *(Chap 4, Class-VII, NCERT)*

(a) Muriatic acid used in household work is diluted form of hydrochloric acid.
(b) HNO_3 is present in maximum amount in acid rain.
(c) Tartaric acid is abundant in grapes and banana.
(d) Vinegar is used as a preservative.

Ans. (b)

Exp. Among the given statements (b) is incorrect as H_2SO_4 is present in maximum amount in acid rain. Acid rain is a rain which is usually acidic i.e. it has elevated levels of hydrogen ions. It is caused by a chemical reaction that begins when compounds like SO_2, NO_2 are released into the air. As, acid rain consists of HNO_3 and H_2SO_4, the pH level of acid rain is in the range of 4-5.

5 Consider the following statements : *(Chap 2, Class-X, NCERT)*

1. Lemon is citrus due to tartaric acid.
2. Citric acid is an organic acid.
3. Formic acid is stronger acid than acetic acid.
4. $FeCl_3$ is not a Lewis acid.

Choose the incorrect statement(s).

(a) Only 1 (b) 2 and 3 (c) 1 and 3 (d) 1 and 4

Ans. (d)

Exp. Among the given statements (1) and (4) are incorrect, whereas statements (2) and (3) are correct. The correct form of statements (1) and (4) are :

Lemon is citrus due to presence of citric acid.

Citric acid is also exists in many other fruits and vegetables. e.g. orange, grape fruits, berries etc.

The Lewis acids are any substances that can accept a pair of non-bonding electrons. In other words, a Lewis acids is an electron pair acceptors. Hence, $FeCl_3$ is a Lewis acid.

6 Match list-I with list-II. *(Chap 4, Class-VII, NCERT)* *(Unit 14, Class-IX, Tamil Nadu Board)*

List-I (Acids)	**List-II** (Sources)
A. Ascorbic acid	1. Apples
B. Malic acid	2. Ant sting
C. Formic acid	3. Grapes
D. Tartaric acid	4. Citrus fruit

Choose the correct answer from the options given below.

	A	B	C	D		A	B	C	D
(a)	3	2	4	1	(b)	2	3	1	4
(c)	4	1	2	3	(d)	3	2	4	1

Ans. (c)

Exp. The correct matching is A-4, B-1, C-2, D-3.

Ascorbic acid Is present in all citrus fruits.

Malic acid Is present in apples.

Formic acid Is present in ant's stings.

Tartaric acid Is present in grapes.

7 Match the following lists and choose the correct code. *(Chap 2, Class-X, NCERT)*

List-I (Chemical compounds)	List-II (Use)
A. Sodium hydroxide	1. For disinfecting water
B. Bleaching powder	2. For removing permanent hardness of water
C. Sodium hydrogen carbonate	3. Soaps and detergents
D. Washing soda	4. Soda-acid fire extinguisher

Codes

	A	B	C	D
(a)	3	1	4	2
(b)	3	1	2	4
(c)	1	3	4	2
(d)	2	1	4	3

Ans. (a)

Exp. The correct matching is A-3, B-1, C-4, D-2.

Sodium hydroxide (NaOH) It is used to manufacture soaps and variety of detergents. It is used to suspend protein and to convert fats to soap. It is generally cheap.

Bleaching powder ($CaOCl_2$) Its used to kill germs and bacteria of water as it is good disinfecting agent.

Sodium hydrogen carbonate ($NaHCO_3$) Soda-acid fire extinguisher consists of sodium hydrogen carbonate and sulphuric acid. Reaction occurring is responsible to exert pressurised water on to a fire.

Washing soda (Na_2CO_3) It is treated with water, carbonate ions from sodium carbonate reacts with calcium and magnesium ions in water. So, calcium carbonate is precipitated out.

8 Among the following, which of the statements are correct? *(Chap 4, Class-VII, NCERT)*

1. Moist baking soda should be applied on ant's bite.
2. Acidic soil should be treated with organic matter to increase fertility.
3. Basic substance must be added with factory wastes.

Codes

(a) 1 and 2
(b) 2 and 3
(c) 1 and 3
(d) None of the above

Ans. (c)

Exp. Statements (1) and (3) are correct. Ant's bite contains formic or methanoic acid which can be neutralised by rubbing moist baking soda as it is basic in nature.

Wastes of many factories contain acid which can harm the aquatic species, if allowed to flow into water bodies directly. So, basic substance should be added for neutralisation of the wastes.

Statement (2) is incorrect because organic matters release acids. So, to neutralise acidic soil, lime or basic substance should be added.

9 Match the following lists and choose the correct codes. *(Chap 2, Class-X, NCERT) (UPPSC Pre 2002)*

List-I (Common name of coumpound)	List-II (Chemical name of coumpund)
A. Neela thotha	1. Sodium bicarbonate
B. Epsom salt	2. Sodium hydroxide
C. Baking soda	3. Magnesium sulphate
D. Caustic soda	4. Copper sulphate

Codes

	A	B	C	D
(a)	3	4	2	1
(b)	4	3	2	1
(c)	3	4	1	2
(d)	4	3	1	2

Ans. (d)

Exp. The correct matching is A-4, B-3, C-1, D-2.

Neela thotha Is the common name of copper sulphate with chemical formula $CuSO_4$. Older name for this compound include blue vitriol, bluestone, vitriol of copper and Roman vitriol.

Epsom salt Is a common name of magnesium sulphate with chemical formula $MgSO_4$. It has an appearance similar to table salt and is often dissolved in baths, so also known as 'bath salt'.

Baking soda Is the common name of sodium bicarbonate having chemical formula of $NaHCO_3$. It is an antacid which is used to relieve heartburn and acid indigestion.

Caustic soda Is the common name of sodium hydroxide. It is an inorganic compound with formula of NaOH. It is a common ingredient in cleaners and soaps.

10 Consider the following statements. *(Chap 2, Class-X, NCERT) (IAS Pre 2005) (Chap 14, Class-XI, NCERT)*

1. Anhydrous sodium carbonate is commonly known as baking soda.
2. Baking soda is used as fire extinguisher.
3. Bleaching powders are produced in Hasenclever plant.

Which of the statement(s) is/are incorrect?

(a) 1, 2 and 3 (b) Only 1
(c) Only 3 (d) 1 and 2

Ans. (b)

Exp. Statement (1) is incorrect because sodium bicarbonate also known as baking soda, used as baking soda in bakery products, while anhydrous sodium carbonate is known as washing soda and is used in detergent.

11 **Match the lists and choose the correct codes.** *(Chap 4, Class-VII, NCERT)*

List-I (Chemical compounds)	List-II (Properties)
A. Vinegar	1. Changes red litmus to blue
B. Sodium chloride	2. Sour in taste
C. Milk of magnesia	3. Major salt of sea
D. Potassium nitrate	4. Used in fertiliser industry

Codes

	A	B	C	D		A	B	C	D
(a)	2	1	4	3	(b)	2	3	1	4
(c)	3	1	4	2	(d)	2	3	4	1

Ans. (b)

Exp. The correct matching is A-2, B-3, C-1, D-4.

Vinegar It consists of acetic acid. It is sour in taste due to its acidic nature.

Sodium chloride It is majorly extracted from sea water, which is also known as common salt.

Milk of magnesia It is basic in nature due to which it changes red litmus to blue.

Potassium nitrate It is a good source of nitrogen and potassium. Hence, it is used in fertiliser industry.

12 **Consider the following statements.**
(Chap 4, Class-VII, NCERT) (Unit 14, Class-IX, Tamil Nadu Board)

1. Antacids are base.
2. Toothpaste is acidic and made up of calcium phosphate.
3. Bases turn red litmus to blue.
4. Soap is basic in nature.

Which of the following statement(s) is/are correct?

(a) Only 3 (b) 1 and 3 (c) 2 and 4 (d) 1, 3 and 4

Ans. (d)

Exp. Among the given statements (1), (3) and (4) are correct. Statement (2) is incorrect. The correct form of statement (2) is, toothpaste is basic and it is made up of clacium hydrogen phosphate, calcium carbonate, aluminium hydroxide, silica, etc. Acidic conditions produced in mouth leads to teeth decay and cavities. Thus, to prevent such problems, there is a need to neutralise acidic condition in mouth. It can be done by using these toothpastes.

13 **Which statement(s) is/are correct about neturalisation reaction?** *(Chap 4, Class-VII, NCERT)*

(a) It occurs between acid and base.
(b) Heat is evolved during the reaction.
(c) Salt and water are produced in this reaction.
(d) All of the above

Ans. (d)

Exp. All the given statements are correct about neutralisation reaction as it is the type of reaction in which acid and base reacts to form salt and water with the evolution of heat.

14 **Consider the following Assertion (A) and Reason (R) and choose the correct code.**
(Chap 2, Class-X, NCERT) (IAS Pre 1999)

Assertion (A) To dilute sulphuric acid, acid is added to water and not water to acid.

Reason (R) Specific heat of water is very high.

Codes

(a) Both A and R are true and R is the correct explanation of A.
(b) Both A and R are true but R is not the correct explanation of A.
(c) A is true but R is false.
(d) A is false but R is true.

Ans. (a)

Exp. Both Assertion (A) and Reason (R) are true and Reason (R) is the correct explanation of Assertion (A).

To dilute sulphuric acid, acid should be added to water which produces heat and energy.

Water has a higher specific heat than the acids, so vessel of cold water will absorb heat on adding acid. If water is added to acid, suddenly more heat would be generated and solution may boil very violently which results in splashing of concentrated acid out of the vessel.

15 **The yellow colour of turmeric changes to red on addition of soap solution. When substance *P* is added to turmeric, there is no change in colour.**

Which of the following is definitely true about substance (*P*)? *(Chap 2, Class-X, NCERT)*

(a) *P* is an acid (b) *P* is not a salt
(c) *P* is not a base (d) *P* is either acid or base.

Ans. (d)

Exp. Turmeric turns red in the base while remains yellow in acidic or neutral substances.

16 **Colour of China rose indicator in basic and acidic solutions respectively are** *(Chap 4, Class-VII, NCERT)*

(a) pink and blue (b) red and blue
(c) green and magenta (d) colourless and pink

Ans. (c)

Exp. Colour of China rose indicator in basic and acidic solutions will be green and magenta respectively. China rose is a natural indicator which turns basic solution to green colour and turns acidic solution to magenta or dark pink. It doesn't show change in colour for neutral solutions.

17 **Which one of the following is an olfactory indicator?** *(Chap 2, Class-X, NCERT)*

(a) Turmeric (b) Clove oil
(c) Phenolphthalein (d) Litmus

Ans. (b)

Exp. Clove oil is an olfactory indicator among the given options. Olfactory indicator is a substance whose smell varies depending on whether it is mixed with an acidic or basic solutions.

Smell of clove oil can be characterised in presence of an acid but cannot be recognised in basic solutions.

18 Which of the following statement is incorrect?
(Chap 2, Class-X, NCERT)

(a) pH of a solution changes from 3 to 6. The H^+ concentration will decrease 1000 times.
(b) pH value of the blood in human body is 7.4.
(c) A solution turns red litmus to blue, pH of the solution is 5.
(d) Decay of tooth enamel starts, when the pH of the mouth is lower than 5.5.

Ans. (c)

Exp. Among the given statements (a), (b) and (d) are correct. While statement (c) is incorrect. The correct form of statement (c) is : If a solution turns red litmus to blue, then it is basic in nature and pH of the solution will be greater than 7. It is negative logarithm of H^+ ion concentration. The ranges goes from 0-14, with 7 being neutral. Whereas greater than 7 indicates a base and less than 7 indicates acid.

19 Which one among the following is not a property of salt? *(Chap 2, Class-X, NCERT)*

(a) Salts have ordered packing arrangements called lattices.
(b) Salts have low melting points but high boiling points.
(c) Salts are brittle.
(d) Salts conduct electricity in molten state.

Ans. (b)

Exp. Statement (b) is not a property of salt because salts have high melting and boiling points. In salts, ionic bonding is present which is very strong and takes lots of energy to break.

20 pH value shows the numeric value of
(Chap 2, Class-X, NCERT) (MPPSC Pre 1996)

(a) quality of chemical used for developing photographic negatives.
(b) analysing the acidic or basic nature of a solution.
(c) analysing the intensity of an earthquake.
(d) analysing for checking purity of milk.

Ans. (b)

Exp. pH value shows the numeric value of analysing the acidic or basic nature of a solution. The solution with pH less than 7 is said to be acidic while with pH more than 7 is basic in nature. Neutral solution has a pH value 7. The logarithm of the reciprocal of hydrogen ion concentration in mole per litre is measured by pH scale from 0 to 14.

21 Which of the following statements is incorrect?
(Chap 2, Class-X, NCERT)

(a) Methyl orange in basic solution is yellow in colour.
(b) Aqueous solution of acids conducts electricity.
(c) Acid reacts with certain metals to form hydrogen gas.
(d) None of the above

Ans. (d)

Exp. None of the given statements are incorrect.
Methyl orange is an indicator which is orange in neutral solution, red in acidic solution and yellow in basic solution. Aqueous solution of acid contains free ions and conduct electricity.
On reaction with some metals, acid produces hydrogen gas and metal salts, e.g. aluminium metal reacts with dilute hydrochloric acid give aluminium chloride and hydrogen gas.

$$\underset{\text{Aluminium}}{2Al} + \underset{\text{Hydrochloric acid}}{6HCl} \longrightarrow \underset{\text{Aluminium chloride}}{2AlCl_3} + \underset{\text{Hydrogen}}{3H_2 \uparrow}$$

22 Consider the following statements.
(Chap 2, Class-X, NCERT)

1. Ant sting contains methanoic acid.
2. Increased pH of mouth results in tooth decay.
3. Milk of magnesia is used as antacids.
4. pH of acid rain falls above 5.6.

Which of the statement(s) given above is/are correct?

(a) 1 and 3
(b) 1 and 2
(c) 2 and 3
(d) 1 and 4

Ans. (a)

Exp. Statements (1) and (3) are correct.
Sting of ant contains methanoic acid. On biting, ant injects the acidic liquid into the skin.
Milk of magnesia is basic in nature. It neutralises acidic substances. Hence, used as antacids to neutralise the excess acid of stomach.
Statements (2) and (4) are incorrect because tooth decay can occur when pH of mouth becomes below 5.5 which means decreased pH of mouth causes tooth decay.
Acid rain is acidic in nature. Therefore, pH of acid rain is low which is below 5.5.

Chapter 6

Metals

Metals

Corrosion/Alloy/Properties

Metals

- Electropositive, tendency to form positive ion by losing electron.

Corrosion

- Oxidative deterioration of metal surface by the action of environment to form unwanted corrosion products.
- Corrosion of iron is called rusting.

Alloy

- Homogeneous mixtures of two or more metals or a metal and a non-metal, Alloy of metal with Hg (mercury) is called amalgam.

Physical Properties

- Hard, except alkali metals.
- All (except mercury) exist as solid state.
- Lustrous, malleable, ductile and sonorus.
- Good conductors of heat and electricity because of the presence of free electrons.

Chemical Properties

- Metals exhibit many chemical properties.
  - **Reaction with Oxygen**
    Metals + Oxygen $\longrightarrow$ Metal oxides (Basic in nature)
  - **Reaction with Water**
    Metal + Water $\longrightarrow$ Metal oxide + Hydrogen (Main product)
  - **Reaction with solution of other metals** More reactive metals displace the less reactive. metals from their salt solution. e.g. $A + BC \rightarrow AC + B$
  - **Reaction with Dilute Acids** Reactive metals generally form salt and hydrogen with HCl or H_2SO_4 , but not with HNO_3.

Some other Important Organic Compounds

Extraction of Metals

- Earth's crust is the major source of metals.
- The compounds in the form of which metal occur naturally are called minerals.
- The minerals from which metal is extracted profitably are called the ores and the Impurities associated with them are called gangue.

Concentration of Ores

- Removal of unwanted materials like gangue or impurities from ore is called concentration, dressing or benefaction.
  - **Hydraulic Washing** This is based on difference in gravities of ore and gangue particles. It is a type of gravity separation. e.g. ores of iron (Fe_2O_3 and Fe_3O_4).
  - **Magnetic separation** It is based on difference in magnetic properties of ore and gangue. e.g. ores of tungsten from cassiterite (SnO_2) Fe_3O_4.
  - **Froth Flotation Method** It is used for removing gangue from sulphide ores. Collectors (pine oils) and froth stabilisers (cresol are used in this method).
  - **Leaching** It is used if the ore is soluble in some suitable solvent. e.g. leaching of bauxite ore with conc. NaOH.

Organic Compounds Containing Carbon, Hydrogen and Oxygen

Extraction of Crude Metals from Concentrated Ores

- Isolation of metals from concentrated ores involve two major steps.
- **Conversion to Oxide** Metal is first converted into oxide.
  - **Calcination** Heating of ore with or without the presence of air. It is done in case of carbonate, hydroxide and oxide ores of metals.
  - **Roasting** Heating of ore in a regular supply of air. It is Done only for sulphide ore.
- **Reduction of Oxide to Metal** The oxide is then reduced to metal.
  - **Smelting** Metal extracted, either as a element or as a compound from its ore by heating beyond the melting point, in the presence of redusing agent such as coke.
  - **Aluminothermic Process** Oxides of metals such as Cr and Mn are reduced by Al.
  - **Auto-reduction** It is used for metals low in the activity series. The oxides of these metals such as Cu, Hg, Pb can be reduced to metals by heating alone.
  - **Electrolytic method** It is used for metals high in the activity series such as Na, Al, Ca.

Reactivity Series of metals

- Decreasing order of reactivity.
- K > Na > Ca > Mg > Al > Zn > Fe > Sn>Pb > H > Cu > Hg > Ag > Au.
- **Some Other Important Metals**
  - Tungsten (W) used to make bulb filament.
  - Titanium (Ti) used to make boats.
  - Caesium (Cs) used in photochemical cell.

SOURCE *New NCERT Class IX Chap 2* (Is Matter Around Us Pure), *Chap 3* (Atoms and Molecules)
New NCERT Class X Chap 2 (Acids, Bases and Salts), *Chap 3* (Metals and Non-metals)
Tamil Nadu Board Class IX (Matter Around Us)

1 **Consider the following statements.**

(Chap 3, Class-X, NCERT)

1. Metals are generally hard.
2. Mercury is hard in nature and is not poisonous.
3. Mercury usually enters human food chain from aquatic animals.

Which of the statement(s) given above is/are incorrect?

(a) 1 and 3 (b) Only 1
(c) Only 2 (d) 1, 2 and 3

Ans. (c)

Exp. Statement (2) is incorrect because mercury is liquid at room temperature and may have toxic effects on the nervous, digestive and immune systems and on lungs, kidneys, skin and eyes.

2 **Which one of the following is the hardest metal?**

(Chap 3, Class-X, NCERT)

(a) Diamond (b) Iron
(c) Platinum (d) Tungsten

Ans. (d)

Exp. Tungsten is the hardest metal. It also has highest melting point among the given options. It is often used in electrical and military applications.

3 **The heaviest natural element is**

(Chap 3, Class-X, NCERT) (UP Lower Sub Pre 2004)

(a) uranium (b) mercury (c) gold (d) calcium

Ans. (a)

Exp. Uranium is the heaviest naturally occurring element with an atomic number of 92. It is a pure form of silver coloured heavy metal. Its most common isotope is uranium-238 which has a nucleus containing 92 protons and 146 neutrons. It has a density of 19.05 g/cm^3.

4 **Which statement regarding metals is not correct?**

(Chap 3, Class-X, NCERT)

(a) Mercury metal is the best conductor of electricity.
(b) Gold metal is dissolved in mixture of hydrochloric acid and nitric acid.
(c) Lead is hard and inflexible metal.
(d) Lead metal is used in storage battery.

Ans. (c)

Exp. Statement (c) is not correct as lead is soft and malleable metal. It has a relatively low melting point. It is a heavy metal and tarnishes to a dull grey colour when exposed to air.

5 **Sodium vapour lamp is usually used as street light, because** *(Chap 3, Class-X, NCERT) (UPPSC Pre 2007)*

(a) these are cheap.
(b) light from this is monochromatic and will not split through water droplets.
(c) it is pleasing to the eyes.
(d) it is brightly illuminating.

Ans. (b)

Exp. Sodium vapour lamp is usually used as street light because light from this is monochromatic and will not split through water droplets.

It is a gas discharge lamp that uses sodium in an excited state to produce light. It causes less light pollution than mercury vapour lamps.

6 **Consider the following statements about calcium.**

1. It forms basic oxide with air. *(Chap 3, Class-X, NCERT)*
2. It floats over water.
3. It replaces sodium from sodium chloride.

How many statement(s) given above is/are incorrect?

(a) Only one (b) Only two
(c) All three (d) None of these

Ans. (a)

Exp. Only one Statement (3) is incorrect about calcium because sodium is more reactive than calcium. Therefore, calcium cannot replace sodium from sodium chloride. Hence, no reaction will take place.

7 **Which of the following statement is a characteristic of metals?** *(Chap 3, Class-X, NCERT)*

(a) They have lowest number of valence electrons.
(b) They are brittle in nature.
(c) They are capable to form anions easily.
(d) None of the above

Ans. (a)

Exp. Among the given statements, only statement (a) is a characteristic of metals as metals have lowest number of valence electrons.

Statements (b) and (c) are not characteristics of metals as generally they are hard, malleable and ductile in nature. They release electrons to acquire noble gas configuration and form cation easily.

8 **Match the following lists and choose the correct codes.** *(Chap 3, Class-X, NCERT)*

List-I (Element)	List-II (Properties)
A. Gold	1. Best conductor of heat and electricity
B. Lead	2. Metal found in highest amount
C. Aluminium	3. It can be drawn into thinnest wire.
D. Silver	4. Minimum heat conducting metal

Codes

	A	B	C	D		A	B	C	D
(a)	1	3	2	4	(b)	2	3	4	1
(c)	3	2	4	1	(d)	3	4	2	1

Ans. (d)

Exp. The correct matching is A-3, B-4, C-2, D-1.

Gold It is most flexible metal and can be drawn into thinnest wire. It is used to make ornaments or objects of any shape using.

Lead It is minimum heat conducting metal. It is malleable, ductile, soft, dense and a poor conductor of heat and electricity.

Aluminium This metal found in highest amount. It constitutes 8% by weight in Earth crust.

Silver It is best conductor of heat and electricity as its electrons are free to move but it is too expensive to use silver wirings.

9 Consider the following statements.
(Chap 3, Class-X, NCERT)

1. Gold is the most ductile metal.
2. Metal like copper and silver are good conductor of heat.
3. Some alkali metals are so soft that they can be cut with a knife.

Which of the statement(s) given above is/are correct?

(a) 1 and 2 (b) 1 and 3
(c) 2 and 3 (d) All of these

Ans. (d)

Exp. All the given statements are correct. Gold is the most ductile metal as it can be converted into thin wire. Metal like silver and copper are good conductors of heat as they provide minimum resistance.

Some alkali metals like sodium, potassium and lithium are very soft that they can be cut with a knife.

10 Which one of the following statement is incorrect?
(Chap 2, Class-X, NCERT) (Unit 4, Class-IX, Tamil Nadu Board)

(a) Goldsmith use aqua-regia, which is prepared by mixing nitric acid and hydrochloric acid in 1 : 3 ratio.
(b) Aluminium oxide react with sodium hydroxide to form sodium aluminate.
(c) Metal oxide reacts with acid to produce base.
(d) Lead and mercury are comparatively poor conductors of heat.

Ans. (c)

Exp. Among the given statements only (a), (b) and (d) are correct, whereas statement (c) is incorrect. The corrected form of statement (c) is, metal oxides react with acids to produce salt and water.

These chemical compounds are formed by the reaction of metals with oxygen. eg. magnesium reacts with oxygen to form magnesium oxide.

11 Consider the following Assertion (A) and Reason (R) and choose the correct code.
(Chap 3, Class-X, NCERT) (IAS Pre 1998)

Assertion (A) Sodium metal is stored under kerosene.

Reason (R) Metallic sodium melts when exposed to air.

Codes

(a) Both A and R are true and R is the correct explanation of A.
(b) Both A and R are true but R is not the correct explanation of A.
(c) A is true but R is false.
(d) A is false but R is true.

Ans. (c)

Exp. Assertion (A) is true, but reason (R) is false. Sodium is kept in kerosene to prevent it from coming in contact with oxygen present in the air. Because it will react with the oxygen and forms sodium oxide.

This is a strongly exothermic reaction in which a lot of heat is evolved. Thus, sodium is kept under kerosene.

12 Consider the following statements regarding the chemical reactions of metal.
(Chap 3, Class-X, NCERT) (Chap 27, Module-6, NIOS)

1. Potassium reacts violently with cold water to produce hydroxide and hydrogen gas with heat.
2. The reaction of calcium with water is more violent.
3. Dilute sulphuric acid reacts with metal to produce salt.
4. Iron replaces copper from its sulphate solution.

How many statement(s) given above is/are correct?

(a) Only one (b) Onle two
(c) Only three (d) All four

Ans. (c)

Exp. Only three Statements (1, 3 and 4) are correct, while one Statement (2) is incorrect. The corrected form of statement (2) is, the reaction of calcium with water is less violent. The bubbles of hydrogen gas evolved and get stick to the surface of calcium. Heat evolved is not sufficient for the hydrogen to catch fire.

13 Consider the following statements about roasting.
(Chap 3, Class-X, NCERT)

1. In this, the ores are generally converted into metal oxides.
2. In this, ores become porous and moisture is removed.
3. In this process, ore is heated below its melting point.

Which of the given statements are correct?

(a) 1 and 2 (b) 2 and 3
(c) 1 and 3 (d) 1, 2 and 3

Ans. (a)

Exp. Statements (1) and (2) are correct about roasting.

In roasting, ores are generally converted into metal oxides. It makes ores porous and removes moisture. In this process, ores are heated at high temperature in the presence of air.

Statement (3) is incorrect because roasting involves heating at high temperature whereas in calcination, ore is heated below its melting point.

14 Consider the following Assertion (A) and Reason (R) and choose the correct code. *(Chap-3, Class-X, NCERT)*

Assertion (A) Lime, silica and magnesium oxide are commonly used as refractory materials in lining of furnace.

Reason (R) These can be withstand very high temperature.

Codes

(a) Both A and R are true and R is the correct explanation of A.
(b) Both A and R are true but R is not the correct explanation of A.
(c) A is true but R is false.
(d) A is false but R is true.

Ans. (a)

Exp. Both Assertion (A) and Reason (R) are true and Reason (R) is the correct explanation of Assertion (A).
Lime, silica and magnesium oxide are commonly used as refractory materials in lining of furnace. They are heat resistance and difficult to melt. They can withstand very high temperature present in furnace.

15 **Match the following lists and choose the correct code.** *(Chap 3, Class-X, NCERT) (IAS Pre 2000)*

List-I (Industrial process)	List-II (Industry)
A. Cracking	1. Rubber
B. Smelting	2. Petroleum
C. Hydrogenation	3. Copper
D. Vulcanisation	4. Edible fats

Codes

	A	B	C	D		A	B	C	D
(a)	3	2	1	4	(b)	2	3	4	1
(c)	2	3	1	4	(d)	3	2	4	1

Ans. (b)

Exp. The correct matching is A-2, B-3, C-4, D-1.
Cracking This technique is used in oil refineries whereby large and complex molecules are broken down into smaller and lighter components.
Smelting Copper smelting process separate element copper from copper concentrates through multiple sulphide oxidising stages.
Hydrogenation It is a process of addition of hydrogen in the presence of catalysts like palladium or nickel, to unsaturated hydrocarbon yield saturated hydrocarbons. Catalysts are the substances that cause a reaction to occur or proceed at a different rate without the reaction itself being affected.
Vulcanisation It is the process of heating of natural rubber with sulphur at appropriate temperature range between 375-415 K to improve its physical properties.

16 **Which one of the following statement is correct?** *(Chap 3, Class-X, NCERT)*

(a) Calcite is an important ore of aluminium.
(b) Malachite is one of the ore of iron mineral.
(c) Monazite is an ore of thorium.
(d) Toys industries used mica as a raw material.

Ans. (c)

Exp. Among the given statements only (c) is correct. The corrected form of statement (a), (b) and (d) are as :
(a) Bauxite is an important ore of aluminium having formula Al_2O_3.
(b) Hematite is an ore of iron having formula Fe_2O_3.
(d) In electrical industries mica is used as a raw material. It is one of the most indispensable minerals. Due to its dielectric strength and insulating properties, it is used in electrical industries.

17 **Which of the following is an incorrect statement about minerals and ores?** *(Chap 3, Class-X, NCERT)*

(a) All minerals are ores.
(b) Feldspar, quartz, mica are examples of minerals.
(c) Minerals are the native form in which various metals exist.
(d) Ores are usually used to extract metals economically.

Ans. (a)

Exp. Statement (a) is incorrect about minerals and ores because all minerals are not ores as some of the minerals have unwanted substances. All ores are minerals and metal can be extracted commercially.

18 **The softest mineral, talc (soapstone) is mainly** *(Chap 3, Class-X, NCERT) (RAS/RTS Pre 1999)*

(a) manganese silicate (b) sodium silicate
(c) sodium phosphate (d) magnesium silicate

Ans. (d)

Exp. Talc is a mineral which is mainly hydrated magnesium silicate with formula $Mg_3Si_4O_{10}(OH)_2$.
On the Mohs hardness scale, the softest mineral talc is rated 1 and the hardest mineral, the diamond is rated 10. In loose form, talc is the widely used substance known as talcum. It occurs as foliated to fibrous masses and in an exceptionally rare crystal form.

19 **Match the following lists and choose the correct code.** *(Chap 3, Class-X, NCERT)*

List-I (Ores)	List-II (Metals)
A. Monazite	1. Iron
B. Bauxite	2. Silver
C. Haematite	3. Thorium
D. Argentite	4. Aluminium

Codes

	A	B	C	D		A	B	C	D
(a)	2	1	4	3	(b)	3	4	1	2
(c)	3	1	4	2	(d)	3	4	2	1

Ans. (b)

Exp. The correct matching is A-3, B-4, C-1, D-2.
Monazite It is an important ore for thorium, lanthanum and cerium. Extensive deposits of monazite are found in Southern India.
Bauxite It is an ore of aluminium, which is found in the form of hydrated aluminium oxides.
Haematite It is an ore of iron which is found in the form of Fe_2O_3.
Argentite It is an ore of silver which is found in the form of silver glance having formula Ag_2S.

20 Which of the following pairs will give displacement reactions ? *(Chap 3, Class-X, NCERT) (UPPSC Pre 2010)*

(a) NaCl solution and copper metal.
(b) $MgCl_2$ solution and aluminium metal.
(c) $FeSO_4$ solution and siver metal.
(d) Ag NO_3 solution and copper metal.

Ans. (d)

Exp. Among the given reactions, (d) is an example of displacement reaction. In this reaction, copper replaces the silver cations in the process of copper itself being oxidised to copper II cations and going into solution Hence, silver metal precipitates out and a copper II nitrate solution with remain.

$$Cu(s) + 2AgNO_3(aq) \rightarrow Cu(NO_3)_2(aq) + 2Ag(s)$$

21 Which of the following statement is incorrect about stainless steel? *(Chap 3, Class-X, NCERT)*

(a) It is known as inox steel.
(b) It is an alloy of iron, cobalt and nickel.
(c) It is corrosion resistant.
(d) Molybdenum is added to increase corrosion resistance in reducing acids.

Ans. (b)

Exp. Statement (b) is incorrect about stainless steel, because stainless steel (stain-free iron) is an alloy whose constituent elements are as follows

Iron - 89.4%	Chromium - 10.0%
Manganese - 0.35%	Carbon - 0.25%

22 Consider the following statements. *(Chap 3, Class-X, NCERT)*

1. Brass is an alloy of copper and zinc.
2. Magnetite is the main ore of aluminium.
3. Mercurius solubilis mainly contains mercury.
4. Potassium nitrate is a chemical used in photography.

Which of the statement(s) given above is/are correct?

(a) 1 and 2 (b) 1 and 3 (c) 2 and 3 (d) 1, 3 and 4

Ans. (b)

Exp. Statements (1) and (3) are correct.

Brass is an alloy of copper and zinc, whereas mercurius solubilis contains mercury.

Statements (2) and (4) are incorrect because magnetite (Fe_3O_4) is an ore of iron. It is the most magnetic of all the naturally occurring minerals on earth.

Silver bromide (AgBr) is used in photography because it is very sensitive to the light.

23 Which of the following statement is incorrect? *(Chap 3, Class-X, NCERT)*

(a) Alloying helps in improving the properties of a metal.
(b) An alloy is a heterogeneous mixture of two or more metals.
(c) The melting point of an alloy is less than that of pure metals.
(d) An alloy is made up of two or more chemical elements.

Ans. (b)

Exp. Statement (b) is incorrect because alloy is a homogeneous mixture of two or more elements, of which at least one is a metal.

24 The important metal used with iron to make it rust free is *(Chap 3, Class-X, NCERT) (CGPSC Pre 2011)*

(a) aluminium (b) carbon (c) chromium (d) tin

Ans. (c)

Exp. The important metal used with iron to make it rust free is chromium. It is used with iron as it protects iron from corrosion, rust and make it high temperature resistance. The resultant alloy is stainless steel.

25 Consider the following Assertion (A) and Reason (R) and choose the correct code. *(Chap 3, Class-X, NCERT) (UP Lower Sub Pre 1998)*

Assertion (A) Normally, it has been seen that iron goods covered with a brown powder called rust when they are unsheltered in the atmosphere.

Reason (R) Rust or the brown powder is the result of deposition of tannin.

Codes

(a) Both A and R are true and R is the correct explanation of A.
(b) Both A and R are true but R is not the correct explanation of A.
(c) A is true but R is false.
(d) A is false but R is true.

Ans. (c)

Exp. Assertion (A) is true but Reason (R) is false because rust is iron oxide (not tannin), a usually red oxide formed by the redox reaction of iron and oxygen in the presence of water or air moisture. Tannin is a pale-yellow to light brown substance secreted from plants and used chiefly in tanning leather, dyeing fabric, making ink and in various medical applications.

26 Consider the following statements *(Chap 3, Class-X, NCERT)*

1. Copper is used for coating in galvanisation.
2. Tarnishing of silver is occur due to the formation of Ag_2S.
3. Corrosion is accelerated by the presence of impurities.

How many statement(s) given above is/are correct?

(a) Only one (b) Only two (c) All three (d) None of these

Ans. (b)

Exp. Only two Statements (2 and 3) are correct but one Statement (1) is incorrect. Zn is used for coating in galvanisation. It is the process of applying a protective zinc coating to iron or steel, to prevent rusting.

Corrosion is a natural process that converts a refined metal into a more chemically stable oxide. It is the gradual deterioration of materials by chemical reaction with their environment. Rusting is one of the form of corrosion. In this the formation of rust (A mixture of iron oxides) on the surface of iron objects takes place.

Chapter 7

Non-Metals

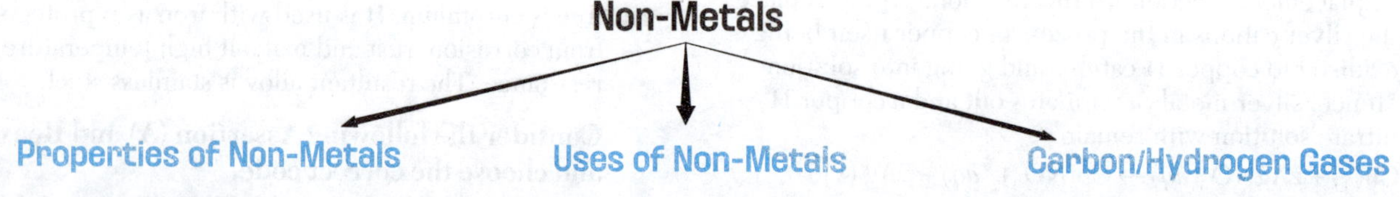

Properties of Non-Metals

Non-Metals

- Electronegative elements, tendency to form anion.
- Poor conductors of heat and electricity.
- e.g. Carbon, iodine, sulphur, oxygen, hydrogen etc.

Physical Properties

- Metallic lusture, conductivity britleness, malleability, ductility, soft (except diamond).
- Low melting and boiling point and highly soluble.
- All (except bromine) exist as solid or gaseous.
- Also show displacement reaction like metal.

Chemical Properties

- **Reaction with Oxygen**
  Non-metals + O_2 $\longrightarrow$ Oxides (Main product) (Acidic)
- **Reaction with Chlorine**
  form various chlorides.
  e.g. $P_4 + 6Cl_2 \longrightarrow 4PCl_3$
- **Reaction with hydrogen**
  form corresponding hydrides.
  e.g. $N_2 + 3H_2 \longrightarrow 2NH_3$

Uses of Non-Metals

Nitrogen N_2

- 78% by volume of the atmosphere, 46% in urea.
- **Compound**
  - Ammonia (NH_3) pungent smell & colourless gas.
  - Nitric acid (NHO_3) use in explosives.

Sulphur (S)

- 16th most abundant element and constitutes 0.03-0.19 by mass of earth's crust.
- **Compound**
  - Sulphur dioxide (SO_2) acts as disinfectant and preservatives.
  - Sulphuric acid (H_2SO_4) used in fertilizers.

Halogen (Group 17)

- Highly reactive non-metallic elements.
- F and Cl are fairly abundant and I are less.
- Insoluble fluorides, cryolite & fluorapatite.
- Astative is a radioactive element.

Noble gases (Group 18)

- All gases are chemically unreactive.
- Xe and Rn are rarest elements also known as stranger gas.
- He-nuclear reactor.
- Ne-fluorescent bulb.

Other Uses of Non-metals

- Used for the growth of plants.
- During the purification of water.
- Iodine blue colour is used as antiseptic.

Carbon/Hydrogen Gases

Carbon

- 17th most abundant element. Stable
- Isotopes 12-C and 13-C Radioactive isotope 14-C.

Allotropes of Carbon (Crystalline and amorphous)

- Diamond (sp^3- hybridisation)
- Graphite (sp^2- hybridisation)
- Fullerens (Pure form of C)
- Buckminster fullerene (sp^2-hybridisation)

Hydrogen

- Proton, electron but no neutron, exists as diatomic (H_2) molecule, 1st configuration, alkali metal as well as halogen properties.
- **Isotopes** - Protium (${}_1H^1$), Deuterium (${}_1H^2$) and Tritium (${}_1H^3$).
- **Compound**
  - Water (high specific heat, thermal conductivity, dipole moment, surface tension etc.)
  - Soft water (free from salts of Ca^{2+} & Mg^{2+}).
  - Hard water (contains Ca^{2+} & Mg^{2+}).
- **Temporary Hardness** Boiling and clarks method.
- **Permanent Hardness** Heavy water (D_2O) exhaustive electrolysis Hydrogen perioxide (H_2O_2) control environmental pollution and used as effluents.

SOURCE *New NCERT Class VIII Chap 3 (Coal and Petroleum), Chap 4 (Combustion and Flame), New NCERT Class X Chap 3 (Metals and Non-metals), Chap 4 (Carbon and Its Compounds) Tamil Nadu Board Class X (Carbon and its Compounds)*

1 Which of the following statement is incorrect?

(Chap 3, Class-VIII, NCERT)

(a) Coal, petroleum and natural gas are all known as fossil fuels.
(b) Coal is used in thermal power plants to produce electricity.
(c) Coal tar is a colourless, thin liquid with pleasant smell.
(d) Coal gas is used as a source of heat rather than light.

Ans. (c)

Exp. Among the given statements only (c) is incorrect. The corrected form of statement (c) is, coal tar is a black, thick liquid with an unpleasent smell. It is a mixture of about 200 substances. Products obtained from coal tar are used as starting materials for manufacturing of various substances.

2 Consider the following statements :

(Chap 4, Class-X, NCERT)

1. Coal is a sedimentary organic rock that contains a lot of carbon.
2. Charcoal is used in making lead pencils.
3. Thermodynamically, diamond is the most stable form of carbon.

How many statement(s) given above is/are correct?

(a) Only 1 (b) 2 and 3
(c) 1 and 3 (d) All of these

Ans. (a)

Exp. Among the given only one statement (1) is correct but two statements (2 and 3) are incorrect.

Lead pencils are made up of graphite and clay. Clay gives the hardness while graphite gives the blackness and softness to the pencil.

Thermodynamically, the most stable form of carbon is graphite. It has high melting point and high specific heat. Graphite contains one delocalised electron per carbon. These cause greater attraction between carbon atoms hence, giving stronger bonds more stability to the structure.

3 Which one of the following statement is incorrect?

(Chap 4, Class-X, NCERT)

(a) Graphite is a naturally occurring hardest substance on the earth.
(b) Graphite is used as lubricant in heavy machines.
(c) Diamond and graphite cannot have the same crystal structure.
(d) Oxo form is not an additional form of carbon.

Ans. (a)

Exp. Among the given statements only (a) is incorrect while (b), (c) and (d) are correct. The corrected form of statement (a) is, diamond is a naturally occurring hardest substance on the earth. It is a mineral composed of pure carbon. It is known as gemstone because of their extreme hardness. Graphite occurs naturally and is the most stable form of carbon.

4 Consider the following statements.

(Chap 4, Class-X, NCERT)
(Unit 11, Class-X, Tamil Nadu Board)

1. Carbon forms large number of organic compounds due to the allotropy.
2. Buckminster fullerene contains 60 carbon atoms.
3. Carbon exists mostly in combined state.

Which of the statements given above is/are correct?

(a) 1 and 2 (b) 1, 2 and 3 (c) 2 and 3 (d) 1 and 3

Ans. (c)

Exp. Among the given statements, only (2) and (3) are correct while statement (1) is incorrect. The correct form of statement (1) is as, carbon element which lead to the formation of a very large number of organic compounds due to catenation and tetravalency.

The property of carbon due to which its atom can join with one another to form long carbon chains is called catenation. Since, the valency of carbon is 4, it is capable of bonding with four other atoms such as H, O, N, S etc., giving rise to large number of compounds.

5 Which of the following statements about diamond and graphite is true?

(Chap 4, Class-X, NCERT) (BPSC Pre 2022)

(a) They have same crystal structure
(b) They have same degree of hardness
(c) They have same electrical conductivity
(d) More than one of the above
(e) None of the above

Ans. (e)

Exp. Statements (a), (b) and (c), all are incorrect because diamond and graphite cannot have the same degree of hardness and crystal structure due to different arrangements and bonding of carbon atoms. They do not have same electrical conductivity because graphite is a good conductor of electricity while diamond does not conduct electricity.

6 Which of the following statements is correct?

(Chap 4, Class-X, NCERT)

(a) Fullerenes have only six-membered carbon rings.
(b) Fullerenes are open cage structure-like ice.
(c) Diamond is thermodynamically the most stable allotrope of carbon.
(d) Graphite is slippery and hard therefore it is used as a dry lubricant in machines.

Ans. (d)

Exp. Statement (d) is correct because in graphite, carbon atoms are strongly bonded in sheets but the bond between the sheets are weak. It shows lower shearing strength due to which it is used as dry lubricants in machines.

Statements (a), (b) and (c) are incorrect because Fullerene (C-60) have 20 six-membered rings and 12 five-membered rings of carbon atoms.

Fullerene are large class of allotropes of carbon, having cage-like molecule with a shape like soccer ball.
Diamond is not thermodynamically stable as it converts into graphite by a spontaneous process.
Graphite is the most thermodynamically stable allotrope of carbon.

7 Glass can be etched or scratched by which of the following? *(Chap 4, Class-X, NCERT) (IAS Pre 1999)*

1. Diamond
2. Hydrofluoric acid
3. *Aqua-regia*
4. Conc. sulphuric acid

Codes

(a) 1 and 4 (b) 2 and 3 (c) 1 and 2 (d) 2 and 4

Ans. (c)

Exp. Glass can be etched or scratched by diamond and hydrofluoric acid. Hydrofluoric acid chemically eats away at the glass substrate and causes etching in the glass surface. Diamond helps in physically grinding the glass surface which results in scratching.

8 Which one of the following pairs is not correctly matched? *(Chap 4, Class-X, NCERT) (UPPSC Mains 2017)*

(a) Dry ice – Solid carbon dioxide
(b) Sevin – Insecticide
(c) Teflon – Polymer containing fluorine
(d) Fullerene – Organic compound containing fluorine

Ans. (d)

Exp. Statement (d) is not correctly matched as fullerene is an allotrope of carbon. It is the cage-like molecule of fullerene which is composed of 60 carbon (C-60) atoms. It has 20 six-membered cages and 12 five-membered cages and its design resembles a soccer ball.

9 Buckminster-fullerene is *(Chap 4, Class-X, NCERT)*

(a) an allotrope of carbon.
(b) a polymer of fluorine.
(c) an isotope of carbon heavier than CCl_4.
(d) None of the above

Ans. (a)

Exp. Buckminster-fullerene is an allotrope of carbon in which clusters of 60 atoms of carbon bound together in polyhedral structure composed of 20 hexagons and 12 pentagons.

10 Match the following lists and choose the correct code. *(Chap 3, Class-X, NCERT) (Chap 27, Module-6, NIOS)*

List-I (Element)	List-II (Properties)
A. Gold	1. Lightest non-metallic element.
B. Graphite	2. Liquid non-metallic element.
C. Bromine	3. Most malleable element.
D. Hydrogen	4. Non-metal which is best conductor of electricity.

Codes

	A	B	C	D		A	B	C	D
(a)	3	2	1	4	(b)	3	2	4	1
(c)	2	4	1	3	(d)	3	4	2	1

Ans. (d)

Exp. The correct matching is A-3, B-4, C-2, D-1.
Gold It is the most malleable element.
Graphite It is a non-metal. Its crystal consists of layers of carbon atoms. Each C-atom joined to three other carbon atoms by strong covalent bonds to form flat hexagonal rings. However, the fourth electrons of each carbon atom is free which make it a good conductor of electricity.
Bromine Among all the non-metals, bromine exist in liquid state at room temperature and is a member of halogen group (17th).
Hydrogen It is the lightest non-metallic element as it contains only one proton and one electron.
Its atomic mass is 1u.

11 Consider the following statements about oxygen. *(Chap 4, Class-VIII, NCERT)*

1. It promotes rapid combustion.
2. It can be toxic at elevated partial pressures.
3. Rockets use liquid oxygen as their oxidiser.
4. It is a colourless and odourless gas.

Which of the statement(s) given above is/are correct?

(a) 1, 2, 3 and 4 (b) 1 and 2 (c) 1, 2 and 3 (d) 1, 2 and 4

Ans. (a)

Exp. All the given statements are correct about oxygen. It promotes rapid combustion as it is flammable. It can be toxic at elevated partial pressures. Liquid oxygen is most common cryogenic liquid oxidiser propellant for spacecraft rocket applications.
Pure form of oxygen is colourless, odourless and tasteless.

12 Water is used as a fire extinguisher because *(Chap 4, Class-VIII, NCERT)*

(a) it cools the combustible substance in order to bring the temperature below its ignition point.
(b) it prevents the supply of air.
(c) Both 'a' and 'b'
(d) it releases CO_2

Ans. (c)

Exp. Water is used as a fire extinguisher as it prevents the supply of air and provides cooling effect. It cools the combustible substances by bringing the temperature below its ignition point.

13 Match the following lists and choose the correct codes. *(Chap 4, Class-X, NCERT)*

List-I (Compound)	List-II (Component)
A. Water gas	1. Ammonia
B. Stranger gas	2. Methane
C. Tear gas	3. $CO + H_2$
D. Bio gas	4. Xenon

Codes

	A	B	C	D
(a)	2	1	4	3
(b)	3	4	1	2
(c)	3	4	2	1
(d)	2	3	4	1

Ans. (b)

Exp. The correct matching is A -3, B-4, C-1, D -2.

Water gas It is a mixture of carbon monoxide and hydrogen produced by passing steam over red hot coke.

Stranger gas Xenon gas is also known as stranger gas as its volume is very low in the atmosphere. Xenon terms is derived from greek word 'xenos' which means foreign or strange. Also, the unique property of xenon makes it peculiar due to which it behaves in different manner.

Tear gas Ammonia is used in tear gas. It is a chemical weapon that causes severe eye and respiratory pain, skin burning, vomiting and even blindness.

Bio gas It is a mixture of methane, carbon dioxide and small quantities of other gases produced by anaerobic digestion of organic matter in an oxygen free environment.

14 Consider the following statements. *(Chap 8, Class-XI, NCERT) (BPSC Pre Re-exam 2022)*

1. Addition of salt to pure water increases the boiling points of water and decreases the freezing point of water.
2. When methyl alcohol is added to water, boiling point of water decreases.

Which of the above statements is/are correct?

(a) Salt and methyl alcohol are same in behaviour
(b) Only 1
(c) Only 2
(d) Both 1 and 2
(e) None of the above/More than one of the above

Ans. (d)

Exp. Both the statement (1) and (2) are correct. When salt is added to pure water it decrease its freezing point and increases its boiling point.

While, when methyl alcohol is added to water, boiling point of water decreases due to hydrogen bonding.

15 Permanent hardness of water is due to the presence of *(Chap 4, Class-XI, NCERT)*

(a) sulphate of calcium and magnesium
(b) calcium bicarbonate sulphate
(c) magnesium bicarbonate
(d) chloride of silver and potassium

Ans. (a)

Exp. Permanent hardness of water is due to the presence of dissolved sulphate of calcium and magnesium. It cannot be removed by simply boiling. To remove the permanent hardness, the hard water should be treated with washing soda.

16 Consider the following statements

Hard water is not suitable for *(Chap 4, Class-XI, NCERT)*

1. drinking
2. washing clothes with soap
3. use in boilers
4. irrigating crops

Which of these statements are correct?

(a) 1 and 2 (b) 2 and 3 (c) 1, 2 and 4 (d) 1, 2, 3 and 4

Ans. (d)

Exp. Hard water is not suitable for drinking, washing clothes with soap, in boilers and irrigating crops etc.

Hard water is named as 'hard' due to presence of highly dissolved minerals specifically sulphates and chlorides of calcium and magnesium. Hard water is salty and therefore it is not used for drinking.

It is difficult to wash clothes with hard water as it requires more soap and leaves a messy scum that cannot be washed out easily.

When hard water is boiled, it leaves deposits of calcium and magnesium salts. These deposits reduces the efficiency of boilers.

If salt level increases in irrigating water, it becomes harder and hard water blocks the xylem tissue of the plants and thus, not suitable for irrigation.

17 The gases employed for respiratory activities of divers are *(Chap 3, Class-X, NCERT) (UPPSC Mains 2014)*

(a) oxygen, nitrogen and helium
(b) oxygen and helium
(c) oxygen and argon
(d) oxygen and neon

Ans. (a)

Exp. The gases employed for respiratory activities of divers are by oxygen, nitrogen and helium gases. Divers carry cylinders which contain oxygen, helium and nitrogen gases.

Helium generates less airway resistance than air and thereby requires less mechanical energy to ventilate the lungs. Helium is much less soluble in water than many other gases such as nitrogen. The low solubility means it does not enter the blood stream even under pressure.

18 Consider the following statements. *(Chap 2, Class-X, NCERT)*

1. Nitric acid is used in the production of fertilisers.
2. Sulphuric acid is used in the production of fertilisers.

Which of the statement(s) given above is/are correct?

(a) Only 1 (b) Only 2
(c) Both 1 and 2 (d) Neither 1 nor 2

Ans. (c)

Exp. Both the statements (1) and (2) are correct.

Nitric acid is used in the production of ammonium nitrate and calcium ammonium nitrate which find applications as fertilisers. Sulphuric acid produces ammonium sulphate on reaction with ammonia and ammonium sulphate formed is an important fertiliser.

19 Consider the following Assertion (A) and Reason (R) and choose the correct code. *(Chap 3, Class-X, NCERT)*

Assertion (A) Elements placed below hydrogen in electrochemical series does not react with concentrated HNO_3.

Reason (R) HNO_3 is a strong oxidising agent.

It oxidises these metals.

Codes

(a) Both A and R are true and R is the correct explanation of A.

(b) Both A and R are true but R is not the correct explanation of A.

(c) A is true but R is false.

(d) A is false but R is true.

Ans. (b)

Exp. Both Assertion (A) and Reason (R) are true but Reason (R) is not the correct explanation of Assertion (A).

Elements placed below hydrogen in electrochemical series does not react with concentrated HNO_3 because they cannot replace hydrogen and hence, do not usually react with nitric acid. Concentrated HNO_3 is a powerful oxidising agent and can oxidise free hydrogen to water.

20 Which of the following is not correct? *(Chap 3, Class-X, NCERT)*

(a) Boric acid is used in pharmaceutical industry and also as a food preservative.

(b) Dry ice is solid carbon dioxide.

(c) Nitric oxide is laughing gas.

(d) Water gas is a mixture of carbon monoxide and hydrogen.

Ans. (c)

Exp. Statement (c) is not correct because nitric oxide (NO) is not a laughing gas. Nitrous oxide having formula N_2O is known as laughing gas.

At room temperature, it is a colourless non-flammable gas, and has a slightly sweet scent and taste.

21 Arrange the following substances in chronological order of their first synthesis in lab

(Unit 11, Class-X, Tamil Nadu Board) (UPPSC Pre 2019)

1. Black gold
2. Fullerene
3. Graphene
4. Kevlar

Select correct answer from the codes given below.

(a) 1 2 3 4 (b) 4 2 3 1 (c) 2 4 3 1 (d) 4 1 2 3

Ans. (b)

Exp. The correct order of their first synthesis in lab is 4 2 3 1.

Kevlar is made by a condensation reaction of an amine and acid chloride.

Fullerene is an allotrope of carbon whose molecule consists of carbon atoms joined by single and double bonds.

Graphene is a single layer of carbon atoms, tightly bound in a hexagonal honeycomb lattice.

Black gold is a term applied to oil or petroleum, which is black when it comes out of the ground and is worth a great deal of money.

Chapter 8

Carbon Compounds

Carbon Compounds

Petroleum

Organic Compounds

- Carbon compound except its oxides, carbonates and hydrogen carbonate salts.
- **Petroleum** Mixture of hydrocarbon mainly aliphatic with lesser amounts of aromatic hydrocarbons.
- **Petrochemical** Petroleum and natural gas.

Classification

- Acylic or open chain compound (consist straight or branched chain).
- Alicyclic or closed chain compound (homocyclic or heterocyclic)
- Aromatic compounds (ring compounds e.g. benzene)
- Homologous series (same functional group; straight chain alkanes)

Homologous Series A series of compounds having same functional group but a difference of $-CH_2$ unit (14 unit mass) between two successive members. e.g. methane(CH_4), ethane(C_2H_6), propane(C_3H_8), butane(C_4H_{10}) etc.

Isomerism

- Identical molecular but different configuration or properties.
  - **Structural Isomerism** same molecular formula but different structures.
  - **Stereoisomerism** difference in relative position of their atoms or molecules in space.
- They are two types
  - Geometrical
  - Optical

Carboxylic Acid

- **Carboxylic Acids** $C_nH_{2n}O_2$
  - **Formic Acid** HCOOH prepared by distillation of water with red ants.
  - **Acetic Acid** (CH_3COOH) obtained from pyroligneous acid 4-6% aqueous solution is called vinegar.
  - **Oxalic Acid** (dicarboxylic acid) Used in metallurgy.
  - **Lactic Acid** monohydroxy tricarboxylic acid. Present in milk
  - **Salicylic Acid** (crystalline aromatic acid). Used in medicines.
  - **Citric Acid** (monohydroxy tricarboxylic acid). Occurs in all citrus fruits.
- **Esters** $C_nH_{2n}O_2$ or $C_nH_{2n+1}COOR$. Ethyl acetate is used for making artificial perfumes, scented colour, dyes, etc.

Hydrocarbons

- Compounds of hydrogen and carbon only.

Saturated Hydrocarbons

- Single bond, Alkanes of paraffin Formula - C_nH_{2n+2}

Unsaturated Hydrocarbons atleast one multiple bonds (double, triple or both).

- Alkenes C_nH_{2n} and C—C double bond along with single bond.
- Alkynes C_nH_{2n-2} and have atleast one C—C triple bond along with single bond.
- Aromatic hydrocarbons arenes contain benzene ring. e.g. toluene.

Organic Compounds

Organic compounds containing C, H and O

- **Alcohols** $C_nH_{2n+1}OH$; presence identified by esterification.
- **Methanol** wood spirit, colourless poisonous liquid.
- **Ethanol** Ethene + water → Ethanol; colourless volatile liquid.
- **Ethylene glycol** dihydric alcohol with sweet taste.
- **Glycerol** Hygroscopic substance use in explosives.
- **Phenols** Hydroxy derivative of benzene; presence identified by ferric chloride.
- **Ethers** $R-O/Ar-O$; $C_nH_{2n+2}O$. Diethylether ($C_2H_5OC_2H_5$)
- **Aldehydes** CHO functional group; $C_nH_{2n}O$ identified by Tollen's regent, fehling's solution and Schiff's reagent formaldehyde (HCHO) used as tissue fixation.
- **Ketones** $>C=O$ functional group; $C_nH_{2n}O$ or $(C_nH_{2n+1})_2CO$.
- **Chloroform** $CHCl_3$ used as anaesthesia
- **Iodoform** CHI_3 is prepared in haloform reaction and insoluble in water and soluble in alcohol and ether.
- **Chlorofluorocarbons (CFCs freons)** Extremely stable, unreactive and used in refrigeration and A.C.
- **Aniline** $C_6H_5NH_2$; amine derivative and used in the; preparation of drugs.
- **Methyl isocyanate** CH_3NC ; used in the production of rubbers.
- **Gammexane or BHC** used as an insecticide.
- **Naphthalene** $C_{10}H_8$; used as an germicide and moth repellant.

SOURCE

New NCERT Class VIII Chap 3 *(Coal and Petroleum),* ***Chap 4*** *(Combustion and Flame),* ***New NCERT Class X Chap 2*** *(Acids, Bases and Salts),* ***Chap 4*** *(Carbon and its Compounds),* ***New NCERT Class XI Chap 9*** *(Hydrocarbons),* ***New NCERT Class XII Chap 7*** *(Alcohols, Phenols & Ethers),* ***Chap 8*** *(Aldehydes, Ketones & Carboxylic Acids),* ***Tamil Nadu Board Class X*** *(Carbon and its Compounds),*

1 In all bio compounds, the most necessary fundamental element is *(Chap 4, Class-X, NCERT)*

(a) sulphur (b) carbon (c) oxygen (d) nitrogen

Ans. (b)

Exp. Carbon is the most necessary fundamental element of all bio compounds or organic compounds.

The organic compounds are a large class of chemical compounds in which one or more atoms of carbon are covalently linked to atoms of other elements, most commonly hydrogen, oxygen or nitrogen.

2 Consider the following statement regarding carbon dioxide? *(Chap 3, Class-VI, NCERT)* *(Unit 11, Class-X, Tamil Nadu Board)*

1. Its aqueous solution is acidic.
2. It forms carbonates on reacting with metal hydroxides.
3. Its molecular structure is tetrahedral in shape.

Which statements (s) given above is/are correct?

(a) Only 3 (b) 1 and 3 (c) 1 and 2 (d) 1, 2 and 3

Ans. (c)

Exp. Among the given statements, (1) and (2) are correct. While correct form of statements (3) is, molecular structure of carbon dioxide is linear and arranged like $O{=}C{=}O$ which makes the bond angle of $CO_2 = 180°$.

3 Consider the following statements about fuel. *(Chap 4, Class-VIII, NCERT)*

1. A good fuel is one which is readily available and cheap.
2. Incomplete combustion of coal and petroleum gives carbon monoxide gas.
3. Burning of coal and diesel does not release sulphur dioxide gas.

Which of the statement(s) given above is/are correct?

(a) 1 and 2 (b) 1 and 3 (c) 2 and 3 (d) All of these

Ans. (a)

Exp. Statements (1) and (2) are correct, while statement (3) is incorrect. Burning of coal and diesel releases sulphur dioxide gas. It is an extremely suffocating and corrosive gas. sulphur and nitrogen dissolve in rain water and cause acid rain.

4 Match the following lists and choose the correct code. *(Chap 3, Class-VIII, NCERT) (RAS/RTS Pre 2013)*

List-I (Fuel gas)	List-II (Major constituents)
A. CNG	1. Carbon monoxide, hydrogen
B. LPG	2. Butane, propane
C. Coal gas	3. Methane, ethane
D. Water gas	4. Hydrogen, methane, carbon monoxide

Codes

	A	B	C	D		A	B	C	D
(a)	2	1	3	4	(b)	2	4	3	1
(c)	3	2	4	1	(d)	3	2	1	4

Ans. (c)

Exp. The correct matching is A-3, B-2, C-4, D-1.

CNG Methane and ethane are mainly stored at high pressure in CNG. It is compressed to less than 10% of the volume it occupies at standard atmospheric pressure.

LPG It is made when propane and butane are separated from natural gas and liquefied at high pressure.

Coal gas It consists of hydrogen, methane and carbon monoxide. It is produced when coal is heated strongly in the absence of air.

Water gas It comprises of carbon monoxide and hydrogen. It is obtained by passing steam over coke.

5 Consider the following statements. *(Chap 3, Class-VIII, NCERT)*

1. Coal, petroleum and natural gas are fossil fuels.
2. Gasohol is a mixture of benzene and alcohol.
3. Geothermal energy is non-conventional energy source.
4. Gobar gas contains mainly methane.

Which of the statements given above is/are correct?

(a) 1 and 2 (b) 2 and 3 (c) 1, 2 and 3 (d) 1, 3 and 4

Ans. (d)

Exp. Statements (1), (3) and (4) are correct.

Fossil fuels are hydrocarbons. Primarily coal, fuel oil or natural gas formed from the remains of dead plants and animals. Geothermal energy is non-conventional energy source. It is heat derived from the surface of Earth. Gobar gas consists of methane.

Statement (2) is incorrect because gasohol is a mixture of ethanol and gasoline.

6 In the heavy vehicles, diesel is used as fuel because *(Chap 3, Class-VIII, NCERT)*

(a) it has more mileage and safe for the engine.
(b) it is less costly and useful for the fuel savings point of view.
(c) it has high power and economic savings.
(d) it is cheaper with comparison to the petrol.

Ans. (c)

Exp. Diesel has high power and economic savings due to which it is used as fuel in heavy vehicles. It can provide high torque than petrol engines which helps heavy vehicles to carry a high load like goods and passengers.

7 Which of the following is the by-product derived from the refining process of petroleum? *(Chap 3, Class-VIII, NCERT)*

(a) Petrol (b) Charcoal (c) Coal (d) Asphalt

Ans. (d)

Exp. The by-product derived from the refining process of petroleum is asphalt. It is also known as bitumen. It is a sticky, black and highly viscous liquid or semi-solid form of petroleum. It is used in road construction, bituminous waterproofing product, sealing flat roofs etc.

8 Which of the following statement is incorrect? *(Chap 3, Class VIII, NCERT)*

(a) Coke is used in manufacture of steel.
(b) Charcoal is used to treat poisoning.
(c) Graphite is used in lubricants and polishes.
(d) Coke is used as an oxidising agent in metallurgy.

Ans. (d)

Exp. Statement (d) is incorrect, the correct form of statement (d) is as; It is used as reducing agent in metallurgy. It is an impure form of carbon. It is formed when coal is strongly heated in the absence of air.

9 Which of the following pairs can be the successive members of a homologous series? *(Chap 4, Class-X, NCERT)*

(a) C_3H_8 and C_4H_{10}
(b) C_2H_2 and C_2H_4
(c) CH_4 and C_3H_6
(d) C_2H_5OH and C_4H_8OH

Ans. (a)

Exp. Among the given pairs C_3H_8 and C_4H_{10} are successive members of a homologous series. Compounds having the same general formula and similar properties are called homologous series. Members of this series have almost same chemical properties due to same functional group. Any two successive members in this series differ in their molecular formula by —CH_2— unit.

10 Which of the following is the correct sequence in increasing order of molecular weights of the hydrocarbons? *(Chap 4, Class-X, NCERT) (IAS (Pre) 2001)*

(a) Methane, ethane, propane and butane
(b) Propane, butane, ethane and methane
(c) Butane, ethane, propane and methane
(d) Butane, propane, ethane and methane

Ans. (a)

Exp. The increasing order of molecular weight of the hydrocarbons is as follows

Methane < ethane < propane < butane

The molecular formulas and weights for given hydrocarbons are as follows

Methane; CH_4, Molecular weight, 16
Ethane; C_2H_6, Molecular weight, 30
Propane; C_3H_8, Molecular weight, 44
Butane; C_4H_{10}, Molecular weight, 58

11 Consider the following statements. *(Chap 9, Class-XI, NCERT) (Chap 28, Module-6, NIOS)*

1. The old name of alkenes is paraffins.
2. Ethane is the carbon compound. It's molecular formula is CH_4.
3. Ethanol is the main constituent of all alcoholic drinks.

Choose the incorrect statements (s) given above.

(a) 1 and 2
(b) Only 1
(c) Only 3
(d) 2 and 3

Ans. (a)

Exp. Statements (1) and (2) are incorrect because the old name of alkenes is olefins. These are a class of chemicals made up of hydrogen and carbon with one or more pairs of carbon atoms linked by a double bond. The molecular formula of methane is CH_4.

12 Fruit ripening is promoted by which of the following? *(Chap 9, Class-XI, NCERT) (UPRO/ARO Pre 2014)*

(a) Carbon dioxide
(b) Sulphur dioxide
(c) Nitrogen
(d) Ethylene

Ans. (d)

Exp. Fruit ripening is promoted by ethylene. This gas is an important natural plant hormone. Fruit ripening is accompanied by increase in rate of respiration. Due to increase respiration, complex carbohydrates are broken down into simpler sugars and cell wall becomes soft.

13 Which of the following statement is incorrect? *(Chap 4 & 9, Class-X, NCERT)*

(a) A hydrocarbon in which two carbon atoms are joined by a double bond is called as an alkene.
(b) Ethene is used in welding industry.
(c) Methane is the main component of natural gas.
(d) Acetylene is obtained by mixing calcium carbide and water.

Ans. (b)

Exp. Statement (b) is incorrect, as acetylene is used in welding industry instead of ethene. It is a raw material for preparing plastics.

Methane is the main component of natural gas. It contains smaller amount of carbon dioxide and water vapours.

14 Consider the following statements about acetylene. *(Chap 9, Class-XI, NCERT) (IAS Pre 1998)*

1. It is used in welding industry.
2. It is a raw material for preparing plastics.
3. It is easily obtained by mixing silicon carbide and water.

How many statement(s) given above is/are correct?

(a) Only one (b) Only two (c) All three (d) None of these

Ans. (b)

Exp. Only two Statements (1 and 2) are correct about acetylene. It is also called as ethyne having formula C_2H_2. It is used in welding. Acetylene is used as raw material in plastic industry.

One Statement (3) is incorrect because the mixture of calcium carbide and water produces acetylene.

$$\underset{\text{Calcium carbide}}{CaC_2} + \underset{\text{Water}}{2H_2O} \longrightarrow \underset{\text{Calcium hydroxide}}{Ca(OH)_2} + \underset{\text{Acetylene}}{C_2H_2}$$

15 Consider the following statements about aromatic hydrocarbons. *(Chap 9, Class XI, NCERT) (Unit 11, Class-X, Tamil Nadu Board)*

1. Benzene ring is highly unsaturated hydrocarbon.
2. Aromatic hydrocarbons are polar molecules.
3. These are immiscible with water but readily miscible with organic solvents.

Which of the statement(s) given above is/are correct?
(a) 1 and 3 (b) 1 and 2 (c) 2 and 3 (d) All of these

Ans. (a)

Exp. Among the given statements (1) and (3) are correct about hydrocarbon. The corrected form of statement (2) is; aromatic hydrocarbons are non-polar molecules and are usually colourless liquids or solids with a characteristic aroma, they burn with sooty flame.

16 **Numbers of sigma and pi-bonds in benzene are**
(Chap 4, Class-X, NCERT) (CGPSC Pre 2014) (BPSC Pre 2020)

(a) 3, 3 (b) 3, 6 (c) 12, 3 (d) 12, 6
(e) None of the above/More than one of the above

Ans. (c)

Exp. Number of sigma and pi-bonds in benzene are 12 and 3 respectively. It is an important organic compound with chemical formula C_6H_6. Its chemical structure can be described as a hexagonal ring with three alternating double bonds and contains 6 sigma bonds between carbon atoms and 6 sigma bonds between carbon and hydrogen atoms.

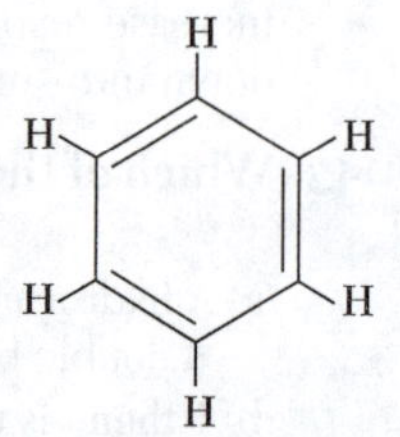

(Structure of Benzene)

17 **Alcohol obtained in the saponification process is**
(Chap 4, Class-X, NCERT)

(a) ethyl alcohol (b) methyl alcohol
(c) wood spirit (d) glycerol

Ans. (d)

Exp. Alcohol obtained in the saponification process is glycerol. Saponification is a process by which triglycerides are reacted with sodium or potassium hydroxide to produce glycerol and a fatty acid salt called soap.

18 **Which of the following statement is incorrect?**
(Chap 7, Class-XII, NCERT)

(a) Boiling point of alcohol increases with increase in the number of carbon atom.
(b) Ether have high boiling point than alcohol.
(c) Methyl alcohol is known as wood spirit.
(d) Methyl alcohol is volatile and colourless flamable liquid.

Ans. (b)

Exp. Statement (b) is incorrect because alcohols have high boiling point in comparison to other classes of compounds like ether, haloalkane etc. It is due to the presence of intermolecular hydrogen bonding in them which is lacking in ethers.

19 **Consider the following statements.**
(Chap 4, Class-X, NCERT)

1. The alcohol which is 99% pure is called absolute alcohol.
2. Ethyl alcohol which cannot be used for the beverage purpose is called denatured alcohol.
3. The mixture of purified spirit and petrol is called power alcohol.

Which of the statement(s) given above are correct?
(a) 1 and 2 (b) 1 and 3 (c) 2 and 3 (d) All of these

Ans. (d)

Exp. All the given statements are correct.
Absolute alcohol is a liquid alcohol that is 99% pure alcohol by weight. It is found in alcoholic beverages. Denatured alcohol is used identically to ethanol which cannot be used for the beverage purpose. Power alcohol is a mixture of purified spirit and petrol. It is useful in the field of automobiles to generate energy for its operations.

20 **Consider the following statements?**
(Chap 4, Class-X, NCERT)

1. In presence of oxidising chemicals, alcohols are transformed to carboxylic acids.
2. Each carbon atom in graphite linked to 4 other carbon atoms.
3. Diamond is hardest substance and allotropes of carbon element.
4. C_nH_{2n} is a general formula of unsaturated carbon compounds.

Which of the above statements is/are incorrect?
(a) 1 and 2 (b) Only 3
(c) 3 and 4 (d) Only 2

Ans. (d)

Exp. Graphite is an allotrope of carbon which is linked to three other carbon atoms. Thus, among the given statements (2) is incorrect.

21 **Consider the given four statements about ethanol and choose the correct answer from the given options.** ***(Chap 4, Class-X, NCERT)***

1. It is the main constituent of all alcoholic drinks.
2. It is not a good solvent.
3. It is soluble in water in all proportions.
4. It cannot be used as an additive in petrol.

Codes
(a) 1 and 2 (b) 1 and 3
(c) 2 and 4 (d) 1 and 4

Ans. (b)

Exp. Statements (1) and (3) are correct because ethanol is the main constituent of all alcoholic drinks and it is soluble in water in all proportions.
Statements (2) and (4) are incorrect because it is considered as a universal solvent and it can be combined with petrol in any concentration.

22 **The offending substance in the liquor tragedies leading to blindness etc., is**
(Unit 11, Class-X, Tamil Nadu Board) (IAS Pre 1996)

(a) ethyl alcohol (b) amyl alcohol
(c) benzyl alcohol (d) methyl alcohol

Ans. (d)

Exp. Methyl alcohol is the offending substance in the liquor tragedies leading to blindness. It is a colourless liquid. Its smell is like a pungent, unpleasant and intense flavour.

23 **Glucose is converted to ethyl alcohol by the enzyme** *(Chap 7, Class-XII, NCERT), (BPSC Pre 2020)*

(a) maltase (b) invertase
(c) zymase (d) diastase
(e) None of the above/More than one of the above

Ans. (c)

Exp. Glucose is converted to ethyl alcohol by the zymase enzyme. Zymase catalyses the fermentation of sugar (glucose and fructose) into ethanol and carbon dioxide. This enzyme is used in the preparation of ethanol and alcoholic beverages commercially, whereas other options like invertase enzyme convert sucrose (cane sugar) into glucose and fructose. Maltase enzyme converts maltose into glucose, while diastase enzyme converts starch into maltose.

24 **Which of the following statement is correct regarding denatured alcohol?** *(Chap 7, Class-XII, NCERT)*

(a) The mixing of colour and methanol to ethanol for the purpose of industrial use.
(b) It is formed when alcohol reacts with oxygen.
(c) The product of ethanol reacting with concentrated sulphuric acid.
(d) The product of alcohol reacting with sodium.

Ans. (a)

Exp. Denatured alcohol is ethanol that has additives to make it poisonous badtasting, foul smelling or nauseating to discourage its recreation of consumption.

25 **Match List-I with List-II and select the correct answer using the codes given below the lists.** *(Chap 9, Class-XI, NCERT)*

	List-I		List-II
A.	Functional group —OH	1.	Benzene
B.	Heterocyclic	2.	Ethene
C.	Unsaturated	3.	Alcohol
D.	Carbocyclic	4.	Furan

Codes

	A	B	C	D		A	B	C	D
(a)	2	1	4	3	(b)	3	4	2	1
(c)	2	3	1	4	(d)	1	4	3	2

Ans. (b)

Exp. The correct matching is A-3, B-4, C-2, D-1.

Functional groups Are group of atoms that define the function of the hydrocarbon.

The functional group —OH is present in alcohol.

Heterocyclic compounds are cyclic compounds with the ring containing carbon and other element.

Furan is a heterocyclic compound as it contains O-atom in cyclic ring.

An organic compound containing one or more double or triple bond called unsaturated compound.

Ethene contains double bond so, it is unsaturated.

Benzene is a six membered C-atom ring, it is also called carbocyclic.

26 **Dehydration of ethanol by concentrated sulphuric acid at 413 K forms** *(Chap 7, Class-XII, NCERT)*

(a) diethyl ether (b) ethene (c) ester (d) acetic acid

Ans. (a)

Exp. Dehydration of ethanol by conc. sulphuric acid at 413 K forms diethyl ether. Ethanol can be dehydrated at 170°C with an excess of conc. sulphuric acid to give ethene. Ester is formed due to the reaction of ethanol with carboxylic acid.

Ethanol is oxidised by $K_2Cr_2O_7$ to form acetic acid.

27 **Which of the following compound does not contain a carboxylic acid group?** *(Chap 8, Class-XII, NCERT)*

(a) Picric acid (b) Vinegar (c) Salicylic acid (d) Benzoic acid

Ans. (a)

Exp. Picric acid does not contain a carboxylic acid group. Chemically, it is known as 2, 4, 6-trinitrophenol. Its structure is as follows

OH
O_2N NO_2
NO_2

28 **Which of the following statement is incorrect about ethers?** *(Chap 7, Class-XII, NCERT)*

(a) Ether is used as an anaesthetics and pain killer.
(b) Ethers do not have a net dipole moment.
(c) The general formula of ether is $C_nH_{2n+2}O$.
(d) Ethers are least reactive of the functional groups.

Ans. (b)

Exp. Statement (b) is incorrect because C—O bond in ethers are polar and thus, ethers have a net dipole moment. The weak polarity of ethers do not appreciably affect their boiling points.

29 **Which of the following statement is incorrect?** *(Chap 8, Class-XII, NCERT)*

(a) Acetone is used to preserve biological specimens in the laboratories.
(b) Solubility of aldehydes decreases on increasing the length of alkyl chain.
(c) Formaldehyde is use to prepare bakelite.
(d) Methanoic acid is used in rubber.

Ans. (a)

Exp. Statement (a) is incorrect because aqueous solution of formaldehyde called formalin is used to preserve biological specimens in the laboratories. It is also used as preservation in foods and products like antiseptics and cosmetics.

30 **Which of the following statements are incorrect?** *(Chap 2, Class-X, NCERT) (RAS/RTS Pre 2016)*

1. Sugarcane juice is fermented to form vinegar.
2. Vinegar has acetic acid.
3. Benzoic acid is present in vinegar.
4. Vinegar is used as a preservative.

Codes

(a) 1 and 2 (b) Only 3 (c) 1, 3, and 4 (d) 1, 2, and 3

Ans. (b)

Exp. Statement (3) is incorrect because benzoic acid is not present in vinegar instead it contains acetic acid. It is used as food preservative and in the manufacture of cosmetics, plastic and insect repellants.

31 Match the lists and choose the correct codes. *(Chap 8, Class-XII, NCERT)*

List-I (Acid)	List-II (Uses)
A. Formic acid	1. Photography
B. Acetic acid	2. Dyeing
C. Salicylic acid	3. Jelly
D. Oxalic acid	4. Medicines

Codes

	A	B	C	D
(a)	4	3	1	2
(b)	1	2	3	4
(c)	2	3	4	1
(d)	3	1	2	4

***Ans.* (c)**

Exp. The correct matching is A -2, B -3, C -4, D -1.

Formic acid It is used in rubber, dyeing and elctroplating industry. The chemical formula of formic acid is HCOOH.

Acetic acid It is used to form various organic compounds like alcohol. The chemical formula of acetic acid is CH_3COOH.

Salicylic acid It is used in the medicines.

Oxalic acid In black and white photography, oxalic acid was used for the toning solution. It is an organic compound with formula $C_2H_2O_4$.

32 Which one of the following pairs is not correctly matched? *(Chap 8, Class-XII, NCERT) (UP Lower Sub Pre 2015)*

	List-I (Compound)	List-II (Source)
(a)	Lactose	Sour milk
(b)	Acetic acid	Vinegar
(c)	Formic acid	Red ants
(d)	Lactic acid	Milk

***Ans.* (a)**

Exp. Pair (a) is not corretly matched as lactic acid is found in sour milk. Lactose is a milk sugar. Lactic acid is produced by the fermentation of lactose.

33 Consider the following Assertion (A) and Reason (R) and choose the correct code. *(Chap 8, Class-XII, NCERT)*

Assertion (A) Formic acid is a stronger acid than acetic acid.

Reason (R) Formic acid is an organic acid.

Codes

(a) Both A and R are true and R is the correct explanation of A.
(b) Both A and R are true but R is not the correct explanation of A.
(c) A is true but R is false.
(d) A is false but R is true.

***Ans.* (b)**

Exp. Both Assertion (A) and Reason (R) are true but Reason (R) is not the correct explanation of Assertion (A). Formic acid (HCOOH) and acetic acid (CH_3COOH) both are organic acids. Acetic acid contains an electron donating methyl group (CH_3) while formic acid has no such electron donating group and hence, it is stronger acid than acetic acid.

34 Consider the given three statements about acetic acid. *(Chap 8, Class-XII, NCERT)*

1. It is obtained by oxidation of methanol in the presence of alkaline $KMnO_4$.
2. It is used as preservative.
3. It is soluble in water.

How many statement(s) given above is/are correct.

(a) Only one (b) Only two
(c) All three (d) None of these

***Ans.* (b)**

Exp. Only two Statements (2 and 3) are correct, while one Statement (1) is incorrect. As acetic acid is obtained by oxidation of ethanol in the presence of alkaline $KMnO_4$.

The reaction involve in this case is as follows

$$\underset{\text{Ethanol}}{CH_3CH_2OH} + [O] \xrightarrow{\text{Alkaline } KMnO_4} \underset{\text{Acetic acid}}{CH_3COOH}$$

Chapter 9

Food Preservatives and Biomolecules

Food Preservatives and Biomolecules

Food Preservatives

Fats and Oils

- **Triglycerides** (Ester bond)
- • Saturated-Fats
- • Unsaturated-Oils
- **Higher fatty acids :** Palmitic acid, stearic acid, oleic acid, etc.
- **Phospholipids** Phosphorus containing fat.

Food Preservation

- Prevent spoilage of food.
- Common preservatives : Salt, sugar, vegetable oil, sodium benzoate, sodium metabisulphite.
- Salt of sorbic acid and propanoic acid also used as preservatives.
- Low temperature ; Reduce rate of biochemical reaction.

Antioxidants

- Chemicals to prevent oxidation of food, e.g. BHA, BHT, lecithin, etc.
- Sources of some antioxidants are fruits and vegetables (Vitamin-E vegetables oils.)
- Vitamin C- Fruit and Vegetables.
- Polyphenolic antioxidants - Tea, Coffee, Soyabean etc.

Artificial Sweetening Agents

- **Saccharin :** *Ortho*-sulphobenzimide ; 550 times as sweet as cane sugar.
- **Aspartame :** Widely used sweetner ; 100 times as sweet as cane sugar.
- **Alitame :** High potency sweetner ; 2000 times as sweet as cane sugar.
- **Sucralose :** Trichloro derivative of sucrose ; 600 times sweeter than sucrose.

Carbohydrates/Protein

Biomolecule

- **Complex** Carbohydrates, proteins, nucleic acids, lipid etc.
- **Simple** Vitamins and minerals.

Carbohydrates (Polyhydroxy aldehydes or ketones)

- **Classification** (basis of hydrolysis)
- • **Monosaccharides** Simple form e.g. triose, tetrose.
- • **Oligosaccharides** (2-10 monosaccharide unit) e.g. sucrose, molecule : disaccharide.
- • **Polysaccharides** (Large number of monosaccharide unit) e.g. starch, cellulose.
- **Physical Properties**
- • **Sugar** e.g sucrose
- • **Non-sugar** e.g. All polysaccharides
- **Reducing properties**
- • **Reducing carbohydrate** (reduce Tollen's reagent and Fehling's solution)
- • **Non-reducing carbohydrate** (unable to reduce Tollen's reagent and Fehling's solution.)
- **Common Carbohydrate** Glucose (dextrose), Fructose (fruit sugar), Sucrose (invert sugar), Maltose (malt sugar), Lactose, starch (amylose and amylopectin), Cellulose and Glycogen.

Protein

- Most abundant biomolecules (polymer of α-amino acids)
- Amino acids contain amino ($-NH_2$) & carboxyl ($-COOH$) functional group.
- Amino acid α, β, γ and δ.
- Held together by **peptide bond**.
- Dipeptide (2AA); Tripeptide (3AA); Tetrapeptide (4AA); Pentapeptide, Hexapeptide and Polypeptide.
- **Classification**
- · **Fibrous Protein** Polypeptide chains Sun parallel (hydrogen and disulphide bond) e.g. Myosin, keratin, etc.
- · **Globular Protein** Polypeptide chains coils into spherical shape e.g. Insulin, albumin, etc.
- **Denaturation** Physical changes lead to chaos in hydrogen bonds; helix becomes uncoiled. e.g. Coagulation of egg and curdling.

SOURCE ***New NCERT Class XII Chap 10*** *(Biomolecules)*, ***Old NCERT Class XII Chap 16*** *(Chemistry in Everyday Life)*

1 Which of the following statement is incorrect? *(Chap 10, Class-XII, NCERT)*

(a) The main component of honey is maltose.
(b) Fructose is sweetest sugar than sucrose.
(c) Milk contains major amount of lactose.
(d) Natural fructose is called as leavulose.

Ans. (a)

Exp. Among the given statements (a) is not correct. The corrected form of (a) is given as : The main component of honey is fructose. Along with fructose, it composed primarily of water and glucose. Honey is a sweet, viscous, edible fluid which constitutes about 17% of water.

2 Match List-I with List-II and choose the correct answer using the codes given below *(Chap 10, Class-XII, NCERT)*

	List-I (Different Sugar)		List-II (Main Component)
A.	Grape sugar	1.	Fructose
B.	Fruit sugar	2.	Sucrose
C.	Milk sugar	3.	Natural sweetener
D.	Table sugar	4.	Glucose
E.	Stevia	5.	Lactose

Codes

	A	B	C	D	E		A	B	C	D	E
(a)	2	4	5	3	1	(b)	1	3	4	5	2
(c)	4	1	5	2	3	(d)	1	4	5	3	2

Ans. (c)

Exp. The correct matching is A-4, B-1, C-5, D-2, E-3.

Grape sugar contains naturally occurring glucose. Molecular formula of glucose is $C_6H_{12}O_6$. It is the most abundant monosaccharide.

Fruit sugar It is the common name of fructose found in many plants. It is also a monosaccharide having formula $C_6H_{12}O_6$.

Milk sugar It is the common name of lactose. Its sub-units are galactose and glucose. It is present in the natural milk.

Table sugar It is the common name of sucrose. It is a disaccharide made of glucose and fructose.

Stevia It is a natural sweetener. It is a great sugar alternative. It has almost no calories. Thus, it may play a role in weight management.

3 Consider the following assertion (A) and reason (R). *(Chap 10, Class-XII, NCERT)*

Assertion (A) Invert sugar is more sweet than sucrose.

Reason (R) Invert sugar is obtained by the hydrolysis of sucrose.

Select the correct answer from the codes given below.

(a) Both A and R are true and R is the correct explanation of A.
(b) Both A and R are true but R is not the correct explanation of A.
(c) A is true but R is false.
(d) A is false but R is true.

Ans. (b)

Exp. Both (A) and (R) are true but (R) is not the correct explanation of (A).

Invert sugar is made by hydrolysis of disaccharide sucrose into glucose and fructose. Invert sugar is sweeter than sucrose due to free fructose crystals in it.

4 Which of the following pairs is/are correctly matched? *(Chap 10, Class-XII, NCERT)*

1. Beetroot – Sugar
2. Honey – Glucose and fructose
3. Cotton – Cellulose
4. Milk – Lactose

Select the correct answer using the code given below.

(A) 1, 2 and 3 (B) 2, 3 and 4
(C) 1, 2 and 4 (D) 1, 2, 3 and 4

Ans. (d)

Exp. All the given pairs i.e., 1, 2, 3 and 4 are correctly matched.

Beetroot are low in calories with zero cholesterol and small amount of fat. However, its root is high in sugar and carbohydrates.

Honey contains approximately 40% fructose, 30% glucose and 17% water. The remaining being sugar, carbohydrates, vitamins and minerals.

Cotton fabrics are the purest form of cellulose.

Milk contains the major amount of lactose (approximately 13 gms) out of all dairy products.

5 Which of the following statement is incorrect? *(Chap 10, Class-XII, NCERT)*

(a) Fructose is an artificial sweetner.
(b) Aspartame is stable only under cold condition.
(c) Cellulose occurs exclusively in plants.
(d) Glucose is the main sugar metabolised by the body for energy.

Ans. (a)

Exp. Statement (a) is incorrect. The corrected form of statement (a) is given as : fructose is not a artificial sweetener. It is present in honey, other fruits, so it is also known as fruit sugar.

Sucralose, alitame, aspartame are some example of artificial sweetener. Mainly diabetic prefer to use artificial sweeteners.

6 Which of the following statements about carbohydrates is not true? *(Chap 10, Class-XII, NCERT)*

(a) Glucose is commercially obtained from starch upon hydrolysis.
(b) Maltose on hydrolysis gives glucose and fructose.
(c) Lactose composed of galactose and glucose.
(d) Cellulose is a straight chain polysaccharide of glucose.

Ans. (b)

Exp. Among the given statement (b) is not true. Maltose on hydrolysis gives two unit of glucose. It is also known as malt sugar and used in alcohol production. Its chemical formula is $C_{12}H_{22}O_{11}$.

7 Which of the following statements about fat is not true? *(Chap 10, Class-XII, NCERT)*

(a) They mainly contain saturated esters.
(b) These are esters of glycerol with higher fatty acids.
(c) These are soluble in water but insoluble in organic solvents.
(d) Saturated triglycerides are called fats.

Ans. (c)

Exp. Fats are insoluble in water but soluble in organic solvents like benzene, carbon tetrachloride etc. These are the major food reserve of organisms and are responsible for several functions. Some examples of food that contain fats are butter, oil, nuts, meat, fish and some dairy products.

8 Which of the following is a common refrigerant used in the domestic refrigerator? *(Chap 16, Class-XII, NCERT)*

(a) Neon (b) Oxygen (c) Freon (d) Helium

Ans. (c)

Exp. Freon (CCl_2F_2) is a common refrigerant used in the domestic refrigerator. It is used for heat transfer to keep the internal compartment of refrigerator cool and ensures that food is kept at proper temperature.

9 Aspartame is an artificial sweetener sold in the market. It consists of amino acids and provides calories like other amino acids. Yet, it is used as a low-calorie sweetening agent in food items. What is the basis of this use? *(Chap 16, Class-XII, NCERT) (IAS Pre 2011)*

(a) Aspartame is as sweet as table sugar, but unlike table sugar, it is not readily oxidised in the human body due to lack of requisite enzymes.
(b) When aspartame is used in food processing the sweet taste remains, but it becomes resistant to oxidation.
(c) Aspartame is as sweet as sugar but after ingestion into the body, it is converted into metabolites that yield no calories.
(d) Aspartame is several times sweeter than table sugar, hence food items made with small quantities of aspartame yield fewer calories on oxidation.

Ans. (d)

Exp. Aspartame ($C_{14}H_{18}N_2O_5$) is several times (200 times) sweeter than table sugar, hence food items made with small quantities of aspartame yield fewer calories on oxidation. It is an artificial, non-saccharide, sweetener used as a sugar substitute in some foods and beverages. When heated, it breaks down into amino acids and loses its sweetness, so it can not be used for baked food.

10 Consider the following statements about protein. *(Chap 10, Class-XII, NCERT)*

1. These are necessary for maintenance of the body.
2. These are polymers of β-amino acids.
3. These are usually represented by a four letter symbol.

How many statement(s) given above is/are incorrect?

(a) Only one
(b) Only two
(c) All three
(d) None of the above

Ans. (b)

Exp. Only two Statements (2 and 3) are incorrect because proteins are polymers of α-amino acid.

Amino acids contain amino (—NH_2) and carboxyl (—COOH) functional groups. Depending upon the relative position of amino group with respect to carboxylic group, the amino acids can be classified as α, β, γ or δ.

Each amino acid is usually represented by a three letter symbol.

11 Consider the following statements. *(Chap 16, Class-XII, NCERT)*

1. Ranitidine is an antacids.
2. Brompheniramine is an antihistamines.
3. Noradrenaline is a tranquilizer.
4. Aspirin is a non-narcotic analgesic.

Which of the above statements are correct?

(a) 1 and 2
(b) 3 and 4
(c) 2 and 3
(d) 1, 2, 3 and 4

Ans. (d)

Exp. Among the given statements 1, 2, 3 and 4 are correct.

Antacids These substance neutralizes the stomach acidity and is used to relieve heartburn.

Anthistamines These medicines treat allergy symptoms by blocking the effects of histamine.

Tranquilizer These drugs are taken to reduce tension or anxiety.

Analgesic These druges are taken the relieve pain.

12 Which of the following statement is incorrect? *(Chap 10 & 16, Class-XII, NCERT)*

(a) Sodium benzoate is used in the preservation of food stuff.
(b) Benzoic acid is used in food preservation.
(c) Refrigeration helps in food preservation by destroying enzyme action.
(d) Fructose is sweeter than glucose and maltose.

Ans. (c)

Exp. Refrigeration helps in food preservation by reducing the rate of biochemical reactions in food. It slows down the growth and reproduction of micro-organism.

Enzymes are proteins that help to speed up the rate of metabolism or the chemical reactions in our body. All living things have enzyme.

13 Match List-I with List-II and select the correct answer using the codes given below the lists.
(Chap 16, Class-XII, NCERT) (BPSC Pre 2016)

List-I (Substance)	List-II (Application)
A. Aspartame	1. Synthetic rubber
B. Freon	2. Anti-histamine
C. Neoprene	3. Artificial sweetener
D. Benadryl	4. Refrigerant

Codes

	A	B	C	D		A	B	C	D
(a)	1	3	4	2	(b)	2	4	1	3
(c)	3	4	1	2	(d)	3	1	2	4

(e) None of these/More than one of these

Ans. (c)

Exp. The correct matching is A-3, B-4, C-1, D-2.

Aspartame It is an artificial sweetener which is 200 times sweetener than table sugar.

Freon Are used as refrigerants. It is a trade name for a class of chemicals known as chlorofluorocarbon or CFC's.

Neoprene It is also known as polychloropene. It is one of the first synthetic rubber products.

Benadryl It is an anti-histamine. It is used for relief from symptoms related to fever, cold or respiratory allergy.

14 Match list-I with list-II and select the correct answer using the codes given below the lists.
(Chap 16, Class-XII, NCERT)

List-I (Artificial sweetener)	List-II (Sweeter than cane sugar)
A. Saccharin	1. 600 times
B. Aspartame	2. 2000 times
C. Alitame	3. 550 times
D. Sucralose	4. 100 times

Codes

	A	B	C	D
(a)	1	3	4	2
b)	2	4	3	1
(c)	1	2	4	3
(d)	3	4	2	1

Ans. (d)

Exp. The correct matching is A-3, B-4, C-2, D-1.

Saccharin It is ortho-sulphobenzimide. It is 550 times as sweet as cane sugar. It appears to be entirely inert and harmless, when taken.

Aspartame It is 100 times as sweet as cane sugar. Its use is limited to cold foods and soft drinks because it is unstable at cooking temperature.

Alitame It is high potency sweetener. It is about 2000 times as sweet as cane sugar.

Sucralose It is a trichloro derivative of sucrose. It is 600 times sweeter than sucrose. Its appearance, colour and taste are like sugar.

15 Which of the following statement(s) about the artificial sweetening agents is/are true?
(Chap 16, Class-XII, NCERT) (HPSC Pre 2021)

1. Ortho-sulphobenzimide is the first popular artificial sweetening agent.
2. Ortho-sulphobenzimide is also called as saccharin.
3. Ortho-sulphobenzimide is about 100 times as sweet as cane sugar.

Choose the correct answer from the options given below

(a) Only 1 (b) 2 and 3
(c) 1 and 3 (d) 1 and 2

Ans. (d)

Exp. Statements (1) and (2) are correct, while statement (3) is incorrect because ortho-sulphobenzimide is about 550 times as sweet as cane sugar.

Chapter 10

Chemistry in Everyday Life

Chemistry in Everyday Life

Fibres/Plastic/Drugs

- **Fibres** (Long thread - like structure)
  - **Natural Fibres** Obtained from plants. e.g. Cotton, hemp, etc.
  - **Semisynthetic Fibres** Obtained by treated natural fibres with some chemicals. e.g. Cellulose, viscose rayon.
  - **Synthetic Fibres** Obtained from chemicals. e.g. Nylon, polyester, etc.
- **Plastic**
  - Polymer with linear or cross-linked arrangement of unit.
  - **Thermoplastic** Deform easily on heating and bends easily. e.g. PVC, polythene.
  - **Thermosetting Plastic** Moulded plastic cannot be softened again by heating. e.g. Bakelite and melamine.
- **Drugs**
  - **Drugs** Chemicals of low molecular masses, used in medicines.
  - **Antipyretics** Bring down body temperature e.g. Aspirin, paracetamol etc.
  - **Analgesics** Reduce pain , e.g. Morphine.
  - **Antibiotics** Inhibit or kill microorganisms e.g. Penicillin. erthromycin etc.
  - **Antiseptic** Prevent growth of microorganism (not ingested like antibiotics) e.g., Dettol, soframicine.
  - **Disinfectants** Applied to inanimate objects e.g. Phenol.
  - **Sulpha Drugs** Drugs contain sulphur and nitrogen only e.g. Sulphapyridine etc.
  - **Anaesthesia** Cease the sense organs e.g. Cocaine, diazepam.
  - **Antacids** Reduce or neutralise acidity e.g. Sodium hydrogen carbonate.

Glass/Chemicals in Food

- **Glass**
  - Homogeneous mixture of silicates (Na_2O . CaO . $6SiO_2$). Proper proportion of silica, soda cullet, and lime stone.
  - **Annealing of Glass** Glass cools slowly becomes opaque and cooled rapidly become brittle and fragile.
  - **Coloured Glass** Mixing colour substance in molten state of glass.
    - **Water glass** Na_2SiO_3, safety glass layer of vinyl acetate, resin; optical fibre use in telecommunication.
  - **Glass Wool** Fireproof, tensile strength.
- **Chemicals in Food**
  - **Artificial sweetning agents** Chemical substance which provide sweetness.
  - **Food preservatives** Protect food against microorganisms.
  - **Antioxidants** Inhibit oxidation of other molecule.
- **Fertilizers**
  - **Nitrogenous** (Ammonia and its derivative) Ammonium sulphate; calcium ammonium nitrate and Urea.
  - **Phosphatic** Superphosphate of lime and Thomas slag.
  - **Potash** Potassium chloride, potassium nitrate and potassium sulphate.
  - **Nitrogen-Phosphorus** Calcium superphosphate nitrate, ammoniated phosphate, sulphate and dihydrogen ammoniated phosphate.
  - **Nitrogen-Phosphorus & Potassium** Three main nutrients in the soil.

Fertilizers/Dyes/ Cleansing agents

- **Fertilizers**
  - Nitrogen, Phosphorus, Potassium (NPK) called complete fertilizers.
- **Dyes**
  - Used to impart permanent colour to fabric, food stuffs etc.
  - **Basis of Application** Acid dyes, basic dyes, direct dyes, disperse dyes, fibre reactive, dyes, vat dyes, mordant dyes .
  - **Basis of Chemical Composition** Azo dyes, phthalein dyes, Indlgold dyes, anthraquinone dyes, tripheny, methane dyes.
- **Cleansing Agents (removal of fats)**
  - **Soaps** (*m*COONa) biodegradable compounds; toilet soaps, floating soaps, transparent soaps and medicated soaps.
  - **Detergents** ($C_{18}H_{29}NaO_3S$) stronger than soaps: anionic detergents, cationic detergents and non-ionic detergents.
    - **Common Cleansing Agent**
      - Sodium carbonate
      - Sodium Hypochlorite
      - Ammonia solution
      - Borax

SOURCE *Old NCERT Class XI Chap 14* (Environmental Chemistry), *Old NCERT Class XII Chap 16* (Chemistry in Everyday Life), *Tamil Nadu Board Class X* (Carbon and its compounds)

1 Consider the following statements. *(Chap 16, Class-XII, NCERT)*

1. Antipyretics are used to bring down the body temperature in case of high fever.
2. Analgin, phenacetin and paracetamol are the common examples of antipyretics.
3. Paracetamol and aspirin act as analgesics as well as antipyretics.

Which of the statements given above are correct?

(a) 1 and 2 (b) 2 and 3
(c) 1 and 3 (d) All of these

Ans. (d)

Exp. All the given statements are correct. Antipyretics help to prevent or reduce fever. Examples of antipyretics are analgin, phenacetin and paracetamol. Aspirin and paracetamol act as both analgesic which reduces pain and antipyretics which reduces fever.

2 Consider the following statements about antiseptics. *(Chap 16, Class-XII, NCERT)*

1. It can kill or prevent the growth of microorganisms.
2. It can be applied to the skin.
3. 1% solution of phenol acts as an antiseptic.

Which of the statement(s) given above is/are correct?

(a) Only 1 (b) Only 2 (c) 1 and 2 (d) 1, 2 and 3

Ans. (c)

Exp. Statements (1) and (2) are correct about antiseptics. Antiseptics kill or prevent the growth of microorganism and can be applied to skin.
They are safe to apply on living tissues. Thus, they are generally applied on the wounds, cuts, ulcers and diseased skin surface. For example furacin, soframycin are examples of antiseptics.
Antiseptics are also added to body powder and breath purifiers, to reduce the odour produced as a result of bacterial decomposition of organic matter on the body or in the mouth.
Statement (3) is incorrect because 1% solution of phenol is used as a disinfectant and 0.2% solution of phenol is an antiseptic.

3 Which of the following is the correct statement about birth control pills? *(Chap 16, Class-XII, NCERT)*

(a) It contains estrogen only.
(b) It contains progesterone only.
(c) It contains a mixture of estrogen and progesterone derivatives.
(d) It contains progesterone which enhances ovulation.

Ans. (c)

Exp. Birth control pills essentially contain a mixture of synthetic estrogen and progesterone derivatives, using birth control Pills is a type of female hormonal birth control method which is very effective at preventing pregnancy.

4 A drug effective in the treatment of pneumonia, bronchitis, etc is *(Chap 16, Class-XII, NCERT)*

(a) streptomycin
(b) chloramphenicol
(c) penicillin
(d) sulphaguanidine

Ans. (c)

Exp. The correct drug is penicillin. It was discovered by Alexander fleming. It is an antibiotic.

5 The main cause of acidity in the stomach is *(Chap 16, Class-XII, NCERT)*

(a) release of extra gastric acids which decreases the pH level.
(b) indigestion and pain in the large intestine.
(c) increase of the pH level in the stomach.
(d) release of extra bile juice which increases alkaline medium in the stomach.

Ans. (a)

Exp. The main cause of acidity in the stomach is release of extra gastric acids which decreases the pH level. Sometime stomach produces too much acid that is hydrochloric acid, which can lead to acidity.
Foods like citrus food, tomatoes, onions, chocolate, coffee, cheese, spicy food or large meal are the most common cause of acidity. Some chemical substances which remove the excess acid in the stomach and raise the pH at appropriate level are called antacids, e.g. sodium hydrogen carbonate, a mixture of aluminium and magnesium hydroxide etc.

6 Which of the following is used as tranquiliser? *(Chap 16, Class-XII, NCERT)*

(a) Naproxen (b) Tetracycline
(c) Chlorpheniramine (d) Equanil

Ans. (d)

Exp. Equanil is used as tranquiliser. A tranquiliser refers to a drug which is designed for the treatment of anxiety, fear, tension, agitation and disturbances of the mind, specifically to reduce states of anxiety and tension.

7 Which of the following statement is incorrect? *(Chap 16, Class-XII, NCERT)*

(a) Drugs are chemicals of low molecular masses.
(b) Antacids reduces acidity in the stomach.
(c) Antiseptics does not prevent the growth of microorganism.
(d) Antibiotics are used to treat infections.

Ans. (c)

Exp. Among the given statement, (c) is incorrect. The corrected form of statement (c) is ; Antisepctics is a chemical which either kill or prevent the growth of microorganisms. These are applied to living tissues such as wounds, cuts and diseased skin surfaces. Dettol, iodoform, boric acid, phenol, etc., are examples of antiseptics.

8 Consider the following statements

(Chap 16, Class-XII, NCERT)

1. Aspirin is obtained from tree.
2. Penicillin and aspirin are antiseptic.
3. Chloramphenicol is an antibiotic drug.

Which of the above statements are correct?

(a) 1 and 3 (b) 2 and 3 (c) 1 and 2 (d) All of these

Ans. (a)

Exp. Among the given statements, (1) and (3) are correct. While statement (2) is incorrect. The corrected form of statement (2) is, Penicillin is an antibiotics which is used to treat or prevent bacterial infections. Aspirin is analgesic medicine obtained from tree.

9 Which of the following statement is incorrect?

(Chap 16, Class XII, NCERT)

(a) Chloroxylenol is an example of analgesic.
(b) Sulpha drug is an antibacterial drug.
(c) Paracetamol is antipyretic medicines.
(d) Aspirin is antipyretic medicine, it is used to relieve pain.

Ans. (a)

Exp. Among the given statements, only (a) is incorrect. The corrected form of statement (a) is, chloroxylenol is an example of antiseptic. This chemical either prevent the growth of microorganisms or kill them but are not harmful to the living human tissues. Dettol is a mixture of chloroxylenol and terpineol which is used as an antiseptic for wounds, cuts, etc.

10 Consider the following statements.

(Chap 16, Class XII, NCERT)
(Unit 11, Class-X, Tamil Nadu Board)

1. Detergents help in removal of fats.
2. Potassium soaps are soft to the skin than sodium soaps.
3. Hard water contains calcium and magnesium ions.

Which of the above statements are correct?

(a) 1 and 2 (b) 2 and 3 (c) 1 and 3 (d) All of these

Ans. (d)

Exp. All the given statements are correct. Detergents help in removal of fats. Potassium is a relatively softer metal than sodium. Therefore, potassium soaps are soft to the skin than sodium soaps.

Hard water contains calcium and magnesium ion. These ions form insoluble calcium and magnesium soaps respectively when these are dissolved in hard water.

$$\underset{\text{(soap)}}{2C_{17}H_{35}COONa} + CaCl_2 \longrightarrow 2NaCl + \underset{\substack{\text{Insoluble calcium stearate}\\ \text{(soap)}}}{(C_{17}H_{35}COO)_2Ca}$$

11 Which of the following statement is incorrect?

(Chap 16, Class-XII, NCERT)

(a) Cutting oil is used in the manufacture of soaps.
(b) Soap removes grease by emulsification.
(c) Detergents used for cleaning clothes are sulphonates.
(d) Potassium salts of long chain carboxylic acids are soaps.

Ans. (a)

Exp. Among the given statement (a) is incorrect. The corrected form of statement (a) is, vegetable oil is used in the manufacture of soaps.

The purpose of vegetable oil in making a soap is to provide a natural and moisturising base for the soap. Its purpose is to provide benefits such as clearing heat, detoxification, sterilization, stopping itch etc.

12 Which of the following statement is incorrect?

(Chap 14, Class-XI, NCERT)

(a) Urea does not effect the pH of soil.
(b) Potassium chloride and potassium nitrate are phosphatic fertilizers.
(c) Potassium nitrate is the example of potash fertilizers.
(d) NPK fertilizers are obtained by mixing nitrogen and phosphate fertilizers.

Ans. (d)

Exp. The corrected form of incorrect statement (d) is, NPK fertilizers are obtained by mixing all three types of fertilizers nitrogenous, phosphate and potash in proper quantity. They supply three main nutrients. i.e. nitrogen, phosphorus and potassium to the soil.

13 With reference to chemical fertilizers in India, consider the following statements.

(Chap 14, Class-XI, NCERT)

1. At present, the retail price of chemical fertilizers is market-driven and not administered by the Government.
2. Ammonia, which is an input of urea, is produced from natural gas.
3. Sulphur, which is a raw material for phosphoric acid fertilizer, is a by-product of oil refineries.

Which of the following statements given above is/are correct?

(a) Only 2 (b) Both 2 and 3 (c) Only 3 (d) 1, 2 and 3

Ans. (b)

Exp. Statements (2) and (3) are correct.
while statement (1) is incorrect because urea is a main chemical fertilizer and MRP of urea is statutorily fixed by the government.

14 What can be the impact of the excessive/ inappropriate use of nitrogeneous fertilizers in agriculture? *(Class-XI, NCERT) (IAS Pre 2015)*

1. The proliferation of nitrogen-fixing microorganisms in soil can occur.
2. The increase in the acidity of soil can take place.
3. Leaching of nitrate to the groundwater can occur.

Select the correct answer using the codes given below.

(a) 1 and 3 (b) Only 2 (c) 2 and 3 (d) 1, 2 and 3

Ans. (c)

Exp. Statements (2) and (3) are correct. While statement (1) is incorrect. This is because fertilisers in agriculture increase inputs of nutrients to soils affecting their pH value.

15 Pasteurisation is related to *A* here and during this process calcium absorption is *B*, here *A* and *B* respectively are *(Chap 16, Class-XII, NCERT)*

(a) sterilisation of milk; not changed
(b) dehydration of milk; not changed
(c) fermentation of milk; not changed
(d) distillation of milk; not changed

Ans. (a)

Exp. Pasteurisation is related to sterilisation of milk. It is a process in which milk is heated to a particular temperature for a set amount of time in order to kills microbes in food and drinks which facilitates its preservation and safety.

During this process calcium absroption in not changed. In this process, the milk is heated at about 63°C for 30 minutes or at about 72°C for 15 minutes to ensure that any harmful bacteria is not alive.

This process was invented by French scientist Louis Pasteur in 1864.

16 On the labels of bottles, some soft drinks are claimed to be acidity regulators. They regulate acidity using *(Chap 16, Class-XII, NCERT)*

(a) carbon dioxide
(b) bicarbonate salt
(c) Both 'a' and 'b'
(d) carbon dioxide and lime

Ans. (b)

Exp. Some soft drinks regulate acidity using bicarbonate salts. They regulate pH level in the body as well as in bottle. They breakdown to form sodium and bicarbonate in water which is helpful to neutralise acid.

17 Which of the following compound is used as food preservative? *(Chap 16, Class-XII, NCERT)*

(a) Nitric acid and sodium benzoate
(b) Potassium chloride and sodium chloride
(c) Sodium benzoate and sodium sorbate
(d) Sodium chloride and potassium chloride

Ans. (c)

Exp. Sodium benzoate and sodium sorbate are used as food preservative. It is used to prevent spoilage of food from bacteria, yeasts and molds. It also keeps freshness in food by helping to slow or prevent changes in colour, flavour and texture.

18 Preparation of 'Dalda or Vanaspati' ghee from vegetable oil involve which of the following process? *(Chap 13, Class-XI, NCERT)*

(a) Hydrolysis
(b) Oxidation
(c) Hydrogenation
(d) Ozonolysis

Ans. (c)

Exp. Preparation of 'Dalda or Vanaspati' ghee from vegetable oil involve process of hydrogenation.

Oils are entities that contain esters of unsaturated fatty acids and dalda contains saturated fatty acids.

Unsaturated fatty acids can be converted to saturated fatty acids by hydrogenation which is basically a reduction reaction.

19 Consider the following statements. *(Chap 14, Class-XI, NCERT)*

1. Cooking in the presence of baking soda causes a quick loss of vitamin C.
2. Vitamin C is easily oxidised in alkaline medium.

Which of the following statement(s) given is/are correct?

(a) Only 1
(b) Both 1 and 2
(c) Only 2
(d) None of the above

Ans. (b)

Exp. Both statements (1) and (2) are correct.

Vitamin C is chemically ascorbic acid which when comes in contact with baking soda that is alkaline in nature. It gets oxidised to dehydroascorbic acid.

Due to this, it causes a quick loss of vitamin C and gets oxidised easily.

20 Which of the following vegetable oil does not contain essential fatty acids? *(Chap 14, Class-XI, NCERT)*

(a) Sunflower oil
(b) Mustard oil
(c) Coconut oil
(d) Groundnut oil

Ans. (a)

Exp. Sunflower oil does not contain essential fatty acids. It is high in essential vitamin E.

While mustard oil, coconut oil and groundnut oil contain fatty acids. Fatty acids are the building blocks of the fat in our body and in the food we eat.

Chapter 11

Environmental Chemistry

Environmental Chemistry

Environment and Stratospheric Pollutions

Environment

- **Environment component** Biotic and abiotic.
- **Environment pollution** Undesirable changes in our surroundings.
- **Pollutant toxicity** Synergism.
- **Pollutants** It can be classified into following two categories
  - **Biodegradable** (Degradable by microorganisms) e.g. discarded vegetables, waste sludges, etc.
  - **Non-biodegradable** (Degrade slowly or remain unchanged) e.g. DDT,

Global Warming

- The increase in the average temperature of earth's atmosphere and oceans.
- Causes : Burning of fossil fuels, increasing greenhouse gases, burning forests etc.
- Deleterious changes in the environment results in odd climatic changes.

Greenhouse Effect

- Thermal radiation absorbed by atmospheric greenhouse gas and re-radiated in all direction, results in elevation of average surface temperature.
- Major greenhouse gases : CO_2, CH_4, N_2O and CFCs.

Acid Rain

- Presence of certain acids in rain water (pH : below 5.6), majorly NO_2 and SO_2 along with HCl.
- Oxides settle down on ground, fog and snow.

Stratospheric Pollution

- Ozone layer (stratosphere) absorbs UV-radiation (cause skin cancer and cataracts).
- **Freon** : Dangerous CFCs
- Decomposition products react with ozone form CO which further reacts with oxygen and produces chlorine atom.

Smog

- Serious air pollutant (Smog) = Smoke + fog
- **Classical smog Reducing Smog** Cool and humid climate, Smoke react with fog.
- **Photochemical Smog Oxidising Smog** Warm, dry and sunny climate, Sunlight on unsaturated hydrocarbons and nitrogens.
  - Photochemical Smog Presence of ozone, PAN, NO_2; can have a tremendous impact on humans, animals, plants and materials.
- Prevented by controlling the formation and release of primary precursor and plantation of certain plants.
- **Bhopal Gas Tragedy** (December, 1984) Methyl Isocyanate (MIC)

Water Pollution and Oil Zapper/Green Chemistry

Water Pollution

- Contamination of water by water pollutants.
- **Point Source** (Easily identifiable source)
- **Non-point Source** (source cannot be easily identified)
- **BOD** (Biochemical Oxygen Demand) less than 5 ppm.
- **Major Pollutants** Pesticides, PCBs, detergents, fertilizers.
- Petroleum products or oils mainly pollute sea water.
- **Eutrophication** Nutrition enrichment of water increase plant population, which kills animals life (lack of dissolved oxygen).

Oil Zapper

- Clean oil spills by using bacteria known as bioremediation process. this technique developed by TERI.
- Oil zapper reacts with hydrocarbon materials present in oil sludge convert them into harmless CO_2 and H_2O.

Green Chemistry

- Production of daily use chemicals.
- Reactants converted completely into useful environment-friendly product in the presence of mild and environment friendly reagent.
- **In Day to Day life**
  - **Dry Cleaning of Clothes** Tetrachloroethane replaced by liquified CO_2.
  - **Bleaching of Paper** Chlorine replaced by H_2O_2.
  - **Synthesis of Chemicals** Ethanol from ethene and ethanol gives acetaldehyde $CH_2 = CH_2 + O_2 \xrightarrow{\text{Catalyst}} CH_3 + CHO$ (90%)

SOURCE *Old NCERT Class X Chap 15* (Our Environment), *Old NCERT Class XI Chap 14* (Environmental Chemistry)

1 **Consider the following statements** *(Chap 14, Class-XI, NCERT)*

1. Nitrogen is a greenhouse gas.
2. Methanogen bacteria increase greenhouse effect by producing methane.
3. Carbon monoxide is colourless, odourless gas and highly poisonous.

How many statement(s) given above is/are correct?

(a) Only one (b) Only two (c) All three (d) None of these

Ans. (b)

Exp. Only two Statements (2 and 3) are correct, while one Statement (1) is incorrect. Nitrogen is not a greenhouse gas because it is transparent to infrared light. Oxides of nitrogen are important in process of creation of tropospheric ozone which is a green house gas.

2 **Which of the following pairs is mismatched?** *(Chap 14, Class-XI, NCERT)*

(a) Fossil fuel burning – Release of CO_2
(b) Nuclear power – Radioactive wastes
(c) Solar energy – Greenhouse effect
(d) Biomass burning – Release of CO_2

Ans. (c)

Exp. Pair (c) is mismatched. Solar energy is not related to greenhouse effect as solar energy systems or power plants do not produce air pollution or greenhouse gases.

3 **The increasing amount of carbon dioxide in the air is slowly raising the temperature of the atmosphere because it absorbs** *(Chap 14, Class-XI, NCERT)*

(a) the water vapour of the air and retains its heat.
(b) infrared part of solar radiation.
(c) the ultraviolet part of the solar radiation.
(d) all the solar radiations.

Ans. (b)

Exp. The increasing amount of carbon dioxide in the air is slowly raising the temperature of the atmosphere because it absorbs infrared part of solar radiation.
It is confined to troposphere only. Deforestation and excessive burning of fossil fuels increase the level of CO_2 and disturb the atmosphere.

4 **The protocol which decided to completely phase Out CFCs is** *(Chap 15, Class-X, NCERT)*

(a) Cartagena protocol (b) Stockholm convention
(c) Montreal protocol (d) Kyoto protocol

Ans. (c)

Exp. Montreal protocol decided to completely phase out chlorofluorocarbons (CFCs). It was designed in 1987 to stop the production and import of ozone depleting substances and reduce their concentration in the atmosphere to protect the Earth's ozone layer.

5 **Which of the following statement is incorrect?** *(Chap 15, Class-X, NCERT)*

(a) UV radiations of the sun is absorbed by ozone layer.
(b) UV radiations cause skin cancer and catoracts in human.
(c) Freon is a dangerous chlorofluorocarbon used in refrigerator.
(d) Chlorofluorocarbon is not responsible for ozone layer depletion.

Ans. (d)

Exp. Among the given statement (d) is incorrect. The corrected form of statement (d) is, chlorofluorocarbons are mainly responsible for ozone depletion in the stratosphere. These are used as coolants in refrigerators and air conditioners. CFCs reach the stratosphere and produce active chlorine in the presence of UV radiation.

6 **Among the following statements, which one is incorrect?** *(Chap 15, Class-X, NCERT)*

(a) Chlorofluorocarbons (CFCs) are responsible for ozone layer depletion.
(b) Greenhouse effect is responsible for global warming.
(c) Acid rain is mostly because of oxides of nitrogen and sulphur.
(d) Ozone layer doesn't permit infrared radiation from the Sun to reach the Earth.

Ans. (d)

Exp. Statement (d) is incorrect because ozone layer only restricts the entry of ultraviolet harmful rays coming from the Sun to reach the Earth.

7 **Which of the following statement is incorrect about classical smog ?** *(Chap 14, Class-XI, NCERT)*

(a) Its main components are produced by the action of sunlight on compounds produced by the automobiles and factories.
(b) It produces in cold and humid climate.
(c) It contains compounds of reducing nature.
(d) It contains smoke, fog and sulphur dioxide.

Ans. (a)

Exp. Statement (a) is incorrect about classical smog as components of photochemical smog are produced by the action of sunlight on compounds produced by the automobiles and factories.
Whereas classical smog is the smog that occurs in cold and humid climate and contains compounds like SO_2.

8 **Which of the following statements about photochemical smog is incorrect?** *(Chap 14, Class-XI, NCERT)*

(a) It has high concentration of reducing agents.
(b) It has low concentration of oxidising agents.
(c) It can be controlled by controlling the release of NO_2, hydrocarbons, ozone etc.
(d) Plantation of some plants like pinus helps in controlling photochemical smog.

Ans. (b)

Exp. Statement (b) is incorrect about photochemical smog because it has high concentration of oxidising agents. Hence, it is also known as oxidising smog.

9 **BOD value less than 5 ppm indicates a water sample to be** *(Chap 14, Class-XI, NCERT)*

(a) rich in dissolved oxygen (b) poor in dissolved oxygen
(c) highly polluted (d) not suitable for aquatic life

Ans. (a)

Exp. Water considered to be pure if it has BOD less than 5 ppm whereas highly polluted water has BOD more than 17 ppm. Thus, water having BOD less than 5 ppm is rich in dissolved oxygen. Biochemical Oxygen Demand, (BOD) is a measure of organic material present in water.

10 BOD (Biological Oxygen Demand) is connected with *(Chap 14, Class-XI, NCERT)*

(a) microbes and organic matter (b) organic matter
(c) microbes (d) inorganic matter

Ans. (a)
Exp. BOD (Biological Oxygen Demand) is connected with microbes and organic matter. It represents the amount of oxygen consumed by bacteria and other microorganisms while they decompose organic matter under aerobic conditions at a specified temperature.

11 Match the following lists and choose the correct Code. *(Chap 14, Class-XI, NCERT)*

List-I (Element)	List-II (Disease)
A. Arsenic	1. Minamata
B. Lead	2. Skin cancer
C. Cadmium	3. Itai-Itai
D. Mercury	4. Dyslexia

Codes

	A	B	C	D		A	B	C	D
(a)	2	4	3	1	(b)	2	3	4	1
(c)	2	1	4	3	(d)	2	4	1	3

Ans. (a)
Exp. The correct matching is A-2, B-4, C-3, D-1.
Arsenic Drinking water containing this element is associated with an increased risk of skin cancer thickening and discoloration of the skin, problem with blood vessels, high blood pressure etc.
Lead High doses of lead results in development of irritability, mental dullness, memory loss termed as dyslexia.
Cadmium Its exposure causes Itai-Itai disease. Cadmium exposure produced as a result of human activities related to industrialisation.
Mercury Its poisoning cause neurological disease known as minamata. It is caused by the daily consumption of large quantities of aquatic animals that very heavily contaminated with toxic chemicals.

12 Which statements are correct for eutrophication? *(Chap 14, Class-XI, NCERT)*

1. It is the phenomenon of nutrient enrichment of a water body.
2. It depletes the level of dissolved oxygen in water.
3. Human activities are mainly responsible for eutrophication.

Codes

(a) 1 and 3 (b) 1 and 2 (c) 2 and 3 (d) 1, 2 and 3

Ans. (d)
Exp. All the given statements are correct about eutrophication process in which nutrient enriched water bodies support a dense plant population, which kills animal life by depriving of oxygen and results in subsequent loss of biodiversity is known as eutrophication.

13 Consider the following statements about water. *(Chap 14, Class-XI, NCERT)*

1. Sodium chloride is used to melt snow and ice in the colder climates.
2. Water can be polluted by mixing pesticides.
3. Water does not dissolve organic chemicals.

Which of the given statement(s) is/are correct?

(a) Only 2 (b) 1 and 2 (c) Only 3 (d) 1 and 3

Ans. (b)
Exp. Among the given statements, (1) and (2) are correct. The corrected form of incorrect statement (3) is, water being an excellent solvent, dissolves most of the inorganic and organic chemicals that make it contaminated.

14 Which one of the following practices will not come under green chemistry? *(Chap 14, Class-XI, NCERT)*

(a) Soap made of vegetable oils instead of synthetic detergents.
(b) H_2O_2 for bleaching purpose instead of chlorine.
(c) Bicycle for travelling instead of petrol diesel based vehicle.
(d) Plastic cans for neatly storing substances.

Ans. (d)
Exp. Using plastic cans does not come under green chemistry. Green chemistry is the different process and methods that helps in minimising the effects of pollution and eliminating the hazardous substances. It takes care that no products adds to the environmental pollution.

15 Which of the following statement is incorrect? *(Chap 14, Class-XI, NCERT)*

(a) Water has high specific heat and low volatility.
(b) Water is cost effective and non-inflammable solvent.
(c) Paper is bleached by using tetrachloroethene.
(d) Tetrachloroethene is used for dry cleaning purposes.

Ans. (c)
Exp. Among the given statements, only (c) is incorrect. The corrected form of statement (c) is, paper was bleached by using chlorine, but because of its harmful effects. Now it has been replaced by hydrogen peroxide which works better in the presence of a suitable catalyst.

16 Environmental benefits of green chemistry include *(Chap 14, Class-XI, NCERT)*

(a) Fewer raw materials and natural resources.
(b) Cleaner production technologies and reduced emissions.
(c) Smaller quantities of hazardous waste to be treated and disposal of.
(d) All of the above

Ans. (d)
Exp. All the statements given above are correct. If we follow green chemistry guidelines, then environmental benefits are as follows

- there is less emission of poisonous gases.
- technology improves and is more cleaner.
- disposal of dangerous waste is avoided.

Introduction to Biology and Classification of Living Beings

Introduction to Biology and Classification of Living Beings

Living World and Biodiversity

Introduction to Biology (Study of living beings)

- **Zoology** Study of animals
  Aristotle [Father of zoology]
- **Botany** Study of plants
  Theophrastus [Father of Botany]
- **Microbiology** Study of microbes
  Louis Pasteur [Father of microbiology]

Features of Living Organism

- Protoplasm, cell structure, Nutrition, Excretion, Reproduction, Movement, Metabolism [anabolism + catabolism]

Biodiversity

- Megadiverse Regions (e.g. India etc.)

Classification

- It is the scientific arrangement of an organism in a specific hierarchical series of groups on the basis of similarities and differences.
- **Basis of Classification**
  - Cell structure, Body structure
  - Nutrition → Autotrophic, Heterotrophic

Taxonomy

- It deals with naming and describing of living organisms. Each classification represents a rank and it termed as taxon.

Binomial Nomenclature

- Proposed by Carolus Linnaeus in his book named *Systema Naturae*.
- Scientific name composed of two components.
  Homo ↓ (Generic name) *sapiens* ↓ (Specific name)

- RH Whittaker proposed five kingdom classification

Monera

- Unicellular prokaryotes, well-defined nucleus absent.
- **Archaebacteria** (Living fossils)
- **Eubacteria** (Rigid cell wall)
- **Cyanobacteria** (Blue-green algae, contain chlorophyll-*a*, heterocysts)

Protista

- Unicellular eukaryotes, membrane bound cell organelle are present.
- Mode of Nutrition is either autotrophic or heterotrophic.
- Nucleus is developed, ribosomes are present (80S and 70S)
- **Protozoans** (Animal - like behaviour)
- **Amoeboid** (e.g. *Amoeba*)
- **Flagellated** (e.g. *Trypanosoma*)
  - **Ciliated protozoans** (e.g. *Paramecium*)
  - **Sporozoans** (e.g.

Fungi

- Eukaryotic, non-green organisms.
- Chitinous cell wall, Saprophytic.
- Mode of Reproduction is through. **Asexual** (spores) **Sexual** (gametes), and **Vegetative**

Plantae

- Multicellular, eukaryotes, cellulosic cell wall, autotrophic
- **Cryptogamae** Do not have external flower or seeds
  - **Thallophyta** (e.g. Algae)
  - **Bryophyta** (e.g. Moss)
  - **Pteridophyta** (e.g Ferns)

Classification of Living Organism

- **Phanerogamae** (Seeds are present and they have well-differentiated reproductive tissues.)
  - **Gymnosperms** Non-flowering plants
  - **Angiosperms** Flowering plants
    (i) **Monocots** (e.g. Maize)
    (ii) **Dicots** (e.g. Pea)

Animalia (Multicellular, eukaryotes without cell wall.)

- **Porifera** (e.g. *Spongilla*)
- **Coelenterata** (e.g. *Hydra)*
- **Platyhelminthes** (e.g. *Tapeworm*)
- **Nematoda** (e.g. *Ascaris* (Roundworm)]
- **Annelida** [e.g. *Hirudinaria* (leech)]
- **Arthropoda** (e.g. *Periplaneta cockroach*)
- **Mollusca** (e.g. *Octopus*)
- **Echinodermata** (e.g. *Asterias*)
- **Protochordata** (e.g. *Amphioxous*)
- **Chordata**
  - **Pisces** Bony fish (e.g. *Exocoetus*)
    (i) **Cartilaginuous fish** (e.g. Sharks)
    (ii) **Amphibia** (e.g. Frogs)
  - **Reptilia** (e.g. Snakes)
  - **Aves** (e.g. Crow)
  - **Mammalia** (e.g. Elephant)

Viruses

- It is an infectious microbe which replicate only inside host, consisting of a segment of nucleic acid (either DNA or RNA), e.g., Tobacco Mosaic Virus. (TMV)

Viroids

- It is an infectious agent of plant similar to a virus, that contain circular stands of RNA without protein coating.

SOURCE ***New NCERT Class VI*** *(The Living Organisms : Characteristics and Habitats)*, ***Old NCERT Class IX*** *(Diversity in Living Organisms)*, ***New NCERT Class XI*** *(The Living World)*, ***New NCERT Class XI*** *(Biological Classification)* ***New NCERT Class XI*** *(Plant Kingdom)*, ***New NCERT Class XI*** *(Animal Kingdom)*

1 Consider the following statements.
(Chap 1, Class-XI, NCERT)

1. Binomial nomenclature was given by Carl Linnaeus.
2. The first word in a biological name represents the species, while the second component the generic epithet.
3. All taxonomic categories together constitute the taxonomic hierarchy.

Which of the statement(s) given above is/are incorrect?

(a) Only 2 (b) Only 3
(c) 1 and 2 (d) 2 and 3

Ans. (a)

Exp. Statement (2) is incorrect as binomial nomenclature is the biological system of naming the organisms in which the name is composed of two terms, where the first word in a biological name represents the genus, while the second component represents the species of the organisms. For example, the scientific name of the tiger is presented as *Panthera tigris.*

Panthera represents the genus while *tigris* represents a particular species or specific epithet.

2 In a taxonomic hierarchy the correct sequence in descending order of number of animals is
(Chap 1, Class-XI, NCERT)

(a) Kingdom → Phylum → Order → Family → Class → Genus → Species
(b) Species → Genus → Family → Order → Class → Phylum → Kingdom
(c) Kingdom → Phylum → Class → Order → Family → Genus → Species
(d) Species → Genus → Order → Class → Family → Phylum → Kingdom

Ans. (c)

Exp. The correct sequence in descending order of number of animals is
Kingdom → Phylum → Class → Order → Family → Genus → Species.

The above given sequence represent the taxonomic hierarchy, i.e., the system of arranging taxonomic categories or taxon in a descending order. It was first introduced by Linnaeus (1751) and hence, it is also known as Linnaean hierarchy.

3 Which of the following statement is incorrect?
(Chap 2, Class -XI, NCERT)

(a) Protista includes unicellular eukaryotic organisms.
(b) Whittaker considered cell structure, mode and source of nutrition for classifying the organisms in to five kingdoms.
(c) Both Monera and Protista may be autotrophic and heterotrophic.
(d) Monerans have well-defined nucleus.

Ans. (d)

Exp. Statement (d) is incorrect as Monera are single-celled organisms without a well-defined nucleus. Their DNA is naked, i.e. without histone proteins. It lies inside the cytoplasm in coiled form.

This is called nucleoid or false nucleus. Moneran cell wall contains peptidoglycan or murein (no cellulose), but the membrane bound cell organelles are not present. These are the oldest microorganisms on the earth.

Rest of the statements are correct.

4 Consider the following Assertion (A) and Reason (R) and choose the correct code. *(Chap 2, Class-XI, NCERT)*

Assertion (A) Fungi are heterotrophic eukaryotic organisms having cell wall made up of chitin.

Reason (R) Fungi use decaying organic material as food and become multicellular at certain stages of life.

Codes

(a) Both A and R are true and R is the correct explanation of A
(b) Both A and R are true, but R is not the correct explanation of A
(c) A is true, but R is false
(d) Both A and R are false

Ans. (b)

Exp. Both Assertion (A) and Reason (R) are true, but Reason (R) is not the correct explanation of Assertion (A). The organisms belonging to Fungi are heterotrophic (i.e. consume the food from the environment) eukaryotic organisms. Some of them use decaying organic material as food and are therefore called saprotrophs. Other require a living protoplasm of a host organism for food. They are called parasites. Many of them have the capacity to become multicellular organisms at certain stages in their lives.

5 Consider the following pairs.
(Chap 4, Class-XI, NCERT) (Chap 1, Class-XII, NCERT)
(JKPSC Pre 2023)

1. *Planaria* – Budding
2. *Spirogyra* – Fragmentation
3. *Amoeba* – Regeneration
4. Yeast – Fission

How many pairs given above are correctly matched?

(a) Only one pair (b) Only two pairs
(c) Only three pairs (d) All four pairs

Ans. (b)

Exp. Only two pairs are correctly matched. These can be explained as

Spirogyra reproduces by fragmentation, in which the filament breaks into several pieces. Each piece grows as a new individual.

Yeasts are generally defined as unicellular fungi without fruiting bodies, which propagate by fission.

Planaria reproduces by the process of binary fission and regeneration.

Amoeba is an unicellular organism. It reproduces asexually by the process of binary fission.

6 Phylum-Mollusca contains soft bodied animals characterised of *(Chap 4, Class-XI, NCERT) (MPPSC Pre 2023)*

1. They are second largest phylum in animal kingdom.
2. They are generally bilaterally symmetrical.
3. They are only terrestrial animals.
4. They are having muscular foot.

Which of the statements given above is/are correct?

(a) Only 1 (b) 1, 2 and 4
(c) 1, 2 and 3 (d) 1 and 4

Ans. (b)

Exp. Statements (1), (2) and (4) are correct as phylum-Mollusca contains soft bodied animals.

They are second largest phylum in animal kingdom.

Statement (3) is incorrect and can be corrected as Molluscs are terrestrial or aquatic animals.

7 Which one of the following statement is not correct? *(Chap 4, Class-XI, NCERT) (IAS Pre 2002)*

(a) All echinoderms are viviparous.
(b) Roundworm has no circulatory system.
(c) In bony fishes, swim bladder is usually present.
(d) In cartilaginous fishes, fertilisation is internal.

Ans. (a)

Exp. Statement (a) is not correct as echinoderm is the common name given to any member of the phylum–Echinodermata of marine animals.

The adults are recognisable by their (usually five point) radial symmetry and include such well-known animals as starfish, sea urchins, sand dollars and sea cucumbers. Most animals of phylum– Echinodermata are oviparous. Oviparous animals lay eggs, with little or no other embryonic development within the mother.

8 Which of the following is a true fish? *(Chap 4, Class-XI, NCERT) (RAS/RTS Pre 1997)*

(a) Starfish (b) Jellyfish (c) Hagfish (d) Seahorse

Ans. (d)

Exp. Seahorse is a true fish. It is the name given to 47 species of small marine fish in the genus–*Hippocampus*, which is a bony fish. Rest options like starfish or sea stars are star-shaped echinoderms belong to the class–Asteroidea. Jellyfish (Cnidaria) and hagfish (Cyclostomata) are also not true fishes.

9 Amongst the following organisms, which one does not belong to the group-Aves? *(Chap 4, Class-XI, NCERT) (UPPSC Mains 2011)*

(a) Bat (b) Crow (c) Eagle (d) Parrot

Ans. (a)

Exp. Bats do not belong to the group-Aves (birds). Bats are mammal of the order–Chiroptera whose forelimbs form webbed wings, making them the only mammals naturally capable of true and sustained flight. Bats are called mammals, as they have hairs on their body, possess mammary glands and give birth to young ones directly.

Chapter 02

Cell

Cell

Discovery of Cell and Cell Theory

Cell

- Smallest unit of life that can exist independently and can perform activities of life.
- Hence, called "building blocks of life".

Discoveries of Cell

- Cell discovered by Robert Hooke (1665)
- **First living cell** Antonie van Leeuwenhoek (1670)
- **Nucleus** Robert Brown (1831)
- **Protoplasm** Purkinje (1839)

Cell Theory

- It is given by Schleiden and Schwann, it states that all plants and animals are composed of cell, the basic unit of life.
- **Types of Organisms**
  Based on number of cells, organisms are divided into two categories.
  - **Unicellular Organism** Made up of single cell, e.g. *Amoeba*.
  - **Multicellular Organism** Made up of many cells, e.g. Plants and animals.

Shape of Cells

- **Fixed Shape** (e.g. Plant and animals cells)
  - Elliptical (e.g. Fat cell)
  - Spherical (e.g. Ovum)
  - Spindle-shaped (e.g Smooth muscle)
  - Knobbed thread (e.g. Sperm)
- **Pleomorphic** (Shapes can be changed) (e.g. *Amoeba*)

Size of Cells

- **Smallest cell** Mycoplasma (0.1-0.5 m)
- **Largest cell** Ostrich (18 cm)
- **Longest cell** Nerve cells (Neurons).

Types and Components of Cell

Types of Cell

- **Prokaryotic Cells**
  - They lack membrane bound organelles. DNA is naked and circular without a nuclear membrane.
  - Mesosomes and 70S ribosomes are the sites of protein synthesis.
  - e.g. Bacteria and Archaea cells.
- **Eukaryotic Cells**
  - Membrane bound organelles are present.
  - DNA is linear with a nuclear membrane.
  - 80S ribosomes are present
  - e.g. Plant and Animals cells.

Structural Organisation of a Cell

- **Components of Cell**
- **Plasma Membrane** Outer Covering [flexible; Lipid + Protein]
- **Cytoplasm** Living part of cell
- **Nucleus** Brain of cell
- **Cell Wall** Present in only plant cells.
- **Cell Organelles** Membrane bound structures found within the cell
  - Endoplasmic Reticulum (RER & SER)
  - Golgi Apparatus • Lysosome
  - Mitochondria
  - Plastids Chromoplasts (coloured) chloroplasts (green) and leucoplasts (colourless)
  - Vacuole • Cytoskeleton
  - Centrosome • Microbodies

Cell Cycle and Division

Cell Cycle

- Sequential event by which a cell duplicates its genome; synthesise new cell constituents.
- **Interphase** (Resting phase). It comprises of
  (i) G_1-phase (1st gap phase) Increase in size
  (ii) S-phase (Synthesis phase) copies its DNA
  (iii) G_2-phase (2nd gap phase) Prepares to divide
- **M-phase** (Dividing phase) Period of actual division.
  - Some cells exit G_1-phase to enter the inactive state called **quiescent stage** [G_0-phase].
  - **Mitosis** (Equational Division)
- Results in formation of two diploid daughter cells with identical genetic composition
  (i) **Prophase** First and longest phase of cell division, condensation of chromosomal material.
  (ii) **Metaphase** Short and simple phase Chromosomes move towards the equatorial plate.
  (iii) **Anaphase** Chromosomes splits and the sister chromatids separate to move towards opposite poles.
  (iv) **Telophase** Identity of chromosome is lost as discrete elements. Nucleolus, Golgi complex and ER reform.
  - **Meiosis** (Reductional division) It results in the formation of four daughter cells as number of chromosomes reduced to half.

SOURCE *Old NCERT Class VIII (Cell : Structure and Functions), New NCERT Class IX (The Fundamental Unit of Life) New NCERT Class XI (Cell : The Unit of Life), New NCERT Class XI (Cell Cycle and Cell Division), NIOS Chap 21 Module 5*

1 **Robert Hooke discovered the cell by observing the** *(Chap 5, Class-IX, NCERT)*

(a) onion peel cells
(b) cork slice
(c) cheek cell
(d) pond water

Ans. (b)

Exp. Robert Hooke discovered the cell in 1665 by observing the cork slice.

Cork is a substance which comes from the bark of a tree. When he looked at thin slice of cork using microscope, he saw that the cork resembled the structure of a honeycomb consisting of many small compartments and called these compartments as 'cells'.

2 **Which of the following is true about cell?** *(Chap 5, Class-IX, NCERT)*

1. The free-living cells in the pond water was first observed by the Purkinje.
2. The cell theory was presented by Schwann and Robert Brown.
3. Virchow suggested that all cells arise from pre-existing cells.

Codes

(a) 1 and 3 (b) Only 3
(c) Only 2 (d) 2 and 3

Ans. (b)

Exp. Statement (3) is true about cell. Virchow in 1855 suggested that all cells divide and new cells arise from pre-existing cells (*Omnis cellula-e-cellula*).

Statements (1) and (2) are not true because the free-living cells in pond water was first discovered by Leeuwenhoek in 1674. Purkinje in 1839 coined the term 'protoplasm' for the fluid substance of the cell.

The cell theory, that all the plants and animals are composed of cells and that the cell is the basic unit of life, was presented by two biologists, Schleiden (1838) and Schwann (1839).

3 **Choose the incorrectly matched pair.** *(Chap 8, Class-XI, NCERT)*

(a) Largest cell Ostrich
(b) Smallest cell Mycoplasma
(c) Spindle-shape cells Nerve cells
(d) Spherical cells RBCs

Ans. (c)

Exp. Pair (c) is incorrectly matched as muscle cells are spindle-shaped cells found in the human body.

They are spindle-shaped because they are responsible for the contraction and relaxation of body.

Nerve cells are the branched cell in our body. The nerve cells receive and transfers messages, thereby helping to control and coordinate the working of different parts of the body.

4 **Which of the following is incorrect difference between plant cell and animal cell?** *(Chap 5, Class-IX, NCERT)*

	Plant cell		Animal cell
(a)	Cell membrane present	–	Cell membrane present
(b)	Chloroplast present	–	Chloroplast absent
(c)	Vacuoles absent	–	Vacuoles present
(d)	Nucleus present	–	Nucleus present

Ans. (c)

Exp. Pair (c) is the incorrect difference between plant cell and animal cell.

This is because vacuole is a membrane bound cell organelle present in both plant and animal cells.

Plant cell has a big central vacuole unlike a number of small vacuoles in animal cells. The plant vacuole occupy more than 80% of the volume of the cell.

5 **Choose the incorrectly matched pair.** *(Chap 5, Class-IX, NCERT)*

(a) Hypotonic solution – Cell will swell up
(b) Hypertonic solution – Cell will shrink
(c) Plasmolysis – Cell will remain same
(d) Isotonic solution – Cell will stay same size

Ans. (c)

Exp. Pair (c) is incorrectly matched as plasmolysis is the process by which a plant cell loses water when placed in a hypertonic solution (a solution having a higher amount of solutes than the cell).

The actual process behind this is the movement of water outwards due to osmosis, resulting in the shrinkage of the entire cell.

6 **Plasma membrane is built up of** *(Chap 5, Class-IX, NCERT) (UPPSC Mains 2008)*

(a) lipids (b) proteins
(c) carbohydrate (d) Both 'a' and 'b'

Ans. (d)

Exp. The plasma membrane is built up of lipids (phospholipids and cholesterol) and proteins.

Lipids are arranged in a bilayer. They are arranged within the membrane with the polar head towards the outer side and the hydrophobic tail towards the inner part.

Proteins can be classified as integral or peripheral. Peripheral proteins lies on the surface of the membrane, while the integral proteins are partially or totally buried in the membrane.

7 **How does the plant cell differ from the animal cell?** *(Chap 8, Class-VIII, NCERT) (UPPSC Pre 1991)*

(a) Mitochondria
(b) Cell wall
(c) Presence of protoplasm
(d) Cell nucleus

Ans. (b)

Exp. The plant cell differ from the animal cell on the basis of cell wall as it is a unique structure present in plant cells. It is found as an outer covering to the plasma membrane. It is absent in animal cells.

The main functions of the cell wall are to provide structure, support and protection to the cell. The cell wall in plants is composed mainly of cellulose and contains three layers in many plants. The three layers are the middle lamella, primary cell wall and secondary cell wall.

8 Which of the following is correct about nucleus? *(Chap 8, Class-XI, NCERT)*

(a) It has single-layered covering called nuclear membrane.

(b) Chromosomes are composed of DNA and protein.

(c) Eukaryotes have an undefined nuclear region called nucleoid.

(d) Functional segments of DNA are chromatin.

Ans. (b)

Exp. Statement (b) is correct about nucleus. The nucleus contain chromosomes which carry genetic information for inheritance of features from parents to next generation. Chromosomes are composed of DNA and protein. DNA molecules contain the information necessary for constructing and organising cells.

Statements (a), (c) and (d) are incorrect because the nucleus has a double-layered covering called nuclear membrane. The nuclear membrane has pores which allow the transfer of material from inside the nucleus to the outside.

In prokaryotes like bacteria, the nuclear region of the cell may be poorly defined due to the absence of a nuclear membrane. Such an undefined nuclear region containing only nucleic acid is called nucleoid.

Functional segments of DNA are called genes.

9 Choose the correct statement regarding Endoplasmic Reticulum. *(Chap 5, Class-IX, NCERT)*

1. Rough Endoplasmic Reticulum (RER) is involved in the protein synthesis and secretion.
2. Smooth Endoplasmic Reticulum (SER) is the site for synthesis of carbohydrate.
3. Rough Endoplasmic Reticulum (RER) also has role in detoxifying many poisons and drugs.
4. Smooth Endoplasmic Reticulum (SER) is the site for manufacture of fat molecules.

Codes

(a) 1 and 2 (b) 1 and 4
(c) 2 and 3 (d) 1 and 3

Ans. (b)

Exp. Statements (1) and (4) are correct regarding Endoplasmic Reticulum.

Rough Endoplasmic Reticulum (RER) is actively involved in the protein synthesis and secretion. Rough Endoplasmic Reticulum (RER) are extensive and continues with the outer membrane of nucleus.

The Smooth Endoplasmic Reticulum (SER) is the major site for synthesis of lipid. In animal cells, lipids like steroid hormones are synthesised in Smooth Endoplasmic Reticulum (SER).

Statements (2) and (3) are incorrect because Smooth Endoplasmic Reticulum (SER) is the site for the synthesis of fat molecules or lipids, important for cell function. In liver cells Smooth Endoplasmic Reticulum (SER) plays a crucial role in detoxifying many poisons and drugs.

10 Which of the following cell organelles play the most significant role in protein synthesis? *(Chap 5, Class-XI, NCERT) (IAS Pre 2001)*

(a) Lysosome and centrosome

(b) Endoplasmic Reticulum and ribosomes

(c) Golgi apparatus and mitochondria

(d) Lysosome and mitochondria

Ans. (b)

Exp. Endoplasmic Reticulum and ribosomes play the most significant role in protein synthesis.

Ribosomes are present on the outer surface of Rough Endoplasmic Reticulum (RER).

The attached ribosomes make proteins that will be used inside the cell and export out of the cell.

11 Which of the following is incorrectly matched? *(Chap 5, Class-IX, NCERT)*

(a) Thread-like structures – Chromosomes

(b) Extension of plasma membrane – Mesosomes

(c) Large vacuoles – Cheek cells

(d) Small vacuoles – Animal cells

Ans. (c)

Exp. Pair (c) is incorrectly matched because cheek cells are animal cells and have many small vacuoles. On the contrary, plant cell vacuoles are large, that help to maintain the turgidity of the cell and store important substances including wastes.

In plants, the tonoplast facilitates the transport of a number of ions and other materials against concentration gradients into the vacuole.

12 Match the following lists and choose the correct code. *(Chap 5, Class-IX, NCERT)*

List I		List II	
A.	Protoplasm	1.	Robert Brown
B.	Nucleus	2.	Robert Hooke
C.	Golgi apparatus	3.	Purkinje
D.	Cell wall	4.	Camillo Golgi

Codes

	A	B	C	D		A	B	C	D
(a)	3	4	2	1	(b)	3	1	2	4
(c)	3	4	1	2	(d)	3	1	4	2

Ans. (d)

Exp. The correct matching is A-3, B-1, C-4, D-2.
'Protoplasm' term was coined by Purkinje in 1839 for the fluid substance of the cell.
Nucleus as a cell organelle was discovered by Robert Brown in 1831. Later the material of the nucleus stained by the basic dyes was given the name chromatin by Flemming.
'Golgi apparatus' first described by Camillo Golgi. He observed densely stained reticular structures near the nucleus.
These were later named Golgi bodies after him.
Robert Hooke in 1665 discovered cell wall.
It is a rigid and a non-living structure which forms an outer covering of the plasma membrane in plants and fungi. It is absent in animal cells.

13 Which of the following is not the function of Golgi apparatus? *(Chap 5, Class-IX, NCERT)*

(a) They are involved in storage, modification and packaging of products in vesicles.
(b) They are involved in the formation of ribosomes.
(c) In Golgi apparatus, complex sugars may be made from simple sugars.
(d) They are important sites for the formation of glycolipids and glycoproteins.

Ans. (b)

Exp. Statement (b) is not the fuction of Golgi apparatus This cell organelle helps in processing and packaging of proteins and lipid molecules.
The material synthesised near the Endoplasmic Reticulum (ER) is packaged and dispatched to various targets inside and outside the cell through the Golgi apparatus.
In some cases, complex sugars may be made from simple sugars in the Golgi apparatus. The Golgi apparatus is also involved in the formation of lysosomes.
The nucleolus, dark staining, round and dense structure present within the nucleus of eukaryotic cells are associated with ribosome formation.

14 Golgi bodies are the stacks of flattened sacs or small vesicles generally located near the nucleus. Similar structures in a plant cells are called *(Chap 21, Module-5, NIOS)*

(a) Lysosmoes (b) Dictyosomes
(c) Leucoplasts (d) Chromoplasts

Ans (b)

Exp. Dictyosomes are net-like structures of flat, membrane-bound cavities called cisternae that comprises the Golgi apparatus. Proteins are stored, modified, sorted and packed into vesicles in the dictyosomes for transport.

15 Which organelle in the cell, other than the nucleus, contains DNA? *(Chap 8, Class-XI, NCERT) (IAS Pre 2001)*

(a) Centriole (b) Golgi apparatus
(c) Lysosome (d) Mitochondrion

Ans. (d)

Exp. Among the given options mitochondrion in the cell contains DNA which is a genetic material responsible for transmitting parental characters to their offspring. The matrix of the mitochondria as well as chloroplast contain a few RNA molecules, ribosomes (70S) and components required for the synthesis of proteins.

16 Choose the correct statement regarding lysosomes. *(Chap 5, Class-IX, NCERT)*

1. They contain powerful digestive enzymes.
2. These enzymes are made by Smooth Endoplasmic Reticulum (SER).
3. They are the membrane bound organelles formed by the process of packaging in the Golgi apparatus.

Codes

(a) 1 and 2 (b) 2 and 3
(c) 1 and 3 (d) Only 1

Ans. (c)

Exp. Statements (1) and (3) are correct regarding lysosomes.
Lysosomes are the membrane bound organelles formed by the process of packaging in the Golgi apparatus. Lysosomes help to keep the cell clean by digesting any foreign material. This is done because they contain powerful digestive enzymes capable of breaking down all organic material.
Statement (2) is incorrect because lysosomal enzymes are synthesised by the Rough Endoplasmic Reticulum (RER) and exported to the Golgi apparatus.

17 Which of the following organelles is the sites of aerobic respiration? *(Chap 8, Class-XI, NCERT)*

(a) Ribosome (b) Mitochondria
(c) Cell membrane (d) Centrosome

Ans. (b)

Exp. Mitochondria is called 'Powerhouse' of the cell because they are the site of aerobic respiration and they produced cellular energy in the form of ATP.
The mitochondrion (Plural mitochondria) is a membrane bound organelle found in most eukaryotic cells. Mitochondria range form 05-1.0μ in diameter. These structures have their own genome.

18 Chloroplasts are able to make their own proteins because they *(Chap 8, Class-XI, NCERT)*

(a) have their own DNA and ribosomes
(b) release energy in the form of ATP
(c) have two coverings instead of one
(d) have porous outer membrane

Ans. (a)

Exp. Chloroplasts are able to make their own proteins because they have their own DNA and ribosomes. Chloroplasts are double membranous cell organelles where photosynthesis occurs. The inner matrix (called stroma) of chloroplast contains dissolved enzymes, starch granules and many copies of chloroplast genome (DNA along with ribosomes).

19 **Consider the following pairs.** *(Chap 8, Class-XI, NCERT)*

1. Chloroplast - yellow or orange colour
2. Chlorophyll - green colour
3. Leucoplasts - orange colour
4. Chromoplast - white or colourless

Which of the pairs given above is/are incorrectly matched?

(a) 1 and 2 (b) 3 and 4 (c) Only 3 (d) 1 and 3

Ans. (b)

Exp. Pairs (3) and (4) are incorrectly matched as Leucoplasts are white or colourless plastids. They are primary organelles in which materials such as starch, oils and protein granules are stored.

It is divided into three groups–amyloplasts (which store starch), elaioplasts (store lipids) and aleuroplasts (store proteins).

The chromoplast contain fat soluble carotenoid pigments like carotene, xanthophylls, etc. This gives the part of a plant a yellow, orange or red colour.

20 **The organelles that are included in the endomembrane system are** *(Chap 5, Class-XI, NCERT)*

(a) Endoplasmic Reticulum, Mitochondria, Ribosomes and Lysosomes.
(b) Endoplasmic Reticulum, Golgi complex, Lysosomes and Vacuoles.
(c) Golgi complex, Mitochondria, Ribosomes and Lysosomes.
(d) Golgi complex, Endoplasmic Reticulum, Mitochondria and Lysosomes.

Ans. (b)

Exp. The organelles that are included in the endomembrane system are Endoplasmic Reticulum (ER), Golgi complex, lysosomes and vacuoles. They are considered in the endomembrane system because their functions are coordinated. Since the functions of the mitochondria, chloroplast and peroxisomes are not coordinated with the above components. These are not considered as part of the endomembrane system.

21 **Choose the incorrectly matched pair.** *(Chap 5, Class-IX, NCERT)*

(a) Endoplasmic reticulum – Membrane biogenesis
(b) Mitochondria – ATP generation
(c) Lysosomes – Digestive enzymes
(d) Golgi apparatus – Osmoregulation and excretion

Ans. (d)

Exp. Pair (d) is incorrectly matched as Golgi apparatus is involved in storage, modification and packaging of products in vesicles.

The material synthesised near the Endoplasmic Reticulum (ER) is packaged and dispatched to various targets inside and outside the cell through the Golgi apparatus.

It is also an important site for the formation of glycolipids and glycoproteins.

The contractile vacuole helps in regulating the quantity of water inside a cell performing osmoregulation and excretion in *Amoeba*.

Rest all the pairs are correctly matched.

22 **Match the following lists and choose the correct code.** *(Chap 5, Class-IX, NCERT)*

	List I		List II
A.	Nucleus	1.	Protein factory
B.	Ribosomes	2.	Protection and rigidity to the cell
C.	Chloroplast	3.	Control centre of the cell
D.	Cell wall	4.	Perform photosynthesis

Codes

	A	B	C	D
(a)	3	4	2	1
(b)	3	1	4	2
(c)	3	1	2	4
(d)	3	4	1	2

Ans. (b)

Exp. The correct matching is A-3, B-1, C-4, D-2.

Nucleus It acts as control centre for the activities of the cell.

It contains the cell's hereditary information and controls the cell growth and reproduction. It regulates all the cellular activities by controlling the enzymes required for cellular processes.

Ribosomes These are called protein factory of the cell because they are site for protein synthesis.

Chloroplasts These are the green plastids that function as the site of photosynthesis, i.e. helps in the synthesis of organic food. These are double membrane bound, DNA and ribosome containing semiautonomous cell organelle.

Cell wall It is the additional layer surrounding the cell membrane in plants. It provides protection and structural strength to the plant.

23 **Which of the following is/are the function(s) of the vacuoles?** *(Chap 5, Class-IX, NCERT)*

1. They are the storage sacs for solid or liquid contents.
2. They provide turgidity and rigidity to the cell.
3. They play important roles in expelling excess water and product from the cell.
4. They have role in the transportation of the water and food outside the cell.

Codes

(a) 1 and 2 (b) 2 and 3
(c) 1, 2 and 4 (d) Only 1

Ans. (a)

Exp. Statements (1) and (2) are considered as the functions of vacuoles.

These are the membrane bound space found in the cytoplasm. Vacuoles are the storage sacs for solid or liquid contents.

In plant cells, vacuoles are full of cell sap and provide turgidity and rigidity to the cell. Many important substances in the life of plant cell are stored in vacuoles. These include amino acids, sugars, various organic acids and some proteins.

Statements (3) and (4) are incorrect and can be corrected as In some unicellular organisms, contractile vacuoles also play an important role in expelling excess water and some wastes from the cell. Vacuoles cannot transport water and food outside the cell.

24 Consider the following statements regarding cell division. *(Chap 8, Class -XI, NCERT)*

1. There are two types of cell division mitosis and meiosis.
2. Mitosis can occur in both in diploid and haploid cells.
3. Mitosis is the equational division.

Which of the statements given above is/are true?

(a) 1, 2 and 3
(b) 1 and 3
(c) 1 and 3
(d) Only 1

Ans. (a)

Exp. All the given statements (1), (2) and (3) are true regarding cell division.

Cell division happens when a parent cell divides into two or more cells called daughter cells.

There are two types of cell division rarely, mitosis and meiosis. Mitosis is the equational division, while meiosis is both equational and reductional division.

Mitosis can occur in both diploid and haploid cells and meiosis occurs only in the diploid cells.

Mitosis usually results in the production of diploid daughter cells with identical genetic complement.

Meiosis usually results in the production of four haploid daughter cells.

25 Consider the following statements regarding mitosis. *(Chap 10, Class -XI, NCERT) (Chap 21, Module-5, NIOS)*

1. Mitosis or the equational division is usually restricted to the diploid cells only.
2. Mitosis results in the production of haploid daughter cells.
3. Mitosis helps in wound healing and replacement of cells lost during wear and tear.
4. In animals, mitosis takes place in reproductive organs.

Which of the statements given above is/are true?

(a) 1 and 2 (b) 2 and 4 (c) 1 and 3 (d) Only 3

Ans. (c)

Exp. Statements (1) and (3) are true regarding mitosis. In mitosis, a cell give rise to two identical daughter cells. Mitosis is needed for growth and repair of worn out parts. It is responsible for the growth of an organism by addition of new cells. It is the method of asexual reproduction in single-celled organism.

Meiosis is necessary for sexual reproduction. In animals, meiosis takes place in reproductive organs, i.e., testis and ovary.

26 Arrange the following categories in the order of mitotic cell division. *(Chap 10, Class-XI, NCERT)* ***(JKPSC Pre 2023)***

1. Prophase 2. Metaphase
3. Anaphase 4. Telophase

The correct order is

(a) 1, 2, 3, 4 (b) 3, 2, 1, 4 (c) 3, 4, 1, 2 (d) 1, 4, 3, 1

Ans. (a)

Exp. The correct order is 1, 2, 3, 4.

Mitosis is divided into the following four stages : *Prophase Chromosomes* Condense, nuclear membrane and nucleolus disappear.

Metaphase Chromosomes are arranged on the equatorial plate of the cell.

Anaphase Chromosomes are pulled to the poles by spindle fibres.

Telophase Nuclear membrane and nucleolus start to reform and the correct order of stages in mitotic cell division is prophase, metaphase, anaphase and telophase.

Chapter 03

Tissues

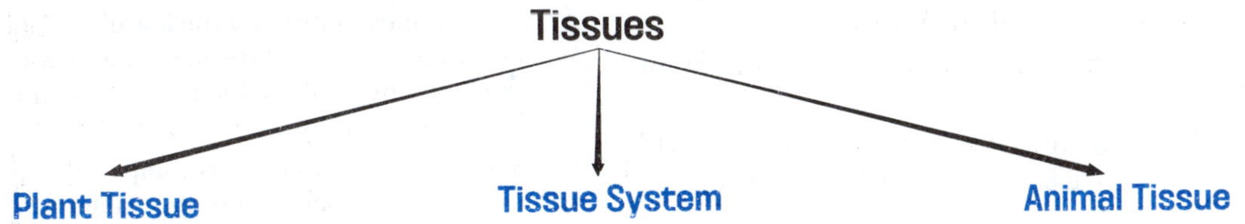

Plant Tissue

Tissue
- Group of cells that are structurally similar and carry out specific function.

Plant Tissue
- Dead cells which provide mechanical support to the plant. It is of two types

(i) **Meristematic Tissue** Cells which actively divide throughout their life.
- **Apical meristem** Found at apices of main root and shoots. Help in growth of the plant.
- **Intercalary Meristem** Found at base of leaves, help in longitudinal growth.
- **Lateral Meristem** Found along the lateral side of stem and roots, help in secondary growth.

(ii) **Permanent Tissue / Mature Tissue** Cells which have lost their ability to divide further.
- **Simple Permanent Tissue** Made up of similar type of cells

(i) **Parenchyma** Living and simple tissue
- **Chlorenchyma** Contain chloroplast.
- **Aerenchyma** Contain air spaces.

(ii) **Collenchyma** Living cell that provides mechanical support to the plants.

(iii) **Sclerenchyma** Contain dead cells Sclerenchyma fibres occur in parts which require mechanical strength, sclereids found in hard parts of plant.
- **Complex Permanent Tissue** Made up of more than one type of cells.

(i) **Xylem** Help in conduction of water and minerals-(unidirectional).

(ii) **Phloem** Help in conduction of

Tissue System

Plant Tissue System
- Tissue which perform similar functions, irrespective of their position constitute a tissue system.
- **Epidermal Tissue System** Form the outermost covering of the whole plant body.
  - **Epidermis** Outermost layer of main plant body. Cells are elongated and compactly arranged to from continuous layer.
  - **Stomata** Opening present in aerial part of plants, especially leaves.
  - **Epidermal Appendages** Outgrowth present on epidermis of plants.
- **Ground Tissue System** Tissues except epidermis and vascular bundles constitute ground tissue system
  - **Hypodermis** Region below the epidermis.
  - **Cortex** Present between epidermis and endodermis
  - **Endodermis** Innermost layer of cortex.
- **Vascular Tissue System** Composed of xylem and phloem, originate from procambium and apical meristem.
  - **Radial** Found mainly in roots.
  - **Conjoint** Same bundle on same radius.
  - **Concentric** Tissue is completely surrounded.

Animal Tissue

Animal Tissue
- Made up of more than one type of cell and are more complex as compared to plant tissue.
- **Epithelial Tissue**
  - **Simple Epithelial Tissue** Formed from single layer of cell.

(i) **Squamous epithelium** (e.g. Skin,etc.)

(ii) **Cuboidal epithelium** (e.g. Pancreatic ducts)

(iii) **Columnar Epithelium** (e.g. Fallopian tube)

(iv) **Glandular Epithelium** (Formed from columnar cell or cuboidal cell)
- **Unicellular gland** (e.g. Goblet cells)
- **Multicellular gland** (e.g. Salivary gland)

- **Connective Tissue**
  - **Proper Connective Tissue**

(i) **Loose Connective Tissues** Adipose Tissue and Areolar Tissue

(ii) **Dense Connective Tissue** White fibrous connective tissue (from tendon) and Yellow fibrous connective tissue (from ligament)

(iii) **Skeletal Connective Tissue** Cartilage, etc.

(iv) **Vascular Connective Tissue** Lymph, etc.

- **Muscular Tissue**
  - **Striated Muscle** Found in tongue, etc.
  - **Non-striated Muscle** Found in stomach etc.
  - **Cardiace Muscle** Found in heart, etc.
- **Nervous Tissue** This tissue makes up brain and the spinal cord.

SOURCE New NCERT Class IX *(Tissues)*, New NCERT Class XI *(Anatomy of Flowering Plants)*, New NCERT Class XI *(Structural Organisation in Animals)*

1 **Consider the following statements regarding meristematic tissue.** *(Chap 6, Class-IX, NCERT)* *(IAS Pre 2011)*

1. Apical meristem results in primary growth and increase in the length of stem and root.
2. Lateral meristem results in secondary growth and is present at the base of the leaves.
3. Intercalary meristem is found at the internodes of the leaves.

Which of the statement(s) given above is/are correct?

(a) 1 and 2 (b) 1 and 3 (c) 2 and 3 (d) Only 1

Ans. (b)

Exp. Statements (1) and (3) are correct regarding meristematic tissue. Apical meristem is present at the growing tips of stems and roots and increases the length of the stem and the root. Intercalary meristem is meristem at the base of the leaves or the internodes on twigs.

Statement (2) is incorrect because lateral meristem is found in the mature regions of roots and shoots of any plant. The girth of the stem or root increases due to lateral meristem (cambium). These are responsible for producing the secondary tissues.

2 **Which one of the following pairs is an example of lateral meristem?** *(Chap 6, Class -XI, NCERT)*

(a) Phellogen and phelloderm
(b) Phellogen and fascicular cambium
(c) Procambium and phelloderm
(d) Inter fascicular cambium and phellem

Ans. (b)

Exp. Phellogen and fascicular cambium are examples of lateral meristem.

Plants need a new protective covering due to the secondary growth. For this reason, the permanent living cells in outer region become meristematic and give rise to secondary lateral meristem called phellogen.

Fascicular cambium is also a secondary lateral meristem.

3 **Match the following lists and choose the correct codes.** *(Chap 6, Class -IX, NCERT)*

List I	List II
A. Parenchyma	1. It provides buoyancy to the plant.
B. Collenchyma	2. It provides support to the plant and stores food.
C. Sclerenchyma	3. It provides flexibility and allows easy bending in various parts of a plant.
D. Aerenchyma	4. It makes the plant hard and stiff.

Codes

	A	B	C	D		A	B	C	D
(a)	2	3	4	1	(b)	2	4	3	1
(c)	2	1	4	3	(d)	2	3	1	4

Ans. (a)

Exp. The correct matching is A-2, B-3, C-4, D-1.

Parenchyma tissue - It is a type of permanent tissue. It consists of relatively unspecialised cells with thin cell walls. This tissue provides support to plants and also stores food.

Collenchyma tissue - It is composed of elongated living cells of uneven primary thick walls, which possess hemicellulose, cellulose and pectin materials. The flexibility in plants is due to collenchyma. It allows easy bending in various parts of a plant without breaking.

Sclerenchyma tissue - It is composed of dead cells that have heavily thickened walls containing lignin and a high cellulose content. It is the tissue which makes the plant hard and stiff.

Aerenchyma tissue - It is a modified parenchyma, where the cells are arranged with regular air spaces to facilitate diffusion of gases to provide buoyancy to aquatic plants.

4 **Consider the following Assertion (A) and Reason (R) and choose the correct code.** *(Chap 6, Class -IX, NCERT)*

Assertion (A) Husk of a coconut tree is hard and stiff.

Reason (R) It is made up of a type of permanent tissue, i.e. sclerenchymatous tissue.

Codes

(a) Both A and R are true and R is the correct explanation of A.
(b) Both A and R are true, but R is not the correct explanation of A.
(c) A is true, but R is false.
(d) Both A and R is false.

Ans. (a)

Exp. Both Assertion (A) and Reason (R) are true and Reason (R) is the correct explanation of Assertion (A). Sclerenchymatous tissue makes up the husk of coconut.

Walls of sclerenchyma are lignified, which make them thick. These tissues causes the plant to become stiff and hard. These walls are so thick that there is no internal space inside the cell. This tissue is present in stems, around vascular bundles, in the veins of leaves and in the hard covering of seeds and nuts. It provides strength to the plant parts.

5 **Choose the incorrectly matched pair.** *(Chap 6, Class-IX, NCERT)*

(a) Sclerenchyma – no internal space
(b) Parenchyma – very less intercellular space
(c) Collenchyma – very little intercellular space
(d) Sclerenchyma – large intercellular space

Ans. (d)

Exp. Only pair (d) is incorrectly matched as Sclerenchyma consists of long, narrow cells with thick and lignified cell walls having a few or numerous protoplasts.

Intercellular spaces are lacking in sclerenchyma tissue because the cells are dead and the cell walls have become thickened due to the deposition of lignin, which function as a cement. Sclerenchyma provides strength to the plant.

6 Consider the following statements. *(Chap 6, Class -IX, NCERT)*

1. Parenchyma tissue provides support to the plant and also conducts water to the other parts.
2. The flexibility in plants is due to collenchyma.
3. Sclerenchyma makes the plant hard due to the presence of chitinous walls.

Which of the statement(s) given above is/are incorrect?

(a) 1 and 2 (b) 2 and 3 (c) 1 and 3 (d) Only 2

Ans. (c)

Exp. Statements (1) and (3) are incorrect. Parenchyma tissue provides support to plants and also stores food.

Xylem tissue conducts water to the other parts of the plant. Sclerenchyma tissue makes the plant hard due to the presence of lignified walls.

7 Which of the following is not true about the complex permanent tissue? *(Chap 6, Class -IX, NCERT)*

(a) Xylem and phloem together constitute a vascular bundle.
(b) Except phloem fibres, phloem cells are dead cells.
(c) Xylem consists of tracheids, vessels and xylem parenchyma and xylem fibre.
(d) Phloem consists of sieve tubes, companion cells, phloem fibres and phloem parenchyma.

Ans. (b)

Exp. Statement (b) is not true about complex permanent tissue and can be corrected as except phloem fibres, phloem cells are living cells.

Phloem transports food materials, usually from leaves to other parts of the plant.

Phloem is composed of sieve tube elements, companion cells, phloem parenchyma and phloem fibres. Sieve tubes are tubular cells with perforated walls.

The companion cells are specialised parenchymatous cells, which are closely associated with sieve tube elements. Phloem parenchyma is made up of elongated, tapering cylindrical walls which have dense cytoplasm nucleus. Phloem fibres are made up of sclerenchymatous cells.

8 Vessels and companion cells are the characteristic features of *(Chap 6, Class -XI, NCERT) (IAS Pre 1999)*

(a) Gymnosperms (b) Angiosperms
(c) Pteridophytes (d) Fungi

Ans. (b)

Exp. Companion cells are the characteristic features of the phloem in angiosperms. It is closely associated with the development and function of a sieve-tube element.

A vessel element or vessel member is one of the cell type found in xylem, the water conducting tissue of plants. Vessel elements are typically found in flowering plants (angiosperms) but absent in most gymnosperms such as conifers. So, vessels and companion cells are the characteristic features of angiosperms and absent in gymnosperms, pteridophytes and bryophytes.

9 A tracheid is distinguished from a vessel element on the basis of *(Chap 6, Class -XI, NCERT) (IAS Pre 1999)*

(a) length
(b) thickness
(c) side-wall pitting
(d) end wall perforation

Ans. (d)

Exp. A tracheid is distinguished from a vessel element on the basis of end wall perforation. Vessel elements have perforated end walls, whereas tracheids have primary wall material present on their end walls.

10 Periderm includes *(Chap 6, Class-XI, NCERT) (IAS Pre 2005)*

(a) phelloderm, collenchyma and cortex
(b) phellem, cambium and cortex
(c) all the tissues between epidermis and pith
(d) phellogen, phellem and phelloderm

Ans. (d)

Exp. Structurally, the periderm includes three parts, i.e., a meristem known as phellogen or cork cambium, the layer of cells cut off by phellogen on the outer side, the phellem or cork. The cells cut off by phellogen towards inner side constitute the phelloderm.

11 Consider the following statements. *(Chap 6, Class-XI, NCERT) (IAS Pre 2002)*

1. Epidermis and cortex of monocot roots are similar to those of dicot roots.
2. Hypodermis of dicot stem consists of sclerenchymatous cells.
3. The cells of bundle sheath in maize leaf serve as temporary storage cells.
4. The dicot leaf is hypostomatic.

Which of statements given above are correct?

(a) 1 and 2 (b) 2, 3 and 4
(c) 1, 3 and 4 (d) 1, 2, 3 and 4

Ans. (c)

Exp. Statements (1), (3) and (4) are correct.

Epidermis and cortex of monocot roots are similar to those of dicot roots. Epidermis is the single outermost layer. The outer wall of cells form unicellular hairs, which helps in absorption of water from the soil.

Cortex is situated below the epidermis up to endodermis. It is multilayered parenchymatous tissue with intercellular spaces.

There are a number of large and small vascular bundles in maize leaf. Each bundle is surrounded by a layer of thin walled cells called bundle sheath. The cells of bundle sheath contain starch to serve as temporary storage cells.

The upper epidermis in the leaves of dicots lack stomata and chloroplast, while stomata are confined to lower epidermis. Therefore, dicot leaf is hypostomatic, i.e. stomata occur more on the lower side.

Statement (2) is incorrect as hypodermis of dicot stem is collenchymatous and of monocot is sclerenchymatous.

12 The annual rings are not formed in monocot stems because *(Chap 6, Class-XI, NCERT)*

(a) Cambium is present

(b) there is no secondary growth due to the absence of cambium

(c) Vascular bundle are not arranged in a ring

(d) All of the above

Ans. (b)

Exp. The annual rings are not formed in monocot stems because there is no secondary growth due to the absence of cambium. Annual rings are formed due to the activity of cambium.

Cambium is the meristematic layer responsible for cutting off vascular tissues–xylem and phloem. Initially, it is present in patches as a single layer between vascular bundles. Later during the development, it forms a complete ring.

13 Which of the following is not correct about the epithelial tissue ? *(Chap 6, Class-IX, NCERT)*

(a) It covers most organs and the cavities with in the body.

(b) They are loosely packed and form a continuous sheath.

(c) They have little intercellular space between them.

(d) It plays a role in exchange of material between the body and the external environment.

Ans. (b)

Exp. Statement (b) is not correct about the epithelial tissue as epithelial tissue cells are tightly packed and form a continuous sheath.

They have only a small amount of cementing material between them and almost no intercellular spaces. It covers most organs and cavities within the body. It also forms a barrier to keep different body systems separate. It also plays an important role in regulating the exchange of materials between the body and the external environment and also between different parts of the body. The skin, the lining of the mouth, the lining of blood vessels, lungs alveoli and kidney tubules are all made up of epithelial tissue.

14 Choose the incorrectly matched pair. *(Chap 6, Class -IX, NCERT)*

(a) Squamous epithelium – Walls of blood vessels and air sacs of lungs

(b) Cuboidal epithelium – Lining of kidney tubules

(c) Columnar epithelium – Lining of mouth

(d) Ciliated epithelium – Inner lining of bronchioles

Ans. (c)

Exp. Pair (c) is incorrectly matched as columnar epithelium form, the inner lining of the intestine and stomach and helps in secretion and absorption.

The columnar epithelium facilitates movement across the epithelial barrier. In the respiratory tract, the columnar epithelial tissue cells has cilia, which are hair-like projections on the outer surface of epithelial cells.

15 Match the following lists and choose the correct code. *(Chap 6, Class -IX, NCERT)*

	List I		List II
A.	Tendons	1.	Connects bone to bone.
B.	Areolar tissue	2.	Supports internal organs.
C.	Ligaments	3.	Storage of fats.
D.	Adipose tissue	4.	Connects muscles to bone.

Codes

	A	B	C	D		A	B	C	D
(a)	1	2	4	3	(b)	4	2	1	3
(c)	1	4	2	3	(d)	4	1	3	2

Ans. (b)

Exp. The correct matching is A-4, B -2, C -1, D -3.

Tendons - These are fibrous tissues that connect muscles to bones. They have great strength, but limited flexibility.

Areolar tissue - It is found between the skin and muscles, around blood vessels and nerves and in the bone marrow. It supports the internal organs and helps in repair of tissues.

Ligaments - These are bands of tough elastic tissues that connect two bones to each other. Ligaments contain, very little matrix.

Adipose tissue - It is found below the skin and between internal organs. Adipose tissue helps to store energy in the form of fat, cushion internal organs and insulate the body.

16 Consider the following statements about connective tissue. *(Chap 6, Class -IX, NCERT)*

1. Blood is the fluid connective tissue, which transports gases, hormones and waste material to different parts of the body.
2. Cartilage matrix is composed of calcium and phosphorus compound.
3. Bone is a strong and non-flexible tissue.

Which of the statement(s) given above is/are incorrect?

(a) 1 and 2 (b) 1 and 3

(c) Only 1 (d) Only 2

Ans. (d)

Exp. Statement (2) is incorrect because bone matrix is composed of calcium and phosphorus compounds. Cartilage matrix is composed of glycosaminoglycans, proteoglycans, collagen fibres and elastin.

17 Consider the following statements.

(Chap 6, Class -IX, NCERT)

1. Areolar connective tissue is found between the skin and muscles, around blood vessels and nerves and in the bone marrow.
2. Fat storing adipose tissue is found below the skin and between internal organs.

Which of the statement(s) given above is/are correct?

(a) Only 1 (b) Only 2
(c) Both 1 and 2 (d) Neither 1 nor 2

Ans. (c)

Exp. Both the statements (1) and (2) are correct.

Areolar connective tissue is found between the skin and muscles, around blood vessels and nerves and in the bone marrow. It contains fibroblasts macrophages and mast cells. It fills the space inside the organs, supports internal organs and helps in repair of tissues.

Fat storing adipose tissue is a type of loose connective tissue located mainly below the skin and between internal organs. The cells of this tissue are filled with fat globules. Storage of fats also lets it act as an insulator.

18 Consider the following pairs. *(Chap 6, Class -IX, NCERT)*

1. Skeletal muscles - voluntary muscles
2. Smooth muscles - voluntary muscles
3. Cardiac muscles - involuntary muscles

Which of the pairs given above is/are correctly matched?

(a) 1 and 2 (b) 2 and 3
(c) 1 and 3 (d) 1, 2 and 3

Ans. (c)

Exp. Pairs (1) and (3) are correctly matched.

Skeletal muscles, also called voluntary muscles are mostly attached to bones and helps in body movement.

These muscles are long cylindrical, unbranched and multinucleate. They are also called striated muscles.

Cardiac muscles, also called involuntary muscles present only in the heart. Heart muscles cells are cylindrical, branched and uninucleate. The muscles of the heart show rhythmic contraction and relaxation throughout life.

Pair (2) is incorrectly matched because smooth muscles are involuntary muscles. The smooth muscles fibres taper at both ends and do not show striations.

19 Which of the following statement is correct about muscular tissue ? *(Chap 6, Class -IX, NCERT)*

(a) Voluntary muscles also called skeletal muscles are long, cylindrical, unbranched and multinucleated.
(b) Smooth muscles are spindle-shaped and multinucleated.
(c) Cardiac muscles are unbranched and multinucleated.
(d) Voluntary muscles are skeletal muscles and smooth muscles.

Ans. (a)

Exp. Statement (a) is correct about muscular tissue. Skeletal muscles are called voluntary muscles. They are long, cylindrical, unbranched and multinucleated. They are closely attached to skeletal bones. They help in body movements and also protect the internal organs and tissues from any injury.

Statements (b), (c) and (d) are incorrect as smooth muscles are spindle-shaped and uninucleated. Cardiac muscles are cylindrical, branched and uninucleated. Voluntary muscles are skeletal muscles. Involuntary muscles include smooth muscles and cardiac muscles.

20 Choose the incorrect statement about the nervous tissue. *(Chap 6, Class -IX, NCERT)*

(a) Nervous tissue is made up of neurons that receive and conduct impulses.
(b) The brain, spinal cord and nerves are all composed of nervous tissue.
(c) A neuron consists of cell body axon and dendrites.
(d) The single long part is called dendrite and branched parts are called axons.

Ans. (d)

Exp. Statement (d) is incorrect about the nervous tissue. A neuron consists of a cell body with a nucleus and cytoplasm, from which long thin hair-like parts arise. Usually each neuron has a single long part, called the axon and many short, branched parts called dendrites. The main function of nervous tissue is to receive stimuli and send signals to the brain and spinal cord.

21 Match the following lists and choose the correct code. *(Chap 6, Class -IX, NCERT)*

	List I (Tissues)		List II (Parts of body)
A.	Epithelial tissue	1.	Bone
B.	Connective tissue	2.	Iris of the eye
C.	Muscular tissue	3.	Brain
D.	Nervous tissue	4.	Skin

Codes

	A	B	C	D		A	B	C	D
(a)	4	2	1	3	(b)	2	1	3	4
(c)	4	1	2	3	(d)	4	1	3	2

Ans. (c)

Exp. The correct matching is A-4, B-1, C-2, D-3.

Epithelial tissue - It forms the outer covering of the skin and also lines the body cavity. It forms the lining of respiratory, digestive, reproductive and excretory tracts.

Connective tissue - It is the most abundant tissue in the body. It performs special function of linking and supporting other tissue organs of the body. The different types of connective tissue are areolar tissue, adipose tissue, bone, cartilage and blood.

Muscular tissue - Smooth muscular tissues are found in the iris of the eye, in ureters and in the bronchi of the lungs.

Nervous tissue - It is found in the brain, spinal cord and nerves.

Chapter 04

Genetics

Genetics

Heredity and Inheritance

Gene

- Functional unit of heredity.

Heredity

- The process of transmission of traits or characters from parents to offspring.

Mendel's Laws of Inheritance

- Observed during experimenting with the pea plant.
- **Law of Dominance** In heterozygous condition only one member of a pair expresses itself.
- **Law of Segregation** Gamete receives only one of two factors.
- **Law of Independent Assortment** Segregation of one pair occurs independently of other.

Non-Mendelian Inheritance

- **Incomplete Dominance** Intermediate character between two parental characteristics. e.g. *Mirabilis*. Jalapa (4' O clock plant)
- **Co-dominance** Two alleles of gene are equally dominant and express themselves even when they are together. (e.g. ABO blood grouping in human)

Mutation

- Sudden heritable change in DNA sequence, which result in changes in the genotype and phenotype of an organism. It leads to variation.

Sex Determination

- Process by which sex of a newborn individual is determined.
- **ZZ- ZW type** ZZ (male)Homozygous, ZW (female) Heterozygous, e.g. Birds
- **XX-XY type** XX (female)XY (male), e.g. Human beings

Disorder and Genetic Code

Chromosomal Theory of Inheritance

- Chromosomes segregate at the time of gamete formation.

Genetic Disorders

- It is a condition that is caused by an abnormality in an individual's DNA.
- **Mendelian Disorders** Caused alternation or mutation in the single gene.
  - **Autosomal dominant** (e.g. Muscular dystrophy)
  - **Autosomal recessive** (e.g. Sickle cell anaemia)
  - **Sex-linked** (e.g. Haemophilia)
- **Chromosomal Disorders** A condition caused due to absence, excess or abnormal arrangement of one or more chromosomes. e.g. Down's Syndrome (trisomy of 21).

Genetic Code

- Sequence of nucleotides in mRNA that contains information for protein synthesis.

Human Genome Project (HGP)
[Mega Project launched in the 1990]

- To identify all the estimated gene in human DNA.
- To determine the sequence of the 3 billion base pairs.

DNA Fingerprinting

Technique used to identify individuals by characteristics of their DNA & is also called genetic fingerprinting.

- Variable Number Tandem Repeats are used as a genetic markers.

DNA and RNA

DNA

- Genetic material in most of the living organism. It is composed of sugar (deoxyribose), phosphate group and nitrogenous bases i.e.
  (i) **Purines** (Adenine, Guanine)
  (ii) **Pyrimidines** (Thymine, Cytosine)

DNA Replication

- DNA molecule produces exact copies of its own structure.
- Semi-conservative method of DNA replication.
- DNA molecule serve as template for the synthesis of new strand.

DNA Packaging

- Eight histone proteins form a histone octamer around which a negatively charged DNA is wrapped.

Central Dogma of Molecular Biology

$$\text{DNA} \underset{\text{Reverse transcription}}{\overset{\text{Transcription}}{\rightleftharpoons}} m\text{RNA} \xrightarrow{\text{Translation}} \text{Protein}$$

Replication

RNA

(First genetic material to be discovered)

- Consist of uracil in place of thymine as nitrogenous base.
- RNA occurs in three main types
  (i) ***r* RNA** Help in protein synthesis.
  (ii) ***t* RNA** Transfer specific amino acid which corresponds to mRNA sequence.
  (iii) ***m* RNA** Carries genetic information from DNA.

Gene Expression and Transcription

- It result in the formation of a polypeptide.
- RNA polymerase enzyme helps in the transfer of information from DNA strand to RNA.

SOURCE *New NCERT Class X (Heredity), New NCERT Class XII (Principles of Inheritance and Variation), New NCERT Class XII (Molecular Basis of Inheritance)*

1 Which of the following statement is incorrect? *(Chap 8, Class-X, NCERT)*

(a) Mendel performed his work on 'law of inheritance' on pea plant.
(b) Mendel is known as father of genetics.
(c) Mendel's inheritance pattern was based on sexual reproduction.
(d) Mendel's experiment ratio was 2 : 2.

Ans. (d)

Exp. Statement (d) is incorrect because the phenotypic ratio of Mendel's monohybrid cross was 3 : 1. From this ratio, law of dominance is derived.

This ratio was shown by the second filial generation of offspring from parents and involved single character. It suggested that dominant trait is present three times as often as recessive trait.

2 Match the following lists and choose the correct code. *(Chap 4, Class-XII, NCERT)*

List I		List II
A. Monohybrid cross	1.	T and t
B. Test cross	2.	TT
C. Alleles	3.	TT × tt
D. Homozygous tall	4.	Tt × tt

Codes

	A	B	C	D		A	B	C	D
(a)	1	4	2	3	(b)	3	4	1	2
(c)	4	3	1	2	(d)	3	4	2	1

Ans. (b)

Exp. The correct matching is A-3, B-4, C-1, D-2.

Monohybrid cross - It is a cross between two individuals with dominant, homozygous genotypes. It results in phenotypes having opposite genetic traits from each other.

Test cross - It is a cross done or made between F_1-generation and its pure recessive form.

Alleles - These are alternate form of a gene. These contribute to organisms phenotype.

Homozygous tall - Its trait is denoted by T and T alleles, whereas homozygous dwarf plant have genotype tt.

3 A married couple adopted a male child. A few years later, twin boys were born to them. The blood group of the couple is AB positive and O negative. The blood group of the three son is A positive, B positive and O positive. The blood group of the adopted son is *(Chap 4, Class-XII, NCERT) (IAS Pre 2011)*

(a) O positive
(b) A positive
(c) B positive
(d) Cannot be determined on the basis of the given data

Ans. (a)

Exp. In the given case, the blood group of the couple is AB positive and O negative, then their biological son blood group must be A or B. Hence, we can say that the blood group of the adopted son is O positive.

Blood group were discovered in the 20th century by Karl Landsteiner. The RBCs had specific substances on their surface. The two important blood group classification in humans are the ABO and the Rh systems.

4 Which one of the following is caused by the expression of a recessive gene present on sex chromosome? *(Chap 4, Class-XII, NCERT) (IAS Pre 1994)*

(a) Rheumatism
(b) Nervous shock
(c) Muscular dystrophy
(d) Cerebral haemorrhage

Ans. (c)

Exp. Muscular dystrophy is caused by a recessive gene present on X-chromosome (i.e. one of the sex-chromosome found in humans). A person with this disease has genotype $44 + X^mX^m$ or $44 + X^mY$. In muscular dystrophy, abnormal genes interfere with the production of proteins needed to form healthy muscle. It is an inheritable disease.

5 Haemophilia is a genetic disease carried by *(Chap 5, Class-XII, NCERT) (IAS Pre 1993)*

(a) women, appear in women.
(b) women, appear in men.
(c) men, appear in women.
(d) men, appear in men.

Ans. (b)

Exp. Haemophilia is a genetic disease carried by women and it appears in men. It is a sex-linked recessive disease in which clotting of blood takes a long time in a patient (up to 24 hours) due to lack of thromboplastin protein in blood plasma.

Women carry it while it appears in men (because men have one X-chromosome but women have two). It is also called bleeder's disease, which was first found in Queen Victoria, so it is also known as royal haemophilia.

6 In the context of genetic disorder, consider the following. *(Chap 4, Class-XII, NCERT) (IAS Pre 2009)*

A woman suffers from colour blindness, while her husband does not suffer from it. They have a son and a daughter.

Which one of the following statements is most probably correct ?

(a) Both children will suffer from colour blindness.
(b) Daughter will suffer from colour blindness, while son will not suffer from it.
(c) Both children will not suffer from colour blindness.
(d) Son will suffer from colour blindness, while daughter will not suffer from it.

Ans. (d)

Exp. In the given context, statement (d) is correct. If a colourblind woman marries a normal man, their sons will be colourblind, while daughters will be carrier.

Colour blindness is inherited in an X-linked recessive pattern. The genes are located on the X-chromosome which is one of the two sex-chromosomes.

In males (who have only one X-chromosome) one genetic change in each cell is sufficient to cause the condition. Males are affected by X-linked recessive disorders much more frequently than females. A characteristics of X-linked inheritance is that father cannot pass X-linked traits to their sons.

7 Phenylketonuria (PKU) is an example of an inborn error of metabolism. This error refers to *(Chap 4, Class-XII, NCERT) (IAS Pre 1993)*

(a) hormonal overproduction
(b) atrophy of endocrine glands
(c) inherited lack of enzyme
(d) non-disjunction

Ans. (c)

Exp. Phenylketonuria (PKU) is a disease caused by a metabolic disorder inherited due to lack of enzyme as a recessive trait. The dominant gene 'P', in this case, codes for the enzyme, phenylalanine hydroxylase, formed in the liver cells. This enzyme catalyses conversion of phenylalanine to tyrosine.

In homozygous recessive genotypes, the absence of this enzyme causes a high level of phenylalanine in blood and tissues fluids. The phenotypic effects include a progressive mental retardation starting a few month after birth, seizures, and anomalies of teeth enamel and bones.

8 Down's syndrome is a genetic disorder, which is caused due to change in the *(Chap 4, Class-XII, NCERT)*

(a) number of the chromosome
(b) structure of the chromosome
(c) structure of DNA
(d) structure of RNA

Ans. (a)

Exp. Down's syndrome is a genetic disorder, which is caused due to change in the number of chromosomes. In this, 21st pair of chromosome are 3 instead of 2. So, the chromosome group is 2X + 1 (chromosome number 21) = 47. This syndrome is also known as Mongolian idiocy.

9 Identify the mismatched pair of disease and its related symptom. *(Chap 4, Class-XII, NCERT)*

(a) Phenylketonuria – Urine turns black when exposed to air
(b) Down's syndrome – Physical and mental retardation
(c) Klinefelter's syndrome – Sterile males
(d) Turner's syndrome – Sterile females

Ans. (a)

Exp. Pair (a) is the mismatched pair.

Phenylketonuria is an inherited error of metabolism which is caused by deficiency of phenylalanine hydroxylase that converts phenylalanine to tyrosine. The deficiency of this enzyme (Phenylalanine hydroxylase) leads to an over production of phenylalanine that accumulates in the cerebrospinal fluid, resulting in mental retardation.

10 Match the following lists and choose the correct code. *(Chap 4, Class-XII, NCERT)*

List I	List II
A. Turner's syndrome	1. Autosomal recessive trait
B. Klinefelter's syndrome	2. Change in α and β-chains of haemoglobin
C. Thalassemia	3. Increase in chromosome number
D. Sickle-cell anaemia	4. Decrease in chromosome number

Codes

	A	B	C	D		A	B	C	D
(a)	4	3	2	1	(b)	1	2	3	4
(c)	3	1	4	2	(d)	2	4	1	3

Ans. (a)

Exp. The correct matching is A-4, B-3, C-2, D-1.

Turner's syndrome In this syndrome there is decrease in number of chromosomes from 44 + XX to 44 + XO. It is a condition that affects only female and results when one of the X-chromosome is partly or completely missing.

Klinefelter's syndrome There is increase in chromosome numbers from 44 + XY to 44 + XXY. In this syndrome, there is an additional copy of X-chromosome. Thus, the affected male is sterile.

Thalassemia It is caused due to the change in α and β-chains of haemoglobin. It is a blood disorder characterised by abnormal haemoglobin production.

Sickle-cell anaemia It is an autosomal recessive trait in which RBCs' shape becomes sickle-like. The cells die early, leaving a shortage of healthy red blood cells (sickle-cell anaemia) and can block blood flow causing pain (sickle-cell crisis).

11 Consider the following. *(Chap 4, Class-XII, NCERT), (Chap 25, Module-5, NIOS)*

1. Haemophilia
2. Cystic fibrosis
3. Sickle-cell anaemia
4. Down's syndrome

How many of the above are Mendelian disorders?

(a) Only one (b) Only two (c) Only three (d) All

Ans. (c)

Exp. Only three from the above are Mendelian disorders. Haemophilia, cystic fibrosis and sickle-cell anaemia are examples of Mendelian disorders in human.

Mendelian disorders are the genetic disorders caused at single genetic locus.

Haemophilia is a type of sex-linked recessive disorders.

Cystic fibrosis and sickle-cell anaemia are a type of autosomal recessive disorder.

Down's syndrome is genetic disorder appeared due to the presence of trisomy in chromosome 21. It is also known as non-Mendelian inheritance.

12 Choose the correct matched pair.

(a) Unit of heredity – DNA *(Chap 5, Class-XII, NCERT)*
(b) A segment of DNA – RNA
(c) The sugar present in DNA – Ribose
(d) Double helical structure of DNA – Watson and Crick

Ans. (d)

Exp. Option (d) is the correct matched Pair. (a), (b) and (c) are incorrectly matched and can be corrected as A gene is the basic physical and functional unit of heredity. Genes are made up of DNA. Also we can say that gene is the segment of DNA that codes for a functional protein. Genes are inherited from parents to offspring. They carry genetic information from one generation to another.

The sugar in DNA is deoxyribose, which contains one less hydroxyl group than RNA's ribose. The bases in DNA are adenine, thymine, guanine and cytosine.

13 Consider the following statements. *(Chap 5, Class-XII, NCERT)*

1. The pyrimidines found in RNA are thymine and guanine.
2. The genomic RNA is double-stranded in wound tumour virus and reovirus.
3. The genome of virus in corona virus is single-stranded RNA.

Which of the statements given above is/are incorrect about RNA?

(a) 1 and 2 (b) 1 and 3 (c) Only 1 (d) Only 2

Ans. (c)

Exp. Statement (1) is incorrect for RNA as the pyrimidines in RNA are guanine and uracil. The given pyrimidines which are thymine and guanine are present in DNA. Rest of the statements are correct.

14 Identify the incorrect statement with respect to RNA. *(Chap 5, Class-XII, NCERT)*

(a) Cytosine is common to both DNA and RNA.
(b) RNA was the first genetic material.
(c) RNA being a catalyst, is less reactive than DNA and hence more stable.
(d) RNA has uracil in place of thymine.

Ans. (c)

Exp. Statement (c) is incorrect. RNA acts as a catalyst, is highly reactive and hence unstable.

Statements (a), (b) and (d) are correct.

Cytosine falls in the category of pyrimidines and is present in both DNA and RNA.

It was the first genetic material that also worked as a catalyst. It has uracil in place of thymine, just contrary to what is present in DNA.

15 Nobel Prize winning scientist James Dewey Watson is known for his work in which area ? *(Chap 5, Class-XII, NCERT) (IAS Pre 2008)*

(a) Metallurgy (b) Meteorology
(c) Environmental protection (d) Genetics

Ans. (d)

Exp. Nobel Prize winning scientist James Dewey Watson is known for his work in genetics.

He was an American molecular biologist, geneticist and zoologist, best-known as one of the co-discoverers of the structure (double helix model) of DNA in 1953 with Francis Crick. Watson, Crick and Maurice Wilkins were awarded with a Nobel Prize in 1962 in Physiology or Medicine for their discoveries concerning the molecular structure of nucleic acids and its significance for information transfer in living material.

16 Who discovered the principle of jumping genes? *(Chap 5, Class-XII, NCERT) (IAS Pre 1993)*

(a) Gregor Johann Mendel (b) Thomas Hunt Morgan
(c) Barbara McClintock (d) Watson and Crick

Ans. (c)

Exp. Barbara McClintock discovered the principle of jumping genes. She found in her study that there are some spots on the grains of corn by the hereditary changes done by jumping genes. Then the conclusion was given that every cell has the part of DNA (transposon) which are important in development.

17 Arrange the following in order of accuracy needed to perform the process given below. *(Chap 5, Class-XII, NCERT)*

1. Replication 2. Transcription 3. Translation

Codes

(a) $1 > 2 > 3$ (b) $3 > 2 > 1$ (c) $1 > 3 > 2$ (d) $2 > 1 > 3$

Ans. (a)

Exp. The correct sequence of process occurring in the cell are replication, transcription and translation.

During replication, DNA is copied, during transcription, the *m*RNA is formed on DNA and during translation, protein synthesised by using the codes present on *m*RNA.

18 'Microsatellite DNA' is used in the case of which one of the following? *(Chap 5, Class-XII, NCERT), (Chap 25, Module-5, NIOS)*

(a) Studying the evolutionary relationships among various species of fauna
(b) Stimulating 'stem cells' transform into diverse functional tissue
(c) Promoting clonal propagation of horticulture plants
(d) Assessing the efficacy of drugs by conducting series of drug trials in a population

Ans. (a)

Exp. 'Microsatellite DNA' is used in studying the evolutionary relationships among various species of fauna. Microsatellite DNA also known as Short Tandem Repeats (STRs), is a type of repetitive DNA sequence composed of short repeated units. It is widely used in molecular biology and genetics for various applications. By analysing the variation in microsatellite DNA sequence among different individuals or species scientists can gain insights into genetic diversity, population structure and evolutionary history.

Evolution

Evolution

Origin of Life and Theory of Organic Evolution

- **Evolution**
  - Sequence of gradual changes occuring from simple life forms to complex life forms.
- **Origin of life**
  - **Biogenesis** Life originates from pre-existing life.
  - **Spontaneous generation** Life came out from dead and decaying matter.
  - **Cosmozic theory / Panspermia** The unit of life (spores) were transferred to earth.
  - **Big Bang Theory** states that life has originated due to great explosion, hydrogen and helium came into existence.
  - **Chemical Evolution Theory** states that life has originated from non-living inorganic and organic molecules.
- **Organic Evolution**
  - Evolution that occurs in an individual organism over time and results in genetic alterations in a species or within a group of species.
- **Theories of Organic Evolution**
  - **Lamarckism** Inheritance of acquired character use of organ, e.g. Neck of giraffe.
  - **Neo-Lamarckism** Focuses on the direct effect of environmental change, only germ cells modification are transferred to next generation.
  - **Darwinism** Natural Selection, Limited Natural Resource. Struggle for existence, survival of fittest.
  - **Neo-Darwinism** Dissimilarities among offsprings of sexually reproducing organism occur by mutation.
  - **Theories of Mutation** Proposed by **Hugo de Vries**. Mutation are sudden change which occur in DNA sequence.

Evidence Organic Evolution

- **Fossils**
  - Traces of living organisms that lived millions of years ago, e.g., dead insects carried in hot mud.
  - **Petrified Fossils** (e.g. Teeth)
  - **Mould Fossils** (e.g. Jelly fishes)
  - **Unaltered Fossils** (e.g. Mammoths)
  - **Compressed Fossils** (e.g. Plant fossils)
  - **Print Fossils** (e.g. Mollusc shells).
- **Morphology & Comparative Anatomy**
  - **Homologous Organs**
    - Same structure, but have different function, e.g. Forelimb of man and cat.
  - **Analogous Organs**
    - Same function but have different structure. e.g. Wings of insects and bird etc.
  - **Vestigial Organs**
    - Non-functional organs in animals but were functional in their ancestors. e.g. Vermiform appendix.
  - **Atavism**
    - Reappearance of certain ancestral characters. e.g. Power of moving pinna in humans.

Speciation and Human Evolution

- **Speciation**
  - It is defined as the evolutionary formation of new biological species.
  - **Factors Causing Speciation**
    - **Gene Flow** Movement of genes, occurs when inbreeding continues and it lead to production of more generations.
    - **Genetic Drift** Random change in frequency of genes in a population.
    - **Natural Selection** Organism that are more adapted to their environment are more likely to survive.
- **Human Evolution**
  - **Human Ancestors**
    - ***Dryopithecus and Ramapithecus*** Hairy and walked like Gorillas.
    - ***Australopithecus africans*** hunt with stone and ate fruits.
    - ***Homo habilis***
  - First human like Organism.
    - ***Homo erectus***
  - Did not eat meat, brain capacity: 650-680 cc.
    - ***Homo sapiens neanderthalenis***
  - Hide to protect their body, brain capacity: 1400 cc.
    - ***Homo sapiens***
  - Skeletal remains, appearance of modern man's chin and rounded skill brain capacity: 1350 cc.

SOURCE *New NCERT Class X* (Heredity), *New NCERT Class XII* (Evolution),

1 **'*Archaeopteryx*' is a connecting link between which of the following classes of animal?**

(Chap 6, Class-XII, NCERT) (RAS/RTS Pre 2008)

(a) Amphibia and Aves
(b) Reptilia and Aves
(c) Reptilia and Mammalia
(d) Aves and Mammalia

Ans. (b)

Exp. '*Archaeopteryx*' is a connecting link between Reptilia and Aves. It is a creature in which we found the character of both reptiles and birds. It is one of the oldest known birds. It is the first bird modified from reptiles.

2 **The book on, '*The Origin of Species*' was written by**

(Chap 6, Class-XII, NCERT) (BPSC Pre 2019)

(a) Linnaeus
(b) Lamarck
(c) Mendel
(d) Darwin

Ans. (d)

Exp. The book on '*The Origin of Species*' (1859); was written by Charles Darwin. In this, he explained natural selection.

The book by favoured races in the struggle for life means of natural selection or the preservation.

It is considered to be the foundation of evolutionary biology.

3 **Choose the incorrectly matched pair.**

(Chap 6, Class-XII, NCERT)

(a) Wings of insects and birds – Analogous organs
(b) Forelimb of human and frog – Homologous organs
(c) Pelvic girdle in human – Vestigial organ
(d) Occurs due to natural selection – Variation

Ans. (c)

Exp. Pair (c) is matched incorrectly as vestigial organs. These organs were functional in primitive times by the species, but now they do not have any functional role, e.g. nictitating membrane, vermiform appendix, etc., in human. Pelvic girdle is not a vestigial organ.

4 **Darwin's theory of natural selection is based on**

(Chap 6, Class-XII, NCERT) (MPPSC Pre 1997)

(a) overproduction
(b) struggle for existence and variation
(c) survival of the fittest
(d) All of the above

Ans. (d)

Exp. Darwin's theory (1859) of natural selection is based on three principles, i.e., over-production (i.e. number of offspring produced is greater in number), struggle for existence and variation among the members and survival of the fittest individual during unfavourable conditions.

It states that the organisms change with time due to the changes in physical and behavioural traits, which are inherited over generations.

5 **Match the following and select the correct answer using the code given below.**

(Chap 6, Class-XII, NCERT) (IAS Pre 1998)

List I		List II	
A.	Theory of mutation	1.	Beadle and Tatum
B.	Theory of evolution	2.	Jacob and Monod
C.	One gene one enzyme hypothesis	3.	Darwin
D.	Operon concept	4.	de Vries

Codes

	A	B	C	D		A	B	C	D
(a)	3	4	1	2	(b)	4	3	1	2
(c)	4	3	2	1	(d)	3	4	2	1

Ans. (b)

Exp. The correct matching is A-4, B-3, C-1, D-2.

Theory of mutation - It was given by Hugo de Vries. According to his idea, new species are formed from the sudden and unexpected emergence of alternation in their defining traits.

Theory of evolution - It was given by Darwin. It states that evolution happens by natural selection.

One gene one enzyme hypothesis - It was proposed by George Beadle and Edward Tatum, is the idea that each gene is responsible for producing a single enzyme that in turn affects a single step in a metabolic pathway.

Operon concept - It was proposed by French microbiologists Jacob and Jacques Monod in 1960s. It explains the regulation of gene action.

6 **Consider the following statements.**

(Chap 6, Class-XII, NCERT)

1. JBS Haldane suggested that life must have developed from a simple inorganic molecules.
2. The first primitive organisms would arise from further chemical synthesis of organic molecules.
3. The condition on primitive Earth were high temperature and oxygen.

Which of the statement(s) given above is/are correct?

(a) Only 3 (b) 2 and 3 (c) 1 and 2 (d) 1 and 3

Ans. (c)

Exp. Statements (1) and (2) are correct as

JBS Haldane, a British scientist suggested in 1929 that life must have developed from simple inorganic molecules, which were present on Earth soon after it was formed. He speculated that the conditions on Earth at that time, which were far from the conditions we see today, could have given rise to more complex organic molecules that were necessary for life. The first primitive organisms would arise from further chemical synthesis.

Statement (3) is incorrect because the conditions on primitive Earth were high temperature, volcanic storms, reducing atmosphere containing CH_3, NH_3, etc., but no oxygen.

7 **Consider the following statements about Miller's experiment.** *(Chap 6, Class-XII, NCERT)*

1. Miller created chemical discharge in a closed flask.
2. He observed formation of new organisms.
3. Flask contained water vapour at 800°C.
4. At the end of a week, 15% of the carbon (from methane) had been converted to simple compounds of hydrogen.

Which of the statement(s) given above is/are incorrect?

(a) 1, 2 and 3 (b) Only 2 (c) Only 4 (d) 2 and 4

Ans. (b)

Exp. Statement (2) is incorrect about Miller's experiment as in 1953, SL Miller created conditions similar to primitive earth in a laboratory scale.

He created electric discharge in a closed flask containing CH_4, H_2, NH_3 and water vapour at 800°C. He observed formation of amino acids. At the end of a week, 15% of the carbon (from methane) had been converted to simple compounds of carbon including amino acids, which make up protein molecules.

8 **Consider the following Assertion (A) and Reason (R) and choose the correct code.** *(Chap 8, Class-X, NCERT)*

Assertion (A) All the variations in a species do not have equal chances of surviving in the environment.

Reason (R) Only variations that confer an advantage to an individual organism will survive in a population.

Codes

(a) Both A and R are true and R is the correct explanation of A.
(b) Both A and R are true, but R is not the correct explanation of A.
(c) A is true, but R is false.
(d) Both A and R are false.

Ans. (a)

Exp. Both Assertion (A) and Reason (R) are true and Reason (R) is the correct explanation of Assertion (A).

All the variations in a species do not have equal chances of surviving in the environment. Depending on the nature of variations different individuals would have different kind of advantages. Selection of variants by environment factors forms the basis of evolutionary process. The variations which prove disadvantageous to an individual organism will not survive because the environment factors cannot support it.

9 **Which of the following statements is not true with respect to variations?** *(Chap 8, Class-X, NCERT)*

(a) All variations in a species have equal chance of survival.
(b) Change in genetic composition results in variation.
(c) Selection of variants by environmental factors forms the basis of evolutionary process.
(d) Variation is minimum in asexual reproduction.

Ans. (a)

Exp. Statement (a) is not true with respect to variations. All variations in a species do not have equal chances of survival as only those variations get pass on to the next generation which were favourable during the course of natural selection.

Variations are a result of change in genetic composition. Only variations which are advantageous, get selected by environment, since changes in DNA contribute wholly to the process, variation is least in asexual reproduction.

10 **Which of the following is important for speciation ?** *(Chap 6, Class-XII, NCERT) (Chap 1, Module-1, NIOS) (Mizoram PCS Pre 2023)*

(a) Seasonal isolation
(b) Reproductive isolation
(c) Behavioural isolation
(d) Temporal isolation

Ans. (b)

Exp. Reproductive isolation is important for speciation. It is a process in which two populations of a species are prevented from interbreeding among themselves and this leads to the origin of new species.

11 **According to evolutionary theory formation of a new species is generally due to** *(Chap 6, Class-XII, NCERT)*

(a) sudden creation of nature.
(b) accumulation of variations over several generations.
(c) clones formed during sexual reproduction.
(d) movement of individuals from one habitat to another.

Ans. (b)

Exp. According to evolutionary theory, formation of a new species is generally due to the accumulation of variations over several generations.

These variations keep on adding up in organisms and ultimately leads to evolution of a new species.

12 **What does micro-evolution mean?** *(Chap 6, Class-XII, NCERT)*

(a) Changes are small, even though they are significant.
(b) Changes should be more to create an impact.
(c) Changes in non-reproductive tissues cause evolution.
(d) Changes in reproductive tissues cause evolution.

Ans. (a)

Exp. Micro-evolution means that changes are small, even though they are significant enough to cause evolution. Also, they simply change the common characteristics of a particular species.

Micro-evolution is the change in allele frequencies that occurs over time within a population.

This change is due to four different processes, i.e. mutation, selection, gene flow and genetic drift.

Micro-evolution may lead to speciation, which provides the raw material for macro-evolution.

13 Choose the correct order of given geological periods, oldest one will come first.

(Chap 6, Class-XII, NCERT) (Chap 20, Module-5, NIOS)

(a) Devonian > Triassic > Jurassic > Carboniferous
(b) Devonian > Triassic > Carboniferous > Jurassic
(c) Devonian > Carboniferous > Triassic > Jurassic
(d) Carboniferous > Triassic > Devonian > Jurassic

Ans. (c)

Exp. The correct sequence or order of given geological periods starting from oldest will be

Devonian > Carboniferous > Triassic > Jurassic

Devonian period often called the age of fishes'. It's known for the diversification of fish, the first appearance of amphibians and the spread of forests of land.

Carboniferous period, it is characterised by extensive coal farming forests, the emergence of reptiles and the evolution of amphibians.

Triassic period, it marks beginning of the Mesozoic era. It is known for the rise of the dinosaurs the diversification of reptiles.

Jurassic period, it is renowned for the dominance of dinosaurs, including specing like *Stegosaurus, Brachiosaurus* and Allosaurus. It is a fascinating time in Earths history, known for its lost landscapes and diverse fauna.

14 Dinosaurs were ***(Chap 6, Class-XII, NCERT) (UP UDA/LDA Pre 2001)***

(a) Cenozoic reptiles
(b) Mesozoic birds
(c) Paleozoic amphibians
(d) Mesozoic reptiles

Ans. (d)

Exp. The Mesozoic era is the age of the dinosaurs and lasted almost 180 million years from approximately 250 to 65 million years ago. This era includes three well known periods, called the Triassic, Jurassic and Cretaceous periods.

15 Some dinosaurs had feathers although they could not fly, but birds have feathers that help them to fly. In the context of evolution this means that

(Chap 6, Class-XII, NCERT)

(a) reptiles have evolved from birds.
(b) there is no evolutionary connection between reptiles and birds.
(c) feathers are homologous structures in both the organisms.
(d) birds have evolved from reptiles.

Ans. (d)

Exp. Some dinosaurs had feathers, but they could not fly using them. Feathers have evolved to provide insulation in cold weather, but later were adopted to be used for flight in animals like birds. Thus, we can infer that birds are very closely related to reptiles, since dinosaurs were reptiles.

Chapter 06

Plant Morphology and Physiology

Plant Morphology and Physology

Plant Morphology

Plant Morphology

- Study of outer forms and features of plant organs like roots, stem etc.

Root

Descending portion

- Positively geotropic.
- **Functions of Root** Storage of food; provides fixation to the plants with, soil absorption and transportation of water and mineral salts.
- **Types of Roots**

(i) Tap root Develops from radicle and found in dicot plants. e.g. Carrot.

(ii) Adventitious Root Develops from any part of plant except radicle. e.g. Maize.

Stem

- Ascending organ, developed from plumule, positively phototropic and negatively geotropic.
- **Functions of Stem** Helps in vegetative propagation. Conduction of water and mineral nutrients.
- **Types of stem**
  - **Aerial Stem** Grows above the soil. e.g. Lemons.
  - **Sub-Aerial Stem** Creeps on the ground. e.g. Grass.
  - **Underground Stem** Grows inside the soil. e.g. Banana, etc.
- **Modifications of Stem**
  - **Underground** Corm, etc.
  - **Sub-Aerial** Offset, etc
  - **Aerial** Bulb, etc.

Leaf

- It consists of chlorophyll to perform photosynthesis & have limited growth.
- **Functions of Leaf** Performs photosynthesis, acts as site of transpiration storage of food, protection of buds.
- **Modification of Leaf**
  - **Leaf Hooks** (e.g. *Doxantha*)
  - **Leaf Bladders** (e.g. Bladderwort)
  - **Phyllodes** (e.g. *Acacia Melanoxylon*)
  - **Scale leaves** (e.g. *Garlic*)
  - **Coloured leaves** (e.g. *Poinsettia*)

Flower

- Reproductive structure in angiospermic plants.
- **Parts of Flower**
  - Calyx (sepals)
  - Corolla (Petals)
  - Androecium (male reproductive part)
  - Gynoecium (female reproductive part)

Inflorescence

- Arrangement and distribution of flower over a plant.
  - Racemose & Cymose inflorescence are two type of inflorescence

Fruit

- Mature or ripened ovary, developed after fertilisation
  - **True fruits** (e.g. Mango)
  - **False fruits** (e.g. Apple)
  - **Parthenocarpic fruits** (e.g. Banana)

Seed (Ripened Ovule)

- Seed coat
- Endosperm
- Cotyledons
- Embryo

Plant Physiology

Transport in Plants

- Transport of water & minerals, translocation of organic solutes, mineral nutrition in plants.

Photosynthesis in Plants

- Absorption of light energy by chlorophyll.
- Conversion of light into chemical energy.

Respiration in Plants

- Process of biochemical oxidation of nutrients in the presence of specific enzymes to release energy for metabolic activities.

Excretion in Plant

- Respiration [Gaseous waste like CO_2 and O_2]
- Transpiration [resins and gums],Cell

Plant Hormones

- Chemical messengers present in plant which control and coordinate in them.
  - **Auxin (IAA)** Apical dominance
  - **Cytokinin (Zeatin)** Delay senescence
  - **Gibberllins (GA)** Breaking dormancy
  - **Ethylene (gaseous)** Fruits ripening
  - **Abscisic acid (Stress Hormone)** Promotes abscission

Coordination in Plants

- Occurence of movement of plant either towards stimulus or away from it is called directional or tropic movement.

Reproduction in Plants

- Flowers perform the functions or reproduction in plants.
- **Asexual** Vegetative propagation
- **Sexual** Gametogenesis→Pollination→Fertilisation→Fruit and seed formation.

SOURCE **New NCERT Class VI** *(Getting to Know Plants),* **New NCERT Class VII** *(Nutrition in Plants), (Respiration in Organisms), (Transportation in Animals and Plants), (Reproduction in Plants),* **New NCERT Class X** *(Life Processes), (Control and Coordination),* **Old NCERT Class XI** *(Transport in Plants), (Mineral Nutrition),* **New NCERT Class XI** *(Morphology of Flowering Plants), (Photosynthesis in Higher Plants), (Respiration in Plants), (Plant Growth & Development),* **Old NCERT Class XII** *(Reproduction in Organisms),* **New NCERT Class XII** *(Sexual Reproduction in Flowering Plants),* **Tamil Nadu Board Class X** *(Plant Anatomy and Plant Physiology)*

1 **Match the following lists and choose the correct code.** *(Chap 4, Class-VI, NCERT)*

	List I		List II
A.	Herbs	1.	Plants with weak stems that cannot stand upright, but spread on the ground.
B.	Shrubs	2.	Plants with weak stems that take support and climb up.
C.	Trees	3.	Plants with green tender stem, usually short.
D.	Creepers	4.	Plants develop branches near the base of stem. The stem is hard, but not very thick.
E.	Climbers	5.	Plants are very tall and have hard and thick stem.

Codes

	A	B	C	D	E
(a)	3	4	5	1	2
(b)	1	2	3	4	5
(c)	4	3	2	1	5
(d)	5	1	2	4	3

Ans. (a)

Exp. The correct matching is A-3, B-4, C-5, D-1, E-2.

Plants with green and tender stems are called herbs. They are usually short and may not have many branches.

Some plants develop branches near the base of stem. The stem is hard, but not very thick. Such plants are called shrubs.

Some plants are very tall and have hard and thick stem. The stems have branches in the upper part, much above the ground. Such plants are called trees.

Plants with weak stems that cannot stand upright, but spread on the ground are called creepers, while those that take support and climb up are called climbers.

2 **Choose the incorrectly matched pairs about anatomy of leaf.** *(Chap 4, Class-VI, NCERT)*

1. Part of leaf by which it is attached to the stem – Lamina
2. The broad green part of leaf – Veins
3. Lines on the leaf – Midrib
4. A prominent line in the middle of the leaf – Petiole

Codes

(a) 1 and 2 (b) 3 and 4
(c) 1, 3 and 4 (d) 1, 2, 3 and 4

Ans. (d)

Exp. All the pairs, i.e., 1, 2, 3 and 4 are incorrectly matched about anatomy of leaf. The part of leaf by which it is attached to the stem is called the petiole.

The broad green part of the leaf is called lamina. The lines on the leaf lamina are called veins. A prominent line in the middle (median vein) of the leaf is called midrib.

It produces thinner lateral veins which in turn branch to form veinlets. The lamina is the site of photosynthesis, transpiration and other metabolic activities.

3 **Which of the following statements are correct?** *(Chap 4, Class-VI, NCERT)*

(a) The design made by veins in a leaf is called the leaf venation.
(b) Net-like design on both sides of midrib, the venation is called reticulate.
(c) When the veins of leaves are parallel to one another, it is called parallel venation.
(d) All of the above

Ans. (d)

Exp. All the statements are correct.

Venation is the arrangement of veins in the blade of a leaf. The veins are composed of vascular tissues which are vital for the transport of food and water. If the design is net-like on both sides of midrib, is called reticulate venation. For example, coriander, rose, oak, etc.

If the design made by veins is parallel to one another in a leaf, it is called parallel venation. For example, grass, wheat, maize, etc.

4 **The part of root that increases the surface area of root for the absorption of water and mineral nutrients dissolved in water is** *(Chap 7, Class-VII, NCERT)*

(a) Xylem (b) Root hairs
(c) Phloem (d) Vascular tissue

Ans. (b)

Exp. Plants absorb water and minerals by the roots. The roots have hair. The root hairs increase the surface area of the root for the absorption of water and mineral nutrients dissolved in water. The root hair is in contact with the water present between the soil particles.

5 **Choose the incorrectly matched pair.** *(Chap 8, Class-VII, NCERT)*

1. Vegetative parts – Root, stems and leaves
2. Reproductive part – Flowers
3. Reproductive organs – Stamen, pistil

Codes

(a) 1 and 2 (b) 2 and 3
(c) 1, 2 and 3 (d) None of these

Ans. (d)

Exp. All the pairs are correctly matched.

The vegetative parts of plants are root, stems and leaves. These are not involved in reproduction. Reproductive part of plant is flower. These flowers contain reproductive organs, i.e., stamen and pistil which help in producing male and female gametes for reproduction in plants.

6 **Match the following lists and choose the correct code.** *(Chap 8, Class-VII, NCERT)*

List I (Vegetative propagation)	List II (Examples)
A. By leaf buds	1. Potato
B. By cutting	2. Rose
C. By eye bud	3. *Bryophyllum*

Codes

	A	B	C		A	B	C
(a)	1	2	3	(b)	3	2	1
(c)	1	3	2	(d)	2	1	3

Ans. (b)

Exp. The correct matching is A-3, B-2, C-1.

Bryophyllum has buds on the margins of leaves. These buds can germinate into new *Bryophyllum* plant.

Cutting of rose or champa with a node can be sown into soil and develops root. This cutting then forms a completely new plant.

Potato can be vegetatively propagated by the scars called as eyes present on them.

7 **The upward and downward growth of shoots and roots can be towards** *(Chap 6, Class-X, NCERT)*

(a) gravity (b) water
(c) chemical (d) All of these

Ans. (d)

Exp. The upward and downward growth of shoots and roots towards gravity, called geotropism, towards water called hydrotropism and towards chemicals called chemotropism.

Tropisms or tropic movements are growth movements of a plant parts in response to an external stimulus in which the direction of stimulus determines the direction of response.

8 **Which of the following statements are correct for chlorophyll?** *(Chap 1, Class-VII, NCERT)*

1. It is a green coloured pigment.
2. It helps capture the energy of sunlight.
3. It is present in mitochondria of leaves.

Codes

(a) 1 and 2 (b) 2 and 3
(c) 1 and 3 (d) 1, 2 and 3

Ans. (a)

Exp. Statements (1) and (2) are correct for chlorophyll. It is a pigment that give plants a green colour and it help plants to prepare their own food by capturing sunlight during photosynthesis.

Statement (3) is incorrect because chlorophyll is present in chloroplast of all photosynthetic organisms including green plants, cyanobacteria and algae.

9 **Consider the following statements and choose the incorrect one.** *(Chap 1, Class-VII, NCERT)*

(a) Component of food necessary for our body are nutrients.
(b) Some plants are heterotrophs.
(c) The mode of nutrition in which organisms make food by themselves from simple substances is called autotrophic.
(d) CO_2 from air is taken in through the tiny pores present on the leaves called guard cells.

Ans. (d)

Exp. Statement (d) is incorrect because during gaseous exchange in plants, the 'in' and 'out' of carbon dioxide and oxygen occur by the tiny pores present on the leaves called the stomata. These pores are enclosed by special cells called guard cells which are kidney-shaped in dicots and dumb-bell shaped in monocots.

10 **Consider the following plants.** *(Chap 8, Class-VII, NCERT) (IAS Pre 2002)*

1. *Bougainvillea* 2. Carnation
3. Cocoa 4. Grapes

Which of these plants are propagated by stem cuttings?

(a) 1 and 2 (b) 2, 3 and 4
(c) 1, 2 and 4 (d) 1, 2, 3 and 4

Ans. (d)

Exp. All the given plants can be propagated by stem cuttings. Propagation of plants by stem cutting is the most popular plant propagation method for woody shrubs and ornamental plants.

This is also a good technique for house plants. Some of the plants propagated by stem cuttings are sugarcane, grapes, rose, cocoa, carnation, *Duranta, Bougainvillea,* etc. Although in plants like cocoa, propagation by seeds is also popular.

11 **Match the following lists and choose the correct code.** *(Chap 1, Class-XII, NCERT) (CGPSC Pre 2013)*

List I	List II
A. Rhizome	1. Garlic
B. Tuber	2. Jimikand or Suran
C. Bulb	3. Ginger
D. Corm	4. Potato

Codes

	A	B	C	D
(a)	1	2	3	4
(b)	3	4	2	1
(c)	3	4	1	2
(d)	3	1	2	4

Ans. (c)

Exp. The correct matching is A-3, B-4, C-1, D-2

Tubers, rhizomes, corms and bulbs actually all serve the same purpose, but in a different way. These are underground storage units which act as storehouse for water and nutrients.

Plants that have rhizomes include ginger, turmeric, sugarcane, etc.

Common example of plants with tuber include potatoes, *Cassava* and *Dahlia.*

Examples of bulbs include onion, garlic, turnip, *Amaryllis, Narcissus.*

Examples of corm include jimikand, *Crocus, Colocasia,* etc.

12 **Consider the following types of fruits and their edible parts.** *(Chap 1, Class-XII, NCERT)*

1. Banana – Mesocarp
2. Coconut – Pericarp
3. Strawberry – Thalamus
4. Mango – Juicy aril

Which of the above is correctly matched ?

(a) 1 and 2 (b) 2 and 4
(c) 1 and 3 (d) 3 and 4

Ans. (c)

Exp. A true fruit is a ripened ovary that develops after fertilisation. Ovule develops into seeds and the ovary wall matures into fruit wall which is called pericarp. Mesocarp is middle pulpy part of the fruit, e.g. banana, mango. Endocarp is hard and stony part of the fruit, e.g. coconut.

Sometimes along with ovary, other floral parts like thalamus, receptacle or calyx may develop as part of fruit, such fruits are called false fruit, e.g. apple, pear, strawberry.

13 **Match the following lists and choose the correct code.** *(Chap 5, Class-XI, NCERT)*

List I		List II	
A.	Raceme	1	Mulberry
B.	Catkin	2.	*Achyranthes*
C.	Spadix	3.	Mustard
D.	Spike	4.	Banana

Codes

	A	B	C	D		A	B	C	D
(a)	1	2	3	4	(b)	3	1	4	2
(c)	3	4	2	1	(d)	3	2	4	1

Ans. (b)

Exp. The correct matching is A-3, B-1, C-4, D-2.

Raceme, catkin, spadix, spike and spikelet are the type of racemose inflorescence.

Raceme In this type of inflorescence, flowers present on the floral axis are stalked and arranged acropetally, e.g. mustard.

Catkin In this type of inflorescence, the axis is pendulous bearing unisexual flowers, e.g. mulberry.

Spadix In this type of inflorescence, the axis is fleshy and enclosed by a large showy bract, e.g. *Colocasia*, banana.

Spike In this type of inflorescence, the flower are sessile, e.g. *Achyranthes* (Latzira).

14 **Match the following lists and choose the correct code.** *(Chap 5, Class-XI, NCERT)*

List I		List II	
A.	Marginal	1.	China rose
B.	Parietal	2.	*Dianthus*
C.	Free central	3.	Pea
D.	Axile	4.	Cucumber

Codes

	A	B	C	D		A	B	C	D
(a)	2	3	1	4	(b)	3	4	2	1
(c)	3	2	1	4	(d)	4	3	1	2

Ans. (b)

Exp. The correct matching is A-3, B-4, C-2 , D-1.

Marginal, parietal, free central, axial and basal are different types of placentation found in plants.

Marginal The ovary is monocarpellary and one chambered and ovules are arranged along the fused margin of the single carpel, e.g. pea, gram.

Parietal Ovary is polycarpellary and syncarpous, having one chamber and ovules are attached on its inner wall where margin of adjoining carpels meet, e.g. mustard, cucumber.

Free central Ovary is syncarpous and polycarpellary, but unilocular as septate are absent. In the central part of the ovary, the placenta bears many groups of ovules, e.g. *Dianthus*, primula.

Axile The ovary is polycarpellary syncarpous, having many chambers. Ovules present on the placenta develop from the central axis formed by the fusion of the margins of two or more carpels, e.g. China rose, tomato, bhindi.

15 **The first step in the seed germination is imbibition of water which induce the**

(Unit 12, Class-X, Tamil Nadu Board)
(Tamil Nadu PCS Pre 2022)

(a) stimulation of plumule (b) breaking dormancy
(c) growth of radicle (d) resumes metabolic activities
(e) answer not known

Ans. (d)

Exp. The first step in seed germination is indeed the imbibition of water. Imbibition refers to the process of water being absorbed by the seed, causing it to swell and become hydrated. This process triggers enzymatic activity and metabolic changes, leading to the activation of hormones, such as gibberellin. Gibberellin play a crucial role in initiating processes including the mobilisation of stored nutrients and the growth of the embryo.

16 **Choose the incorrect statement about transpiration.** *(Chap 7, Class-VII, NCERT)*

(a) Water evaporates through the stomata present on the surface of the leaves by transpiration.
(b) A suction pull is generated in the plant by transpiration.
(c) Water is transported to great heights in the tall trees by transpiration.
(d) Transpiration heats the plant.

Ans. (d)

Exp. Statement (d) is incorrect because transpiration cools the plant as it helps in temperature regulation. During transpiration, evaporation of water molecules from cells of a leaf creates a suction which pulls water from the xylem cells of roots in order to pull water to great heights in the tall trees. Thus, transpiration helps in the absorption and upward movement of water and minerals dissolved in it from roots to the leaves.

17 Which of the following statements are true ?

(Unit 12, Class-X, Tamil Nadu Board) (CGPSC Pre 2023)

1. Small pores in epidermis of leaf are called stomata.
2. Guard cells present in the stomata are helpful in exchange of gases with atmosphere.
3. Transpiration takes place through stomata.

Codes

(a) 1 and 2 (b) 1 and 3 (c) 2 and 3 (d) 1, 2 and 3

Ans. (d)

Exp. Statements (1), (2) and (3) are true.

Small pores in epidermis of leaf are called stomata. Guard cells present in them are helpful in exchange of gases with the atmosphere.

Transpiration takes place through stomata.

18 Which of the following process does not occur during photosynthesis? *(Chap 4, Class-VI, NCERT)*

(a) Leaves prepare their food in the presence of sunlight and a green coloured pigment chlorophyll.
(b) Water and carbon dioxide are used for this.
(c) Oxygen is given out in the process and food prepared by leaves gets stored in different parts of plant.
(d) Production of new seeds and flowers by plant.

Ans. (d)

Exp. Production of new seeds and flowers by plant is not an action of photosynthesis. Photosynthesis helps in making food for plant. The process requires water and sunlight along with CO_2, whereas oxygen gas is released in the process. Food produced during photosynthesis is stored as starch.

19 The byproduct of photosynthesis is

(Chap 5, Class-X, NCERT) (BPSC Pre 2019)

(a) CO_2 (b) O_2 (c) energy (d) sugar
(e) None of the above/More than one of the above

Ans. (b)

Exp. Photosynthesis occurs in membrane bound structures called the chloroplast. The main product of photosynthesis is glucose, which is the molecule that produces energy to run the processes of the cell. Oxygen is mainly a byproduct of photosynthesis.

20 Consider the following Assertion (A) and Reason (R) and choose the correct code. *(Chap 5, Class-X, NCERT)*

Assertion (A) Desert plants do not perform photosynthesis.

Reason (R) Photosynthesis occurs in green parts of a plant.

Codes

(a) Both A and R are true and R is the correct explanation of A.
(b) Both A and R are true, but R is not the correct explanation of A.
(c) A is true, but R is false.
(d) A is false, but R is true.

Ans. (d)

Exp. Assertion (A) is false, but Reason (R) is true. Desert plants perform photosynthesis. They take up carbon dioxide at night and prepare an intermediate which is acted upon by the energy absorbed by the chlorophyll during the day. They have leaves modified into spines but in them, photosynthesis occurs *via* their green stem.

Chlorophyll is a green pigment that plays a vital role in photosynthesis. It resides in the chloroplasts of plants and helps to convert carbon dioxide and water into oxygen and glucose using sunlight. Thus, photosynthesis occurs in green parts of the plant.

21 Consider the given statements about algae.

(Chap 1, Class-VII, NCERT)

1. Algae can be seen as slimy, green patches in ponds or stagnant water bodies.
2. Algae are green due to chlorophyll.
3. Algae prepare their own food.

Which of the statements given above are correct?

(a) 1 and 2 (b) 1 and 3 (c) 2 and 3 (d) 1, 2 and 3

Ans. (d)

Exp. All the statements are correct about algae.

Algae can be seen as slimy, green patches in ponds or stagnant water bodies. They contain chlorophyll which gives them green colour. Algae can also prepare their own food by the process of photosynthesis as they have chlorophyll.

22 Identify the insectivorous plant in the following.

(Chap 1, Class-VII, NCERT) (IAS Pre 2008)

(a) Pitcher plant (b) Passion flower plant
(c) Night queen (d) Flame of the forest

Ans. (a)

Exp. Pitcher plant is an insectivorous plant. It is a plant having pitcher-like or jug-like structure which is modified part of leaf. The apex of the leaf forms a lid which can open and close the mouth of the pitcher. Inside the pitcher, there are hair which are directed downwards. When an insect lands on the pitcher, the lid closes and the trapped insect gets entangled into the hair. The lid closes and insect is trapped. The insect is digested by the digestive juices secreted in the pitcher and its nutrients are absorbed. Such insect eating plants are insectivorous plants.

23 Nitrogen fixing bacteria present in the nodules of the root of leguminous plants are

(Chap 1, Class-VII, NCERT) (UKPSC Pre 2007)

(a) saprophytic (b) parasitic (c) symbiotic (d) protolytic

Ans. (c)

Exp. Nitrogen fixing bacteria present in the nodules on the roots of the leguminous plants are symbiotic. During nitrogen fixation, bacteria such as *Rhizobium* convert nitrogen (N_2) gas into ammonium compounds (NH_4OH). These bacteria live in the roots of leguminous plants including alfalfa, clover, peas and beans. Some blue-green algae can also fix nitrogen.

24 **Which of the following is symbiotic bacteria which help to take up atmospheric nitrogen for plants?** *(Chap 1, Class-VII, NCERT)*

(a) *Rhizopus* (b) *Rhizobium* (c) *Penicillium* (d) *Neurospora*

Ans. (b)

Exp. *Rhizobium* is a bacterium found in soil that helps in fixing nitrogen in leguminous plants. These perform symbiosis resulting in the formation of nodules on roots of leguminous plants. In these nodules, the bacteria reduce nitrogen into ammonia used by the host plant.

25 **Consider the following Assertion (A) and Reason (R) and choose the correct code.** *(Chap 1, Class-VII, NCERT) (UPRO/ARO Pre 2016)*

Assertion (A) *Cuscuta* (Amarbel) is an example of parasitic plant.

Reason (R) It gets its nutrition from the leaves of the host plant.

Codes

(a) Both A and R are true and R is the correct explanation of A.
(b) Both A and R are true, but R is not the correct explanation of A.
(c) A is true, but R is false.
(d) A is false, but R is true.

Ans. (c)

Exp. Assertion (A) is true, but Reason (R) is false.

Cuscuta is a rootless, yellow coloured plant with a slender stem which twines around the stem of the host. It is an example of parasitic angiosperm. It develops haustorial which enters the host plant forming contact with xylem and phloem of the host. It absorbs the prepared food, water and minerals from the host plant. It is thus heterotrophic in nutrition.

26 **Which of the following statements is correct about translocation?** *(Chap 5, Class-X, NCERT)*

(a) The translocation in phloem is achieved by utilising energy from ATP.
(b) Transport of solute products of photosynthesis is called translocation.
(c) Translocation of food and other substances take place in the sieve tubes.
(d) All of the above

Ans. (d)

Exp. All the above statements are correct with regard to translocation. Transport of soluble products of photosynthesis is called translocation and it occurs in the part of the vascular tissue known as phloem.

Besides the products of photosynthesis, the phloem transport amino acids and other substances. These substances are specially delivered to the storage organs of roots, fruits and seeds and to growing organs.

The translocation of food and other substances take place in the sieve tubes with the help of adjacent companion cells both upward and downward. The translocation in phloem is achieved by utilising energy from ATP.

27 **Consider the following statements about transport in plants.** *(Chap 5, Class-X, NCERT)*

1. The effect of root pressure in transport of water is less in night.
2. Transpiration pull becomes effective during night.
3. If the distance between soil-containing organs and chlorophyll containing organs is large, then the raw material easily diffuse to all parts of plant.
4. At the roots, cells in contact with soil passively takes up ions.

Which of the statements given above are incorrect?

(a) 1 and 2 (b) 3 and 4 (c) 1 and 3 (d) All of these

Ans. (d)

Exp. All the given statements are incorrect.

The effect of root pressure in transport of water is effective at night due to stomatal closure.

During the day when the stomata are open, the transpiration pull becomes the major driving force in the movement of water in the xylem.

If the distance between soil containing organs and chlorophyll containing organs is small, energy and raw materials can easily diffuse to all parts of the plant body but if the distance become large because of changes in plant body design, diffusion processes will not be sufficient to provide raw material to leaves and energy in roots. At roots, cells in contact with the soil actively take up ions.

28 **Match the following lists and choose the correct code.** *(Chap 12, Class-XI, NCERT) (Unit 12, Class-X, Tamil Nadu Board)*

	List I		List II
A.	Glycolysis	1.	Inner membrane of mitochondria
B.	Krebs' cycle	2.	Cytoplasm
C.	Electron transport chain	3.	Mitochondrial matrix

Code

	A	B	C		A	B	C
(a)	1	3	2	(b)	3	2	1
(c)	2	3	1	(d)	2	1	3

Ans. (c)

Exp. The correct matching is A-2, B-3, C-1.

Glycolysis (Glucose splitting) It is the breakdown of one molecule of glucose (6 carbon) into two molecules of pyruvic acid (3 carbon). Glycolysis takes place in cytoplasm of the cell.

Krebs' cycle This cycle occurs in mitochondrial matrix. At the end of glycolysis , 2 molecules of pyruvic acid enter into mitochondria. The oxidation of pyruvic acid into CO_2 and water takes place through this cycle. It is also called Tricarboxylic Acid (TCA) cycle.

Electron transport chain This is accomplished through a system of electrons carrier complex called electron transport chain located on the inner membrane of mitochondria.

29 Which one of the following is not a plant hormone?
(Chap 13, Class-XI, NCERT) (UPPSC Mains 2011)

(a) Cytokinin (b) Auxin (c) Insulin (d) Gibberellin

Ans. (c)

Exp. Insulin is an animal hormone produced by the pancreas from islets of Langerhans. Cytokinin, ethylene, gibberellin and auxin are plant hormones which help in control and coordination in plant. The plant hormones (also known as phytohormones) are such organic substances which are formed in one tissue or organ of the plants and are then transported to other sites where they produce specific effects on growth and development.

30 Match the following lists and choose the correct code.
(Chap 13, Class-XI, NCERT)

List I (Plant Hormones)	List II (Functions)
A. Auxin	1. Helps plant to bend towards light.
B. Gibberellin	2. Helps in the growth of the stem.
C. Cytokinin	3. Promotes cell division.
D. Abscisic acid	4. Inhibits growth.

Codes

	A	B	C	D		A	B	C	D
(a)	1	2	3	4	(b)	4	3	2	1
(c)	4	1	2	3	(d)	3	2	1	4

Ans. (a)

Exp. The correct matching is A-1, B-2, C-3, D-4.

Auxin It helps plant to bend towards light as it is produced at the tip of the plant. The chief natural auxin is Indole-3-Acetic Acid (IAA- $C_{10}H_9O_2N$). IAA is the most common auxin found in plants.

Gibberellin It helps in the growth of stem. It promotes shoot growth mainly by accelerating the roles of cell elongation and cell division in the sub-apical meristem region where young internodes are developing.

Cytokinin In plants, it promotes cell division and thus also helps in fruit ripening. The kinetin and zeatin act as cytokinins. These control cell division, morphogenesis, counter action of apical meristem, breaking the dormancy, delay of senescence, etc.

Abscisic acid It is an inhibitory plant hormone which inhibits plant growth. It is thus widely used as spraying agent on the trees to regulate dropping of fruits.

31 Which of the following is a correct statement about reproduction in plants? *(Chap 7, Class-X, NCERT)*

(a) In budding, a small bulb-like projection coming out from yeast cell remains attached to the parent cell and form a new yeast cell.

(b) In fragmentation, a fern breaks up into two or more fragments and each fragment grows into a new individual.

(c) Under favourable condition, a spore in algae germinates and develops into a new individual.

(d) In China rose, reproduction occurs by means of stamen and pistil.

Ans. (d)

Exp. Statement (d) is correct.

Mustard, China rose, *Petunia*, etc., are angiosperms, i.e. flower bearing plants. They reproduce by sexual reproduction by means of stamen and pistil.

Statements (a), (b) and (c) are incorrect because in budding, the small bulb-like projection coming out from the yeast cell (bud) gradually grows and gets detached from the parent cell and forms a new yeast cell.

Fragmentation occurs in algae, where an algae breaks into two or more fragments. These fragments or piece grow into new individuals.

Under favourable conditions, a spore of fern or moss germinate and develops into a new individual.

Spore formation also occurs in fungus.

32 Which of the following statements is/are correct?
(Chap 7, Class-X, NCERT)

(a) Flower containing either only pistil or only stamens are called unisexual flowers.

(b) Flowers which contain both stamen and pistil are bisexual flowers.

(c) In sexual reproduction, a male and a female gamete fuse to form a zygote.

(d) All of the above

Ans. (d)

Exp. All the statements are correct.

Flowers which contain either only pistil or only stamens are called unisexual flowers. Flowers which contain both stamens and pistil are called bisexual flowers. Corn, papaya and cucumber produce unisexual flowers whereas mustard, rose and *Petunia* have bisexual flowers.

In sexual reproduction, male gamete from the stamen fuses with the female gamete from the ovary/pistil to form a zygote.

33 A .... consists of stigma, style and ovary. Ovary contains one or more .... *(Chap 8, Class-VII, NCERT)*

(a) pistil, ovules

(b) ovule, female gamete

(c) pistil, female gamete

(d) ovule, pistil

Ans. (a)

Exp. A pistil consists of stigma, style and ovary. Ovary contains one or more ovules. The female gamete or the egg is formed in an ovule.

Stigma is small and sticky landing structure. The pollen grains from the same or different flowers stick to it. Style is a thin stalk like structure that holds the stigma. Ovary is a base of the style or the lower part of the pistil and contains the ovules, which contain the female gamete.

34 The transfer of pollen from the anther to the stigma of a flower is *(Chap 7, Class-X, NCERT)*

(a) fertilisation (b) fusion

(c) pollination (d) transportation

Ans. (c)

Exp. The transfer of pollen from the anther to the stigma of a flower is called pollination. If the pollen lands on the stigma of the same flower or another flower of the same plant, it is called self-pollination.

When the pollen of a flower lands on the stigma of a flower of a different plant of the same kind, it is called cross-pollination.

35 Consider the following types of organisms. *(Chap 1, Class-XII, NCERT) (IAS Pre 2012)*

1. Bat 2. Bee 3. Bird

Which of the above is/are pollinating agent/agents?

(a) 1 and 2 (b) Only 2
(c) 1 and 3 (d) 1, 2 and 3

Ans. (d)

Exp. All of the given animals are agents of pollination. Pollination is the act of transferring pollen grains from anther (having male gametes) of a flower to the stigma (female part).

It is a pre-requisite for fertilisation. Fertilisation allows the flower to develop fruits and seeds. Bees are the most important pollinating agent.

Pollination by bees and butterflies often occurs in the flowers which bloom in the day time. Hummingbird pollinated flowers, which appear in warm colours like red, yellow and orange. Bat is also a pollinating agent of many flowers.

36 Which of the following actions is incorrect? *(Chap 8, Class-VII, NCERT)*

(a) Ripened ovary is embryo.
(b) Seeds develop from ovule.
(c) Zygote develops into an embryo.
(d) Seed dispersal prevents competition between plants and its own seedling for sunlight, water and minerals.

Ans. (a)

Exp. Statement (a) is incorrect because ripened ovary is called fruit. After fertilisation, the ovary grows into a fruit and other parts of the flower fall off.

Seeds develop from the ovules. The seed contains an embryo enclosed in a protective seed coat.

Zygote develops into embryo after fertilisation. The process involves cell division. Dispersal of seed prevents competition between the plant and its own seedling for resources like sunlight, water and minerals. It also enables plants to invade new habitats.

37 In a bisexual flower, if androecium and gynoecium mature at different times, the phenomenon is known as *(Chap 1, Class-XII, NCERT) (IAS Pre 2002)*

(a) dichogamy (b) herkogamy
(c) heterogamy (d) monogamy

Ans. (a)

Exp. In a bisexual flower, if androecium and gynoecium mature at different time the phenomenon is known as dichogamy. It is of two types; (i) Protandry, (ii) Protogyny. Protogyny is a condition of flower in which female parts mature before the male ones, while protandry is the condition in which male part of flower mature before the female ones.

38 Consider the following statements regarding pollen grains. *(Chap 1, Class-XII, NCERT)*

1. Pollen grains are spherical in shape and have a multilayered wall.
2. Pollen grain exine has a prominent aperture called germ pores.
3. Pollen grains can be well preserved as fossils.
4. Pollen grains of several species may also cause severe allergies.

Which of the statements given above are incorrect?

(a) 1 and 2 (b) 3 and 4
(c) 1, 2 and 3 (d) Only 1

Ans. (d)

Exp. Statement (1) is incorrect because pollen grains which represent male gametophytes, are spherical in shape and have a bilayered wall-outer exine and inner intine.

39 Match the following lists and choose the correct code. *(Chap 1, Class-XII, NCERT)*

List I (Pollination)	List II (Features)
A. Autogamy	1. Transfer of pollen from anther to stigma of a different plant.
B. Geitonogamy	2. Transfer of pollen within the same flower.
C. Xenogamy	3. Transfer of pollen from another flower of the same plant.

Codes

	A	B	C
(a)	2	3	1
(b)	1	2	3
(c)	3	2	1
(d)	2	1	3

Ans. (a)

Exp. The correct matching is A-2, B-3, C-1.

Autogamy In this type, pollination is achieved within the same flower by transfer of pollen grain from the anther to the stigma of the same flower.

Geitonogamy Transfer of pollen grains from the anther to the stigma of another flower of the same plant. Genetically, it is similar to autogamy. Since, the pollen grains comes from the same plant.

Xenogamy Transfer of pollen grains from anther to the stigma of a different plant. This is the only type of pollination, which during pollination brings genetically different type of pollen grains to the stigma.

Chapter 07

Human Physiology

Human Physiology

Nutrition, Skin and Excretion

Nutrients

- Substances which provide nourishment to living organism.

Organic Substances

- **Carbohydrates** Monosaccharide, Disaccharide, Polysaccharide
- **Proteins** Kwashiorkor, Marasmus.
- Fats Stored source of energy
- **Vitamins** The organic compounds. They can be either

(i) Fat Soluble (Vitamins-A, D, E and K).
(ii) Water Soluble (Vitamins-B and C)

Inorganic Substances

- **Minerals**
  - **Bulk minerals** (e.g. Calcium etc.)
  - **Trace minerals** (e.g. Copper, iron etc.)
- **Water** Controls body temperature and help in excretional activities.

Skin

- Largest organ of the body has following layers
  - **Epidermis** Stratum corneum, stratum lucidum, stratum granulosum (Keratohyalin granules and lamellae granules).
  - **Dermis** Papillary & Reticular dermis.
- **Derivatives of Skin**
  - Hair and hair follicle.
  - Glands of the skin.

Excretion

- Process of removal of metabolic waste from the body of an organism.

Digestive, Skeletal and Nervous system

Mechanism of Urine Formation

- Glomerular Filtration (Ultrafiltration)
- Reabsorption (99% filtrate reabsorbed)
- Secretion (Renal Tubules)

Digestive System

- **Alimentary Canal** Mouth→Buccal cavity → Pharynx Oesophagus → Stomach → Small intestine → large intestine.

Skeletal System

It comprises of

- **Axial skeleton** (80 bones) Skull (40 bones), Sternum, Ribs (12 pairs) and vertebral column (33 bones)
- **Appendicular skeleton** (126 bones) Hind limb, forelimb, pelvic girdle and pectoral girdle.

Joints

- Place of articulation between two or more bones or between a bone and a cartilage
- **Classification of Joints Fibrous** (Immovable Joints), **Cartilaginous** (Slightly Movable Joints), **Synovial** (Freely Movable Joints), joints.

Nervous System

- **Central Nervous System (CNS)**
  - Brain receives and processes sensory information. Spinal cord conducts signals to and from the brain.
- **Peripheral Nervous System (PNS)**
- **Autonomic Nervous System (ANS)**
  - Sympathetic and parasympathetic.

Endocrine and Circulatory system

Endocrine System

- **Hypothalamus**
- **Pituitary** (anterior and posteriors)
- **Pineal gland**
- **Pancreas** (acts as both endocrine and exocrine glands)
- **Adrenal gland**
- **Thymus gland**
- **Thyroid gland**
- **Testis** (in males) **and ovary** (in females)

Human Reproduction

- Male Reproductive System
- Female Reproductive System
- Gametogenesis
- Menstrual cycle
- Fertilisation and implantation

Circulatory System

- **Blood** Plasma (55%), Blood cells (45%) - RBCs, WBCs and Platelets
- **Lymph** Tissue Fluid
- **Heart** (Pumping organ)
- **Blood vessels** Arteries, veins and capillaries

Respiration

- Biochemical oxidation of nutrients to release of nutrients to release energy for metabolic activities.
- Mechanism-Inspiration, expiration, gaseous exchange, (lungs) oxygen transport, gaseous exchange (tissue), transport of CO_2.

SOURCE *New NCERT Class VII (Nutrition in Animals, Respiration in Organisms, Transportation in Animals and Plants), New NCERT Class VIII (Reproduction in Animals, Reaching the Age of Adolescence), New NCERT Class X (Life Processes, Control and Coordination, How do Organisms Reproduce), New NCERT Class XI (Breathing and Exchange of Gases, Body Fluids and Circulations, Excretory Products and Their Elimination, Locomotion and Movement, Neural Control and Coordination, Chemical Coordination and Integration), Old NCERT Class XI (Digestion and Absorption) New NCERT Class XII (Human Reproduction, Reproductive Health) Tamil Nadu Board Class X (Transportation in plants and circulatfonin Animals)*

1 Consider the following statements regarding human digestive system. *(Chap 5, Class-X, NCERT)*

1. The oral cavity has a number of teeth and a muscular tongue.
2. The tongue is the fleshy muscular organ attached at the back floor of the buccal cavity.
3. Human beings form two sets of teeth during their life time. This type of dentition is called thecodont.
4. Incisors are the sharply pointed teeth which help in grinding of food.

Which of the statements given above are correct?

(a) 1 and 2 (b) 2 and 4 (c) 3 and 4 (d) 1 and 3

Ans. (a)

Exp. Statements (1) and (2) are correct.

The oral cavity also known as mouth is the hollow cavity that allows food and air to enter the body.

It contain many organs such as the teeth, tongue and the ducts of the salivary glands. The tongue is a muscular organ in the mouth and is covered with moist, pink tissue called mucosa.

Statements (3) and (4) are incorrect.

Human beings form two sets of teeth during their life time. This type of dentition is called diphyodont.

Whereas in thecodont dentition, the base of the tooth is enclosed in jaw sockets. Incisors are narrow edged teeth present at the front of the mouth which are adapted for cutting of food whereas canines are sharply pointed teeth and molars and premolars help in grinding of food.

2 Which of the following is not a digestive enzyme? *(Chap 5, Class-X, NCERT)*

1. Trypsin 2. Gastrin 3. Ptyalin 4. Pepsin

Codes

(a) 1 and 2 (b) Only 2 (c) 2 and 3 (d) 1 and 4

Ans. (b)

Exp. Trypsin, ptyalin and pepsin are digestive enzymes whose secretion is performed by pancreas, salivary gland and stomach, respectively.

Gastrin is a peptide hormone that stimulates secretion of gastric acid (HCl) by the parietal cells of the stomach and aids in gastric motility. It is released by G-cells in the pyloric antrum of the stomach, duodenum and pancreas.

3 Choose the incorrect pair. *(Chap 6, Class-X, NCERT)*

(a) Rennin – liver (b) Pepsin – stomach
(c) Ptyalin – mouth (d) Trypsin – pancreas

Ans. (a)

Exp. Pair (a) is incorrect because rennin also called chymosin, is a protein digesting enzyme. It curdles milk by transforming the caseinogen into insoluble casein.

It is found only in human infants and cud chewing animals. Rennin is synthesised by the chief cells of the stomach.

Rest of the pairs are correctly matched.

4 Consider the following statements with reference to human body. *(Chap 16, Class-XI, NCERT)*

1. The common bile duct releases its content in stomach.
2. The pancreatic duct releases its content in small intestine.

Which of the following statement(s) given above is/are correct?

(a) Only 1
(b) Only 2
(c) Both 1 and 2
(d) Neither 1 nor 2

Ans. (b)

Exp. Only statement (2) is correct as pancreatic enzymes such as trypsin, lipase and amylase are released in the small intestine through pancreatic duct.

Statement (1) is incorrect because the common bile duct releases its content in small intestine.

5 Consider the following Assertion (A) and Reason (R) and choose the correct code. *(Chap 2, Class-VII, NCERT) (IAS Pre 2008)*

Assertion (A) In human body, the liver has an important role in fat digestion.

Reason (R) Liver produces two important fat digesting enzymes.

Codes

(a) Both A and R are true and R is the correct explanation of A.
(b) Both A and R are true, but R is not the correct explanation of A.
(c) A is true, but R is false.
(d) A is false, but R is true.

Ans. (c)

Exp. Assertion (A) is true, but Reason (R) is false.

The liver does not produce fat-digesting enzymes.

It detoxifies chemical and metabolises drugs. The liver has multiple functions such as secretion of bile, storage of fat, synthesis of urea, glycogenesis, gluconeogenesis and glycogenolysis, etc.

Although the bile lacks digestive enzymes, yet it plays an important role in the digestion, especially in digestion of fats by bringing about their emulsification.

6 Digestion of lipids takes place in the presence of which of the following? *(Chap 2, Class-VII, NCERT) (UPPSC Mains 2016)*

1. Bile acids
2. Lipase
3. Pepsin

Codes

(a) Only 1 (b) 1 and 3
(c) 1 and 2 (d) 1, 2 and 3

Ans. (c)

Exp. Most of the lipids in our food are present in the form of simple fats or triglycerides. Lipase enzyme plays an important role in the digestion of lipids. Lipase breaks down lipids into fatty acids and monoglycerides.

Bile probably contains no digestive enzyme. Yet it plays an important role in the digestion and absorption of fat. It facilitates emulsification of fats. Pepsin is a protein digesting or proteolytic enzyme.

7 Match the following lists and choose the correct code. *(Chap 16, Class-XI, NCERT) (UPPSC Mains 2008)*

List I	List II
A. Salivary amylase	1. Protein digestion
B. Trypsin	2. Starch digestion
C. Lipase	3. Fat digestion

Codes

	A	B	C		A	B	C
(a)	1	2	3	(b)	2	1	3
(c)	2	3	1	(d)	1	3	2

Ans. (b)

Exp. The correct match is A-2, B-1, C-3.

Salivary amylase (ptyalin) It is secreted by salivary glands present in our mouth. It helps in digestion of starch into maltose and dextrin.

Trypsin It is a protein digesting enzyme, which breaks down protein in the small intestine. It is secreted by the pancreas as inactive trypsinogen.

Lipase It helps in fat digestion. It is secreted by pancreas and released in small intestine. Lipases are a sub-class of the esterases.

8 Choose the incorrectly matched pair. *(Chap 16, Class-XI, NCERT)*

(a) Salivary glands – salivary amylase
(b) Gastric glands – mucus
(c) Pancreas – pepsin
(d) Liver – bile

Ans. (c)

Exp. Pair (c) is incorrectly matched as pancreas secretes trypsin, lipase and amylase enzymes for the digestion of proteins, fats and carbohydrates, respectively. Whereas pepsin is secreted by stomach that helps in breakdown of proteins. Rest are correctly matched pairs.

9 Consider the following characteristics. *(Chap 2, Class-VII, NCERT) (UPPSC Mains 2008)*

1. This is the second largest gland of the human body.
2. Its secretion comes out from a characteristic type of cells and is alkaline.
3. Its secretion is said to be complete digestive juice.

The above characteristics are attributed to which of the following?

(a) Liver (b) Spleen (c) Pancreas (d) Salivary glands

Ans. (c)

Exp. The given characteristics are attributed to pancreas as it is the second largest gland in human body. It secretes enzymes such as trypsin, lipase and amylase which are released in small intestine for complete digestion of food. Acinar cells within the pancreas produce these enzymes. These enzymes needs alkaline (basic) medium to get activated which is provided by liver as bile juice.

10 Which of the following statements is not correct regarding the secretion in the stomach? *(Chap 2, Class-VII, NCERT)*

(a) The mucus protects the lining of the stomach from HCl.
(b) HCl creates an acidic medium which facilitates the action of enzyme pepsin.
(c) Pepsin helps in the breakdown of starch.
(d) HCl kills many bacteria that enter along with the food.

Ans. (c)

Exp. Statement (c) is incorrect regarding the secretion in the stomach because pepsin helps in the breakdown of proteins.

It helps in the digestion of protein with the help of HCl secreted by the stomach. HCl changes a protein called pepsinogen into pepsin.

Rest of the statements are correct.

11 Enzyme trypsin and pepsin works in *(Chap 16, Class-XI, NCERT)*

(a) basic and acidic medium, respectively.
(b) acidic and basic medium, respectively.
(c) acidic medium only.
(d) neutral medium only.

Ans. (a)

Exp. Trypsin is secreted by the pancreas as trypsinogen which gets activated in the presence of alkaline (basic) medium provided by bile juice. Pepsin is secreted by stomach as pepsinogen which gets activated by the acidic medium provided by HCl.

12 Consider the following Assertion (A) and Reason (R) and choose the correct code. *(Chap 2, Class-VII, NCERT) (IAS Pre 2005)*

Assertion (A) All the proteins in our body are digested in small intestine only.

Reason (R) The protein digesting enzymes from the pancreas are released into the small intestine.

Codes

(a) Both A and R are true and R is the correct explanation of A.
(b) Both A and R are true, but R is not the correct explanation of A.
(c) A is true, but R is false.
(d) A is false, but R is true.

Ans. (d)

Exp. Assertion (A) is false, but Reason (R) is true. Protein digestion begins in the stomach with the action of an enzyme called pepsin. Pepsin is the active protein digesting enzyme of the stomach. Protein-digesting enzyme, i.e. trypsin is produced in an inactive form in the pancreas and is activated in the small intestine, where it digests protein. Duodenum is the first and shortest segment of the small intestine. In the duodenum, trypsin catalyses the hydrolysis of peptide bonds, breaking down proteins into smaller peptides.

Enzymes continue to breakdown polypeptides and peptides into amino acids. As amino acids are very small, they are able to be absorbed through the small intestine lining and into the bloodstream.

13 Which of the following changes is catalysed by the enzyme trypsin? *(Chap 5, Class-X, NCERT) (RAS/RTS Pre 1999)*

(a) Proteins to peptones
(b) Proteins to peptides
(c) Protein to amino acid
(d) Starch to glucose

Ans. (c)

Exp. In the duodenum, trypsin catalyses the hydrolysis of peptide bonds, breaking down proteins into smaller peptides. The peptide products are then further hydrolysed into amino acids *via* other proteases, rendering them available for absorption into the bloodstream.

14 Which one of the following is the correct sequence in the order of decreasing length of the three structural part of the small intestine in the human body? *(Chap 16 Class-XI, NCERT) (IAS Pre 2007)*

(a) Jejunum-Duodenum-Ileum
(b) Ileum-Duodenum-Jejunum
(c) Jejunum-Ileum-Duodenum
(d) Ileum-Jejunum-Duodenum

Ans. (d)

Exp. The small intestine is divided into three structural parts ileum, jejunum, duodenum. The duodenum is a short structure (about 20-25 cm long) continuous with the stomach and shaped like 'C'. It surrounds the head of the pancreas. The duodenum contains Brunner's glands, which produce a mucus-rich alkaline secretion containing bicarbonate. The jejunum is the midsection of the small intestine, connecting the duodenum to the ileum. It is about 2.5 m long and contains the plicae circulares and villi that increases its surface area.

The ileum is the final section of the small intestine. It is about 3.5 m long and contains villi similar to the jejunum.

15 Consider the following statements about small intestine. *(Chap 16, Class-XI, NCERT)*

1. Small intestine receives secretions from the liver and the pancreas.
2. It is the site for the complete digestion of carbohydrates, proteins and fats.
3. The inner lining of the small intestine has numerous finger-like projections called villi which helps in digestion of food.

Which of the statements given above are correct?

(a) 1 and 3
(b) 1 and 2
(c) 2 and 3
(d) 1, 2 and 3

Ans. (b)

Exp. Statements (1) and (2) are correct about small intestine as it receives secretions such as bile juice from liver and trypsin, lipase and amylase from pancreas.

It is a site of complete digestion and absorption of digested food. Digestion of carbohydrates, fats and proteins gets completed in small intestine. The digested products are absorbed in small intestine.

Statement (3) is incorrect because the inner lining of the small intestine has numerous finger-like projections called villi which helps in absorption of digested food.

16 Consider the following statements for human digestive system. *(Chap 2, Class-VII, NCERT)*

1. The end products of digestion in small intestine are amino acids, glucose, glycerol and fatty acids.
2. The unabsorbed food is sent into the large intestine where more villi absorbs water from the material.
3. The food is mixed thoroughly with saliva with the help of tongue.

Which of the statements given above are correct?

(a) 1 and 2
(b) 1, 2 and 3
(c) 2 and 3
(d) 1 and 3

Ans. (b)

Exp. Statements (1), (2) and (3) are correct for human digestive system as small intestine is the site of complete digestion of food.

Hence, proteins breakdown into amino acids, carbohydrates breakdown into glucose and fats breakdown into glycerol and fatty acid.

In large intestine, the water is absorbed through villi from the undigested or unabsorbed food.

Tongue helps in mixing of food thoroughly with saliva to make the digestion of food easy.

17 Which of the following is not true about cellular respiration? *(Chap 14, Class-XI, NCERT)*

(a) In all cases, the first step is breakdown of glucose into pyruvate molecule.
(b) In the absence of oxygen, pyruvate is converted into lactic acid in yeast.
(c) In the presence of oxygen, pyruvate is breakdown into ethanol, carbon dioxide and energy.
(d) The cramps occur when muscle cells respire anaerobically.

Ans. (a)

Exp. The food material taken in during the process of nutrition is used in cells to provide energy for various life processes. Some organisms uses oxygen to breakdown glucose completely into carbon dioxide and water.

Some use other pathways that do not involve oxygen. In all cases, the first step is the breakdown of glucose, into three carbon molecules called pyruvate. Further, the pyruvate may be converted into ethanol and carbon dioxide.

This process occurs in yeast during fermentation.

In the mitochondria, pyruvate is converted into carbon dioxide and water when there is lack of oxygen in our muscle cells, the pyruvate is converted into lactic acid. This cause cramps in the muscles.

18 Which one of the following biotransformations provide maximum energy to the human body? *(Chap 6, Class-VII, NCERT) (UPPSC Mains 2015)*

(a) ADP - AMP (b) ATP - ADP
(c) ADP - ATP (d) AMP - ADP

Ans. (b)

Exp. Adenosine Triphosphate (ATP) is the high energy molecule that stores the energy. The conversion of ATP to ADP is an extremely crucial reaction for the supplying of energy for life processes. ATP hydrolysis is the final link between the energy derived from food or sunlight and useful work such as muscle contraction.

19 The complete conversion of glucose, in the presence of oxygen, into carbon dioxide and water with release of energy is called *(Chap 6, Class-VII, NCERT) (IAS Pre 1998)*

(a) aerobic respiration (b) anaerobic respiration
(c) glycolysis (d) hydrolysis

Ans. (a)

Exp. The complete conversion of glucose in the presence of oxygen, into carbon dioxide and water with release of energy is called aerobic respiration. Aerobic respiration is divided into three main stages: glycolysis, citric acid cycle and electron transport chain.

Most eukaryotes and prokaryotes use aerobic respiration to obtain energy from glucose.

20 Choose the incorrectly matched pair. *(Chap 16, Class-XI, NCERT)*

(a) Trachea – windpipe
(b) Larynx – epiglottis
(c) Bronchi – cartilaginous ring
(d) Alveoli – air sacs

Ans. (c)

Exp. Pair (c) is incorrect because rings of cartilage are present in the throat to ensure that air passage does not collapse. Cartilage is a flexible tissue which is present in the windpipe or trachea.

It helps the windpipe to move while breathing. These rings balance out the trachea and keep it from bending, while also allowing the trachea to extend long when the person relaxes.

21 Match the following lists and choose the correct code. *(Chap 16, Class-XI, NCERT)*

List I	List II
A. Pharynx	1. Bag-like structures
B. Alveoli	2. Common passage for air and food
C. Bronchioles	3. Subdivision of bronchi
D. Bronchi	4. Subdivision of trachea

Codes

	A	B	C	D
(a)	2	1	3	4
(b)	2	1	4	3
(c)	2	3	1	4
(d)	2	3	4	1

Ans. (a)

Exp. The correct matching is A-2, B-1, C-3, D-4.

Pharynx It is the part of the throat behind the mouth and nasal cavity. It serves both the respiratory and digestive systems by receiving air from the nasal cavity and air, food and water from the oral cavity.

Alveoli These are tiny, irregular-walled and vasculorised bag-like structures in the lungs. They are the smallest passage way in the respiratory system and are richly supplied with a network of blood vessels. They are called as the structural and functional unit of lungs.

Bronchioles These are the subdivision of the bronchi. They carry air into the lungs. Each terminal bronchiole give rise to tiny alveoli.

Bronchi These are the subdivision of the trachea. Each bronchi undergoes repeated divisions to form the secondary and tertiary bronchi and bronchioles.

22 Consider the following statements. *(Chap 14, Class-XI, NCERT)*

1. The opening of the pharynx into the trachea is called glottis.
2. Trachea is thick walled but its walls do not collapse even there is not enough air.
3. An adult human breathes about 16 to 18 times per minute.

Which of the statements given above is/are true?

(a) 1 and 3 (b) 1 and 2
(c) 2 and 3 (d) 2 only

Ans. (a)

Exp. Statements (1) and (3) are correct.

The opening of the pharynx into the trachea is called glottis. Trachea is thin walled, but its walls do not collapse even when there is not enough air in it as it is supported by rings of cartilage. Trachea bifurcates into bronchi.

An adult human breathes about 16 to 18 times per minute. Breathing rate increases during physical exercise, disease, fever, pain and under stress.

23 Read the following statements in connection with Red Blood Corpuscles and with the help of the codes given below find out the correct answer.

(Chap 15, Class-XI, NCERT) (UPPSC Mains 2004)

1. They have iron.
2. They provide red colour to the blood.
3. They provide immunity against certain diseases.
4. They are carrier of oxygen in the blood.

Codes

(a) 1, 2 and 3 (b) 2, 3 and 4
(c) 1, 2 and 4 (d) 1, 2, 3 and 4

Ans. (c)

Exp. Statements (1), (2) and (4) are correct.

Red Blood Cells (RBCs) or red blood corpuscles also called erythrocytes are the most common type of blood cell in the vertebrate organisms. They are principal means of delivering oxygen (O_2) to the body tissues *via* blood.

RBCs take up oxygen in the lungs or gills and release it into tissues while squeezing through the body's capillaries.

The cytoplasm of erythrocytes is rich in haemoglobin, an iron-containing biomolecule that can bind oxygen and is responsible for the red colour of the cells.

RBCs do not play role in providing immunity against any kind of diseases. This is done by WBCs.

24 Consider the following statements about haemoglobin. *(Chap 7, Class-VII, NCERT)*

1. It carries oxygen in the blood.
2. It is iron containing compound.
3. It imports a red colour to the blood.

Which of the statements given above are correct?

(a) 1 and 2 (b) 1, 2 and 3
(c) 2 and 3 (d) 1 and 3

Ans. (b)

Exp. All the statements are correct. The cytoplasm of erythrocytes is rich in haemoglobin, an iron containing compound. It binds with oxygen and transports it to all the parts of the body and ultimately to all the cells. The presence of haemoglobin makes blood appear red.

25 A person with 'AB' blood group is called an universal recipient because of the

(Chap 15, Class-XI, NCERT) (IAS Pre 1995)

(a) lack of antigen in his blood
(b) lack of antibodies in his blood
(c) lack of both antigens and antibodies in his blood
(d) presence of antibodies in his blood

Ans. (b)

Exp. Blood group 'AB' individuals have both A and B antigens on the surface of their RBCs and their blood plasma does not contain any antibodies.

Therefore, an individual with type AB blood can receive blood from any group (with AB being preferable), but cannot donate blood to any group other than AB. Thus, they are known as universal recipients.

26 A man having 'A' blood group met with a serious road accident and the doctors advised for blood transfusion. The relatives were asked to donate blood, whose blood groups were found to be as follows *(Chap 15, Class-XI, NCERT) (RAS/RTS Pre 2013)*

1. Wife-'O' 2. Brother-'AB'
3. Son-'A' 4. Daughter-'O'

Who among the above relations could donate blood to the injured man?

(a) 1 and 2 (b) 2 and 3 (c) 2, 3 and 4 (d) 1, 3 and 4

Ans. (d)

Exp. In above case wife-'O', Son-'A' and Daughter-'O' can donate the blood to concerned person. Blood group 'A' individuals have the A-antigen on the surface of their RBCs and blood serum containing IgM antibodies against the B antigen.

Therefore, group A individual can receive blood only from individuals of groups A or O (with A being preferable) and can donate blood to individuals with type A or AB.

27 Consider the following Assertion (A) and Reason (R) and choose the correct code.

(Chap 15, Class-XI, NCERT) (MPPSC Pre 2008)

Assertion (A) People with AB blood groups are universal recipients.

Reason (R) Red blood cell of blood group AB has no antigen and so agglutination does not occur with any other blood group.

Codes

(a) Both A and R are true and R is the correct explanation of A.
(b) Both A and R are true, but R is not the correct explanation of A.
(c) A is true, but R is false.
(d) A is false, but R is true.

Ans. (c)

Exp. Assertion (A) is true, but Reason (R) is false.

People with AB blood groups are universal recipients because, they have both A and B antigens on the surface of their RBCs and their blood plasma does not contain any antibodies. These individuals with type AB blood can receive blood from any group (with AB being preferable), but cannot donate blood to any group other than AB.

28 Consider the following statements.

(Chap 15, Class-XI, NCERT)

1. A human heart is two sided, four-chambered with muscular walls.
2. An atrioventricular valve separates each auricle from its connecting artery.
3. A semilunar valve separates ventricles and atria.

Which of the statement(s) given above is/are true?

(a) 1 and 2 (b) 2 and 3 (c) Only 1 (d) 1, 2 and 3

Ans. (c)

Exp. Only statement (1) is true as the heart is the muscular organ which pumps blood through the blood vessels of circulatory system. The heart is divided into four-chambers-upper left and right atria and lower left and right ventricles.

Statements (2) and (3) are not true because artioventricular valves are between ventricles and atria. The valve between the right ventricle and right atrium is the tricuspid valve, and the one which is found between the left ventricle and left atrium is known as the mitral valve. Semilunar valves are located between the left ventricle and aorta. It is also found between the pulmonary artery and right ventricle.

29 Consider the following statements. *(Chap 15, Class-XI, NCERT)*

1. Pulmonary artery carries deoxygenated blood from the heart to the lungs.
2. Aorta carries deoxygenated blood from body parts to the lungs.
3. Pulmonary vein is the only vein that carries oxygen rich blood.

Which of the statement(s) given above is/are incorrect?

(a) 1 and 2 (b) 2 and 3 (c) Only 3 (d) Only 2

Ans. (d)

Exp. Statement (2) is incorrect because the aorta is the largest artery in the body which delivers oxygenated blood from the left ventricle to the rest of the body. Aorta performs systemic circulation.

When the blood is pumped into the aorta from the left ventricle, the aorta expands. The walls of aorta are thick since it has to bear high blood pressure from within, as it builds high pressure than the pulmonary artery.

30 Match the following lists and choose the correct code.
(Chap 15, Class-XI, NCERT) (Unit 14, Class-X, Tamil Nadu Board)

List-I	List-II
A. Neutrophils	1. Inflammation
B. Eosinophils	2. Infection
C. Basophils	3. Allergy

Codes

	A	B	C		A	B	C
(a)	1	2	3	(b)	2	3	1
(c)	3	2	1	(d)	2	1	3

Ans. (b)

Exp. The correct matching is A-2, B-3, C-1.

Neutrophils They are large in size and have a 2-7 lobed nucleus. These corpuscles form 60- 65% of the total leucocytes. The numbers are increased during infection.

Eosinophils It has a bilobed nucleus and constitute 2%-3% of the total leucocytes. Their number increases during allergy. It brings about detoxification of toxins.

Basophils They have lobed nucleus. They form 05-1.0% of the total leucocytes. They release chemicals during the process of inflammation.

31 Which of the following is true about the blood vessels? *(Chap 15, Class-XI, NCERT)*

1. Arteries have thick, elastic walls.
2. Veins have high pressure of blood in it.
3. Valves in veins ensures that the blood flows only in one direction.

Codes

(a) 1 and 2 (b) 1, 2 and 3 (c) 1 and 3 (d) Only 3

Ans. (c)

Exp. Statements (1) and (3) are correct.

Arteries carry oxygen rich blood from the heart to all parts of the body. Arteries have thick, elastic walls to withstand the pressure of blood flow from the heart. Blood emerges from the heart under high pressure. Veins contain valves that ensure blood flows in only one direction.

Statement (2) is incorrect because veins carry blood back to your heart from the rest of our body. The pressure of the blood returning to the heart is low, so the walls of veins are much thinner than arteries.

32 Match the following lists and choose the correct code. *(Chap 15, Class-XI, NCERT)*

List I	List II
A. Right ventricle	1. Pulmonary veins
B. Right auricle	2. Pulmonary arteries
C. Left auricle	3. Aorta
D. Left ventricle	4. Vena cava

Codes

	A	B	C	D		A	B	C	D
(a)	2	4	3	1	(b)	2	4	1	3
(c)	4	2	3	1	(d)	4	2	1	3

Ans. (b)

Exp. The correct matching is A-2, B-4, C-1, D-3.

Right ventricle receives deoxygenated blood from the right atrium and pumps it to the lungs *via* the pulmonary arteries.

Right auricle collects deoxygenated blood from the body *via* superior and inferior vena cava.

Left auricle collects oxygenated blood from the lungs *via* pulmonary veins.

Left ventricle pumps the oxygenated blood *via* aorta to the rest of the body.

33 Consider the following statements about lymph. *(Chap 15, Class-XI, NCERT)*

1. It is dark yellow in colour.
2. It always flows only in one direction from tissue to heart.
3. Cells called lymphocytes present in lymph eat up germs and prevent body from infections.

Which of the statements given above is/are true ?

(a) 1 and 2 (b) 2 and 3 (c) Only 3 (d) 1 and 3

Ans. (b)

Exp. Lymph is a circulatory fluid and flows in the lymph vessels. It is light yellow in colour. It always flows only in one direction from tissue to heart and cells called lymphocytes present in lymph eat up germs and prevent body from infections. It returns protein and fluids from circulation to tissues.

34 Consider the following statements regarding human excretory system. *(Chap 5, Class-X, NCERT)*

1. In humans, the excretory system consists of one pair of kidneys, a pair of ureters, a urinary bladder and a urethra.
2. Urine formation involves three main processes, i.e. filtration, reabsorption and secretion.

Which of the statement(s) is/are correct?

(a) Only 1 (b) Only 2
(c) Both 1 and 2 (d) Neither 1 nor 2

Ans. (c)

Exp. Statements (1) and (2) are correct.

In humans, the excretory system consists of a pair of kidneys, one pair of ureters, a urinary bladder and a urethra. Kidneys are located in the abdomen, one on either side of the backbone.

Urine produced in the kidney passes through the ureters into the urinary bladder where it is stored until it is released through the urethra.

Urine formation involves three main processes namely, glomerular filtration, reabsorption and secretion, that takes place in different parts of the nephron.

35 Match the following lists and choose the correct code. *(Chap 16, Class-XI, NCERT)*

List I	List II
A. Kidneys	1. Carry urine from the kidneys to the urinary bladder
B. Ureter	2. Helps in formation of urine
C. Urethra	3. Stores urine
D. Urinary bladder	4. Pass urine outside the body

Codes

	A	B	C	D		A	B	C	D
(a)	2	4	3	1	(b)	2	1	4	3
(c)	2	3	4	1	(d)	2	1	3	4

Ans. (b)

Exp. The correct matching is A-2, B-1, C-4, D-3.

Kidneys These are reddish brown, bean-shaped structures situated between the levels of last thoracic and third lumbar vertebra close to the dorsal inner wall of the abdomen. They mainly help in the formation of urine.

Ureters These are the narrow tubes that carry urine from the kidneys to the urinary bladder. Muscles in the ureter walls continuously tighten and relax, forcing urine downward, away from the kidneys.

Urethra It is a tube that drains urine from the bladder to outside of the body. Urethra length differs in human females and males. In males, it is passage for both urine and semen.

Urinary bladder It is the temporary storage reservoir for urine. Urine is stored in the bladder until the pressure of the expanded bladder leads to the urge to pass it out through the urethra.

36 Match the following lists and choose the correct code. *(Chap 16, Class-XI, NCERT)*

List I	List II
A. Ultrafiltration	1. Ureter
B. Concentration of urine	2. Urinary bladder
C. Transport of urine	3. Henle's loop
D. Storage of urine	4. Malpighian corpuscles

Codes

	A	B	C	D		A	B	C	D
(a)	4	3	1	2	(b)	1	2	4	3
(c)	1	3	2	4	(d)	1	4	2	3

Ans. (a)

Exp. The correct matching is A-4, B-3, C-1, D-2.

Ultrafiltration It occurs at the barrier between the blood and the filtrate in the glomerular capsule in the kidney. The force of hydrostatic pressure in the glomerulus is the driving force that pushes filtrate out of the capillaries and into the slits in the nephron.

Concentration of urine It occurs in the loop of Henle. The loop of Henle creates a negative or low water potential in the medulla tissues to absorbs more water from the fluids present in the collecting duct.

Transport of urine It is done by the ureters. Each ureter is a muscular tube that drains into the bladder. They carry urine from kidneys to the urinary bladder.

Urine It is stored in the urinary bladder. Urine is stored in bladder until the pressure of the expanded bladder leads to the urge to pass it out through the urethra.

37 Which of the following statement is incorrect? *(Chap 16, Class-XI, NCERT)*

(a) Protein free fluid is filtered from blood plasma into the Bowman's capsule.
(b) Urine reaches the bladder from the kidneys through the urethra.
(c) Henle's loop plays an important role in concentrating the urine.
(d) Micturition is carried out by a reflex.

Ans. (b)

Exp. Statement (b) is incorrect because urine produced in kidney passes through the ureter into the urinary bladder where it is stored until it is released through the urethra.

In humans adults, the ureters are usually 20-30 cm long and around 3-4 mm in diameter. The muscular layers are responsible for the peristaltic activity that the ureter uses to move the urine from the kidneys to the bladder.

38 Dialysis is a procedure to remove waste products and excess fluid from the blood. This process is related to which of the body organ?

(Chap 5, Class-X, NCERT) (MPPSC Pre 2004)

(a) Liver (b) Kidney (c) Eyes (d) Brain

Ans. (b)

Exp. Dialysis is a process for removing waste and excess water from the blood and is used primarily as an artificial replacement for lost kidney function in people with kidney failure. Dialysis filtres out unwanted substances and fluids from the blood.

39 When kidneys fail to function, there is accumulation of

(Chap 16, Class-XI, NCERT) (UKPSC Pre 2007)

(a) fats in the body
(b) proteins in the body
(c) sugar in the blood
(d) nitrogenous waste products in the blood

Ans. (d)

Exp. Metabolism refers to all of the body's chemical process, the digestion of food and the elimination of waste. The main nitrogenous wastes are ammonia, urea and uric acid. Urea is formed from gluconeogenesis of amino acids.

Urea is one of the primary components of urine. When kidneys fail to function, there is accumulation of nitrogenous waste products in the blood.

40 Which amongst the following is responsible for the formation of stone in the human kidney?

(Chap 16, Class-XI, NCERT) (UPPSC Pre 2015)

(a) Calcium acetate (b) Calcium oxalate
(c) Sodium acetate (d) Sodium benzoate

Ans. (b)

Exp. Calcium oxalate crystals are the most common cause of kidney stones. These are hard clumps of minerals and other substances that form in the kidneys. These crystals are made from oxalate, i.e. a substance found in food like green leafy vegetables which when combines with calcium forms calcium oxalate.

41 Arrange the following in order with respect to the urine formation in human beings.

(Chap 16, Class-XI, NCERT) (Telangana PCS Pre 2023)

1. Formation of concentrated urine
2. Tubular reabsorption
3. Glomerular filtration
4. Tubular secretion

Choose the correct order.

(a) 1, 3, 2, 4 (b) 3, 2, 4, 1
(c) 2, 1, 4, 3 (d) 1, 4, 2, 3

Ans. (b)

Exp. 3, 2, 4, 1 are the correct order with respect to the urine formation in human beings. Glomerular filtration is the initial step in urine formation and occurs in the renal corpuscle of the nephron within the kidneys.

Tubular reabsorption occurs along the renal tubules, which include the PCT, loop of Henle and DCT. Essential substances such as water, glucose, ions and amino acids are reabsorbed from the renal tubules into the bloodstream.

Tubular secretion involves the active transport of certain substances from the blood within the peritubular capillaries into the renal tubules H^+ ions, K^+ ions, NH_3^+ are actively secreted from the blood into the renal tubules. This process helps in maintaining the acid-base balance of the body and eliminating excess ions or substances.

In the collecting duct, water is reabsorbed concentrating the urine. Antidiuretic Hormone (ADH) plays a crucial role in regulating water reabsorption.

42 Consider the following statements.

(Chap 17, Class-XI, NCERT)

1. Longest bone is found in thigh region of human body.
2. Longest bone in man is femur.

Which of the statement(s) given above is/are true about bone?

(a) Only 1 (b) Only 2
(c) Both 1 and 2 (d) Neither 1 nor 2

Ans. (c)

Exp. Statements (1) and (2) are correct.

The femur is the longest bone found in the human body, It is almost 19.9 inches long and is commonly known as thigh bone. The head of the femur articulates with the acetabulum in the pelvic bone forming the hip joint, while the distal part of the femur articulates with the tibia and patella, forming the knee joint.

43 How many pairs of ribs are there in a human body?

(Chap 17, Class-XI, NCERT) (MPPSC Pre 1995)

(a) 12 (b) 10 (c) 14 (d) 11

Ans. (a)

Exp. The human rib cage is made up of 12 paired (total 24) rib bones. Each are symmetrically paired in right and left side. The ribs are flat, thin bones that together with the sternum make up the rib cage. The ribs provide protection for vital organs in the upper body, including the heart and lungs.

44 Find the incorrectly matched pair.

(Chap 17, Class-XI, NCERT)

(a) Long bone - femur (b) Short bone - tarsals
(c) Flat bone - carpals (d) Irregular bone - skull

Ans. (c)

Exp. Pair (c) is incorrectly matched because the flat bones in the skull are occipital, frontal, parietal, etc. The function of flat bones is to protect internal organs such as brain, heart and pelvic organs.

Femur is a long bone that is subjected to most of the weight of the body. It is extremely hard.

Tarsals are short angular bones which make up ankles. Vertebrae and bones of the skull are irregular.

45 **Which one of the following is the correct descending order of longest bones in the human body?** *(Chap 17, Class-XI, NCERT)*

(a) Femur, fibula, humerus, tibia
(b) Humerus, femur, ulna, fibula
(c) Humerus, femur, tibia, fibula
(d) Femur, tibia, fibula, humerus

Ans. (d)

Exp. The femur is the longest bone found in the thigh. It is 19.9 inches long. Then tibia is larger of the two bones in the lower leg. The top of the tibia connects to the knee joint and the bottom connects to the ankle joint. It is 16.9 inches long.

The fibula is a small bone located on the outside of the leg. It is 15.9 inches long. The humerus is the arm bone between your shoulder and elbow. It is 14.4 inches long.

46 **Match the following lists and choose the correct code.** *(Chap 17, Class-XI, NCERT) (IAS Pre 2001)*

List I (Bones)	List II (Names)
A. Triangular bone	1. Clavicle
B. Collar bone	2. Patella
C. Knee cap	3. Ankle bone
D. Tarsals	4. Scapula

Codes

	A	B	C	D		A	B	C	D
(a)	4	1	3	2	(b)	1	4	2	3
(c)	1	4	3	2	(d)	4	1	2	3

Ans. (d)

Exp. The correct matching is A-4, B-1, C-2, D-3.

Scapula is a large triangular flat bone situated in the dorsal part of the thorax between the second and the seventh ribs.

The clavicle is located between the rib cage and the shoulder blade (scapula). It is bone that connects the arm to the body. This bone is commonly called collar bone.

The patella, also known as knee cap, is a flat, rounded triangular bone which articulates with the femur and covers and protects the knee joint.

Tarsals are angular bones that make up the ankle in the humans. It is the set of 7 irregularly shaped bones.

47 **Choose the correctly matched pair.** *(Chap 17, Class-XI, NCERT)*

(a) Cervical vertebrae - 12 (b) Thoracic vertebrae - 7
(c) Lumbar vertebrae - 5 (d) Sacral vertebrae - 12

Ans. (c)

Exp. Pair (c) is correctly matched as the vertebral column usually consists of 26 vertebrae as follows

(i) Cervical vertebrae -7 (its first vertebra is called as atlas vertebra).
(ii) Thoracic vertebrae -12
(iii) Lumbar vertebrae -5
(iv) Sacral vertebra -1 (5 fused vertebrae)
(v) Coccyx vertebra -1 (4 fused vertebrae)

48 **Which one of the following joints is incorrectly matched?** *(Chap 17, Class-XI, NCERT)*

(a) Ball and socket joint – shoulder
(b) Pivot joint – between atlas and axis
(c) Hinge joint – knee
(d) Gliding joint – elbow

Ans. (d)

Exp. Pair (d) is incorrectly matched as gliding joint is present between the carpals. It is a common type of synovial joint formed between bones that meet at flat or nearly flat articular surface. Rest of the pairs are correctly matched.

49 **Which of the following is the correct description of certain parts of normal human skeleton?** *(Chap 17, Class-XI, NCERT) (MPSC Pre 2023)*

(a) The 9th and 10th pairs of ribs are called floating ribs.
(b) Pelvic girdle occurs in the shoulder region.
(c) Each arm consists of 30 bones.
(d) Glenoid cavity is the depression to which the thigh bones articulate.

Ans. (c)

Exp. Among the given options (c) is the correct description of certain parts of normal human skeleton. The total number of bones in upper arm of human is 30. Humerus (upper arm), radius and ulna (forearm) make up the arm and in the palm there are total of 27 bones; the wrist is made up of carpals (8), metacarpals (5) and 14 phalanges, 3 in each finger and 8 in thumb. So, along with 1 humerus, radius and 1 ulna each, arm has makes 30 bones.

50 **Consider the following statements.** *(Chap 6, Class-X, NCERT)*

1. The peripheral nervous system consists of cranial nerves arising from the brain and spinal nerves arising from the spinal cord.
2. The brain has two major parts forebrain and hindbrain.
3. The hindbrain comprises pons, cerebellum and medulla.
4. Involuntary actions are controlled by midbrain and hindbrain.

Which of the statements given above are correct?

(a) 1, 2 and 4 (b) 1, 3 and 4 (c) 2, 3 and 4 (d) 1, 3 and 2

Ans. (b)

Exp. Statements (1), (3) and (4) are correct. The peripheral nervous system consists of cranial nerves arising from the brain and spinal nerves arising from the spinal cord. The hindbrain comprises of pons, cerebellum and medulla. Involuntary actions are controlled by midbrain and hindbrain.

Actions like vomiting are controlled by the medulla of hindbrain whereas reflexes associated with vision and hearing is controlled by midbrain.

Statement (2) is incorrect because the brain has three major parts; forebrain, midbrain and hindbrain.

51 Which of the following statements are correct about the brain? *(Chap 6, Class-X, NCERT)*

1. Centres for hearing, smell, memory, sight, etc., are located in forebrain.
2. The main thinking part of brain is hindbrain.
3. Involuntary actions like salivation, vomiting, blood pressure are controlled by the medulla in the hindbrain.
4. Cerebellum does not control posture and balance of the body.

Codes

(a) 1 and 2 (b) 1 and 3 (c) 1, 2 and 3 (d) 3 and 4

Ans. (b)

Exp. Statements (1) and (3) are correct.

Centres for hearing, smell, memory, sight, etc., are located in forebrain. Involuntary actions like salivation, vomiting, blood pressure are controlled by the medulla in the hindbrain.

Statements (2) and (4) are incorrect because the main thinking part of brain is the forebrain. Cerebellum is responsible for precision of voluntary action and maintaining the posture and balance of the body.

52 Which of the following is true about cranial meninges? *(Chap 18, Class-XI, NCERT)*

1. The outer layer is known as dura mater.
2. The middle layer is called pia mater.
3. The inner layer is called arachnoid.

Codes

(a) 1 and 2 (b) 1, 2 and 3 (c) Only 1 (d) Only 2

Ans. (c)

Exp. The human brain is well-protected by the skull. Inside the skull, the brain is covered by cranial meninges consisting of an outer layer called dura mater a very thin middle layer called arachnoid and an inner layer called as pia mater.

53 Choose the correctly matched pair. *(Chap 6, Class-X, NCERT)*

1. Medulla oblongata - Centre for regulating swallowing and vomiting.
2. Hypothalamus - Controls body temperature.
3. Cerebellum - Controls blood pressure.

Codes

(a) 1 and 2 (b) Only 1
(c) 1 and 3 (d) 3 and 2

Ans. (a)

Exp. Pairs (1) and (2) are correctly matched.

Medulla oblongata controls the blood pressure, salivation and vomiting. Hypothalamus contains a number of centres which controls body temperature, urge for eating and drinking.

Pair (3) is incorrectly matched because cerebellum is responsible for maintaining the posture and balance of the body.

54 Which of the following statements are correct? *(Chap 18, Class-XI, NCERT)*

1. Sudden action in response to something in environment is called reflex action.
2. Sensory neurons carry signals from spinal cord to muscles.
3. Efferent neurons carry signal from CNS to the effector.

Codes

(a) 1 and 2 (b) 1 and 3
(c) 2 and 3 (d) All of these

Ans. (b)

Exp. Statements (1) and (3) are correct.

Sudden action in response to something in environment is called reflex action. Efferent neurons carry signal from CNS to the effector.

Statement (2) is incorrect because sensory neurons transmits impulses from a receptor, to the central nervous system.

55 Which of the following is not true for endocrine glands? *(Chap 19, Class-XI, NCERT)*

(a) Hypothalamus plays an important role in the release of many hormones.
(b) Thyroxine regulates carbohydrates, proteins and fat metabolism in our body.
(c) Growth hormone regulates the blood sugar level.
(d) Testis and ovaries changes during puberty are associated with testosterone in male and oestrogen in females.

Ans. (c)

Exp. Statement (c) is incorrect because growth hormone is produced by the anterior pituitary. It is responsible for the regulation of several physiological processes such as growth and metabolism.

56 Consider the following statements about pineal gland. *(Chap 19, Class-XI, NCERT)*

1. Pineal gland secretes a hormone called melatonin.
2. This hormone regulates diurnal rhythm in our body.
3. This also influences pigmentation.

Which of the statement(s) given above is/are correct?

(a) 1 and 2
(b) 1, 2 and 3
(c) 1 and 3
(d) Only 1

Ans. (b)

Exp. All statements are correct about pineal gland. The pineal gland is located on the dorsal side of forebrain. It secretes a hormone called melatonin. It plays a very important role in the regulation of 24 hours diurnal rhythm of our body.

It also influences metabolism, body temperature, pigmentation, the menstrual cycle as well as our defence capability.

57 **Which of the following is correct about gland?** *(Chap 19, Class-XI, NCERT)*

(a) Thyroid gland synthesise T_3 and T_4 hormones.
(b) Adrenal gland acts as both exocrine and endocrine glands.
(c) Oxytocin hormone is secreted by pineal gland.
(d) Blood pressure is controlled by parathyroid gland.

Ans. (a)

Exp. Statement (a) is correct about gland.

Thyroid gland synthesise two hormones, tetraiodothyronine or thyroxine (T_4) and triiodothyronine (T_3). Iodine is essential for normal rate of hormone synthesis in thyroid.

Statements (b), (c) and (d) are incorrect and can be corrected as pancreas has got a dual function of an exo as well as endocrine glands. Adrenaline is known as flight or fight hormone as it prepares the body for emergency. Renin and nor-epinephrine both help in controlling blood pressure situations. Oxytoxin is secreted by hypothalamus.

58 **Consider the following statements about pituitary gland.** *(Chap 19, Class-XI, NCERT)*

1. Pituitary gland is situated in brain.
2. The effect of oversecretion of hormone from pituitary gland is increased growth in length.
3. Growth hormone is secreted from pituitary gland.

Which of the statements given above are correct?

(a) 1, 2 and 3 (b) 1 and 2
(c) 2 and 3 (d) 1 and 3

Ans. (a)

Exp. All statements are correct.

Pituitary gland is situated in the brain. Growth hormone is secreted from the anterior pituitary.

Oversecretion of growth hormone stimulates abnormal growth of the body leading to gigantism and low secretion of GH results in stunted growth resulting in dwarfism.

59 **Match the following lists and choose the correct code.** *(Chap 19, Class-XI, NCERT)*

List I (Endocrine glands)	List II (Hormone secreted)
A. Ovary	1. Insulin
B. Pituitary	2. Progesterone
C. Pancreas	3. Growth hormone
D. Adrenal	4. Epinephrine

Codes

	A	B	C	D		A	B	C	D
(a)	3	2	4	1	(b)	2	3	4	1
(c)	2	3	1	4	(d)	3	2	1	4

Ans. (c)

Exp. The correct matching is A-2, B-3, C-1, D-4.

Ovary It produces two groups of steroid hormones called oestrogen and progesterone. These are responsible for development of secondary sexual characters.

Pituitary gland It secretes growth hormone which regulates the growth and development of body. If this hormone is secreted in excess it can cause gigantism and if produced in low quantity then cause cretinism.

Pancreas It secretes hormones called glucagon and insulin. Insulin is secreted by β-cells of the islets of Langerhans. Insulin helps to lower the glucose level in the body.

Adrenal gland It secretes two hormones called adrenaline or epinephrine and nor-epinephrine. These are commonly called as catecholamines. Adrenaline is also called stress hormone.

60 **Match the following lists and choose the correct code.** *(Chap 19, Class-XI, NCERT)*

List I (Hormones)	List II (Secreting glands)
A. Progesterone	1. Thyroid
B. Testosterone	2. Ovaries (females)
C. Thyroxine	3. Testes (males)

Codes

	A	B	C		A	B	C
(a)	2	3	1	(b)	3	2	1
(c)	3	1	2	(d)	1	2	3

Ans. (a)

Exp. The correct matching is A-2, B-3, C-1.

Progesterone It is secreted by ovaries in the human female body. It helps to maintain normal ovarian cycle. It supports pregnancy. It also acts on the mammary glands and stimulates milk secretion.

Testosterone It is secreted by testis in males. They regulate development, maturation and function of the male accessory sex organs.

Thyroxine It is secreted by thyroid gland.

It plays vital role in the digestion, heart and muscle function, brain development and maintenance of bones.

61 **Consider the following statements regarding human brain.** *(Chap 18, Class-XI, NCERT) (Chap 23, Module-5, NIOS)*

1. The inner surface of cerebrum is highly convoluted with rides and grooves.
2. The inner portion of the cerebrum consists of 'white matter'.
3. Cerebrum is the seat of intelligence.

Which of the statement (s) is /are correct?.

(a) Only 1 (b) 1 and 2 (c) 2 and 3 (d) 1 and 3

Ans. (c)

Exp. Statements (2) and (3) are correct.

Cerebrum is the largest portion of the brain. Vertically divided into two halves : right and left cerebral hemispheres. Their outer surface is highly convoluted with ridges and grooves.

The outer portion or the cortex of the cerebrum contains cell bodies of the neurons, which is the basic unit of nervous tissue. Being grayish in colour, it is called the gray matter. The inner portion of the cerebrum consists of 'white matter', which mainly contains the axon or nerve fibres of the neurons. Cerebrum is the seat of intelligence.

62 **Choose the incorrectly matched pair.**
(Chap 2, Class-XII, NCERT)

(a) Acrosome	–	Enzyme filled cap structure on sperm head.
(b) Middle piece	–	Possesses numerous mitochondria.
(c) Sperm tail	–	Facilitates sperm motility essential for fertilisation.
(d) Semen	–	Contains only sperms.

Ans. (d)

Exp. Pair (d) is matched incorrectly because the combined secretion of three glands namely, seminal vesicle, prostate gland, Cowper's gland, together with sperms collectively form semen. Rest are correctly matched.

63 **If the mammalian ovum fails to get fertilised, which one of the following is likely to happen?**
(Chap 2, Class-XII, NCERT)

(a) Corpus luteum will degenerate
(b) Oestrogen secretion further decreases
(c) Primary follicle starts developing
(d) Progesterone secretion rapidly increases

Ans. (a)

Exp. If mammalian ovum fails to get fertilised, then corpus luteum (source of progesterone and oestrogen) will disintegrate and degenerate resulting in decrease in the level of progesterone.

Thus, endometrial lining of uterus sloughs off and menstruation begins, making a new cycle.

64 **Match the following lists and choose the correct code.**
(Chap 2, Class-XII, NCERT)
(Unit 17, Class-X, Tamil Nadu Board)

List I	List II
A. Menstrual phase	1. The Graafian follicle ruptures and releases the ovum (egg)
B. Follicular phase	2. Development of primary follicles
C. Ovulatory phase	3. Emptied Graafian follicle develops into corpus luteum.
D. Luteal phase	4. Primary follicles grow to become a fully mature Graafian follicle

Codes

	A	B	C	D
(a)	2	1	4	3
(b)	2	4	1	3
(c)	4	3	2	1
(d)	3	2	4	1

Ans. (b)

Exp. The correct matching is A-2, B-4, C-1, D-3.

The cyclic events that take place in a rhythmic fashion during the reproductive period of a woman's life is called menstrual cycle.

Menstrual phase occurs for 4 - 5 days in which their is development of primary follicles.

Follicular phase occurs for 6th to 13th day in which primary follicles grow to become a fully mature Graafian follicle.

Ovulatory phase occurs on the 14th day in which the Graafian follicle ruptures and releases the ovum (egg).

Luteal phase occurs for the 15th-28th day in which emptied Graafian follicle develops into corpus luteum.

Chapter 08

Human Health and Diseases

Human Health and Diseases

Health and Diseases

Health

- State of complete physical, mental and social well-being.

Disease

- Any disturbance in the structure or function of any organ or part of the body.
- **Symptoms of Diseases** experienced by the individual who is suffering, e.g. Dizziness, tiredness etc.
- **Sign** an observable phenomenon that can be identified by another person. e.g. High temperature, wound etc.

Types of Diseases

- **Congenital Disease** These diseases occur from the time of birth.
- **Acquired Diseases** These diseases develop after birth. e.g. Cancer, etc.
  - **Acute Disease** Lasts for short period of time, e.g. Common cold.
  - **Chronic Disease** Lasts for a longer time. e.g. Cancer.

Rules for The Treatment of Infectious Diseases

- **Reducing the Impact of Disease** Reducing the effect of the disease by use of medicines.
- **Death of the Casual organism** For an effective treatment, micro-organism causing the disease must be killed.

Methods of Prevention of Infections Diseases

- **Balanced Diet** It plays a major role in successful functioning of immune system.
- **Strong Immune System** It fights with disease causing micro-organisms and kill them.
  - **Vaccination** Dead or attenuated
  - **Immunisation** Immunoglobulin molecules

Communicable Disease/Infectious Disease

- **Airborne Disease** Caused by micro-organism and is transmitted through air. e.g. Common cold.
- **Water Borne Disease** Caused by pathogenic microbes and transmitted by contaminated water. e.g. Diarrhea .
- **Sexually Transmitted Diseases** Diseases that spreads from an infected person to an uninfected person through sexual contact. e.g. AIDS.
- **Vector Borne Disease** Diseases transmitted by the bite of an infected species which surround us e.g. *Aedes*-Dengue .
- **Bacterial Diseases** e.g. Cholera caused by *Vibrio cholerae*.
- **Viral Diseases** e.g. Small pox caused by *Variola* virus.
- **Protozoan Diseases** e.g. Malaria caused by Plasmodium.
- **Fungal Diseases** e.g. Ringworm caused by *Micosporum trichophyton*.
- **Non-Communicable / Non-infectious Disease**
- **Nutrition Deficiency** caused by deficiency of a nutrient. e.g. Kwashiorkor.
- **Allergy** Exaggerated response of immune system to certain agent present in environment. e.g. Skin rashes.
- **Degenerated Disease** Caused due to failure of an organ. e.g. Coronary arteriosclerosis.
- **Respiratory and Skin Diseases** caused due to pollution.
- **Mental Disease** caused due to distortion in the nervous system.

Immunity

Immunity

- Ability of the body to protect itself from disease causing agent.
- **Louis Pasteur** (Father of Immunology)

Types of Immunity

(i) **Innate Immunity** It is present right from birth and also called **natural immunity.**

(ii) **Acquired Immunity** It is acquired during life time of an individual and also known as **adaptive immunity.**

- **Active Acquired Immunity** Immunity developed by the body when it is exposed to antigens.
- **Natural Acquired Active** Immunity Occurs when a person is exposed to a live pathogen.
- **Artificial Acquired Active immunity** (Require commercial production of antigens).

- Vaccine (improves immunity to particular disease).
- Toxoids (Induce antibody formation).
- Viral Vaccine (Prepared from viruses, e.g. Polio).

- **Passive Acquired Immunity** Transfer of actively formed anti-bodies from one person to another.
- **Natural Acquired Passive Immunity** Antibodies transmitted from mother to baby. e.g. mother's milk.
- **Artificial Acquired Passive Immunity** Antibodies acquired from an immune serum medicine e.g. Tetanus.

SOURCE **New NCERT Class VIII** *(Microorganisms : Friend and Foe)*, **Old NCERT Class IX** *(Why do we Fall ill)* **NCERT Class XII** *(Human Health and Disease)*

1 **Consider the following statements.**

(Chap 7, Class-XII, NCERT)

1. Health is a state of being well enough to function well physically, mentally and socially.
2. Health of all organisms depend on their surroundings or their environment.
3. Public cleanliness, good economic condition, social equality and harmony are needed for individual health.
4. Disease means being uncomfortable.

Which of the statements given above are correct?

(a) 1 and 4 (b) 2, 3 and 4 (c) 1 and 3 (d) 1, 2, 3 and 4

Ans. (d)

Exp. All the given statements are correct.

Health is a state of being well enough to function well physically, mentally and socially. The health of all organisms will depend on their surroundings or their environment. The environment includes the physical environment.

Public cleanliness is important for individual health. Good economic conditions and jobs are also important for individual health. Social equality and harmony also play a great role in individual health.

Disease means being uncomfortable. When there is a disease, either the functioning or the appearance of one or more systems of the body will change for the worse. These changes give rise to symptoms and signs of disease.

2 **Which of the following statements is not true about vitamins?** *(Chap 1, Class-VI, NCERT)*

(a) Vitamins help in protecting our body against diseases.
(b) Vitamin-C helps body to fight against many diseases.
(c) Vitamin-A helps our body to use calcium for bones and teeth.
(d) Sunlight is a good source of vitamin-D.

Ans. (c)

Exp. Statement (c) is not true about vitamins. Vitamins help in protecting our body against diseases. Vitamins also help in keeping our eyes, bones, teeth and gums healthy. Vitamins are of different kinds known by different names.

Our body needs all type of vitamins in small quantities. Vitamin-A keeps our skin and eyes healthy. Vitamin-C helps body to fight against many diseases.
Vitamin-D helps our body to use calcium for bones and teeth. Sunlight is a good source of vitamin-D. Vitamin-E act as an antioxidant. Vitamin-K plays role in the blood clot formation.

3 **Which of the following pair is incorrectly matched?**

(Chap 1, Class-VI, NCERT)

(a) Vitamin-C – Oranges (b) Vitamin-D – Fish
(c) Vitamin-A – Papaya (d) Vitamin-K – Sunlight

Ans. (d)

Exp. Pair (d) is incorrectly matched. Vitamins are organic compounds, found in natural foods which are required for normal growth and maintenance of the body.
Both humans and animals require vitamins for their growth. Sunlight is a good source of vitamin-D. Vitamin-K is found in green leafy vegetable, fish, meat, eggs, etc.

Oranges and lemon are a good source of vitamin-C. This vitamin enhances immunity. Papaya is a rich source of vitamin-A.

4 **Consider the following pairs.** *(Chap 1, Class-VI, NCERT)*

	Vitamin/Mineral		Deficiency disease
1.	Iodine	–	Goitre
2.	Iron	–	Scurvy
3.	Calcium	–	Bone and tooth decay
4.	Vitamin-D	–	Night blindness

Which of the pairs given above is/are correctly matched?

(a) 1 and 2
(b) 2 and 3
(c) 1 and 3
(d) Only 3

Ans (c)

Exp. Pairs (1) and (3) are correctly matched.
Deficiency of iodine in our body causes goitre. Symptoms of this include glands in the neck appear swollen, mental disability in children, etc.
Deficiency of calcium leads to bone and tooth decay. In this, bones become weak and tooth decay starts early.
Pairs (2) and (4) are incorrectly matched because
Deficiency of iron cause anaemia. It results into tiredness and shortness of breath.
Deficiency of vitamin-D cause rickets. In this, bones become weak and can easily bent.

5 **From the following pairs, find the one which is correctly matched?** *(Chap 7, Class-XII, NCERT)*
(BPSC Pre Re-exam 2022)

(a) Scurvy – Thiamine
(b) Tuberculosis – ATS
(c) Tetanus – BCG
(d) Malaria – Chloroquine
(e) None of the above/More than one of the above

Ans. (d)

Exp. Pair (d) is correctly matched.
Chloroquine is used for the treatment of malaria.
Scurvy is a disease caused due to the deficiency of vitamin-C.
BCG vaccine is given to prevent tuberculosis and ATS is used for prophylaxis and treatment of tetanus.

6 **Some diseases last for only very short periods of time, these are called ...... disease, but other ailments can last for a long time, even as much as a lifetime and are called ....**
Choose the correct option to fill in the blanks.
(Chap 7, Class-XII, NCERT)

(a) chronic, acute (b) acute, chronic
(c) active, passive (d) passive, active

Ans. (b)

Exp. The manifestations of disease will be different depending on a number of factors. One of the most obvious factors that determine how we perceive the disease is its duration.

Some diseases last for only very short periods of time and these are called acute diseases, e.g. typhoid. Other ailments can last for a long time, even as much as a lifetime and are called chronic diseases.

An example is the infection causing elephantiasis, which is very common in some parts of India.

7 **Consider the following Assertion (A) and Reason (R) and choose the correct code.** *(Chap 7, Class-XII, NCERT)*

Assertion (A) Any disease that causes poor functioning of some parts of the body will affect our general health as well.

Reason (R) All functions of the body are necessary for general health.

Codes

(a) Both A and R are true and R is the correct explanation of A.
(b) Both A and R are true, but R is not the correct explanation of A.
(c) A is true, but R is false.
(d) Both A and R are false.

Ans. (b)

Exp. Both Assertion (A) and Reason (R) are true, but Reason (R) is not the correct explanation of Assertion (A).

Any disease that causes poor functioning of some parts of the body will affect our general health as well. All functions of the body are necessary for general health.

But an acute disease, which gets over very soon, will not have time to cause major effects on general health, while a chronic disease will do so.

8 **Which of the following pairs are correctly matched ?**
(Chap 7, Class-XII NCERT) (Chap 32, Module-7, NIOS) (BPSC Pre 2023)

1. Anorexia – Sleep disorder
2. Insomnia – Eating disorder
3. Dyspnoea – Shortness of breath
4. Anosmia – Partial or full loss of smell

Select the correct answer using the codes given below.

(a) 1 and 2 (b) 2 and 3 (c) 3 and 4 (d) All of these

Ans. (c)

Exp. Pairs (3) and (4) are correctly matched.

Dyspnoea is referred to as shortness of breath. The main symptom of dyspnoea is laboured breathing. Diet and exercise can treat dyspnoea.

Anosmia is the partial or complete loss of the sense of smell. This loss may be temporary or permanent. Irritation to the mucus membranes lining the nose, blockage of the nasal passage, brain or nerve damages are the causes of anosmia.

Insomnia is a common sleep disorder.

Anorexia is an eating disorder.

9 **Species of *Plasmodium* which causes malignant malaria?** *(Chap 7, Class-XII, NCERT) (RAS/RTS Pre 2023)*

(a) *Vivax* (b) *Falciparum*
(c) *Ovale* (d) *Malariae*

Ans. (b)

Exp. *Falciparum* species of *Plasmodium* causes malignant malaria which is the most dangerous form of the disease. Other species of *Plasmodium* (i.e. *vivax, ovale, malariae*) causes benign malaria. Hence, rest options are incorrect because they do not cause malignant malaria.

10 **Consider the following statements.**
(Chap 7, Class-XII, NCERT) (BPSC Pre 2023)

1. Taeniasis is an intestinal infection caused by three species of tapeworm - *Taenia solium, Taenia saginata* and *Taenia asiatica.*
2. When cysts develop in the brain, the condition is referred to a Neurocysticercosis (NCC).

Which of the above statement (s) is / are correct?

(a) Only 1
(b) Only 2
(c) Both 1 and 2
(d) None of the above

Ans. (c)

Exp. Both statements (1) and (2) are correct. This can be explained as

Taeniasis is an intestinal infection caused by 3 species of tapeworm : *Taenia solium* (pork tapeworm), *Taenia saginata* (beef tapeworm) and *Taenia asiatica* (Asian tapeworm). Human can become infected with these tapeworms by eating raw or under cooked beef or pork. Their larva can grow in muscles, eyes, skin and central nervous system. When cysts develop in the brain (CNS) the condition is referred to a Neurocysticercosis (NCC). Common symptoms are seizures, chronic headaches and increased pressure in the brain.

11 **Choose the incorrectly matched pair.**
(Chap 7, Class-XII, NCERT)

(a) Chronic disease – Tuberculosis
(b) Acute disease – Cough and cold
(c) Infectious disease – AIDS
(d) Non-infectious disease – Cold

Ans. (c)

Exp. Pair (c) is incorrectly matched because AIDS (Acquired Immuno Deficiency Syndrome) is not an infectious disease. Diseases where microbes are the intermediate cause are called infectious disease.

As the microbes spread in the community, the diseases they cause will also spread with them, e.g. common cold.

Diseases that are not caused by infectious agents are called non-infectious disease.

For example, some cancers are caused by genetic abnormalities.

12 **Consider the following statements.**

(Chap 7, Class-XII, NCERT)

1. The signs and symptoms of a disease will depend on the tissue or organ which the microbe targets.
2. An active immune system recruits many cells to the affected tissue to kill off the disease causing microbes. This recruitment process is called swelling.
3. Severity of disease manifestations depend on the number of microbes in the body.

How many statement(s) is/are correct?

(a) Only one (b) Only two
(c) All three (d) None of these

Ans. (b)

Exp. Only two statements i.e., (1) and (3) are correct. The signs and symptoms of a disease will depend on the tissue or organ which the microbe targets. If lungs are targeted, then symptoms will be cough and breathlessness. If the liver is targeted, there will be jaundice. The severity of disease manifestations depend on the number of microbes in the body.

If the number of microbes is very small, the disease manifestations may be minor or unnoticed, but if the number of the same microbes is large, the disease can be severe enough to be life - threatening.

Statement (2) is incorrect because an active immune system recruits many cells to the affected tissue to kill off the disease causing microbes. This recruitment process is called inflammation.

13 **Which of the following is not a limitation to dealing with infectious diseases?** ***(Chap 7, Class-XII, NCERT)***

(a) Once someone has a disease, their body functions are damaged and may never recover completely.
(b) Treatment will take time, which means that someone suffering from a disease is likely to be bedridden for sometime even if we can give proper treatment.
(c) The person suffering from an infectious disease can serve as the source from where the infection may spread to other people.
(d) Symptom directed treatment by itself will make the infecting microbe go away and the disease will be cured.

Ans. (d)

Exp. There are three limitations to dealing with infectious diseases. The first is that once someone had a disease, their body functions are damaged and may never recover completely.

The second is that treatment will take time, which means that someone suffering from a disease is likely to be bedridden for sometime even if we can give proper treatment.

The third is that the person suffering from an infectious disease can serve as the source from where the infection may spread to other people. This leads to the multiplication of the above difficulties and may also worsen the case.

It is because of such reasons that prevention of diseases is better than their cure. The symptom directed treatment by itself will never make the infecting microbes go away and cure the disease automatically.

14 **Which of the following pair is incorrectly matched?**

(Chap 2, Class-VIII, NCERT)

	Disease	Mode of Transmission
(a)	Measles	Virus, nasal or throat secretion
(b)	Chicken pox	Virus, through air by coughing and sneezing
(c)	Hepatitis - A	Virus, Faecal-oral route
(d)	Polio	Fungi, droplets or aerosols

Ans. (d)

Exp. Pair (d) is incorrectly matched because polio is an infectious disease caused by polio virus. It is transmitted through contaminated water, or contact with an infected person. This virus cause paralysis and is easily preventable by the polio vaccine.

This virus primarily grows and multiplies in the intestine, from where it can attack the nervous system and will cause polio and paralysis on advanced level.

Measles, chicken pox are transmitted by air and hepatitis-B gets transmitted by water.

15 **Consider the following pairs.**

(Chap 2, Class-VIII, NCERT)

1. Pathogens – Microorganisms causing diseases in human beings, plants and animals.
2. Non-communicable diseases – Microbial diseases that can spread from an infected person to a healthy person through air, water, food or physical contact.
3. Carriers – Insects and animals which carry diseases causing microbes.

How many pair(s) is/are incorrectly matched.

(a) Only one (b) Only two
(c) All three (d) None of these

Ans. (a)

Exp. Only one pair i.e., (2) is incorrectly matched. Microbial diseases that can spread from an infected person to a healthy person through air, water, food or physical contact are called communicable diseases. Examples of such diseases include cholera, common cold, chicken pox and tuberculosis. Pathogens enter our body through air, water or food and cause diseases in humans, plants and animals. They can get transmitted by direct contact with an infected person or carried through an animal.

16 Which of the following statements is/are correct? *(Chap 7, Class-XII, NCERT)*

1. A bacteria, *Helicobacter pylori* is responsible for peptic ulcers.
2. Peptic ulcer disease is no longer a chronic, frequently disabling condition, but a disease that can be cured by treatment with antibiotics.
3. Marshall and Warren received Nobel Prize in 2005 for discovery of peptic ulcer causing bacteria.

Codes

(a) 1 and 2 (b) 1 and 3 (c) 1 and 3 (d) 1, 2 and 3

Ans. (d)

Exp. All statements are correct.

Two Australians made a discovery that a bacterium, *Helicobacter pylori*, was responsible for peptic ulcers. They showed that patients could be cured of peptic ulcer only when the bacteria were killed off from the stomach. After their discovery, peptic ulcers disease was no longer considered a chronic, frequently disabling condition, but a disease that can be cured by a short period of treatment with antibiotics.

For this achievement, Marshall and Warren received the Nobel Prize for Physiology and Medicine in 2005.

17 Identify the correctly matched pair. *(Chap 7, Class-XII, NCERT)*

(a) AIDS – HIV-Roundworm
(b) Sleeping sickness – *Trypanosoma* - Protozoan
(c) Kala-azar – *Leishmania* - Bacteria
(d) Ascariasis – *Ascaris lumbricoides* - Fungi

Ans. (b)

Exp. Pair (b) is correctly matched as *Trypanosoma* is the protozoan organism responsible for sleeping sickness. It is transmitted by tse tse fly bite which have acquired their infection from human beings or from animals harbouring human pathogenic parasites.

Pairs (a), (c) and (d) are matched incorrectly because *Leishmania* is the protozoan organism causing kala-azar. It is caused by the bite from sand flies –the vector of the *Leishmania* parasite.

Adult roundworm *Ascaris lumbricoides* causes ascariasis. Roundworms are type of parasitic worms.

AIDS is caused by HIV (Human Immunodeficiency Virus). By damaging your immune system, HIV interferes with your body's ability to fight infection and diseases.

18 Match the following lists and choose the correct code. *(Chap 7, Class-XII, NCERT)*

	List I (Diseases)		List II (Causes)
A.	Influenza, dengue fever, SARS	1.	Virus
B.	Typhoid, cholera, tuberculosis, anthrax	2.	Bacteria
C.	Skin infections	3.	Fungi
D.	Malaria	4.	Protozoan
E.	Worm	5.	Elephantiasis

Codes

	A	B	C	D	E
(a)	1	2	3	4	5
(b)	5	4	3	2	1
(c)	1	4	3	2	5
(d)	1	2	4	3	5

Ans. (a)

Exp. The correct matching is A-1, B-2, C-3, D-4, E-5.

Diseases like influenza, common cold, dengue fever, AIDS and SARS are caused by viruses. Viral disease are not cured by antibiotics. Only immunological responses within the body can cure them. For this vaccination is done.

Diseases like typhoid fever, cholera, tuberculosis and anthrax are caused by bacteria. These diseases can be cured by taking antibiotics.

Many common skin infections are caused by different kinds of fungi like black fungus disease, white fungus disease, etc. Malaria and kala-azar are caused by protozoan microbes. They need vector for transmission.

Disease like elephantiasis is caused by different species of worms. It affects lymph nodes and lymph vessels.

19 Polio is a viral disease. WHO extends facilities of members nations to fight against polio. *(Chap 7, Class-XII, NCERT) (MPPSC Pre 2022)*

1. It is acute viral infection caused by DNA virus.
2. Poliomyelitis is commonly called as polio.
3. Pulse polio immunisation programme was launched in India in 1995.
4. New polio is already eradicated from India.

Which of the statement(s) given above is/are correct?

(a) 1 and 2 (b) 2 and 3
(c) 2, 3 and 4 (d) 3 and 4

Ans. (c)

Exp. Statements 2, 3 and 4 are correct as poliomyelitis is commonly called as polio. National Immunisation Day (NID) commonly known as pulse polio immunisation programme was launched in India in 1995.

Fortunately, India is free of wild polio virus since 2011. The last case of polio virus in India was reported in Howrah, West Bengal on 13th January 2011. Since then, India has been free of this disease

Statement (1) is incorrect because polio virus is a non-enveloped virus having single-stranded RNA genome.

20 **Consider the following statements about ascariasis.** *(Chap 7, Class-XII, NCERT) (Chap 32, Module-7, NIOS)*

1. It is caused by *Entamoeba histolytica* a protozoan parasite infecting large intestine.
2. Muscular pain, internal bleeding, imparied digestion, colic pain and blockage of intestinal passage.
3. Antihelminthic drugs are used for treatment.

Choose the correct statement.

(a) 1 and 2 (b) Only 1
(c) 2 and 3 (d) 1 and 3

Ans. (c)

Exp. Ascariasis is caused by *Ascaris lumbricoides* (roundworm) that resides in the small intestine. Eggs of the parasite come out along with the faeces of the infected person and contaminate soil, water, plants, etc. It is transmitted by air, housefly and cockroaches that may carry the pathogen from the infected person stool to food water.

Amoebiasis is caused by *Entamoeba histolytica* a protozoan parasitic infecting large intestine.

21 **Disease causing microbes can spread through air *via* little droplets when an infected person sneezes or coughs in all, except** *(Chap 7, Class-XII, NCERT)*

(a) Tuberculosis (b) Pneumonia
(c) Common cold (d) Malaria

Ans. (d)

Exp. Malaria is caused by a *Plasmodium* parasite and transmitted by the bite of infected mosquitoes. This cannot be spread through tiny droplets when an infected person sneezes or coughs.

Disease that can be spread through little droplets thrown out by an infected person who sneezes or cough are called communicable diseases. Examples of such diseases which spread through the air are the common cold, pneumonia and tuberculosis.

22 **Consider the following statements about spread of the given diseases and choose the correct code.** *(Chap 7, Class-XII, NCERT)*

1. AIDS virus can spread through blood to blood contact with infected person or from an infected mother to her baby during pregnancy or through breastfeeding.
2. Cholera can spread through water, if the excreta from someone suffering from this disease, get mixed with the drinking water used by people living nearby. The cholera causing microbes will enter new hosts through the water they drink.

Codes

(a) Statement 1 is true, but 2 is false.
(b) Statement 2 is true, but 1 is false.
(c) Both statements 1 and 2 are true.
(d) Both statements 1 and 2 are false.

Ans. (c)

Exp. Both statements (1) and (2) are true.

AIDS (Acquired Immuno Deficiency Syndrome) is a disease caused by the HIV virus. It can spread through many ways. It can spread by sexual contact, blood to blood contact with infected people or from an infected mother to her baby during pregnancy or through breastfeeding.

Cholera is a bacterial disease caused by the bacterium *Vibrio cholerae*. This type of bacteria is usually present in contaminated foods. The cholera causing microbes will enter new hosts through the water they drink and cause disease in them.

23 **...... is a bacteria that causes disease. If it enters through the mouth, it can stay in the gut lining like typhoid causing bacteria, or it can go to the liver, like the viruses that cause jaundice. Choose the correct option to fill in the blank.** *(Chap 7, Class-XII, NCERT)*

(a) Malaria (b) Tuberculosis (c) Cholera (d) AIDS

Ans. (b)

Exp. Tuberculosis is an infectious disease usually caused by *Mycobacterium tuberculosis* bacteria.

Tuberculosis causing bacteria if enters through the mouth, they can stay in the gut lining like typhoid-causing bacteria, or they can go to the liver, like the viruses that cause jaundice.

It spread from one person to the next through the air when people who have active tuberculosis in their lungs cough, spit, speak or sneeze.

24 **The causative organism of Japanese encephalitis is** *(Chap 7, Class-XII, NCERT)*

(a) protozoans (b) bacteria
(c) roundworm (d) virus

Ans. (d)

Exp. The causative organism of Japanese encephalitis is virus. Encephalitis is an inflammation of the brain that can cause fever, headache, confusion, seizures, and in some cases, death. The Japanese encephalitis virus has an incubation period of 2 to 26 days. The vast majority of infections are asymptomatic, only 1 in 250 infections develop into encephalitis.

25 **The bacterium (*Bacillus anthracis*) which causes anthrax disease was discovered by** *(Chap 2, Class-VIII, NCERT)*

(a) Louis Pasteur (b) Edward Jenner
(c) Alexander Fleming (d) Robert Koch

Ans. (d)

Exp. The bacterium (*Bacillus anthracis*) which causes anthrax disease was discovered by Robert Koch (1876). It mainly affects animals.

Humans can become infected through contact with an infected animal or by inhaling spores. Symptoms onset occurs between one day to over two months, after the infection is contracted.

26 **A carrier is the .... mosquito which carries the parasite of malaria. .... mosquito acts as carrier of dengue virus.** *(Chap 7, Class-XII, NCERT)*

Choose the correct option for the above statement to fill in the blanks.

(a) Male *Aedes*, Female *Anopheles*
(b) Female *Anopheles*, Male *Aedes*
(c) Male *Anopheles*, Male *Aedes*
(d) Female *Anopheles*, Female *Aedes*

Ans. (d)

Exp. There are some insects and animals which act as carriers of disease-causing microbes. An example of a carrier is the female *Anopheles* mosquito which carries the parasite of malaria.

Female *Aedes* mosquito acts as carrier of dengue virus. Other example include housefly.

The flies sit on the garbage and animal excreta, pathogens stick to their bodies. When these flies sit on uncovered food they may transfer the pathogens.

27 **Match the following lists and choose the correct code.** *(Chap 2, Class-VIII, NCERT)*

List I (Vector)	List II (Disease)
A. *Salmonella typhi*	1. Pneumonia
B. *Streptococcus pneumoniae* and *Haemophilus influenzae*	2. Common cold
C. Rhino virus	3. Typhoid
D. *Plasmodium*	4. Malaria

Codes

	A	B	C	D		A	B	C	D
(a)	3	1	2	4	(b)	1	2	3	4
(c)	4	3	2	1	(d)	2	4	1	3

Ans. (a)

Exp. The correct matching is A-3, B-1, C-2, D-4.

Salmonella typhi - It is a pathogenic bacterium which cause typhoid fever in human beings. These pathogens generally enter the small intestine through food and water contaminated with them and migrate to other organs through food.

Streptococcus pneumoniae and *Haemophilus influenzae* - These are responsible for the disease pneumonia in humans, which infects the alveoli of the lungs. The alveoli get filled with fluid leading to severe problems in respiration.

Rhino virus - It cause one of the most infectious human aliments, the common cold. They infect the nose and respiratory passage, but not the lungs.

Plasmodium - It is a tiny protozoan responsible for malaria disease. Different species of *Plasmodium* (*P. vivax*, *P. malariae* and *P. falciparum*) are responsible for different types of malaria.

28 **Which of the following statements are correct for AIDS?** *(Chap 7, Class-XII, NCERT) (IAS Pre 1996)*

1. AIDS is caused by Human Immunodeficiency Virus (HIV).
2. HIV is a member of group of virus called retrovirus.
3. HIV is a RNA virus.
4. Diagnostic test for AIDS is ELISA.

Codes

(a) 1 and 2 (b) 3 and 4
(c) 2, 3 and 4 (d) 1, 2, 3 and 4

Ans. (d)

Exp. All the statements are correct regarding AIDS.

AIDS (Acquired Immuno Deficiency Syndrome) is caused by the Human Immunodeficiency Virus (HIV), a member of group of viruses called retrovirus, which have an envelope enclosing the RNA.

Transmission of HIV-infection generally occurs by sexual contact with infected person, by transfusion of contaminated blood and blood product from infected mother to her child.

A widely used diagnostic test for AIDS is Enzyme Linked Immuno-Sorbent Assay (ELISA). Treatment of AIDS with antiretroviral drugs is only partially effective. They can only prolong the life of the patient, but cannot prevent death, which is inevitable.

29 **Which of the following are associated with diabetes mellitus, a common disease in adults?** *(Chap 7, Class-XII, NCERT) (IAS Pre 1996)*

1. Higher sugar level in blood.
2. Lower sugar level in blood.
3. Lower insulin level in blood.
4. Higher insulin level in blood.

Codes

(a) 2 and 4 (b) 1 and 2 (c) 2 and 3 (d) 1 and 3

Ans. (d)

Exp. When a low level of insulin is secreted from β-cells of pancreatic islets of Langerhans, sugar level enhances in the blood. As a result of it, the probability of diabetes gets increased. This disease is caused in adult human and is called diabetes mellitus person suffering from it feels thirsty.

30 **Which situation of the body is known as cancer?** *(Chap 7, Class-XII, NCERT) (MPPSC Pre 1996)*

(a) End of making new cells, which gradually causes death.
(b) A collection of toxic chemicals in the body and finally death.
(c) Uncontrolled multiplication of cells by which death of sound cells and finally death.
(d) Stop working of mind due to the wound in the body and finally death.

Ans. (c)

Exp. Cancer is caused by the uncontrolled multiplication of cells and by the excess consumption of nutrients from them while other normal cells of body do not get proper nutrients. Finally the normal cells of body end slowly and die at the last.

31 Choose the correct statements about working of antibiotics. *(Chap 7, Class-XII, NCERT)*

1. They commonly block biochemical pathways important for bacteria.
2. Antibiotic penicillin blocks the bacterial processes that build the cell wall.
3. Antibiotics are being produced from bacteria and fungi.
4. Streptomycin, tetracycline and erythromycin are some of the commonly known antibiotics.

Codes

(a) 1 and 2 (b) 3 and 4
(c) 1, 3 and 4 (d) 1, 2, 3 and 4

Ans. (d)

Exp. All the given statements are correct about working of antibiotics. The antibiotics commonly block biochemical pathways important for bacteria. Many bacteria have cell wall to protect themselves.

The antibiotic penicillin blocks the bacterial process that build the cell wall. As a result, the growing bacteria become unable to make cell walls and die easily.

These days number of antibiotics are being produced from bacteria and fungi.

Streptomycin, tetracycline and erythromycin are some of the commonly known antibiotics which are made from fungi and bacteria.

32 Antibiotics do not work against virus infections because *(Chap 7, Class-XII, NCERT)*

(a) viruses do not have cell wall.
(b) viruses are surrounded by a protective protien coat.
(c) viruses do not use biochemical pathways.
(d) All of the above

Ans. (d)

Exp. Antibiotics do not work against viruses because they do not use biochemical pathways at all. Viruses do not have cell walls that can be attached by antibiotics, instead they are surrounded by a protective protein coat.

33 Which of the following statement is correct? *(Chap 2, Class-VIII, NCERT)*

(a) Antibiotics are mixed with the feed of livestock and poultry to check microbial infection in animals.
(b) Antibiotics are not used to control plant diseases.
(c) Vaccines cannot be made on a large scale from microorganisms.
(d) Alexander Fleming in 1929 observed the presence of mould preventing the growth of protozoan.

Ans. (a)

Exp. Statement (a) is correct as the medicines that kill or stop the growth of the disease causing microorganism are called antibiotics. The antibiotics are manufactured by growing specific microorganisms and are used to cure a variety of diseases (both animals and plants). Antibiotics are even mixed with the feed of livestock and poultry to check microbial infection in animals.

Statements (b), (c) and (d) are incorrect and can be corrected as Antibiotics are also used to control many plants diseases like bacterial spot of leaves. These days vaccines are made on a large scale from microorganisms to protect humans and other animals from several disease.

In 1929, Alexander Fleming was working on a culture of disease causing bacteria. He observed that the presence of mould prevented the growth of bacteria. From this, the mould penicillin was discovered.

34 Which of the following pairs is not correctly matched? *(Chap 7, Class-XII NCERT) (Chap 32, Module-7, NIOS) (MPSC Pre 2023)*

(a) Nicotine – Antibacterial properties
(b) Caffeine – Stimulant
(c) Reserpine – Antihypertensive agent
(d) Quinine – Antimalarial drug

Ans. (a)

Exp. Pair (a) is not correctly matched as

Nicotine does not possess antibacterial properties. It is a highly addictive chemical found in tobacco products and acts as a stimulant.

However, it is not known for its antibacterial properties. Nicotine primarily affects the Central Nervous System (CNS) and has various physiological effects on the body, including increased heart rate and blood pressure.

Chapter 09

Environment and Ecology

Environment and Ecology

Environment

Environment

- Includes both biotic and abiotic components that affects the life of an organism.

Categorisation of Environment

- Atmospheres
- Hydrosphere (Blue Planet)
- Lithosphere (29% of the earth)
- Soil (Solid Genesis)

Population

All the organisms of a plant or an animal species, inhabiting in a given area.

- **Population Growth Rate** Percentage variation between the number of individuals in a population at two different times.
  - **Birth** and **immigration** leads to the increase in population.
  - **Death** and **emigration** leads to the decrease in population.
- **Features of Population**
  - Population density
  - Crude Birth Rate
  - Crude Death Rate
  - Sex Ratio • Age Structure
  - Population Growth

Biogeochemical Cycles

- The cyclic flow of nutrients between non-living and living organisms.
- **Types of cycles**
  - Water Cycle • Carbon Cycle
  - Oxygen Cycle • Nitrogen Cycle

Ecology

Ecological Interaction

- The relationship of two different or the same species that live in a specific community.

Types of Interactions

- **Positive Interaction** one or both the species involved is/are benefitted.
  - Commensalism • Proto cooperation
  - Mutualism
- **Negative Interaction** out of the two species, one is negatively affected.
  - Ammensalism • Competition
  - Parasitism • Predation
- **Neutral Interaction** In this type of interaction, the two species neither get benefitted nor harmed.

Ecological Adaptations

- Organism that allows it to survive and reproduce in its natural environment.
  - Adaptation in Aquatic Plants
  - Adaptation in Aquatic Animals
  - Adaptation in Xerophytic Animals & Plants
  - Adaptation in Plants in Mountain Regions
  - Adaptation in Animal living in Mountain

Ecological Pyramids

- Graphical representation of the relationship between the different living organisms at different trophic levels.
  - **Pyramid of number** (represent total no. of organism at each trophic level).
  - **Pyramid of biomass** (represent total weight of organism)
  - **Pyramid of energy** (represent total energy of organism.)

Ecosystem

Food Chain

- Linear sequence of organisms through which nutrients and energy pass as one organism eats another.
- **Types of Food chain**
  - **Predatory Food Chain**
  - **Parasitic Food Chain**
  - **Detritus Food Chain**

Food Web

- Network of various food chain which are interconnected at various trophic levels.

Flow of Energy in an Ecosystem

- It is always unidirectional.
- During the transfer of energy from one trophic level to another only 10% of the total energy is passed to the next.
- Decrease in energy level leads to

Biological Magnification

- Process of increase in the concentration of a toxic chemical (pesticides) with increasing tropic level in a food chain.
- **Pesticides** (Chemical that kills a pest organism.)
- **Insecticides** (use for killing insects)
- **Weedicides** (use for killing weeds)
- **Fungicides** (use for killing fungi)
- **Nematicides** (use for killing nematodes).
- **Rodenticides** (use for killing rodents).

SOURCE *Old NCERT Class VI* (Water), (The Living Organisms and Their Surroundings), *New NCERT Class VI* (Air Around Us), *Old NCERT Class VII* (Weather, Climate and Adaptations of Animals to Climate), (Weather Forest : Our Lifeline, Soil), *Old NCERT Class IX* (Natural Resources) *New NCERT Class X* (Our Environment), *Old NCERT Class X* (Management of Natural Resources), *New NCERT Class XII* (Organisms and Population),*New NCERT Class XII* (Ecosystem), *NIOS Chap 29* Module 7

1 Choose the correctly matched pair. *(Chap 13, Class-X, NCERT)*

(a) The outermost layer of our Earth – Crust.
(b) A series of organisms feeding on one another – Food web.
(c) Each level of the food chain – Crown.
(d) Branchy part of tree above the stem – Trophic.

Ans. (a)

Exp. Pair (a) is correctly matched as the outer most layer of Earth is called crust. The second layer inner to crust is called mantle and the deepest part of Earth is called core.
Pairs (b), (c) and (d) are incorrectly matched because a series of organisms feeding on one another and taking part at various biotic levels form a food chain.
Each level or step of the food chain form a trophic level. Many food chains when are interlinked to each other forms a food web. The branchy part of a tree above the stem is known as the crown.

2 When air comes in contact with a cool surface, it condenses and drops of water appear on the cooled this surface called as *(Chap 11, Class-VI, NCERT)*

(a) water vapour (b) oxygen drops
(c) precipitated water (d) water with dust

Ans. (a)

Exp. When air comes in contact with a cool surface, it condenses and drops of water appear on the cooled surface which is called as water vapour. The presence of water vapour in air is important for the water cycle to occur in nature.

3 Match the following lists and choose the correct code. *(Chap 11, Class-VI, NCERT)*

List I	List II
A. Oxygen	1. Plants and animals produce this gas.
B. Nitrogen	2. Component of air which supports burning.
C. Carbon dioxide	3. Burning of fuel produces this harmful gas.
D. Smoke	4. It does not support burning of candle.

Codes

	A	B	C	D		A	B	C	D
(a)	1	4	3	2	(b)	2	4	1	3
(c)	3	1	4	2	(d)	4	2	3	1

Ans. (b)

Exp. The correct matching is A-2, B-4, C-1, D-3.
Oxygen It is the component of air that supports burning. It is about 21% of all the gases in the atmosphere.
Nitrogen It is the major part of air. It is about 78% of all the gases in the atmosphere. It does not support burning. But it is essential for growth and development of plants.
Carbon dioxide It makes up a small component of the air around us. Plants and animals consume oxygen for respiration and produce carbon dioxide.
Smoke It contains few gases and dust particles. Burning of fuel produces smoke which is often harmful.

4 Our Earth is surrounded by a thin layer of air which extends up to many kilometres above the surface of the Earth and is called *(Chap 13, Class-X, NCERT)*

(a) stratosphere (b) biosphere
(c) atmosphere (d) ozone

Ans. (c)

Exp. Our Earth is surrounded by a thin layer of air. This layer extends up to many kilometres above the surface of the Earth and is called atmosphere. Above the atmosphere there are troposphere, stratosphere, ionosphere and mesosphere.

5 Which of the following statements is incorrect? *(Chap 13, Class-X, NCERT)*

(a) Air on Earth contains mostly nitrogen and oxygen is up to 49%.
(b) Carbon dioxide constitutes up to 95-97% of the atmosphere on Venus and Mars.
(c) The balance of oxygen and CO_2 in the atmosphere is maintained through respiration in plants and animals and by photosynthesis in plants.
(d) Air helps in movement of sailing yachts, aeroplanes, dispersal of seeds, etc.

Ans. (a)

Exp. Statement (a) is incorrect because air contains mostly nitrogen and oxygen. In fact, these two gases together make up 99% of the air. The remaining 1% is constituted by carbon dioxide and a few other gases and water vapour.

6 Consider the following Assertion (A) and Reason (R) and choose the correct code. *(Chap 13, Class-X, NCERT)*

Assertion (A) Our food grains such as wheat, rice, vegetables and fruits and even meat contain varying amounts of pesticide residue.

Reason (R) They cannot always be removed by washing or other means.

Codes

(a) Both A and R are true and R is the correct explanation of A
(b) Both A and R are true, but R is not the correct explanation of A
(c) A is true, but R is false
(d) Both A and R are false

Ans. (b)

Exp. Both Assertion (A) and Reason (R) are true, but Reason (R) is not the correct explanation of (A).
Food grains such as wheat, rice, vegetables and fruits and even meat contain varying amounts of pesticides residue. This is because several pesticides and other chemicals used to protect crops from diseases are either washed down into the soil or into water bodies. From there they are taken up by plants and by aquatic animals. There chemicals do not degrade and they get accumulated progressively at each trophic level and thus cannot be removed by washing or other means.

7 **When pesticides used by us to protect crops from disease is washed down into soil or into water bodies then which of the following organisms will show maximum concentration of that pesticide in its body?** *(Chap 13, Class-X, NCERT)*

(a) Fishes (b) Humans (c) Plants (d) Birds

Ans. (b)

Exp. As humans occupy the top level in any food chain, the maximum concentration of chemicals and pesticides which are non-biodegradable get maximum accumulated in human body due to biological magnification.

8 **Match the following lists and choose the correct code.** *(Chap 6, Class-VI, NCERT)*

List I	List II
A. A-horizon	1. Hard and difficult to dig with a spade
B. B-horizon	2. Have small lumps of rocks with cracks and crevices
C. C-horizon	3. Harder and compact layer
D. Bedrock	4. Soft porous and retain more water

Codes

	A	B	C	D		A	B	C	D
(a)	4	3	2	1	(b)	1	2	3	4
(c)	3	4	1	2	(d)	2	1	4	3

Ans. (a)

Exp. The correct matching is A-4, B-3, C-2, D-1.

The uppermost soil horizon is dark in colour due to humus and minerals. It is soft, porous and can retain more water. It is called top soil or the A-horizon.

The next layer has a lesser amount of humus, but more of minerals. This layer is generally harder and more compact and is called the B-horizon or the middle layer.

The third layer is the C-horizon which is made up of small lumps of rocks with cracks and crevices.

Below this layer is the bedrock which is hard and difficult to dig with a spade.

9 **The day-to-day condition of the atmosphere at a place with respect to the temperature, humidity, rainfall, wind-speed, etc. is** *(Chap 6, Class-VI, NCERT)*

(a) climate (b) weather
(c) climatic index (d) surroundings

Ans. (b)

Exp. The day-to-day condition of the atmosphere at a place with respect to the temperature, humidity, rainfall, wind-speed, etc., is called the weather at that place.

The temperature, humidity and other factors are called the elements of weather.

10 **Consider the following statements.** *(Chap 12, Class-XII, NCERT), (Chap 29, Module 7, NIOS)*

1. The flow of energy in food chain is multidirectional.
2. The amount of energy that is transferred gets lesser and lesser as we go up the food chain.
3. Food chain and food web helps in energy flow and nutrient cycle.

How many statement(s) is/are matched correctly?

(a) Only one (b) Only two
(c) All three (d) None of these

Ans. (b)

Exp. Only two statements i.e. (2) and (3) are correct.

Incorrect statement can be corrected as

We known that food provides, energy and thus in a food chain, energy in passed from one link to another. This energy flow is unidirectional, i.e. the energy which is transferred from one trophic level to the next does not come back.

11 **Which of the following statements is true about troposphere?** *(Chap 13, Class-X, NCERT) (BPSC Pre 2023)*

(a) It is topmost layer of the atmosphere
(b) The temperature at this layer increase with the height
(c) Its average height is 13 km
(d) More than one of the above
(e) None of the above

Ans. (c)

Exp. Statement (c) is true about troposphere. The average height of troposphere is about 13 km. Statements (a) and (b) are incorrect. The troposphere is the lowest layer of Earth, atmosphere. Most of the mass (about 75-80%) of the atmosphere is in the troposphere. The bottom of the troposphere is at Earth's surface. Air is warmest at the bottom of the troposphere near ground level. Air gets colder as one rises through the troposphere.

12 **Which of the following is correctly matched pair?** *(Chap 12, Class-XII, NCERT)*

(a) Amount of living material at a particular time – Standing crop
(b) Breaking of rocks by action of wind, water and climate – Erosion
(c) A vertical section through different layers of the soil – Soil index
(d) Mixture of rock particles and humus – Horizon

Ans. (a)

Exp. Pair (a) is correctly matched as each trophic level has a certain mass of living material at a particular time called as the standing crop.

Pairs (b), (c) and (d) are incorrectly matched because breaking of rocks by action of wind, water and climate is called weathering.

A vertical section through different layers of the soil is called soil profile.

Each layer differs in feel (texture), colour, depth and chemical composition. These layers are referred to as horizons.

Soil is a mixture, containing small particles of rock (of different sizes). It also contains bits of decayed living organisms called humus.

13 Given below is the type of soil and the plant best grown in that. Choose the incorrectly matched pair. *(Chap 6, Class-VI, NCERT)*

(a) Clayey soil + Loamy soil – Wheat and gram
(b) Clay + Organic matter – Paddy
(c) Loamy soil – Lentils and pulses
(d) Sandy loam – All vegetables

Ans. (d)

Exp. Pair (d) is incorrectly matched as climatic factors as well as the component of soil, determine the various types of vegetation and crops that might grow in any region. Clayey and loamy soil are both best to grow cereals like gram and wheat. Such soils are good at retaining water.
For paddy, soil rich in clay and organic matter and having a good capacity to retain water are ideal.
For lentils (masoor) and other pulses, loamy soils, which drain water easily are required. For cotton, sandy loam or loam which drain water easily is required.

14 Consider the following statements. *(Chap 12, Class-XII, NCERT)*

1. The mineral nutrients that are found in a particular soil depends on the rocks it was formed from.
2. The topmost layer of the soil that contain humus and living organisms in addition to the soil particles is called the top soil.
3. The movement of nutrient elements through various components of an ecosystem is called biogeochemical cycle.

How many statement(s) is/are correct?

(a) Only one (b) Only two (c) All three (d) None of these

Ans. (c)

Exp. All the statements are correct. The mineral nutrients that are found in particular soil depends on the rocks it was formed from.
The nutrient content of a soil, the amount of humus present in it and the depth of the soil are some of the factors that decide which plants will thrive on that soil. Thus, the top most layer of the soil that contains humus and living organisms in addition to the soil particles is called top soil.
There is constant transfer of matter and energy between different component of the biosphere. The movement of nutrient elements through various components of an ecosystem is called biogeochemical cycle.

15 Which of the following statement(s) is/are incorrect?

(a) Tropical animals have sensitive hearing and sharp eyesight. *(Chap 6, Class-VI, NCERT)*
(b) Tropical animal's skin colour helps them to camouflage by blending with surroundings.
(c) Animals living in tropical region has very less competition among themselves.
(d) All of the above

Ans. (c)

Exp. Statement (c) is incorrect because the climatic conditions in rainforests are highly suitable for supporting an enormous number and a variety of animals. Since the number are large, there is intense competition for food and shelter in animals living in tropical rain forests.

16 Match the following lists and choose the correct code. *(Chap 11, Class-XII, NCERT)*

List I	List II
A. Predation	1. Monarch butterfly and bird.
B. Competition	2. Flamingoes and resident fishes in South American lake.
C. Commensalism	3. Cattle egret and grazing cattle.
D. Mutualism	4. *Mycorrhizae*.

Codes

	A	B	C	D
(a)	4	1	2	3
(b)	3	2	1	4
(c)	4	3	2	1
(d)	1	2	3	4

Ans. (d)

Exp. The correct matching is A-1, B-2, C-3, D-4.
Predation - The monarch butterfly and bird predator. It is when one organism kills and consume another organism.
Competition - The South American lakes visiting flamingoes and resident fishes compete for their common food the zooplankton in the lake. It is an interaction between organisms or species in which both the organisms are harmed.
Commensalism - The cattle egret and grazing cattle. It is an association between two organisms in which one is benefitted and the other is neither benefitted not harmed.
Mutualism - *Mycorrhizae* are associations between fungi and roots of higher plants. In this association, both organisms are benefitted.

17 Choose the correct statements from the following. *(Chap 11, Class-XII, NCERT)*

1. Natality and immigration increases population density.
2. Mortality and emigration decreases population density.
3. Natality and emigration decreases population density.
4. Mortality and immigration increases population density.

Codes

(a) 1 and 2
(b) 2 and 4
(c) 2 and 3
(d) 1 and 4

Ans. (a)

Exp. Statements (1) and (2) are correct as natality refers to number of birth during a given period and mortality refers to the number of death in a given period.

Immigration is the moving in of individuals from other places to a place and emigration is moving out of individuals from a place to other places.

Statements (3) and (4) are incorrect because natality and immigration contribute to an increase in population density and mortality and emigration leads to decrease in population density.

18 Which of the following statements is correct? *(Chap 11, Class-XII, NCERT)*

(a) Pyramid of energy is always inverted.
(b) Pyramid of biomass in sea is generally upright.
(c) All pyramids of number, energy and biomass are inverted.
(d) In an ecological pyramid same species cannot belong to two or more trophic levels.

Ans. (d)

Exp. Statement (d) is correct as in an ecological pyramid some species belonging to two or more trophic level does not exist.

Rest statements are incorrect and can be corrected as In most ecosystem, all the pyramids of number, energy and biomass are upright.

The pyramid of biomass in sea is generally inverted because biomass of fishes far exceeds that of phytoplanktons. Pyramids of energy is always upright and can never be inverted because flow of energy is only 10% to next trophic level and is unidirectional.

19 Natality refers *(Chap 11, Class-XII, NCERT) (JKPSC Pre 2023)*

(a) to the number of births during a given period in the population that are added to the initial density
(b) to the number of deaths in the population during a given period
(c) to the number of individuals of the same species that have come into the habitat form elsewhere during the time period under consideration
(d) to the number of individuals of the population who left the habitat and went elsewhere during the time period under consideration.

Ans. (a)

Exp. Natality refers to the number of births during a given period in the population that are added to the initial density. It is used to express birth rate.

20 Maternal mortality rate is *(Chap 11, Class-XII, NCERT) (Mizoram PCS Pre 2023)*

(a) female deaths that occurred before the 9th month of pregnancy
(b) the annual number of female deaths per 100,000 live births due to pregnancy
(c) the annual number of female deaths per 10,000 live births due to pregnancy
(d) the death of females the occurred within 3 months of child delivery

Ans. (b)

Exp. The term Maternal Mortality Rate (MMR) refers to the number of maternal deaths per 100,000 live births that are caused by either pregnancy or pregnancy termination, without taking the length and location of the pregnancy into account. The maternal mortality rate is used as a tool to show risk associated with pregnancy in women.

21 Match the following lists and choose the correct code. *(Chap 11, Class-XII, NCERT)*

List I	List II
A. Eurythermal	1. Tolerate a wide range of salinities.
B. Stenothermal	2. Can tolerate and thrive in a wide range of temperature.
C. Stenohaline	3. Restricted to a narrow range of temperature.
D. Euryhaline	4. Restricted to a narrow range of salinities.

Codes

	A	B	C	D
(a)	2	3	4	1
(b)	3	1	2	4
(c)	4	3	1	2
(d)	1	3	2	4

Ans. (a)

Exp. The correct matching is A-2, B-3, C-4, D-1.

A few organisms can tolerate and thrive in a wide range of temperature. They are called eurythermals, but a vast majority of them are restricted to a narrow range of temperature such organisms are called stenothermal.

Some organisms are tolerant to a wide range of salinities, i.e., euryhaline. But others are restricted to a narrow range called stenohaline.

22 Which of the following statements is/are correct? *(Chap 11, Class-XII, NCERT)*

(a) An organism maintain the consistency of its internal environment by a process called homeostasis.
(b) Small animals are rarely found in polar regions.
(c) Bears hibernate to escape winter and snails and fishes go into aestivation to avoid summer.
(d) All of the above

Ans. (d)

Exp. All statements are correct.

Homeostasis is the ability of an organisms to maintain constant internal temperature/environment inside its body.

Very small animals are rarely found in polar region because they tend to loss body heat very fast.

Bears hibernate during winter to escape extreme cold, snails and fishes go into aestivation to avoid summer related problems, i.e. heat and desiccation.

23 Choose the correct example to describe Allen's rule of adaptation in animals. *(Chap 11, Class-XII, NCERT)*

(a) Mammals from colder climate generally have short ears and limbs to minimise heat loss.
(b) Desert lizards bask in the Sun and absorb heat when their body temperature drops below the comfort zone.
(c) Kangaroo rat has the ability to concentrate its urine so that minimal volume of water is used to remove excretory products.
(d) Tribes living in high altitude have high red blood cell count.

Ans. (a)

Exp. Mammals from colder climates generally have short ears and limbs to minimise heat loss. This is called Allen's rule. It is a principle holding that in a warm-blooded animals species having distinct geographic populations, the limbs, ears and other appendages of the animals living in cold climates tends to be shorter than in animals of the same species, living in warm climates.

24 Which of the following statements about soil are correct? *(Chap 6, Class-VI, NCERT)*

1. Weathering of rocks produces small particles of various materials.
2. If soil contains greater proportion of big particles it is called sandy soil.
3. The proportion of five particles is relatively higher then it is called clayey soil.
4. Loamy soil is a mixture of sand, clay and silt.

Codes

(a) 1 and 2 (b) 3 and 4 (c) 1 and 3 (d) 1, 2, 3 and 4

Ans. (d)

Exp. All statements are correct about soil as weathering of rocks produces small particles of various material. These include sand and clay. Three types of weathering are physical, chemical and biological.

If soil contains greater proportion of big particles it is called sandy soil. It is light, warm, dry and tends to be acidic and low in nutrients. If the proportion of five particles is relatively higher, then it is called clayey soil. It is a heavy soil type that is rich in nutrients. Loamy soil is a mixture of sand, clay and another type of soil particle known as silt. This soil type is best for plant growth.

25 All the interacting organisms in an area together with the non-living constituents of the environment form an/a *(Chap 13, Class-X, NCERT)*

(a) biosphere (b) surroundings
(c) ecosystem (d) None of these

Ans. (c)

Exp. All the interacting organisms in an area together with the non-living constituents of the environment form an ecosystem. An ecosystem consists of biotic components comprising of living organisms and abiotic components comprising physical factors surrounding an organism.

26 Which of the following statements about ecosystem is/are incorrect? *(Chap 13, Class-X, NCERT)*

1. A constant input of chemical energy from soil that acts as the basic requirement of an ecosystem to sustain life is called productivity.
2. Garden and crop fields are artificial ecosystem.
3. Forest, ponds and lakes are natural ecosystem.

Codes

(a) Only 1 (b) 2 and 3
(c) 1, 2 and 3 (d) None of these

Ans. (a)

Exp. Statement (1) is incorrect about ecosystem because a constant input of solar energy is the basic requirement for an ecosystem to function and sustain. Primary production is defined as the amount of biomass or organic matter produced per unit area over a time period by plants during photosynthesis. It is expressed in terms of weight (gm^{-2}) or energy (K cal m^{-2}). The rate of biomass production is called productivity.

27 Which of the following cannot be categorised as consumers in an ecosystem? *(Chap 13, Class-X, NCERT)*

(a) Herbivores
(b) Parasites
(c) Omnivores
(d) Microorganisms

Ans. (d)

Exp. Microorganisms cannot be categorised as consumers in an ecosystem. These are decomposers of an ecosystem.

Consumers consume food produced either directly from producers or indirectly by feeding on other consumers. Consumers can be classified as herbivores, carnivores, omnivores and parasites.

28 Which one of the following is the correct sequence of ecosystems in the order of decreasing productivity? *(Chap 12, Class-XII, NCERT)* *(IAS Pre 2013)*

(a) Oceans, lakes, grasslands, mangroves
(b) Mangroves, oceans, grasslands, lakes
(c) Mangroves, grasslands, lakes, oceans
(d) Oceans, mangroves, lakes, grasslands

Ans. (c)

Exp. The correct sequence of ecosystems in the order of decreasing productivity is

Mangroves > Grasslands > Lakes > Oceans.

Productivity is the rate of organic matter or biomass production.

The average ocean productivity is about 50 grams carbon per square meter per year; while the average land productivity is 160 grams carbon per square meter per year.

Salt marshes and mangroves have one of the highest productivity of 3300-6000 grams carbons per square meter per year.

29 Consider the following Assertion (A) and Reason (R) and choose the correct code.

Assertion (A) Phytoplankton grow in abundance in the limnetic zone.

Reason (R) Limnetic zone is open water zone.

(Chap 12, Class-XII, NCERT) (UPPSC Pre 2022)

Codes

(a) Both A and R are true and R is the correct explanation of A
(b) Both A and R are true, but R is not the correct explanation of A
(c) A is true, but R is false
(d) A is false, but R is true

Ans. (a)

Exp. Both Assertion (A) and Reason (R) are true and Reason (R) is the correct explanation of Assertion (A).

This is proved by the fact that the limnetic zone is often known as the open water area (or zone) where the light does not penetrate to the bottom. It is dominated by plankton, i.e., Both phytoplankton and zooplankton. These are mainly the small organisms that plays a crucial role in the aquatic food chain.

30 High juvenile mortality is the characteristic feature of *(Chap 11, Class-XII, NCERT) (Tripura PCS Pre 2023)*

(a) r - selected population
(b) k - selected population
(c) r- and k - selected population
(d) None of the above

Ans. (a)

Exp. High juvenile mortality is the characteristic feature of r - selected population.

The r - selected species are those species that tend to produce a higher number of offspring or progeny. But, they offer less parental care.

31 Choose the correct statements about decomposers. *(Chap 13, Class-X, NCERT)*

1. They breakdown the complex organic substances into simple organic substances called detritus.
2. During decomposition, water soluble inorganic nutrients go down the soil horizon by leaching.
3. Humification ensures that the nutrients of dead plants and animals are released into the soil.
4. Humus is a dark-coloured substance.

Codes

(a) 1 and 4
(b) 1, 2 and 3
(c) 3 and 4
(d) 2, 3 and 4

Ans. (d)

Exp. Statements (2), (3) and (4) are correct about decomposers.

The microorganisms which convert dead plants and animals to humus are known as decomposers and this process is known as decomposition. Its steps include fragmentation, leaching, catabolism, humification and mineralisation.

During leaching, water soluble inorganic nutrients go down into the soil horizon and get precipitated as unavailable salts. Humification leads to accumulation of a dark coloured amorphous substance called humus.

Statement (1) is incorrect because dead plant remains such as leaves, bark, flowers and dead remains of animals including fecal matter constitute detritus, which is the raw material for decomposition.

32 Consider the following Assertion (A) and Reason (R) and choose the correct code. *(Chap 13, Class-X, NCERT)*

Assertion (A) Food chains generally consist of only three or four steps.

Reason (R) There are generally a greater number of individuals at the lower trophic levels of an ecosystem.

Codes

(a) Both A and R are true and R is the correct explanation of A
(b) Both A and R are true, but R is not the correct explanation of A
(c) A is true, but R is false
(d) Both A and R are false

Ans. (b)

Exp. Both Assertion (A) and Reason (R) are true, but Reason (R) is not the correct explanation of Assertion (A).

10% of energy is present at each trophic level which reaches the next level of consumers.

Since, so little energy is available for the next level of consumers, food chains generally consists of only three or four steps.

The loss of energy at each step is so great that very little usable energy remains after four trophic levels. There are generally a greater number of individuals at the lower trophic level of an ecosystem, the greater number is of the producers.

33 Which of the following is the correct sequence of a food chain? *(Chap 11, Class-XII, NCERT) (IAS Pre 2014)*

(a) Diatoms–Crustaceans–Herrings
(b) Crustaceans–Diatoms–Herrings
(c) Diatoms–Herrings–Crustaceans
(d) Crustaceans–Herrings–Diatoms

Ans. (a)

Exp. The correct sequence of a food chain is Diatoms-Crustaceans-Herrings. Diatoms are autotrophs which prepare their own food. Crustaceans are herbivorous animals which feed on diatoms. Herrings are carnivorous animals which feed on crustaceans.

34 With reference to food chains in ecosystems consider the following statements.

(Chap 13, Class-X, NCERT) (IAS Pre 2013)

1. A food chain illustrates the order in which a chain of organisms feed upon each other.
2. Food chains are found within the populations of a species.
3. A food chain illustrates the number of each organisms which are eaten by others.

Which of the statement(s) given above is/are correct?

(a) Only 1 (b) 1 and 2
(c) 1, 2 and 3 (d) None of these

Ans. (a)

Exp. Statement (1) is correct as food chain shows the order/sequence of feeding.

Statements (2) and (3) are incorrect. Food chains are not found within the population of a species because technically, food chain is the sequence of organisms through which the energy flows. If the species starts eating itself, then flow of energy will not proceeds.

Also food chain does not show numbers of each organism eaten by other.

35 Which of the following is not a biogeochemical cycle? *(Chap 12, Class-IX, NCERT)*

(a) Water cycle (b) Nitrogen cycle
(c) Carbon cycle (d) Food cycle

Ans. (d)

Exp. Food cycle is not a biogeochemical cycle.

Rest cycles like water cycle, nitrogen cycle and carbon cycle are biogeochemical cycle. In these cycle there is interaction between organic and inorganic matter present in the biosphere.

36 With reference to the food chains in ecosystem, which of the following kinds of organisms is/are known as decomposer organism/organisms?

(Chap 11, Class-XII, NCERT) (IAS Pre 2013)

1. Virus 2. Fungi 3. Bacteria

Codes

(a) Only 1 (b) 2 and 3 (c) 1 and 3 (d) 1, 2 and 3

Ans. (b)

Exp. Option (2) and (3) are correct.

Decomposers also called saprotrophs, are mostly bacteria and fungi that feed on dead decomposed organisms. Viruses does not feed on dead organisms, they need living host cells to survive. Thus, viruses are not decomposer.

37 Peacock eats a snake, snake eats frog and frog eats insect while insect eats green plant, then position of peacock is *(Chap 12, Class-XII, NCERT)*

(a) primary producer
(b) secondary producer
(c) decomposer
(d) top, at the apex of food pyramid

Ans. (d)

Exp. Green plants → Insects → Frog → Snakes → Peacock

From the above food chain, it is clear that the peacock occupies the top position at the apex of the food pyramid. Hence, it is the top carnivore.

Transfer of food energy from the producers through a series of (biotic components) organisms with repeated eating and being eaten is known as food chain. Producers utilise the solar energy and transform it to chemical form, i.e., ATP during photosynthesis. Thus, food chain involves biotic components and helps in energy flow and transfer of nutrients.

38 Which of the following statements are correct about detritus food chain ? *(Chap 12, Class-XII, NCERT)*

1. This type of food chain starts from dead organic matter.
2. The dead organic matter is broken down into simple nutrients by microorganism.
3. A complex detritus food chain also exist in an aquatic ecosystem.
4. It is the most common food chain found in the terrestrial ecosystem

Code

(a) 1 and 3 (b) 1 and 2
(c) 2 and 4 (d) 2 and 3

Ans. (b)

Exp. Detritus food chain starts from dead organic matter. The dead organic matter is broken down into simple nutrients by microorganism like fungi and bacteria. These simple nutrients and decomposers are then consumed by smaller carnivores which in turn become food for larger carnivores.

A similar detritus food chain also exist in an aquatic ecosystem. Grazing food chain is found both in aquatic as well as grassland ecosystem. It is the most common food chain found in terrestrial ecosystem.

39 Consider the following statements about flow of energy in a trophic level. *(Chap 13, Class-X, NCERT)*

1. Green plants capture about 10% of the energy of sunlight that falls on their leaves.
2. An average of 1% of the food eaten is turned into its energy and made available for the next level of consumers.
3. Each organism is generally eaten by two or more other kinds of organisms.
4. The flow of energy is multidirectional in an ecosystem.

Which of the statement(s) given above is/are incorrect?

(a) 1 and 2
(b) 3 and 4
(c) Only 3
(d) 1, 2 and 4

Ans. (d)

Exp. Statements (1), (2) and (4) are incorrect about flow of energy in a trophic level.

Green plants (producers) in a terrestrial ecosystem capture about 1% of the energy of sunlight that falls on their leaves and convert it into food. Rest of 90% energy is reflected back.

An average of 10% of the food eaten is turned into its own body and made available for the next level of consumers. This is known as Lindeman's 10% law.

These can be corrected as the flow of energy in an ecosystem is always unidirectional. This is because energy cannot go back to its previous level in a food chain.

40 In the grasslands, trees do not replace the grasses as a part of an ecological succession because of *(Chap 12, Class-XII, NCERT) (IAS Pre 2013)*

(a) insects and fungi
(b) limited sunlight and paucity of nutrients
(c) water limits and fire
(d) None of the above

Ans. (c)

Exp. The trees do not replace the grasses as they require more water than grasses and this would lead to water scarcity for other species.

Also, trees are prone to catch fire and the fire spreads swiftly. Due to these reasons trees do not replace the grasses as a part of ecological succession.

41 Match the following lists and choose the correct code. *(Chap 13, Class-X, NCERT)*

List I	List II
A. Autotrophs or producers	1. Fourth trophic level
B. Herbivores or primary consumer	2. First trophic level
C. Large carnivores	3. Third trophic level
D. Small carnivores	4. Second trophic level

Codes

	A	B	C	D		A	B	C	D
(a)	1	2	3	4	(b)	4	3	2	1
(c)	2	4	1	3	(d)	3	2	1	4

Ans. (c)

Exp. The correct matching is A-2, B-4, C-1, D-3.

The autotrophs or the producers are at the first trophic level. They fix up the solar energy and make it available for heterotrophs or the consumers. They perform photosynthesis for making their own food.

The herbivores or the primary consumers come at the second level as they feed on autotrophs.

Small carnivores or the secondary consumers comes at the third level as they feed on primary consumers.

Lastly large carnivores or the tertiary consumers, form the fourth trophic level. They include lion, tigers, etc.

42 Match the following lists and choose the correct code. *(Chap 13, Class-X, NCERT)*

List I	List II
A. Producers	1. Green plants and blue-green algae.
B. Consumers	2. Depends on producers for sustenance.
C. Decomposers	3. Bacteria and fungi.

Codes

	A	B	C		A	B	C
(a)	1	2	3	(b)	3	2	1
(c)	1	3	2	(d)	2	1	3

Ans. (a)

Exp. The correct matching is A-1, B-2, C-3.

The green plants in the ecosystem are called producers. In a terrestrial ecosystem, major producers are autotrophs and woody plants. Likewise producers in an aquatic ecosystem are various species like phytoplankton, algae and higher plants.

All animals depends on plants (producers) directly or indirectly for their food needs. They are hence called consumers and also heterotrophs.

The microorganisms, comprising bacteria and fungi, breakdown the dead remains and waste products of organisms. These microorganisms are the decomposers as they breakdown the complex organic substances into simple inorganic substance.

43 Consider the following processes. *(Chap 12, Class-XII, NCERT) (IAS Pre 2014)*

1. Volcanic action
2. Respiration
3. Photosynthesis
4. Decay of organic matter

Which of the following adds/add carbon dioxide to the carbon cycle on the planet Earth?

(a) Only one
(b) Only two
(c) Only three
(d) All four

Ans. (c)

Exp. Only three processes viz., Volcanic action, respiration and decay of organic matter adds carbon dioxide to the carbon cycle on the planet Earth. However, photosynthesis uses carbon dioxide to produce food and oxygen by the plant.

44 More than 90 per cent of all nitrogen are fixed as ammonia, nitrites and nitrates by soil microorganisms. Symbiotic bacteria associated with leguminous plants fix nitrogen by the formation of root nodules. In which of the following plant nitrogen fixation does not occur? *(Chap 12, Class-XII, NCERT) (Odisha PCS Pre 2023)*

(a) Common beans
(b) Soyabeans
(c) Peanuts
(d) Oats

Ans. (d)

Exp. Nitrogen fixation does not occur in oat plants. It is a vital process where nitrogen gas from the atmosphere is converted into ammonia, nitrates and nitrites, making it available for plants. Soil macroorganisms and symbiotic bacteria, like those associated with leguminous plants, play key role in this nitrogen fixing process. The formation of root nodules is a specific mechanism employed by symbiotic bacteria, (i.e. *Rhizobia*) in association with legumes (common beans, soybeans, peanuts) for nitrogen fixation.

45 Which of the following pairs of bacteria are nitrifying bacteria ? *(Chap 29, Module-7, NIOS)*

1. *Nitrobacter*
2. *Clostridium*
3. *Nitrosomonas*
4. *Pseudomonas*

Codes

(a) 1 and 2 (b) 1 and 3 (c) 2 and 4 (d) 3 and 4

Ans. (b)

Exp. Conversion of ammonia into nitrates is called nitrification. Nitrifying bacteria like *Nitrobacter* and *Nitrosomonas* found in the soil convert ammonia into nitrate.

46 Which of the following statements is incorrect? *(Chap 6, Class-VI, NCERT)*

(a) Birds migrate to warmer regions when winter sets in.
(b) Penguins bodies are streamlined and their feet have webs, making them good swimmers.
(c) Tropical rainforest are found in Rajasthan and Assam in India.
(d) The climatic conditions in rainforests are highly suitable for supporting an enormous number and variety of animals.

Ans. (c)

Exp. Statement (c) is incorrect as tropical rainforests are found in Western Ghats and Assam in India, Southeast Asia, Central America and Central Africa because of continuous warmth and rain, this region supports wide variety of plants and animals.

47 Which one of the following terms describes not only the physical space occupied by an organism, but also its functional role in the community of organisms?

(a) Ecotone *(Chap 11, Class-XII, NCERT) (IAS Pre 2013)*
(b) Ecological niche
(c) Habitat
(d) Home range

Ans. (b)

Exp. In ecology, the term 'niche' describes the role an organisms plays in a community.

A species niche encompasses both the physical and environmental conditions it requires (like temperature or terrain) and the interactions it has with other species (like predation and competition).

Each organism has an invariably defined range of conditions that it can tolerate, diversity in the resources it utilises and a distinct functional role in the ecological system, all these together comprise its niche.

Chapter 10

Biodiversity and Its Conservation

Biodiversity and Its Conservation

Biodiversity

Biodiversity

- Occurence of different types of genes, gene pools, species, habitat and ecosystem in a given region at a given time.
- The term was given by **Edward Wilson**.
- **Levels of Biodiversity**
  - **Genetic Diversity** (e.g. More than 50,000 genetically different straim of rice.)
  - **Species Diversity** (e.g. Western ghats have more amphibian than eastern ghats)
  - **Ecological Diversity** (e.g. Flora fauna found in desert shows difference with these found in grasslands)

Species Diversity on Earth and in India

- According to the IUCN [2004], the total number of plant and animal species described is slightly more than 1.5 million.
- According to **Robert May**, the global species diversity is about 7 million with 70% animal species and 22% fungal and plant species.
- India was one of the 12 mega diversity countries of the world.

Patterns of Biodiversity

- **Latitudinal Gradient** Tropis has more species than temperate or polar areas.
- **Species Area Relationship** Region species richness increase as there is increase in explored area.

Importance of Species Diversity to the Ecosystem

- Communities with more species are more stable as compared with less species.
- Increased diversity contribute to higher productivity.

Loss of Biodiversity

- Refers to the decline or disappearance of biological diversity

Causes of Loss of Biodiversity

- Habitat loss and fragmentation.
- Over exploitation of resources.
- Invasion of foreign species and Coextinction.

Conservation of Biodiversity

Conservation of Biodiversity

Protection, upliftment and management of biodiversity to derive sustainable benefits for present and future generation.

Types

- **In-situ** (on-site) **conservation** Involves conservation of flora and fauna in their natural habitats.
  - **Biodiversity hotspot**
  - **Protected areas**

  (i) Biosphere reserve

  These includes has three main zones as

  - **Core Zone**
  - **Buffer zone**
  - **Transition zone**

  (ii) National Parks

  (iii) Wildlife sanctuary **(iv) Sacred groves**
- **Ex-situ** (off-site) **conservation** Conservation of threatened flora and fauna in special care unit.

The Red list

It is a document that is established for documenting rare and endangered species of animals, plants and fungi that exist within a state or country.

Information in Red Data Book

- It contain colour coded information sheets which are arranged according to the extinction risk of species and sub-species.
- Black → Species confirmed to be extinct.
- Red → Represents the endangered species.
- Amber → Represents vulnerable species.
- White → Represents rare species.
- Green → Represents the species that were formerly endangered but their numbers started to recover.
- Grey → Represents species that are classified as vulnerble, endangered or rare but proper information is not available to classify them properly.

SOURCE *Old NCERT Class VII (Weather, Climate and Adaptations of Animals to Climate), Old NCERT Class VIII (Conservation of Plants and Animals), Old NCERT Class X (Management of Natural Resources), New NCERT Class XII (Biodiversity and Its Conservation), NIOS Chap 30 Module 7*

1 Which of the following statements are correct? *(Chap 13, Class-XII, NCERT)*

(a) Deforestation means clearing of forests and using that land for other purposes.
(b) Biosphere is the part of the Earth in which living organisms exist or which support life.
(c) Biodiversity refers to the variety of organisms existing on the Earth and their relationships with the environment.
(d) All of the above

Ans. (d)

Exp. All the given statements are correct.
Deforestation means clearing of forests and using that land for other purposes.
Biosphere is that part of the Earth in which living organisms exist or which supports life. The biosphere is made up of three parts, called lithosphere, atmosphere and hydrosphere.
Biodiversity or Biological diversity, refers to the variety of organisms existing on the Earth and their interrelationship and relationship with the environment. Biodiversity is usually explored at three levels— genetic diversity, species diversity and ecosystem diversity.

2 Which among the following can be a natural cause of deforestation in an area? *(Chap 13, Class-XII, NCERT)*

(a) Building houses and factories
(b) Procuring land for cultivation
(c) Forest fires and severe droughts
(d) Making furniture or using wood as fuel

Ans. (c)

Exp. Option (c) is correct as human driven and natural loss of trees is called deforestation. The main causes of natural deforestation are drought, forest fires, climate change, floods, etc.
Forest fire is uncontrolled fire in an area of combustible vegetation. It may occur in fields or forests. Drought occurs due to low rainfall, due to which shortage of water occurs. Due to lack of water, the animals and plants living in that area start dying and lead to deforestation.

3 Consider the following events. *(Chap 13, Class-XII, NCERT)*

1. Increase in Earth temperature.
2. Increase in pollution level.
3. Increase in fertility of soil.
4. Decrease in groundwater level.
5. Increase in rainfall.
6. Increase in floods and droughts.

Which of the above events can be considered as a consequence of deforestation?

(a) 1, 2 and 3
(b) 1, 2, 4 and 6
(c) 2, 3 and 4
(d) All of these

Ans. (b)

Exp. Statements (1), (2), (4) and (6) are correct. There are several consequences of deforestation.
It increases the temperature and pollution level on the Earth. It increases the level of carbon dioxide in the atmosphere. Deforestation disturbs the balance in nature. Continuous cutting of trees will affect the fertility of soil. There will be increased chances of natural calamities such as floods and droughts.
The amount of carbon dioxide will increase in the atmosphere resulting in global warming. The increase in temperature on the Earth disturbs the water cycle and may reduce rainfall and cause drought.
Deforestation leads to the change in soil properties. It also decreases the water holding capacity of the soil. The other properties of the soil like nutrient content, texture, etc., also change because of deforestation.

4 Consider the following Assertion (A) and Reason (R) and choose the correct code. *(Chap 13, Class-XII, NCERT)*

Assertion (A) Deforestation decreases water holding capacity of the soil.

Reason (R Properties of the soil like content, texture, etc., change because of deforestation.

Codes

(a) Both A and R are ture and R is the correct explanation of A.
(b) Both A and R are true, but R is not the correct explanation of A.
(c) A is true, but R is false.
(d) A is false, but R is true.

Ans. (b)

Exp. Both Assertion (A) and Reason (R) are true, but Reasons (R) is not the correct explanation of Assertion (A).
Desertification is the degradation process by which a fertile land changes itself into a desert by losing its flora and fauna.
Deforestation is major cause which leads to the change in soil properties. It leads to a decrease in the water holding capacity of the soil. Properties of soil like nutrient content, texture, etc. also change because of deforestation.

5 If you are visiting Pachmarhi Bisophere Reserve then which of the given activities are prohibited there? *(Chap 13, Class-XII, NCERT)*

1. Plantation and cultivation
2. Grazing animals
3. Hunting and poaching
4. Felling of trees

Codes

(a) 1, 2 and 3
(b) 2, 3 and 4
(c) None of these
(d) All of these

Ans. (d)

Exp. Activities like grazing, hunting, felling of tree, forestry or cultivation are strictly prohibited in the biosphere reserve. No human activity is allowed in its core zone. This area is legally protected and has an undisturbed ecosystem. Thus, option (d) is correct.

6 Match the following lists and choose the correct code. *(Chap 13, Class-XII, NCERT)*

List I	List II
A. Sanctuary	1. Area where animals are protected from any disturbance to them and their habitat.
B. National park	2. Area reserved for wildlife where they can freely use the habitats and natural resources.
C. Biosphere reserve	3. Large area of protected land for conservation of wildlife, plant and animal resources and traditional life of the tribals living in the area.

Codes

	A	B	C		A	B	C
(a)	1	3	2	(b)	3	2	1
(c)	1	2	3	(d)	2	1	3

Ans. (c)

Exp. The correct matching is A-1, B-2, C-3.

Sanctuary It is an area where animals are protected from any disturbance to them and their habitat.

National park It is an area reserved for wildlife where they can freely use the habitats and natural resources. They give safe space to animals to breed and survive.

Biosphere reserve It is the large area of the protected land for conservation of wildlife, plant and animal resources and traditional life of the tribals living in the area.

There are three biosphere reserve zones–core, buffer and a transition zone.

7 The practice of controlling the establishment, growth, composition, health and quality of tree to meet diverse needs and values are referred to as. *(Chap 30, Module-7, NIOS)*

(a) Deforestation (b) Reforestation
(c) Silviculture (d) Afforestation

Ans. (c)

Exp. Silviculture is the art and science of controlling the establishment, growth, composition, health and quality of forest and woodlands to meet the diverse needs and values of of landowners and society such as wildlife, habitat, timber, water resources, restoration and recreation on a sustainable basis.

8 Choose the correctly matched pair. *(Chap 13, Class-XII, NCERT)*

(a) Flora – Plants and animals found in an area.
(b) Fauna – Flowers found in an area.
(c) Endemic species – Animals found anywhere in the world.
(d) Ecosystem – All plants, animals and microorganisms in an area along with non-living components.

Ans. (d)

Exp. Pair (d) is correctly matched as an ecosystem is made up of all the plants, animals and microorganisms in an area along with non-living components such as climate, soil, river, deltas, etc.

It comprises of abiotic and biotic components. Abiotic components include air, water, soil, sunlight, temperature, etc. Biotic components include plants, animals, microorganisms, etc.

Pairs (a), (b) and (c) are incorrectly matched because the plants and animals found in a particular area are termed flora and fauna, respectively. Endemic species are those species of plants and animals which are found exclusively in a particular area.

9 Choose the incorrectly matched pair. *(Chap 13, Class-XII, NCERT)*

(a) Western Ghat – Karnataka and Maharashtra
(b) Chanda and Bastar – Uttar Pradesh
(c) Sacred Groves – Meghalaya
(d) Aravalli Hills – Rajasthan

Ans. (b)

Exp. In India, ecologically unique and biodiversity rich regions are legally protected as biosphere reserves, national parks and sanctuaries. In many cultures, tracts of forest were set aside and all the trees and wildlife within are venerated and given total protection. These are called sacred groves.

Chanda and Bastar areas are in Madhya Pradesh. In Meghalaya, the sacred groves are the last refuges for a large number of rare and threatened plants.

10 Consider the following statements. *(Chap 13, Class-XII, NCERT)*

1. India has only 2.4 per cent of the worlds land area.
2. A stable community should show too much variation in productivity from year to year.
3. The Nile perch introduced in Lake Victoria led to extinction of 200 species of cichlid fish.

How many statement(s) is/are correct?

(a) Only one (b) Only two
(c) All three (d) None of these

Ans. (b)

Exp. Only two statements are correct. Ecologists believed that communities with more species, generally, tend to be more stable than those with less species. A stable community should not show too much variation in productivity from year to year, it must be either resistant or resilient to occasional disturbances (natural or man-made) and it must also be resistant to invasion by alien species.

11 Which of the following statement(s) is/are correct? *(Chap 13, Class-XII, NCERT)*

1. Forest (conservation) Act 1980 aimed at preservation and conservation of natural forests and meeting the basic needs of the people living in or near forests.

2. Project Tiger was launched by Indian Government to ensure the survival and maintenance of the tiger population in the country.

Codes

(a) Only 1
(b) Only 2
(c) 1 and 2
(d) Neither 1 nor 2

Ans. (c)

Exp. Statements (1) and (2) are correct. Forest (conservation) Act, 1980 aimed at preservation and conservation of natural forests and meeting the basic needs of the people living in or near the forests. This Act also aims to restore the woods in our country by planting trees and increasing forest growth. The Act gives complete authority to the Central Government to carry out the objectives of the act.

It was revised again in 1988. Project Tiger was launched by the government to protect the tigers in the country. The objective of this project was to ensure the survival and maintenance of the tiger population in the country.

12 Which of the following statements is correctly matched? *(Chap 13, Class-XII, NCERT)*

Common name	Scientific Name
(a) Carrot grass	*Parthenium*
(b) Water hyacinth	*Eichhornia*
(c) African catfish	*Clarias gariepinus*

Codes

(a) 1 and 2
(b) 1 and 3
(c) 1, 2 and 3
(d) 2 and 3

Ans. (c)

Exp. All statements are correctly matched. When alien species are introduced unintentionally or deliberately for whatever purpose, some of them turn invasive and cause decline or extinction of indigenous species.

e.g., Carrot grass (*Parthenium*), water hyacinth (*Eichhornia*). The recent illegal introduction of the African catfish *Clarias gariepinus* for aquaculture purposes is posing a threat to the indigenous catfishes in our rivers.

13 Which of the following statements are correct with reference to 'The Evil Quartet' of biodiversity loss? *(Chap 13, Class-XII, NCERT)*

1. Habitat loss and fragmentation
2. Over-exploitation
3. Alien species invasion
4. Co-extinction

Codes

(a) 1 and 2
(b) 2, 3 and 4
(c) 1, 3 and 4
(d) 1, 2, 3 and 4

Ans. (d)

Exp. All statements are correct. 'The Evil Quartet' of biodiversity loss is a concept that describes the reason that causes extinction of species. There are four main causes which include habitat loss and fragmentation, over-exploitation, alien species invasion and co-extinction. Habitat loss and fragmentation occurs due to large scale human activities and has become the important cause resulting in extinction of plants and animals. Overexploitation of natural resources also lead to extinction of species.

Some of the alien species turn invasive, resulting in decline or extinction of indigenous species.

When a species become extinct, the plant and animal species associated with it in an obligatory way also become extinct.

14 Which of the following statements is incorrectly matched? *(Chap 13, Class-XII, NCERT)*

(a) Amrita Devi Bishnoi in 1731 sacrificed her life along with 363 people to protect Khejri trees in Khejari village, Rajasthan.
(b) Chipko Andolan originated in Reni, Garhwal in 1970s.
(c) Forests cannot be considered as 'biodiversity hotspots.'
(d) Bioprospecting is exploring molecular genetics and species level diversity for products of economic importance.

Ans. (c)

Exp. Statement (c) is incorrect as a biodiversity hotspot is a biogeographic region with significant levels of biodiversity that is threatened by human habitation. Forests serve as the reservoir of biodiversity containing different species of plants, animals and different types of microbes.

They comprise richest diversity of species including the most rare and endangered species. Therefore, forests are often considered as biodiversity hotspots because they have very high level of species richness and a high degree of endemism.

15 *Nepenthes khasiana*, a rare and endangered plant is found in *(Chap 13, Class-XII, NCERT) (UPPSC Mains 2011)*

(a) Himachal Pradesh
(b) Madhya Pradesh
(c) Meghalaya
(d) Uttar Pradesh

Ans. (c)

Exp. *Nepenthes khasiana* is India's only pitcher plant and is named after the Khasi hill region of Meghalaya. They are mostly found in Garo, Khasi and Jaintia hills of Meghalaya.

16 Which of the following statements is incorrect? *(Chap 13, Class-XII, NCERT) (Chap 30, Module-7, NIOS)*

(a) Chipko Movement prevented cutting and felling of trees by hugging them
(b) Van Mahotsav is celebrated in the first week of April
(c) Soil erosion, loss of fertility of soil and lack of vegetation lead to desertification
(d) Social forestry is a means of afforestation

Ans. (b)

Exp. Van Mahotsav is a tree-planting festival that is celebrated in the first week of July from 1 - 7.

It is observed to spread awareness about the importance of forests, woodlands and trees in our lives.

17 Consider the following animals of India.

(Chap 13, Class-XII, NCERT) (IAS Pre 2003)

1. Crocodile
2. Elephant

Which of these is/are endangered species?

(a) Only 1 (b) Only 2
(c) Both 1 and 2 (d) Neither 1 nor 2

Ans. (c)

Exp. According to the Red Data list of International Union for Conservation of Nature (IUCN), crocodile species found in India are in critically endangered category, while Indian elephant is in endangered category. Thus, both are considered endangered species of India.

18 The term 'Sixth mass extinction/sixth extinction' is often mentioned in the news in the context of the discussion of *(Chap 13, Class-XII, NCERT) (IAS Pre 2018)*

(a) Widespread monoculture practices in agriculture and large-scale commercial farming with indiscriminate use of chemicals in many parts of the world that may result in the loss of good native ecosystems.

(b) Fears of a possible collision of a meteorite with the Earth in the near future in the manner it happened 65 million years ago that caused the mass extinction of many species including those of dinosaurs.

(c) Large scale cultivation of genetically modified crops in many parts of the world and promoting their cultivation in other parts of the world which may cause the disappearance of good native crop plants and the loss of food biodiversity.

(d) Mankind's overexploitation/misuses of natural resources, fragmentation/loss of natural habitats, destruction of ecosystems, pollution and global climate change.

Ans. (d)

Exp. The term 'Sixth mass extinction' is used in the context of mankind's over exploitation/misuse of natural resources, fragmentation/loss of natural habitats, destruction of ecosystems, pollution and global climate change.

Currently, the Earth is mainly towards the sixth extinction, which is different from the previous episodes in the rates. The current species extinction rates are estimated to be 100-1000 times faster than in the pre human times and human activities are responsible for the faster rates. If the present rate of species extinction goes on, 50% of these species will be wiped out within next 100 years.

Chapter 11

Agriculture Science and Animal Husbandary

Agriculture Science and Animal Husbandary

Agriculture Science

Agricultural Science

- It deals with food and fibre production and their processing.
- **Crops and Their Classification** When plants of the same kind are grown and cultivated at one place, is called crop.
- **Based on Production** Cereal (Carbohydrate),pulses (protein), Oil seeds (fat and oils), vegetables, spice and fruits (vitamins and minerals) and fodder crops.
  - **Based on Seasons** Crops are of the following types, i.e, Kharif crops, Rabi crops, Zaid crops.

Crop Production Management

- Preperation of soil, sowing, nutrient management (manure and fertiliser) and irrigation.

Irrigation

- Process of supplying water to crop plants.
- **Sources of Irrigation** Canals, Wells Dug well, Tube well, Tanks, River lift system;
- **Modern Techniques** Rainwater Harvesting; Watershed development.
- **Methods** Traditional methods [Pulley, Dhekli chain pump lever system];

Cropping Patterns

- It inclues Mixed Cropping Intercropping, Crop Rotation.

Crop Protection Management

- Reduce chance of getting harm to the crops from weeds, pests, pathogens, insects storage (Biotic or abiotic factor) etc.

Improvement in Crop Production

- **Hybridisation** (Produce High yielding variety by crossing)
- **Types** Intervaritel, Interspecific and Intergeneric.
- **Genetically modified crop**
- **Factors** Higher yield, biotic and abiotic resistance, etc.

Animal Husbandary

Animal Husbandary

- Scientific Management of livestock.

Cattle Farming

- It is done for getting milk and drought labour for agricultural work, e.g., *Bos indicus* and *Bos bubalis*.
- **Breeds of Cattle** Indigenous/local breeds & Exotic/foreign breeds
- **Lactation Period and Requirement** Period of milk production after the birth of a calf.
  - Animal feeds are roughage and concentrates (contain high level of proteins e.g. Cereals like gram and bajra.)
- **Diseases in Cattle** External parasite, Internal parasite .

Poultry Farming

- Rearing of domestic fowls.
- Egg and Broiler production.
- Poultry disease & prevention.

Animal Breeding

- Increase the yield off animals and improve desirable qualities.
- **Inbreeding** Mating between two closely related individuals.
- **Outbreeding** Mating between two unrelated individuals. These includes the following

(i) Out crossing (ii) Cross-breeding
(iii) Interspecific Hybridisation

Bee-keeping

- Method of rearing, care and management of honey bees
- It requires low investments.
- Indian bee — *Apis cerana indica*
- Rock bee — *A. dorsata*
- Little bee — *A. florae*

Fish Culture

- Process of raising desirable species of fishes.
- **Advantage** (Large variety of desired fish)
- **Disadvantage** (Threat to biodiversity)

SOURCE *Old NCERT Class VIII* (Crop Production and Management), *New NCERT Class IX* (Improvement in Food Resources), *Old NCERT Class XII* (Strategies for Enhancement of Food Production), *NIOS Chap 31* Module 7

1 Consider the following crops *(Chap 12, Class-IX, NCERT) (IAS Pre 2013)*

1. Cotton 2. Groundnut
3. Rice 4. Wheat

Which of the above are Kharif crops?

(a) 1 and 4
(b) 2 and 3
(c) 1, 2 and 3
(d) 2, 3 and 4

Ans. (c)

Exp. The crops which are sown in the rainy season are called kharif crops. The rainy season in India is generally from June to September. Paddy, maize, soyabean, groundnut, cotton and rice, etc, are kharif crops.

Crops like wheat, gram, pea, mustard, etc., are example of rabi crops.

2 Which of the following statements with reference to the main cropping seasons in India is /are false? *(Chap 12, Class-IX, NCERT))*

1. The terms 'kharif' and 'rabi' originate from Arabic language where kharif means autumn and rabi means spring.
2. Kharif crops need cold weather for growth and need less water.
3. Rabi crops generally require more water and are called monsoon crops.
4. Zaid is short cropping season during summer months and mostly seasonal fruits and vegetables are grown in this season.

Choose the correct answer from the options given below.

(a) 1 and 2 (b) 1 and 4
(c) 3 and 4 (d) 2 and 3
(e) Question not attempted

Ans. (d)

Exp. Statements (1) and (4) are correct.

Statements (2) and (3) are incorrect because kharif crops are monsoon or autumn crops, that are cultivated and harvested during the Indian Subcontinent's monsoon season.

Rabi crops are the winter crops and are sown in the month from October to December and harvested in the spring season.

3 First dwarf rice variety developed in India was *(Chap 12, Class-IX, NCERT) (UPPSC Mains 2010)*

(a) IR-8 (b) Jaya
(c) Padma (d) Ratna

Ans. (b)

Exp. The first dwarf variety of rice developed in India was Jaya. It was the first paddy variety that emerged from the programme developed by ICAR (Indian Council of Agriculture and Research).

4 Which of the following statements is correct about fertilisers? *(Chap 1, Class-VIII, NCERT)*

(a) It is a natural substance obtained by the decomposition of cattle dung.
(b) It provides a lot of humus to the soil.
(c) It is very rich in plant nutrients like nitrogen, phosphorus and potassium.
(d) It is prepared in the field.

Ans. (c)

Exp. Statement (c) is correct about fertilisers. Fertilisers are chemical substances which are rich in a particular nutrient. It is an inorganic salt prepared in the factories. Fertilisers do not provide any humus to the soil. They are very rich in plant nutrients like nitrogen, phosphorus and potassium. They enhance the water retention capacity of the soil and also increase its fertility. Excessive use of fertilisers makes the soil less fertile. It also disturbs the pH of the soil and reduces microbial activity.

5 The organic manure is considered better than fertilisers because *(Chap 1, Class-VIII, NCERT)*

(a) it enhances the water holding capacity of the soil
(b) it improves the texture of the soil
(c) it increases the number of friendly microbes
(d) All of the above

Ans. (d)

Exp. The organic manure is considered better than fertilisers because it enhances the water holding capacity of the soil. It makes the soil porous, due to which exchange of gases become easy. It increases the number of friendly microbes. It improves the texture of the soil.

Organic manure is derived from animal matter and human excreta. These are obtained naturally and have no harmful impact on the soil.

6 Which of the following is the chief characteristics of 'mixed farming'? *(Chap 12, Class-IX, NCERT)*

(a) Cultivation of both cash crops and food crops
(b) Cultivation of two or more crops in the same field
(c) Rearing of animals and cultivation of crops together
(d) None of the above

Ans. (c)

Exp. Statement (c) is the chief characteristic of mixed farming.

Mixed farming is a system of farming on a particular farm which includes crop production, raising of livestock, etc. In this, the crops and animals components are complement and support each other. For example, the crop farming gives feed to the animals, and in return, the animals can supply fertilisers manure to the crop. So, this reduces the need and cost of fertilisation and animal feed.

It protects the farmer against the risk of poor prices. It is useful in maintaining the soil fertility. It is helpful in economic development.

7 Consider the following pairs. *(Chap 12, Class-IX, NCERT)*

1. Mixed cropping – Growing two or more crops simultaneously on the same piece of land.
2. Intercropping – Growing of two or more crops simultaneously on the same field in a definite manner.
3. Crop rotation – Growing of different crops on a piece of land in pre-planned succession.

Which of the pairs given above are correctly matched?

(a) 1 and 2 (b) 2 and 3
(c) 1, 2 and 3 (d) 1 and 3

Ans. (c)

Exp. Pairs (1), (2) and (3) are correctly matched.

Mixed cropping is growing of two or more crops simultaneously on the same piece of land. This minimise the pest infestation, reduces crop failure and farmers can harvest varieties of produce at the same time. For example, growing wheat and gram on the same land at the same time is mixed cropping.

Growing of two or more crops in a definite row pattern is known as intercropping. It is a sustainable practice that can improve resource usage efficiency, such as nutrients and water, allowing low input agricultural practices.

The growing of different crops on a piece of land in a preplanned succession is called crop rotation. It is a practice to minimise pests and diseases, reduce chemical use, aid in building and maintaining healthy soil and manage nutrient requirement.

8 With reference to drip irrigation, which of the following statement(s) is/are incorrect? *(Chap 1, Class-VIII, NCERT)*

1. In this system, water falls drop by drop at the positions of the roots.
2. Lots of water is wasted in this type of irrigation.

Codes

(a) Only 1 (b) Only 2
(c) Both 1 and 2 (d) Neither 1 nor 2

Ans. (b)

Exp. Statement (2) is incorrect with reference to drip irrigation because water is not wasted in this type of irrigation. It is a boon in regions where availability of water is poor.

9 Which of the following weed causes diseases such as allergy and asthma in human beings? *(Chap 31, Module-7, NIOS)*

(a) *Xanthium* (b) *Parthenium*
(c) *Cyperus rotundus* (d) *Cemazine*

Ans. (b)

Exp. Weeds are useless plants like *Xanthium*, *Parthenium* and *Cyperus rotundus* that grow along with crops in fertile soil.

Weeds like *Parthenium* causes diseases such as allergy and asthma in human beings.

10 Consider the following statements. *(Chap 1, Class VIII, NCERT)*

1. Green Revolution occurred in the Indian agricultural scenario between 1968 and 1988.
2. Multicropping is only possible when we plant crops that require planting for a shorter period of time.
3. Plants containing large number of leaves should be selected for transplantation.

Choose the correct options.

(a) 1 and 3 (b) 1, 2 and 3 (c) Only 3 (d) 1 and 2

Ans. (d)

Exp. The correct statement is 1 and 2.
A big change related to crop farming and food production occurred in the Indian agricultural scenario between 1968 to 1988 and this period is called golden age of agriculture named Green Revolution.
The process of shifting the new plants from the field where they are sown to the main field is called transplantation. Plants, containing at least 4-5 healthy leaves should be selected for transplantation.

11 Match the following lists and choose the correct code. *(Chap 1, Class-VIII, NCERT)*

List I	List II
A. Threshing	1. Removal of unwanted plants
B. Harvesting	2. Separation of grains from the chaff
C. Weeding	3. Supply of water to crops at appropriate intervals
D. Irrigation	4. Cutting of the mature crop manually or by machines

Codes

	A	B	C	D
(a)	2	1	4	3
(b)	2	4	1	3
(c)	4	2	1	3
(d)	4	3	1	2

Ans. (b)

Exp. The correct matching is A-2, B-4, C-1, D-3.

Threshing - It is the process of separation of the grains from the chaff. This is carried out with the help of a machine called 'combine'.

Harvesting - It is the cutting of the mature crop manually or by machines. It is done either by sickle or by a machine called 'harvester'.

Weeding - It involves removal of unwanted and uncultivated plants called weeds. It is necessary since weeds compete with the crop plants for water, nutrients, space and light.

Irrigation - It is the process of supplying water to crops at different intervals. The time and frequency of irrigation vary from crop to crop, soil to soil and season to season.

12 Which of the following is/are Indian cow breeds? *(Chap 12, Class-IX, NCERT)*

1. Jersey 2. Red Sindhi
3. Sahiwal 4. Murrah

Codes

(a) 3 and 4 (b) 2 and 3 (c) 1, 3 and 4 (d) 1, 2, 3 and 4

Ans. (b)

Exp. Option (2) and (3) are correct as Indian cow breeds are Red Sindhi and Sahiwal. The exotic breeds are Jersey and Brown Swiss, etc. The exotic breeds are selected for long lactation periods, while local breeds shows excellent resistance to diseases. The two can be cross-breed to get animals with both the desired qualities. Murrah is an indigenous buffalo breed of India.

13 **Choose the incorrectly matched pair.** *(Chap 12, Class-IX, NCERT)*

(a) Catla – Surface feeders
(b) Mrigals – Middle zone feeders
(c) Rohu – Middle zone feeders
(d) Grass carps – Weed feeders

Ans. (b)

Exp. Pair (b) is incorrectly matched as mrigals and common carps are bottom feeders.

Catla are surface feeders, Rohu feed in the middle zone of the pond and grass carps feed on the weeds.

Together, these species can use all the food in the pond without competing with each other. This increases the fish yield from the pond.

14 **Which of the following fishes is/are found in marine water?** *(Chap 12, Class-IX, NCERT)*

1. Pomphret 2. Tuna 3. Catla 4. Mackerel

Codes

(a) 1 and 2 (b) 1, 2 and 4 (c) 2, 3 and 4 (d) 2 and 4

Ans. (b)

Exp. Popular marine fish varieties include pomphret, mackerel, tuna, sardines and Bombay duck. Some marine fishes of high economic value are also formed in seawater. This includes finned fishes like mullets, bhetki and pearl spots, shellfish such as prawn, mussels and oyster as well as seaweed.

15 **Cross-breeding is done between Indian and exotic poultry breeds for development of which of the following traits?** *(Chap 12, Class-IX, NCERT)*

1. Tolerance to high temperature.
2. High maintenance requirement.
3. Increase in the size of egg-laying bird.
4. Number and quality of chicks.

Codes

(a) 1 and 2 (b) 1 and 4 (c) 2 and 3 (d) 3 and 4

Ans. (b)

Exp. Statements (1) and (4) are correct.

The cross-breeding programmes between Indian and foreign breeds are focused on to develop new varieties for the following desirable traits

- Number and quality of chicks.
- Dwarf broiler parent for commercial chick production.
- Low maintenance requirements.
- Summer adaptation capacity/tolerance to high temperature.
- Reduction in the size of the egg-laying bird with ability to utilise more fibrous cheaper diet formulated using agricultural byproducts.

16 **Match the following lists and choose the correct code.** *(Chap 12, Class-IX, NCERT)*

List I (Scientific name)	List II (Common name)
A. *Apis mellifera*	1. Little bee
B. *Apis florae*	2. Rock bee
C. *Apis dorsata*	3. Italian bee
D. *Apis indica*	4. Indian bee

Codes

	A	B	C	D		A	B	C	D
(a)	1	2	3	4	(b)	2	1	3	4
(c)	3	1	2	4	(d)	4	2	3	1

Ans. (c)

Exp. The correct matching is A-3, B-1, C-2, D-4.

Apis mellifera - It is an Italian bee variety. They are bigger than all other honeybees except *Apis dorsata*. They have high honey collection capacity. They sting less. They stay in a given beehives for long periods, and breed very well.

Apis florae - It is called little bee. It is unique for its morphology, foraging behaviour and defensive mechanisms.

Apis dorsata - It also known as rock bee. These social bees are known for their aggressive defensive strategies and attacking behaviour when disturbed.

Apis cerana indica - It is commonly known as the Indian bee. They are good nectar collector and honey producer. They are more prone to swarming and absconding.

17 **Consider the following pairs.** *(Chap 12, Class-IX, NCERT)*

1. Inbreeding – Mating of two closely related members of same breed
2. Outbreeding – Mating of unrelated members of same breed
3. Cross-breeding – Mating between male and female of different breed.

Which of the above pair(s) is/are correctly matched?

(a) Only 1 (b) 1 and 3 (c) 1 and 2 (d) 1, 2 and 3

Ans. (d)

Exp. All the given pairs are correctly matched.

Inbreeding refers to the mating of closely related individuals within the same breed for 4-6 generations.

Outbreeding is the breeding of unrelated animals, which may be between individuals of the same breed, but having no common ancestors for 4-6 generations (outcrossing) or between different breeds (cross breeding) or different species (interspecific hybridisation).

Cross-breeding allows the desirable qualities of two different breeds to be combined. It is mating between male and female of different breeds.

Chapter 12

Environmental Issues

Environmental Issues

Types of Pollution

Pollution

- Any undesirable change in physical, chemical and biological characteristics of air, water and land etc.
- **Pollutants** Agent causing undesirable change.

Types of Pollution

- **Air Pollution** Undesirable change in the physical, chemical or biological characteristics of air.
  - **Causes** Radio active substances, excessive use of chemicals; deforestation; combustion of fuel.
  - **Harmful Effects** Acid rain, smog, global warming, ozone depletion, respiratory problems.
- **Methods to Control** Use biofuels catalytic correcters, ESP and scrubber etc.
- **Water Pollution** Undesirable change which changes the quality of water.
  - **Causes** Fertilisers and pesticides; industrial waste.
  - **Harmful Effects** Biomagnification, eutrophication, algal Bloom, increased Biochemical oxygen demand.
  - **Methods to Control** Drip irrigation technique, Rain water harvesting, Implementation of water resource management.
- **Soil Pollution** Removal of useful components from the soil and addition of hazardous substances.
  - **Soil Erosion** Removal and thinning of the fertile top soil, **Preventive Measures** Intensive cropping, planting trees and sowing grasses, providing proper drainage, terrace framing.
  - **Harmful Effects** Reduced crop productivity, biomagnification, eutrophication, unfertile soil, disturbance in food chain.
- **Methods to Control** Organic farming, reduce use of chemical fertilisers. Proper disposing of radioactive
- **Noise Pollution** Undesirable high level of sound
  - **Harmful Effects** Impaired hearing ability, breathing problem, stress sleeplessness, increased heartbeat
  - **Method to Control** Sound absorbent material should be used; delimitation of horn-free zone around hospital & schools.

Radioactive Pollution

- Caused due to radiations from different elements used in nuclear power plants and mines.
  - **Harmful Effects** Skin cancer, mutations (sudden change in DNA); cataract, etc.
  - **Method of Control** Proper disposal of radioactive waste, Prohibition of nuclear weapons.

Solid Waste and Its Management

Solid Waste

- On the basis of degradation there are two type of waste
- **Biodegradable Waste** Waste which can be easily degraded by the action of micro-organisms. e.g. Animal bones, fruit and vegetable peels, etc.
- **Non-biodegradable Waste** Waste which cannot be degraded into harmless forms. e.g. Radioactive waste, plastic etc.

Methods of Solid Waste Disposal

- **Recycling** Manage e-waste.
- **Sanitary Landfills** Alternative to open-burning.
- **Composting** Rotting and conversion of biodegrable substances with the help of bacteria and fungi.
- **Biogas Production** Sewage and other biodegradable substances are used for the production of biogas.
- **Open Burning** It involves burning of muncipal waste in open dumps to reduce volume.
  - **Incineration** Burning of substance at high temperature.
  - **Pyrolysis** Thermochemical treatments where material is burnt in closed vessel.

SOURCE *Old NCERT Class VI* (Garbage In, Garbage Out), *Old NCERT Class VII* (Water : A Precious Resource), *New NCERT Class VII* (Wastewater Story), *Old NCERT Class VIII* (Pollution of Air and Water), *Old NCERT Class IX* (Natural Resources), *Old NCERT Class X* (Our Environment), (Management of Natural Resources), *Old NCERT Class XII* (Environmental Issues)

1 **Consider the following characteristics of ozone.** *(Chap 13, Class-X, NCERT)*

1. It is a deadly poison formed by three atoms of oxygen.
2. At the higher level of atmosphere, ozone shields the surface of the Earth from ultraviolet (UV) radiation of the Sun.
3. Bad ozone is formed at stratosphere and good ozone is formed at troposphere.

Which of the above statements is/are incorrect?

(a) Only 3 (b) 1 and 3
(c) 2 and 3 (d) None of these

Ans. (a)

Exp. Statement (3) is incorrect because bad ozone is formed in the lower atmosphere, i.e. troposphere, that harm plants and animals. There is 'good ozone' also which is found in the upper part of the atmosphere called the stratosphere and it acts as a shield absorbing ultraviolet (UV) radiation from the Sun.

2 **Which of the given chemical is responsible for reduction of ozone layer?** *(Chap 13, Class-X, NCERT)*

(a) Methane (b) Carbon dioxide
(c) Chlorofluorocarbons (d) All of these

Ans. (c)

Exp. Chlorofluorocarbons (CFCs) are responsible for reduction in amount of ozone in the atmosphere. These are synthetic chemicals which are used as refrigerant. They are also used in manufacture of aerosol sprays, blowing agents for foams and in packing materials as solvents. In 1987, the United Nations Environment Programme (UNEP) succeeded in forging an agreement to freeze CFCs production at 1986 level.

3 **Industries located in and around Agra like rubber processing, automobile, chemicals and especially the Mathura oil refinery have been responsible for producing pollutants like .... causing acid rains in that area.** *(Chap 13, Class-X, NCERT) (UPPSC Pre 2008)*

(a) Carbon monoxide and sulphur oxide
(b) Sulphur dioxide and nitrogen dioxide
(c) Sulphur oxide and nitrogen oxide
(d) Carbon dioxide and carbon monoxide

Ans. (b)

Exp. The industries located in and around Agra like rubber processing, automobile, chemicals and especially the Mathura oil refinery, have been responsible for producing pollutants like sulphur dioxide and nitrogen dioxide.

These gases react with water vapour present in the atmosphere to form sulphuric acid and nitric acid. These acids drop down with rain, making the rain acidic. This is called acid rain.

Suspended particulate matter such as soot particles emitted by Mathura oil refinery, has contributed towards the yellowing of the marble (taj).

4 **Choose the correctly matched pair about air pollution.** *(Chap 13, Class-X, NCERT)*

(a) Marble cancer – Acid rain
(b) Greenhouse gases – CH_4, CO_2, N_2O, CFCs
(c) Smog – Oxides of nitrogen and fog
(d) All of the above

Ans. (d)

Exp. All pairs (a), (b) (c) and (d) are correctly matched about air pollution.

Smog is made up of smoke and fog. It may contain oxides of nitrogen which combine with other air pollutants and fog to form smog.

Acid rain corrodes the marble of the monuments. This phenomenon is also called 'Marble cancer'.

Greenhouse gases include water vapour, carbon dioxide, methane, nitrous oxide, ozone and some artificial chemical such as chlorofluorocarbons (CFCs). The absorbed energy warms the atmosphere and the surface of the Earth.

5 **With respect to air pollution, consider the following statements.** *(Chap 13, Class-X, NCERT)*

1. Smog causes breathing difficulties such as asthma, cough and wheezing in children.
2. CO produced from incomplete burning of petrol is poisonous as it reduces oxygen carrying capacity of blood.
3. Natural sources of air pollution are forest fires and volcanic eruptions.

Which of the statement(s) given above are correct?

(a) 1 and 2 (b) 2 and 3 (c) 1 and 3 (d) 1, 2 and 3

Ans. (d)

Exp. Statements (1), (2) and (3) are correct.

The substances which contaminate the air are called air pollutants. Natural sources like smoke and dust arising from forest fires or volcanic eruptions are also pollutants. They are added to the atmosphere by certain human activities. Smog is a kind of air pollution, which is made up of smoke and fog. It is composed of nitrogen oxides, sulphur dioxide, ozone smoke and other particulates. The smog causes breathing difficulties such as asthma, cough and wheezing in children.

Vehicles produce high levels of pollutants like carbon monoxide, carbon dioxide, nitrogen oxide and smoke. Carbon monoxide is produced from incomplete burning of fuels such as petrol and diesel. It is a poisonous gas. It reduces the oxygen carrying capacity of the blood.

6 **Regular breathing of air that contains hydrocarbons increases the incidence of which of the following?** *(Chap 13, Class-X, NCERT)*

1. Allergies 2. Cancer
3. Heart disease 4. Cataract
5. Inflammation of cornea

Codes

(a) 1, 2 and 3 (b) 2, 3 and 4 (c) 3, 4 and 5 (d) 1, 4 and 5

Ans. (a)

Exp. Options (1), (2) and (3) are correct. Regular breathing of air that contains hydrocarbons increases the incidence of allergies, cancer and heart diseases. An increase in the content of these harmful substances in air is called air pollution. These substance can also lead to the greenhouse effect and climate change, deplete the ozone and reduce photosynthetic ability of plants. Options (3) and (4) are incorrect as breathing of hydrocarbons in air do not affect our eyes and does not cause cataract or inflammation of cornea.

7 Consequences of global warming are all except

(Chap 13, Class-X, NCERT)

(a) rise in Earth's temperature by 0.6°C
(b) El Nino effect
(c) melting of polar ice caps
(d) decrease in sea level

Ans. (d)

Exp. Increase in the level of greenhouse gases has led to considerable heating of Earth leading to global warming. During the past century, the temperature of Earth has increased by 0.6°C, most of it during the last decade. Rise in temperature leads to deleterious changes in the environment and resulting in odd climatic change (e.g. El Nino effect), thus, leading to increased melting of polar ice caps. This will also lead to rise in sea level that can submerge many coastal areas. Therefore option (d) is incorrect.

8 What will be the decreasing order of the following that contribute to the greenhouse effect?

(Chap 13, Class-X, NCERT)
(CGPSC Pre 2021), (Tripura PCS Pre 2023)

(a) $CO_2 > CH_4 > CFCs > N_2O$
(b) $CH_4 > CO_2 > CFCs > N_2O$
(c) $CO_2 > CFCs > CH_4 > N_2O$
(d) $CO_2 > CH_4 > N_2O > CFCs$

Ans. (a)

Exp. Decreasing order of the gases contributing to the greenhouse effect is CO_2(60%) > CH_4(20%)> CFCs (14%) >N_2O(6%). Greenhouse gases are crucial in keeping our planet at a suitable temperature for life. The major factors contributing to greenhouse gas emissions are the burning of fossil fuels, deforestation, farming and livestock production, etc.

9 Gases that trap heat in the atmosphere and cause global warming are called greenhouse gases. Which of the following combinations are not included under the greenhouse gases?

(Chap 13, Class-X, NCERT) (Odisha PCS Pre 2023)

(a) Carbon dioxide, Methane
(b) Nitrous oxide, Hydrofluorocarbons
(c) Carbon monoxide, Sulphur dioxide
(d) Carbon dioxide, Water vapour

Ans. (c)

Exp. Carbon monoxide and sulphur dioxide are not included under the greenhouse gases.

Greenhouse gases are gases in Earth's atmosphere that trap heat. They allow sunlight to enter, but prevent some of the heat that the Earth reflects from escaping, contributing to the greenhouse effect.

The common greenhouse gases include Carbon dixode (CO_2), Methane (CH_4), Nitrous oxide (N_2O) Chlorofluorocarbons (CFCs) and water vapour. These gases play a significant role in the Earth's climate system and can contribute to global warming when their concentration increase.

10 In relation to ozone which statements are true?

(Chap 13, Class-X, NCERT) (Chap 26, Module-6, NIOS)
(MPSC Pre 2023)

1. Ozone is called protection shield of the Earth.
2. In 1985 it was clear that ozone layer has holes.
3. 16th September is celebrated as World Ozone Day.
4. In 1989 chemicals responsible for ozone depletion are banned to utilise.

Codes

(a) 1, 2 and 3
(b) 2, 3 and 4
(c) 1, 3 and 4
(d) All of the above

Ans. (a)

Exp. Statements 1, 2 and 3 are correct.

Ozone is called protection shield of Earth because it acts as a shield absorbing ultraviolet radiation from the Sun. The portion where ozone layer is thinnest which is known as ozone hole and in 1985 it was clear that ozone layer has hole.

World Ozone Day is celebrated on 16th September every year to spread awareness among people about depletion of ozone layer.

Statement (4) is incorrect because chemical responsible for ozone depletion were banned to utilise in 1987.

11 Which of the following greenhouse gases has the highest atmospheric lifetime?

(Chap 13, Class-X, NCERT) (Mizoram PCS Pre 2023)

(a) CO
(b) N_2O
(c) CH_4
(d) CF_4

Ans. (d)

Exp. CF_4 has the highest atmospheric lifetime among the given gases.

Greenhouse gases or GHGs are gases present in the atmosphere of the Earth which effectively capture and retain heat. An increase in the level of GHGs lead to heating of Earth leading to the global warming.

Among the given gases CF_4 (Carbon tetraflouride) posses longest lifetime of 50,000 years and has a Global Warming Potential (GWP) of around 5000 over a span of 20 years.

12 Increase in concentration of a toxicant at successive trophic level is called *(Chap 13, Class-X, NCERT) (Mizoram PCS Pre 2023)*

(a) biomagnification (b) succession
(c) eutrophication (d) biotransformation

Ans. (a)

Exp. Increase in concentration of toxicant at successive trophic level is called biomagnification. Biomagnification is the term used to describe the amplification of toxicant as it moves up each level of the food chain. The reason for this occurrence is that when an organism gathers a harmful substance that it cannot metabolise, it ends up transferring it to the higher trophic level.

13 Photochemical smog is a resultant of the reaction among *(Chap 13, Class-X, NCERT) (IAS Pre 2013)*

(a) NO_2, O_3 and peroxyacetyl nitrate in the presence of sunlight
(b) CO, O_2 and peroxyacetyl nitrate in the presence of sunlight
(c) CO, CO_2 and NO_2 at low temperature
(d) High concentration of NO_2, O_3 and CO in the evening

Ans. (a)

Exp. Photochemical smog is the chemical reaction of sunlight, nitrogen oxides and volatile organic compounds (hydrocarbons) in the atmosphere. These reactions often result in the formation of ground level ozone and certain airborne particles.

Common examples of primary pollutants that contribute towards photochemical smog include oxides of nitrogen such as nitric oxide, nitrogen dioxide and nitrous oxide and most VOCs (Volatile Organic Compounds). Common examples of secondary pollutants that contribute towards the formation of photochemical smog include aldehydes, tropospheric ozone and Peroxylacyl Nitrate (PAN).

14 Which of the following are some important pollutants released by steel industry in India? *(Chap 13, Class-X, NCERT) (IAS Pre 2014)*

1. Oxides of sulphur 2. Oxides of nitrogen
3. Carbon monoxide 4. Carbon dioxide

Codes

(a) 1, 3 and 4 (b) 2 and 3 (c) 1 and 4 (d) 1, 2, 3 and 4

Ans. (d)

Exp. Option (d) is correct. In steel industries, the steel furnace has coke which reacts with iron ore, releasing iron and generating CO (Carbon monoxide) and CO_2 (Carbon dioxide) gases.

Due to use of coal, pollutants such as oxides of sulphur and oxides of nitrogen are released.

15 Choose the correct pair of impurities causing disease present in wastewater. *(Chap 7, Class-XII, NCERT)*

(a) *Salmonella cholerae* – Cholera
(b) *Vibrio typhi* – Typhoid
(c) Protozoan – Dysentery
(d) All of the above

Ans. (c)

Exp. Pair (c) is correctly matched as dysentery is caused by protozoans. It is a type of infectious diarrhoea. Risk factor includes contamination of food and water with faeces due to poor sanitation.

Pairs (a) and (b) are incorrect because *Vibrio cholerae* causes cholera and *Salmonella typhi* causes typhoid.

16 The term water pollution does not cover the effect like *(Chap 13, Class-VII, NCERT)*

(a) building dams in areas where there is water scarcity
(b) addition of undesirable substance to water bodies that may cause diseases
(c) removal of desirable substances from water bodies
(d) change in temperature of the water body

Ans. (a)

Exp. The term water pollution does not cover the effect like building dams in areas where there is water scarcity. It includes the addition of undesirable substances to water bodies.

These substances could be the fertilisers and pesticides. These could also be disease causing organisms, like the bacteria which cause cholera.

The removal of desirable substances from water bodies. A change in temperature in water bodies would be dangerous for the aquatic organisms. The eggs and larvae of various animals are particularly susceptible to temperature changes.

17 Which of the following statement(s) is/are correct? *(Chap 13, Class-VII, NCERT)*

(a) Sewage is a liquid waste. Most of it is water, along with dissolved and suspended impurities
(b) 22nd March is celebrated as World Water Day
(c) Environment (Protection) Act, 1986 has been passed by Government of India to protect and improve the quality of our environment
(d) All of the above

Ans. (d)

Exp. All statements are correct. Sewage is a liquid waste. Most of it is water, which has dissolved and suspended impurities. It consists of wastewater discharged from residences and from commercial, institutional and public facilities.

World Water Day in an annual United Nations observance day held on 22nd March that highlights the importance of freshwater. The day is used to advocate for the sustainable management of freshwater resources.

In order to control environmental pollution, the Government of India has passed the Environment (Protection) Act in 1986, to protect and improve the quality of our environment (air, water and soil). The purpose of this Act is to implement the decisions of the United Nations Conference on the Human Environment.

18 Which of the following statements is not related to pollution of the Ganga? *(Chap 13, Class-VII, NCERT)*

(a) Coliform bacteria is found in Ganga water
(b) Ganga Action Plan came in 1985 to improve the quality of water in Ganga
(c) Ganga river is 'dead' at many places where the pollution level is low
(d) All of the above

Ans. (c)

Exp. Statement (c) is incorrect for Ganga river.

This is because the Ganga river is dead at many places where the level of pollution is high, where aquatic life is unable to survive.

Ganga river is contaminated because people throw large quantities of garbage, untreated sewage, dead bodies and various harmful things in it.

In 1985, Ganga Action Plan was launched because the quality of the water in the Ganga was very poor. Coliform is a disease-causing microorganism found in human intestine, whose presence in water indicates contamination.

19 In India, the problem of soil erosion is associated with which of the following? *(Chap 12, Class-VII, NCERT) (IAS Pre 2014)*

1. Terrace cultivation
2. Deforestation
3. Tropical climate

Codes

(a) 1 and 2 (b) Only 2
(c) 1 and 3 (d) 1, 2 and 3

Ans. (b)

Exp. Only option (2) is correct. Deforestation is a major cause of soil erosion, perhaps the main cause. Trees and their roots provide the soil with an anchor, as well as shelter from the wind and rain. When forests are wiped out, the land becomes exposed, leaving it vulnerable to being washed or blown away.

Terrace cultivation and tropical climate are not a consequence of soil erosion. Terrace cultivation is a method of growing crops on sides of hills or mountains by planting on graduated terraces build into the slope. Tropical climate is one of five major climate regions found on Earth.

20 Choose the incorrect statement about ecosystem. *(Chap 12,Class-XII, NCERT)*

(a) Decomposers form an important link between the living and non-living component of the ecosystem
(b) In aquatic ecosystem, floating plants called phytoplankton are the only autotrophs
(c) Greater the number of species present in the pond, the stronger and healthier it is
(d) Biotic community refers to populations of various kinds of organisms living together and sharing the same habitat

Ans. (b)

Exp. Statement (b) is incorrect.

Autotrophs form the basis of any biotic system as they trap solar energy to manufacture food for all. In terrestrial ecosystems, the autotrophs are mainly the rooted plants, while in aquatic ecosystems, floating plant called phytoplankton and shallow water rooted plants called macrophytes are the examples of autotrophs.

21 There is a concern over the increase in harmful algal bloom in the sea water in India. What could be causative factors for this phenomenon? *(Chap 13, Class-X, NCERT) (IAS Pre 2011)*

1. Discharge of nutrients from the estuaries.
2. Run-off from the land during the monsoon.
3. Upwelling in the sea.

Codes

(a) Only 1 (b) 1 and 2
(c) 2 and 3 (d) 1, 2 and 3

Ans. (d)

Exp. All statements are correct.

Algal bloom is a rapid increase or accumulation in the population of algae in freshwater or marine water systems.

The causative factors of algal bloom in coastal water of India are upwelling in the seas, formation of mud banks, nutrient discharges from estuaries and run-off from the land during Southwest and Northeast monsoon.

22 Global warming can be controlled by *(Chap 13, Class-X, NCERT)*

(a) reducing deforestation, cutting down use of fossil fuels
(b) reducing reforestation, increasing the use of fossil fuel
(c) increasing deforestation, slowing down the growth of human polulation
(d) increasing deforestation, reducing efficiency of energy usage

Ans. (a)

Exp. Global warming can be controlled by reducing deforestation and cutting down use of fossil fuel, which results into reduction of accumulation of the greenhouse gases. The other ways of reducing global warming are slowing down the growth of human population, improving efficiency of energy usage, etc.

23 In stratosphere, which one of the following elements acts as a catalyst in degradation of ozone and release of molecular oxygen? *(Chap 13, Class-X, NCERT)*

(a) Iron (b) Chlorine
(c) Carbon (d) Oxygen

Ans. (b)

Exp. In stratosphere, chlorine act as a catalyst in the degradation of ozone and release of molecular oxygen. It is released by action of UV rays on chlorofluorocarbons. Chlorine reacts with ozone in a series of chain reactions, converting it into molecular oxygen and nascent oxygen. One active chlorine can destroy 5000 molecules of ozone in one month.

Chapter 13

Biotechnology

Biotechnology

Technique of Biotechnology

Biotechnology

- Deals with the technique of using live organisms or enzymes from organisms
in order to produce different products and processes useful to humans. The

Techniques of Biotechnology

- **Genetic Engineering**
Technique used for modification of genetic material and their introduction into another organism to acquire desirable characteristics.
Paul Berg. Father of Genetic engineering
- **Sterilisation Methods**
Technique used to maintain microbial contamination free condition to enable the growth and manipulation of only desired microbes or cells. Products like vaccines, enzymes, antlblotlcs are obtained by this method.

Recombinant DNA Technology

- Technique in which two genes are combined from two different sources to create a new recombinant gene.
- First created by **Stanley Cohen** and **Herbert Boyer** in 1972.

Ethical Issues in Applications of Biotechnology

- Unpredictable results by genetically modified organisms.
- Environmental Issues and demerits.
- Socio-economics, cultural and Religious Issues.

Process of Biotechnology

Tools of Recombinant DNA Technology

- **Restriction enzymes** (Molecule Scissors). These are of two types
(i) Exonuclease (remove nucleotide from either of the end.)
(ii) Endonuclease (cut at specific position)
- **DNA ligases** (joins two nucleotides)
- **Alkaline Phosphate** (remove phosphate group.)
- **DNA polymerase** (aids *in vitro* synthesis or complementary DNA)
- **Cloning Vectors**
  - Origin of Replication (*ori*)-It controls the copy number of linked DNA and allow autonomous replication.
  - Selectable Marker-Identify and eliminate non-transformants.
  - Cloning sites-It is the site where DNA is inserted into the vector.
- **Competent Host Organism**
  - Ability of a cell to take up foreign DNA cells by methods like heat shock, microinjection and gene gun.

Process of Biotechnology

- Construction of a recombinant DNA molecule.
- Transport into the host cell.
- Multiplication of recombinant DNA molecule within the host cell.
- Division of the host cell.
- Numerous cell divisions resulting in a clone.

Application

In Medicines

- **Geneticaly Engineered Insulin** (Humulin) It's effect is same as insulin produced by the pancreas.
- **Gene Therapy** Technique used for correcting a defective gene through gene manipulation.
- **Stem cell Technology** Used in bone marrow transplantation, brain disease
treatment etc.
- **Molecular Diagnosis**
  - **Polymerase Chain Reaction** (PCR)
  - **Enzyme Linked Immunosorbent Assay** (ELISA)
  - **Blotting Technique.** It includes
- DNA (Southern blotting)
- RNA (Northern blotting)

Transgenic Animals

- Animals that have their DNA manipulated to express and extra gene.
- **Advantages**
  - To study normal physiology and development.
  - Vaccine and chemical safety testing.
  - Biological products, e.g. 1 anti-trypsin treat emphysema.

In Agriculture GM Crops

- More tolerant to abiotic stresses.
- High efficiency of mineral usage by plants.
- Enhance nutritional value of food.
- e.g. *Bt* crops, pest resistant plants, nutrition rich crops.

SOURCE **Old NCERT Class XII** (Reproduction in Animals), **New NCERT Class XII** (Molecular Basis of Inheritance), (Biotechnology : Principles and Processes), (Biotechnology and Its Applications), **Tamil Nadu Board Class X** (Breeding and biotechnology)

1 Which work among these falls into the category of biotechnology? *(Chap 9, Class-XII, NCERT) (IAS Pre 1993)*

(a) Use of the organisms or their substances in industrial processes.
(b) Modernisation of the process of commercial industries to produce the goods used in bio-exploration.
(c) Use of modern technology in research of biological multiplication.
(d) Use of industrial technology to increase the biosphere.

Ans. (a)

Exp. Statement (a) is correct as industrial use of all organisms, their substances or their biological process is known as biotechnology. For example, use of yeast cells for liquor production, use of starter (having microbes) for curd making comes under biotechnology.

2 Which one of the following cuts or break DNA at specific sites and also called as molecular scissors ? *(Chap 9 & 10, Class-XII, NCERT) (Unit 20, Class-X, Tamil Nadu Board)*

(a) Plasmid (b) DNA ligases
(c) Restriction enzymes (d) Transgene

Ans. (c)

Exp. Restriction enzymes cuts or break DNA at specific sites and are called as molecular scissors. It cleaves the phosphodiester bond within DNA.
Plasmid is the small, circular, double stranded DNA molecule found in the cytoplasm of bacteria cell and separated from chromosomal DNA. It can replicate independently.
DNA ligases are molecular glue and the enzymes which help in ligating (joining) the broken DNA fragments.
The DNA fragment is inserted to produce genetic modified organism using DNA techniques in order to produce the desired character is called transgene.

3 Which of the following is used in genetic engineering? *(Chap 9, Class-XII, NCERT) (UPPSC Pre 2015)*

(a) Plastid (b) Plasmid
(c) Mitochondria (d) Ribosome

Ans. (b)

Exp. Plasmid are used in genetic engineering. Bacteria possess extranuclear genetic material consisting of DNA. These extranuclear cytoplasm carries genetic information between cells of the same and even between different species and genera. These are termed as plasmids.

4 A selectable marker is used to *(Chap 9, Class-XII, NCERT)*

(a) help in eliminating the non-transformants, so that the transformants can be regenerated.
(b) identify the gene for a desired trait in an alien organism.
(c) select a suitable vector for transformation in a specific crop.
(d) mark a gene on a chromosome for isolation using restriction enzyme.

Ans. (a)

Exp. A selectable marker helps in identifying and eliminating non-transformants and selectively permitting the growth of the transformants.
Selectable marker is used to identify the cells which are recombinant in a cell culture.
It can provide resistance against a substrate like antibiotic resistance does in a plasmid. It can also inhibit the growth of organisms that does not have the marker gene.

5 Primers are *(Chap 9, Class-XII, NCERT)*

(a) small, chemically synthesised oligonucleotides of about 10-18 nucleotides that are complementary to the region of template DNA.
(b) chemically synthesised oligonucleotides of about 10-18 nucleotides, that are not complementary to region of template DNA.
(c) the double-stranded DNA that need to be amplified.
(d) specific sequences present on recombinant DNA.

Ans. (a)

Exp. Primers are the small, chemically synthesised oligonucleotides of about 10-18 nucleotides that are complementary to the region of template DNA.
In living organisms, primers are short strands of RNA. A primer must be synthesised by an enzyme called primase, which is a type of RNA polymerase, before DNA replication can occur.

6 In order to obtain the pure form of DNA in bacterial cells, it is treated with which of the following enzyme. *(Chap 9, Class-XII, NCERT)*

(a) Lysozyme
(b) Cellulase
(c) Chitinase
(d) Protease

Ans. (a)

Exp. In order to cut the DNA with restriction enzymes , it needs to be in pure form , free from other macro-molecules. This can be achieved by treating the bacterial cells, plant or animal tissue with enzyme such as lysozyme (bacteria), cellulase (plant cells), chitinase (fungus). The proteins can be removed by treatment with protease.

7 Palindrome sequences *(Chap 9, Class-XII, NCERT)*

(a) read opposite on two strands.
(b) read specific sequence in opposite direction.
(c) read same on two strands when orientation of reading is same.
(d) read opposite on two strands when orientation of reading is same.

Ans. (c)

Exp. Palindrome in DNA is the sequence of base pairs which read same on the two strands when orientation of reading is kept the same, e.g.

5′-GAATTC-3′ 3′-CTTAAG-5′

The sequence given above reads the same on both the strands either in 5′ → 3′ direction or in 3′ → 5′ direction.

8 **What is the criterion for DNA fragment's movement on agarose gel during gel electrophoresis?** *(Chap 9, Class-XII, NCERT)*

(a) The larger the fragment size, the farther it moves.
(b) The smaller the fragments size, the farther it moves.
(c) Positively charged fragments move to farther end.
(d) Negatively charged fragments do not move.

Ans. (b)

Exp. Gel electrophoresis is used for the separation of molecules of similar electric charge on the basis of their size. Hence, smaller the size of the DNA fragment, the farther it moves on agarose gel during gel electrophoresis.

9 **Other than resistance to pests, what are the prospects for which genetically engineered plants have been created?** *(Chap 10, Class-XII, NCERT) (IAS Pre 2012)*

1. To enable them to withstand drought.
2. To increase the nutritive value of the product.
3. To increase reliance on chemical pesticides.
4. To reduce post harvest losses.

Codes

(a) 1 and 2 (b) 3 and 4 (c) 1, 2 and 4 (d) 1, 2, 3 and 4

Ans. (c)

Exp. Statements (1), (2) and (4) are correct as genetically modified crops have been created to make crop more tolerant to abiotic stresses (cold, drought, salt, heat). It also helped to reduce post harvest losses. It has increased efficiency of mineral usage by plants and enhanced nutritional value of food, e.g. golden rice etc.

10 **Which one of the following is incorrect about gene therapy?** *(Chap 10, Class-XII, NCERT)*

(a) It was first successfully implemented in 1990.
(b) It is the replacement of defective gene.
(c) It targets the reproductive cells.
(d) The genetic makeup of the patient cell is altered using recombinant DNA technology.

Ans. (c)

Exp. Gene therapy refers to the replacement of defective gene by the direct transfer of functional genes into humans to treat genetic disease or disorder. Gene therapy conducted till date has targeted only somatic (non-reproductive) cells.

11 **Consider the following Assertion (A) and Reason (R) and choose the correct code.** *(Chap 12, Class-XII, NCERT)* *(Unit 20, Class-X, Tamil Nadu Board)*

Assertion (A) The transgenic plants are less stable, with improved nutritional quality.

Reason (R) The transgenic animals are used to produce proteins of medicinal importance.

(a) Both A and R are true and R is the correct explanation of A
(b) Both A and R are true, but R is not the correct explanation of A
(c) A is true, but R is false
(d) A is false, but R is true

Ans. (d)

Exp. Assertion (A) is false, but Reason (R) is true.

One of the most tremendous development of genetic engineering is the production of Genetically Modified (GM) plants and animals. Plants or animals expressing a modified endogenous gene or a foregin gene are called transgenic organism.

The transgenic plants are much stable, with improved nutritional quality, are resistant to diseases and tolerant to various environmental condition.

12 **RNA interference as a method of cellular defence involve** *(Chap 10, Class-XII, NCERT)*

(a) synthesis of *c*DNA and RNA using reverse transcriptase
(b) silencing of specific *m*RNA due to a complementary *ds*RNA
(c) interference of RNA in synthesis of DNA
(d) synthesis of *m*RNA from DNA

Ans. (b)

Exp. RNA interference takes place in all eukaryotic organisms as a method of cellular defence. This method involves silencing of a specific *m*RNA due to a complementary *ds*RNA molecule that binds to and prevents translation of the *m*RNA (silencing).

13 ***Bt*** **toxin protein crystals present in bacterium *Bacillus thuringiensis*, do not kill the bacteria because** *(Chap 10, Class-XII, NCERT)*

(a) bacteria are resistant to the toxin.
(b) bacteria enclose toxins in a special sac.
(c) toxins occur as inactive protoxins in bacteria.
(d) it increases protein content in bacteria.

Ans. (c)

Exp. *Bacillus thuringiensis* forms protein crystals during a particular phase of their growth. These crystals contain toxic insecticidal protein. The *Bt* toxin protein exist as inactive protoxins but once an insect ingest the inactive toxin, it is converted into an active form of toxin.

14 **The American multinational company, Monsanto, has produced an insect-resistant cotton variety that is undergoing field trials in India. A toxin gene from which one of the following bacteria has been transferred to this transgenic cotton?** *(Chap 10, Class-XII, NCERT) (UPPSC Pre 2001)*

(a) *Bacillus subtilis* (b) *Bacillus thuringiensis*
(c) *Bacillus amyloliquefaciens* (d) *Bacillus globigii*

Ans. (b)

Exp. Insect-resistant cotton plants have been genetically engineered by inserting a gene from a bacterium (*Bacillus thuringiensis*). Strains of *Bacillus thuringiensis* produce different toxins which are harmful to different insects. Such variety of cotton is commonly known as *Bt* cotton.

15 Consider the following pairs. ***(Chap 10, Class-XII, NCERT)***

1. cry IAc and cry II Ab – Corn borer
2. cry IAb – Cotton bollworms
3. Nematode – Meloidogyne incognita

How many pair(s) given above is/are correctly matched?

(a) Only one
(b) Only two
(c) All three
(d) None of the above

Ans. (a)

Exp. Only one pair i.e. (a), is correctly matched.
A nematode *Meloidogyne incognita* infects the roots of tobacco plants and cause a great reduction in yield.
While two pairs (1) and (2) are matched incorrectly.
cry IAc and *cry* IIAb genes control cotton bollworms. It provides protection from feeding damage by lepidopteran pests.
cry, IAc, *cry* II Ab and *cry* IAb produce toxins that are formed by introduction of *Bt* genes in plants that help to prevent them from small pests like cotton bollworms and corn borer, respectively.

16 Consider the following Assertion (A) and Reason (R) and choose the correct code. ***(Chap 9, Class-XII, NCERT) (IAS Pre 1999)***

Assertion (A) Dolly was the first cloned mammal.
Reason (R) Dolly was produced by *in vitro* fertilisation.

Codes

(a) Both A and R are true and R is the correct explanation of A.
(b) Both A and R are true, but R is not the correct explanation of A.
(c) A is true, but R is false.
(d) A is false, but R is true.

Ans. (c)

Exp. Assertion (A) is true, but Reason (R) is false.
Dolly was born in Roslin Institute in Scotland on 5th July, 1996 by efforts of Ian Wilmut, Keith Campbell and their colleagues.
She was the first mammal in the world, cloned from adult somatic cell successfully. Dolly was developed by conventional cloning technique, not by *in vitro* fertilisation. *In vitro* fertilisation is accepted widely for effective treatment of infertility.

17 World level program 'Human Genome Project' is related to ***(Chap 6, Class-XII, NCERT), (UPPSC Pre 2001)***

(a) establishment of superman society
(b) identification of colour distinct breeds
(c) genetic improvements of human breeds
(d) identification and mapping of human genes and its sequences

Ans. (d)

Exp. World level program in 'Human Genome Project' is related to identification and mapping of human genes and its sequences. As estimated by scientists, the human genome has approximately 30,000 genes and analysis of majority of genes has been completed.

18 Match the following lists and choose the correct code. ***(Chap 6, Class-XII, NCERT) (IAS Pre 2001)***

List I (Achievement in genetics)	List II (Scientists)
A. Discovery of transduction and conjugation in bacteria	1. Khorana
B. Establish sex linked inheritance	2. Kornberg
C. Isolation of DNA polymerase from *E. coli*	3. Lederberg
D. Establishing the complete genetic code	4. Morgan
	5. Ochoa

Codes

	A	B	C	D		A	B	C	D
(a)	4	3	2	1	(b)	3	4	1	5
(c)	4	3	1	5	(d)	3	4	2	1

Ans. (d)

Exp. The correct matching is A-3, B-4, C-2, D-1.
Bacterial conjugation is the transfer of genetic material between bacterial cells by direct cell-to-cell contact or by a bridge-like connection between two cells, discovered in 1946 by Joshua Lederberg and Edward Tatum.
Morgan was the first to establish the chromosome theory of inheritance. He used fruitflies with eye colour mutations to demonstrate sex-linked inheritance patterns.
Arthur Kornberg in 1956, discovered the first known DNA polymerase (and, indeed, the first known of any kind of polymerase).
Hargobind Khorana was an Indian-American biochemist who shared the 1968 Nobel Prize in Physiology or Medicine with Marshall W. Nirenberg and Robert W. Holley for research that helped to show how the order of nucleotides in nucleic acids, which carry the genetic code of the cell, control the cell's synthesis of proteins.

19 Consider the following Assertion (A) and Reason (R) and choose the correct code. ***(Chap 6, Class-XII, NCERT) (IAS Pre 2000)***

Assertion (A) 'DNA fingerprinting' has become a powerful tool to establish paternity and identity of criminals in rape and assault cases.
Reason (R) Trace evidence such as hair, saliva and dried semen are adequate for DNA analysis.

Codes

(a) Both A and R are true and R is the correct explanation of A.
(b) Both A and R are true, but R is not the correct explanation of A.
(c) A is true, but R is false.
(d) A is false, but R is true.

Ans. (a)

Exp. Both Assertion (A) and Reason (R) are true and Reason (R) is the correct explanation of Assertion (A). DNA fingerprinting, also called DNA typing, DNA profiling, genetic fingerprinting, genotyping or identity testing in genetics, is a method of isolating and identifying variable elements within the base-pair sequence of DNA (deoxyribonucleic acid).

The technique was developed by British geneticist Alec Jeffreys after he noticed that certain sequences of highly variable DNA (known as mini-satellites), which do not contribute to the functions of genes are repeated within genes. DNA fingerprinting is a powerful tool to establish paternity and identity of criminals in rape and assault cases because DNA from trace evidence such as hairs, saliva and dried semen are adequate for DNA analysis.

20 Which of the following statement is incorrect? ***(Chap 10, Class-XII, NCERT)***

(a) Recombinant therapeutics do not induce unwanted immunological response.
(b) Insulin used for diabetes was earlier extracted from pancreas of slaughtered cattle and pigs.
(c) In 1983, Eli Lilly company produced human insulin from a transgenic species of *Rhizobium*.
(d) The first clinical gene therapy was done to cure Adenosine Deaminase (ADA) deficiency.

Ans. (c)

Exp. Statement (c) is incorrect because in 1983, Eli Lilly an American company prepared two DNA sequences corresponding to A and B-chains of human insulin and introduced them in plasmids of *E.coli* to produce insulin chains. Chains A and B were produced separately, extracted and combined by creating disulphide bonds to form human insulin.

21 Which of the following molecular diagnostic techniques help in early detection of a disease?

1. Polymerase chain reaction ***(Chap 10, Class-XII, NCERT)***
2. Recombinant DNA technology
3. ELISA

Codes

(a) 1 and 2 (b) 2 and 3
(c) 1 and 3 (d) 1, 2 and 3

Ans. (d)

Exp. Options (1), (2) and (3) are correct. PCR (Polymerase Chain Reaction) is defined as the DNA replication *in vitro*. It results in selective amplification of a specific region of DNA molecule and is used to generate multiple copies of desired DNA fragment for cloning.

Recombinant DNA technology is the joining together of DNA molecules from two different species. Joining of DNA is done by use DNA ligase enzymes and cutting of DNA is done by using restriction enzymes.

ELISA is Enzyme Linked Immuno Sorbent Assay. It is a commonly used laboratory test to detect antibodies in the blood. An antibody is a protein produced by the body's immune system when it detects harmful substances, called antigens.

22 Transgenic animals serve as model to study many human diseases such as ***(Chap 10, Class-XII, NCERT)***

(a) Alzheimer's disease (b) Cancer
(c) Night blindness (d) Both (a) and (b)

Ans. (d)

Exp. Transgenic animals are specially made to serve as models for human diseases, so that investigation of new treatment for diseases can be conducted. Currently transgenic models exist for many human diseases such as Alzheimer's, cancer, cystic fibrosis, rheumatoid arthritis.

23 Choose the incorrectly matched pair. ***(Chap 10, Class-XII, NCERT)***

(a) PCR – can detect very low amount of DNA
(b) Probe – *ss*DNA or *ss*RNA with a radioactive molecule
(c) ELISA – antigen-antibody interaction
(d) Rosie – first transgenic sheep

Ans. (d)

Exp. Pair (d) is matched incorrectly because in 1997, the first transgenic cow Rosie, produced human enriched milk (2.4 grams per litre). The milk contained the human alpha-lactalbumin and was nutritionally a more balanced product for human babies than natural cow milk.

24 Which of the following statements are correct? ***(Chap 10, Class-XII, NCERT)***

1. GEAC (Genetic Engineering Approval Committee) regulates research, testing and commercial release of GM crops, foods and organisms.
2. Indian Parliament has recently cleared the second amendment of Indian Patents Bill that takes of biopiracy into consideration.
3. In 1997, an American company got patent right on Indian Basmati rice through the US Patent and Trademark Office.
4. In 1997, a transgenic cow was made which produced milk enriched with α-lactalbumin.

Codes

(a) 1 and 2 (b) 3 and 4 (c) 1 and 4 (d) 1, 2, 3 and 4

Ans. (d)

Exp. All the statements are correct.

The Indian Government has set up organisations such as GEAC (Genetic Engineering Approval Committee), which will make decisions regarding the validity of GM research and the safety of introducing GM-organisms for public services.

The Indian Parliament has recently cleared the second amendment of the Indian Patents Bill, that takes such issues into consideration, including patent terms, emergency provisions, research and development initiative.

In 1997, an American company got patent rights on Basmati Rice through the US Patent and Trademark Office.

In 1997, the first transgenic cow, Rosie, produced human enriched milk (2.4 grams per litre). The milk contained the human alpha-lactalbumin.

NCERT MCQ

Practice Set (1-3)

General Science

Scan the QR Code given below to get the PDF of these Practice Sets.